KILL JEFF DAVIS

CAMPAIGNS & COMMANDERS

GREGORY J. W. URWIN, SERIES EDITOR

KILL JEFF DAVIS

The Union Raid on Richmond, 1864

BRUCE M. VENTER

UNIVERSITY OF OKLAHOMA PRESS | NORMAN

Library of Congress Cataloging-in-Publication Data

Venter, Bruce M., 1948–
   Kill Jeff Davis : the Union raid on Richmond, 1864 / Bruce M. Venter.
      pages cm. — (Campaigns and commanders ; volume 51)
   Includes bibliographical references and index.
   ISBN 978-0-8061-5153-3 (hardcover : alk. paper)
   1. Kilpatrick-Dahlgren Raid, Va., 1864. 2. Kilpatrick, Judson,
1836–1881. 3. Dahlgren, Ulric, 1842–1864. I. Title.
   E476.27.V46 2016
   975.5'03—dc23
                        2015021580

Kill Jeff Davis: The Union Raid on Richmond, 1864, is Volume 51 in the
Campaigns & Commanders series.

The paper in this book meets the guidelines for permanence and durability of the
Committee on Production Guidelines for Book Longevity of the Council on Library
Resources, Inc. ∞

1 2 3 4 5 6 7 8 9 10

Interior layout and composition: Alcorn Publication Design

To my daughter, Jessica,
and my wife, Lynne

"[Y]ou may see battles and figures in action or strange faces and costumes in action in endless variety, which you can then re-create in well-drawn forms."

—*Leonardo da Vinci*

Contents

Illustrations

Figures

Maps

Preface

Historians have largely neglected the story of Brigadier General Judson Kilpatrick's 1864 raid on Richmond, an action that only two books have addressed. The better of them, which appeared more than fifty years ago, drew on standard primary sources such as the *Official Records*, regimental histories, published reminiscences, and contemporary newspaper accounts. Now and again popular publications have covered the topic, vividly chronicling the mission but adding little to our understanding of the raid and its principal actors.

Twelve years ago I wrote an article for *Blue & Gray* that added new information about the raid. But my research uncovered far more than the magazine format could accommodate. Since then I have located more sources and materials that have forced me to rethink some of my earlier assumptions. In particular, I have encountered additional unpublished diaries, letters, reminiscences, and government documents specific to the raid that amplify and deepen the record of what happened during those wet, snowy days in late February and early March 1864 and beyond.

This book attempts to weave those newfound sources and perspectives into a fuller account of the Kilpatrick-Dahlgren Raid on Richmond, putting to rest questions previous studies did not answer. This narrative fosters a clearer understanding of Kilpatrick and his leadership, Colonel Ulric Dahlgren and his motives, and Confederate commanders and their capacity to defend Richmond. In the process it endeavors to dispel a miasma of myth and legend generated by unreliable postwar memoirs. Employing manuscript sources previously untapped, this account identifies the black guide who Dahlgren hanged and delineates the chain of custody for the infamous orders found on the colonel's corpse, refuting contemporaneous claims by Federal officials that those documents were Confederate forgeries. Many previously unused sources from raid participants have been incorporated into this study, two of which shed new light on the raid. Reuben Bartley, Dahlgren's signal officer, wrote a ninety-eight-page document heretofore unused by chroniclers of the operation. In addition, army scout James Wood's papers provide enlightening information about the raid and Federal intelligence-gathering efforts prior to its start. Wood's papers also contain a cryptic document written to Dahlgren's brother in arcane Pittman shorthand, which upon transcription further illuminates details of the colonel's activities.

Army archival sources, previously ignored by historians, are used herein to point out the unbounded political clout Ulric Dahlgren's father, Admiral John A. Dahlgren, commanded after his son's death. Such power appears unprecedented in connection with nineteenth-century battlefield deaths. The admiral brought the full force of the Federal government's investigative powers to bear on former Confederates immediately after the war ended in an effort to ferret out what happened to his son's personal effects. The incredible odyssey of Colonel Dahlgren's gold ring, overcoat, crutch, sack coat, prosthesis, horse, saber, boots, gauntlets, and sash is truly a fascinating story never before told, except in musty documents.

This study also emphasizes the importance Kilpatrick placed on Major General Benjamin F. Butler's participation for the raid's success. Butler commanded a sizable number of troops on Virginia's Peninsula at Fort Monroe. There is no question Kilpatrick planned on this force to march up the Peninsula to attack Richmond from the southeast. But Butler failed to come up as planned, which had a major influence on Kilpatrick's decision making during the afternoon of March 1, 1864. If Butler had come up in a timely manner, even if Dahlgren could not cross the James River, it is possible the outcome might have been different.

However much light we shine on it, the Kilpatrick-Dahlgren Raid retains an aura of mystery. In the absence of definitive sources, even the most diligent examiner must at times proffer circumstantial evidence. Thus, the raid is persistently enigmatic in nature.

Of the many cavalry operations conducted by both sides, the 1864 Kilpatrick-Dahlgren Raid stands out as unique. Had circumstance not revealed the malignant orders found on the dead colonel, this action would have disappeared into the crowded archive of other mounted efforts launched to cut enemy communication lines, destroy supply depots, and damage infrastructure like railroads, bridges, and canals. But Kilpatrick's Richmond raid had no precedent. Beyond an ostensible aim of freeing some thirteen thousand Union men held at Libby Prison and on Belle Isle, the raiders had a much more sinister objective—the assassination of the

Confederacy's chief executive and members of his cabinet. Had Dahlgren not been killed, no one would have been the wiser despite the failure. The papers and memorandum book in a pocket of his uniform would have remained in his possession until he returned to Culpeper County. But in the roadside mud of King and Queen County, Virginia, Ulric Dahlgren did die, and from the young colonel's corpse arose the specter of scandal, mayhem, and murder.

Kilpatrick had initiated and led nearly four thousand Union cavalrymen on a raid to capture Richmond and torch the Confederate capital. The sortie, chancy from the start, had promised fame and glory—or at least a leg up for the career-minded officer who might also have seen the glimmer of political possibilities at war's end.

The official record, with its voluminous rendering of the miseries inflicted at Libby Prison and Belle Isle on Union prisoners by a Confederate government unable to address the needs of POWs, offers a glib rationale for the raid. But there was a deeper, darker purpose at work that only came to light with Dahlgren's death.

No doubt the Federal prisoners were suffering excruciating hardships at Rebel hands. The time was ripe for Kilpatrick's fertile mind to solve their problems by freeing them from abuse. Kilpatrick planned an action splendid on paper but foiled by bad weather, lapses in command and control, ignorance of terrain, logistical mishaps, and infinitely permeable efforts at secrecy. He also had personal shortcomings that contributed to what devolved into a pretty mess all the way around for the Union high command and President Abraham Lincoln's administration. Kilpatrick's principal subordinate was hampered by ill health, poor judgment, and a zeal that presupposed the ability to carry out a dangerous mission.

Lincoln had personally approved Kilpatrick's scheme to capture Richmond and free the prisoners. Did he also approve assassinating his Rebel counterpart? While Lincoln scholars see no connection between the president and Dahlgren's secret orders—and rightly so—150 years after the raid, speculation remains as to who authored the lethal though unexecuted sentence for Davis.

At one time or another, Dahlgren and other Federal officers had suggested capturing Richmond. In early February 1864 Butler's plan to take the city included freeing the prisoners and bagging Davis, but it had failed. It was Kilpatrick's scheme that Lincoln bought, a scenario the young general had been rehearsing for all his life. Practiced in politics and oratory, he possessed a ward leader's gift for streetwise strategy and drawing-room palaver—skills that gained him entrance to West Point, advancement in the volunteer army, and finally a face-to-face meeting with the president. Writers and historians fond of caricature have given Kilpatrick short biographic shrift rather than note the qualities that endeared him to most of his troopers, who followed him in headlong mounted charges, through battles, and on raids—some successful, others less so. Diaries and letters speak in this study, telling how the men really felt about the general who came to be known as "Kill-Cavalry."

In the weeks before the raid, Kilpatrick had observed a failed run at Richmond orchestrated by Butler, his former mentor who had political aspirations of his own. Kilpatrick was certain he could do better. Nearly three years' experience in the Federal cavalry had taught him about the need for hard riding and quick execution to accomplish a goal. His uncanny leadership style and brash ambition allowed him only to see success on a path others saw as fraught with failure.

On this foray Kilpatrick not only had loyal lieutenants but also an outsider—a flashy, courageous, arrogant young officer who had something to prove since losing a leg during the Gettysburg Campaign. Ulric Dahlgren's mind was sound, but his command experience was scant and his wound-raddled body unready for campaigning over foreign ground leading men who, while faithful to a fault, had never served under him. His death underpinned the operation's failure. This account, rather than repeat the platitudinous encomia that collected around his tragic end, focuses a more objective lens on the young colonel's failings, bringing them into the proper light of history.

From 1863 until Appomattox, one of the Union's most famous and heralded cavalry commanders was George Armstrong Custer. But Kilpatrick relegated Custer's participation in the raid to a sideshow, spawning internal conflicts in the Third Cavalry Division that may have figured in the raid's outcome. The backstory of these boy generals' animosity toward one another is given a fresh interpretation through the context of the raid.

And what of Richmond's defenders and their seemingly magical rebuff of the Yankee horde? Was there really "not a sound pair of legs" in the city in March 1864 as Lincoln thought? Besides old men and adolescents, were there stout fellows and veterans standing ready to defend the Confederate capital? This study offers a new analysis of Richmond's defenders, mounted and on foot, that is essential to understanding why Kilpatrick and his troopers returned in disarray rather than triumph. In addition, the story of the blue-clad cavalrymen and the horses they rode needs to be told in more detail. The men were loyal, brave, and steadfast in carrying out their duties against a backdrop of wartime political intrigue. Their horses were indeed heroes as well, accomplishing incredible feats without understanding why they were driven so hard and suffered so much; their story is part of this narrative as well.

Acknowledgments

About fifteen years ago, a meeting at Kilroy's restaurant in Springfield, Virginia, laid the foundation for this book. My good friend Horace Mewborn set up dinner with Dave Roth, editor and publisher of *Blue & Gray* magazine. Horace was aware of my seemingly never-ending research on Judson Kilpatrick. After many conversations over ice tea and occasionally red wine, Horace and I came around to the idea that I should write an article on the Kilpatrick-Dahlgren Raid. Horace was a friend of Dave's from his articles on John Mosby and J. E. B. Stuart. Over a prime rib dinner, we sold Dave on the idea of an article on the raid. The ever-congenial publisher readily agreed. In 2003 the article appeared in *Blue & Gray*. Dave was very pleased with it, but I had amassed much more material than I could include in the article. In addition, there was much more to be said about the raid, including placing it all into a larger context. The result is *Kill Jeff Davis: The Union Raid on Richmond, 1864.*

Over the many years it took to complete this book, I have been helped and encouraged by many friends and colleagues.

Dr. Richard J. Sommers, now retired from his position as senior historian at the U.S. Army Heritage and Education Center in Carlisle, Pennsylvania, has been my mentor for many years. Dick shared many insights with me and pointed out sources I might have missed. He was also a reader of this study in manuscript form for the University of Oklahoma Press. His endorsement of my work meant so much to me.

Another person who had a major role in the development of this book is Michael Dolan, senior editor at the Weider History Group. Over the years Mike has corrected, suggested, and improved my writing. From my first article in *Blue & Gray* to the final submission of my manuscript to the Press, he has been there to help. Mike is an editor extraordinaire, plus a great counselor when I needed encouragement. If this book is a good read, it is because Mike Dolan's edits made it a much better narrative.

Charles Rankin, editor in chief and associate director at the University of Oklahoma Press, and Gregory Urwin, senior editor of the Campaigns and Commanders Series, were both instrumental in seeing this project through to completion. No one could have had more patience and understanding than Chuck Rankin. It was a long gestation period, but he shepherded my manuscript through the process with encouragement and genuine support for it. Greg saw merit in my initial proposal and made sure it got to Chuck's desk. Kevin Brock provided excellent editing of the final manuscript. Thanks also to Edward Longacre, who was a reader and offered thoughtful suggestions and comments. James M. McPherson also read the manuscript; his comments were very much appreciated.

Many friends and colleagues provided helpful sources to me over the years. Michael Musick, now retired from the National Archives, showed me a file on Ulric Dahlgren that allowed me to bring to light many aspects about the colonel's service that have never before been revealed in print. His guidance has made this study unique in many ways. Robert E. L. "Bobby" Krick never hesitated to send me material on the raid whenever he came across it. Likewise, my good friends Bob O'Neill and Horace Mewborn sent me relevant material whenever they found it. They also provided loads of encouragement and good-natured chiding over the years to ensure that my study of the raid would be completed.

Clark B. "Bud" Hall is a longtime friend who connected me with the owners of Rose Hill plantation, Dr. John Covington and Don Wells. Gaining access to this historic house was of inestimable value. Eric Wittenberg provided kind words about my research in his biography of Ulric Dahlgren. Others who helped with sources or added encouragement along the way were A. Wilson "Will" Greene, Tom Clemens, John Coski, Ed Bartley, Steve Herrick, the late Don Makely, Nancy Moscheo, Brigadier General Jack Mountcastle, Debbie Hamm, Alice Miller, and members of the King and Queen County Historical Society.

Several gentlemen from the Richmond area provided information in the early stages of my research and are now fast friends: Richard Forrester, Hobson Goddin, and C. Southall Wallace. The Adamson family, owners of Ben Green's plantation house, have always allowed me access to their property when I have conducted tours of the raid. Laura Meadows, Catherine Southworth, and Phyllis Silber, all with the Goochland County Historical Society, helped with the images that appear in this book. Bill Nelson created the excellent maps.

Thanks also to Rick Smith and the officers and troopers of the 2nd U.S. Cavalry/9th Virginia Cavalry reenacting unit, who allowed me the honor of riding with them for three days in September 2012 when they recreated Dahlgren's raid through Goochland County. It was an experience I will never forget.

Librarians at the following institutions were most helpful to me during my research: Library of Congress, National Archives, Library of Virginia, the Bentley and Clements Libraries at the University of Michigan, Vermont Historical Society, Vermont State Library, New York State Library and Archives, U.S. Army Heritage and Education Center (formerly the Military History Institute), University of Virginia's Adelman Library, Abraham Lincoln Presidential Library, Albany Institute of History and Art, University of Vermont's Bailey/Howe Library, Central Michigan University's Clarke Library, Georgetown University's Special Collections, Maine Historical Society, Maine State Library, Massachusetts Historical Society, Michigan State Library and Archives, Colonial Williamsburg's John D. Rockefeller, Jr., Library, U.S. Military Academy's Special Collections, University of North Carolina's Southern Historical Collection, Duke University's Special Collections, Historical Society of Pennsylvania, Indiana State Library, Detroit Public Library's Burton Historical Collection, Wistar Institute Archives, and Western Michigan University's Waldo Library. A special thank you goes to the staff at the Virginia Historical Society Library, one of my favorite places to work.

My daughter, Jessica, was involved in this project early on when we set out together to discover the site where Dahlgren was killed. She has waited a long time to see this work come to fruition. I trust she will be pleased with the result.

And finally, my sincerest gratitude goes to my wife, Lynne, who has lived through many years with Judson Kilpatrick, Ulric Dahlgren, and the troopers who rode with them. Lynne traversed the roads, helped with research in many libraries, photocopied more pages than anyone could ask, listened to more talks on the raid than bearable, and proofread countless pages. No one has done more to help this project become a reality. I could not have done it without her encouragement. She is my strongest supporter and greatest critic. By working together, I think we have accomplished something special.

KILL JEFF DAVIS

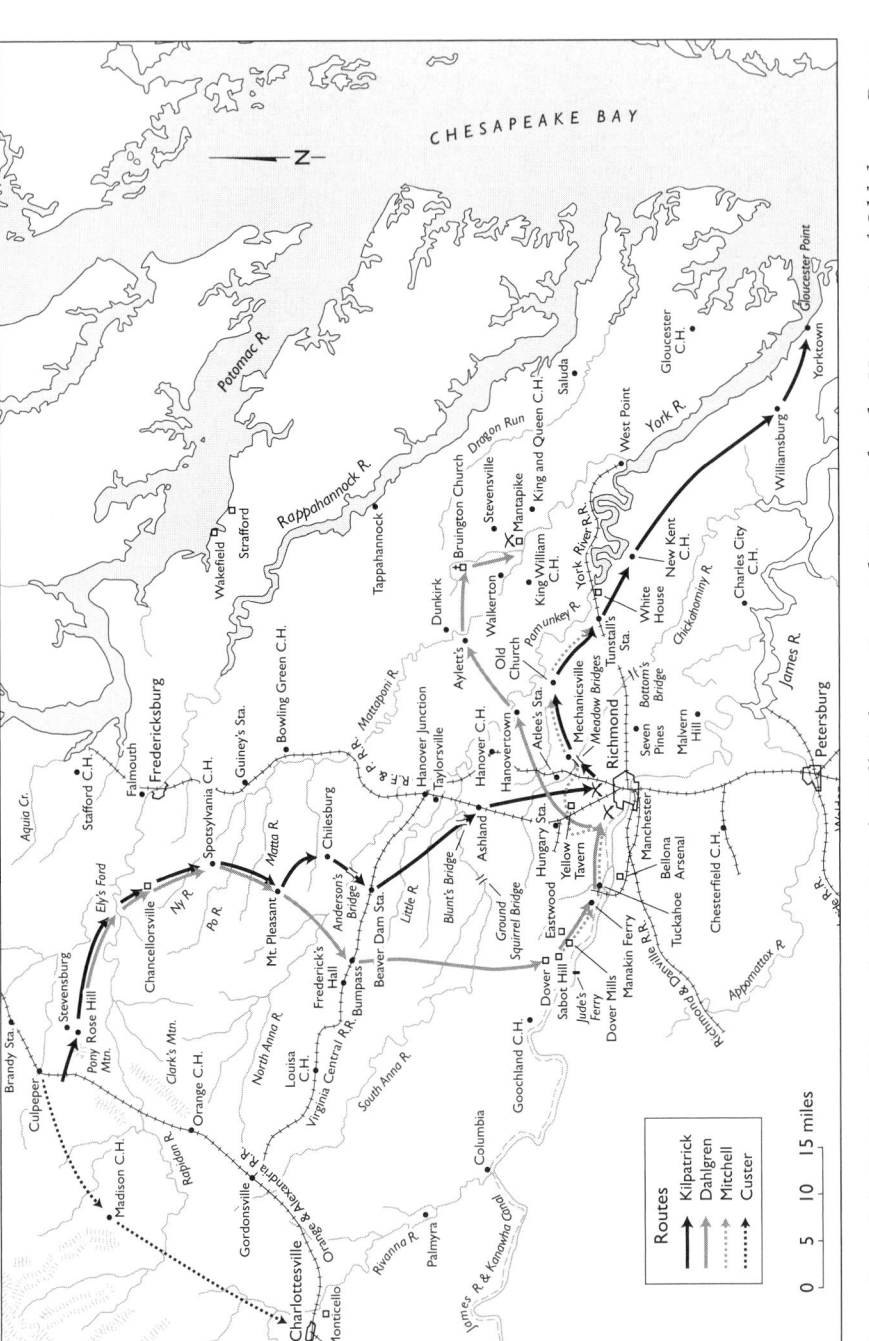

CHESAPEAKE BAY

Overview of the Raid on Richmond, 1864. Map by Bill Nelson. Copyright © 2016 by the University of Oklahoma Press.

CHAPTER I

LITTLE KIL DEPARTS

A column of blue-coated horsemen trotted down a sloppy road in Culpeper County, Virginia, the horses' hooves splashing mud on every animal's belly and each rider's stirrups, boots, and uniform trousers. Several score in number, they were mostly officers with the Army of the Potomac's Third Cavalry Division.

Sunday morning, April 17, 1864, was a rather "cold and unpleasant day," especially for the staff officers in the vanguard. Severe rain the previous evening had left the region's narrow country lanes in wretched shape, worsening conditions brought on by two weeks of miserable weather. But the young aides were unsettled less by the weather than by the reason for the ride. The men were making their way a brief distance—four and a half miles—along the Carolina Road, traveling between the outlying hamlet of Stevensburg and Brandy Station, the nearest stop on the Orange and Alexandria Railroad. Circumstances and emotions made it seem a much longer trip to the depot, where they would give a handshake and one final salute to a man they had come to admire.[1]

At the head of the column was a diminutive figure in officer's livery who bore himself with assurance beyond his twenty-six years, though he felt only despair now. He had led the Third Cavalry Division in "many a hard fight" the last eleven months and, as one trooper put it, "for dash his equal is not in this army."[2] But as the winter was ending, Brigadier General Judson Kilpatrick's storied career had lurched to an abrupt halt. His failed raid on Richmond had placed any idea of promotion on the backburner for another year.

Kilpatrick's musings as he rode to the train depot went unrecorded, but perhaps he reflected on his army career in a war that had seemed tailor made for a dashing cavalry officer and aspiring politician. Back in New Jersey as a youth, he had stumped for his local congressman, who handily won the election. The grateful politician returned the favor by providing an appointment for the young man to the U.S. Military Academy at West Point. It was here that "Little Kil," the nickname his classmates bestowed on him, developed his oratorical skills, giving his class's valedictory address on graduation day in May 1861. His eloquence with words, so essential for nineteenth-century politicians, would serve him well in the army. As one officer recalled, Kilpatrick was "a ready and fluent speaker—an orator, in fact—and had the gift of charming an audience with his insinuating tongue."[3] No doubt Lincoln appreciated the young officer's talent at turning a phrase when they sat together in the Executive Mansion in mid-February 1864.

Instead, the recent raid on Richmond, while thrilling, had brought disaster. The regimental historian of the 3rd Indiana obviously was engaging in understatement when he later wrote: "The raid was not a success, and perhaps never should have been undertaken, but it showed the desperate bravery of the men who took part in it, and no doubt changed the military career of the man who conceived it." A Baltimore newspaper presaged the soldier-scribe's sentiments when, with the raid's outcome still up in the air, its editor wrote: "The enterprise is a bold and daring one, and would need for its success a combination of fortunate circumstances as well as great dash, pluck and expedition. Gen. Kilpatrick may be relied upon for the exhibition of the latter qualities, but we still do not regard success in the affair as more than barely possible." Moreover, Union army brass were not pleased by the debacle; despite the outcome, the "plucky" general was lucky to still wear a star on his shoulder straps.[4]

In the weeks since the raid, speculation had abounded in camp that Kilpatrick was in line for promotion to command of the Cavalry Corps itself, but as always rank-and-file chatter was just that, absurd rumor. A new general in chief of all the Federal armies, Lieutenant General Ulysses S. Grant, had plans for the Army of the Potomac's cavalry all right, but these did not include the man some called "Kill-Cavalry," a sobriquet the young general likely earned for riding his men and his horses equally hard. As his mount cantered down the slushy road, Kilpatrick knew he was no longer destined for a cavalryman's glory. No doubt he was considering his options, as he always had and always would. A Union trooper called him "one of those restless, nervous, energetic and self-reliant spirits who believe in themselves thoroughly, [and] make up in activity what they lack in method."[5]

Nevertheless, the New Jersey native's momentum had degenerated with alarming speed. Three months earlier the New York Herald had quoted inside sources hailing his prowess and his prospects. The newspaper claimed that mention of his name in "Washington dispatches" to the U.S. Senate foreshadowed his promotion to major general. A member of the Kilpatrick claque, the editor declared that the general's "fitness of the appointment is not to be questioned." In wartime, editorial puffery was a daily ration, but the *Herald* seemingly had battlefield facts behind its hoopla. Kilpatrick's "record for the last year is a series of bold, skillful and successful operations of cavalry," the newspaperman trilled, "[a]ll won by personal merit entirely, and not obtained through political influence." Such hyperbole irked one army staff officer; in a skeptical letter home, he told his family that the general "gets all his reputation by newspapers and political influence."[6]

As the Yankee column continued its soggy jaunt toward the train depot, the riders may have considered their first impressions of their commander, particularly his unusual appearance. Perhaps they agreed with a civilian visitor to the army's winter encampment who months earlier described Kilpatrick as "a little man, with loud, swaggering voice, full of fun and profanity, florid face, square, prognathous jaw, firm, large mouth, prominent Roman nose, quick, deep-set, piercing, fearless gray eyes, full square forehead, large round head, large ears, [and] dark, thin, and short hair."[7] In addition, Little Kil's trademark Dundreary whiskers at all times beetled from his face. He stood about five feet seven inches tall, his right shoulder slightly stooped, and had small hands and feet. But his eyes were what caught most people's attention. After the war an artist who interviewed Kilpatrick observed that he "partially closes his china blue eyes and draws down the corners of his mouth which then gives him a peculiar wicked appearance."[8]

A Michigan officer who had served in Kilpatrick's division since the summer of 1863 recalled the general's "face was a marked one, showing his individuality in every line," with a "countenance that once seen, was never forgotten." This same Wolverine remembered that he "was not especially refined in manners and in conversation" but possessed "an intellect that would at times emit flashes so brilliant as to blind those who knew him best to his faults."[9] But Little Kil had several other traits, such as the horsemanship familiar to the men riding behind him that dreary spring day. A Union captain remembered him riding "as though he had been made for the saddle. . . . His well-trained steeds understand him perfectly." On horseback the general's compact frame gave the impression that his bones were made of "iron and his sinews steel."[10]

Staff officers knew most of the enlisted men held Kilpatrick in high regard. His men thought him approachable but "not inclined to be much of a disciplinarian." One soldier said the general "would frequently harangue the men, but his good-natured dash and personal magnetism made him popular." He "had a capacity for rallying his soldiers and getting them into a charge." Indeed, the charge seemed to be his favorite tactic. Another trooper said, "Sometimes this was very successful, and at other times it was not so much so and very costly of men." A more generous officer from New York later wrote that his commander "has undoubtedly his faults, but his men fail to see them, so that to them he is as good as perfect," an attribute sure to win him plaudits from any soldier. But the general's penchant for hurling troopers headlong into assaults on the enemy virtually assured him the nickname "Kill-Cavalry," according to one veteran.[11]

Kilpatrick had a salty way with words too. According to Libbie Custer, the enamoring wife of Brigadier General George Armstrong Custer, Little Kil "used an oath with every sentence he uttered." She might have bridled at the habit, but not his soldiers, who had grown accustomed to officers' imprecation-laden barking. A general able to curse with the best of them had a leg up with the men. An Ohio officer later remembered that Kilpatrick was "energetic and ambitious, a great talker, with a vocabulary which he did not learn at Sunday School, but was a dashing officer whose enthusiasm inspired his men."[12]

The Third Cavalry Division's officers and men knew Kilpatrick best, which made them more forgiving than others in the Army of the Potomac. An officer on Major General George G. Meade's staff scoffed that Little Kil was "certainly an odd looking specimen. His colorless eye, big nose, and narrow forehead, with an indescribable air between a vulgarian & a crack-brain, combine to render him almost laughable. . . . I don't believe he is worth a fig as a general." He was "hard to look at without laughing," this critic added. The staff officer credited Kilpatrick for being "a brave, vigorous man," but one who was "apparently deficient in judgment, a fault in which his two Brigadiers, Davis [sic] and Custer do not much help him."[13]

As his horse splashed across Mountain Run, "a vicious little stream" according to Union cavalry general John Buford, Kilpatrick must have been thinking of his future, which looked bleak. As a New York trooper told a relative back home, "Genl Kilpatrick, yes, our daring, fearless, indefatigable leader—'our little Kil' has been relieved and ere thus is on his way to the West to take a new command."[14] Kill-Cavalry's destiny now rested with Major General William T. Sherman, Grant's choice to lead the western armies. The year before at Vicksburg, Grant had split the South with skill and brute force. Sherman, his favorite subordinate, was poised to splinter the Confederacy again with a plan to march deep into Georgia, breaking the Rebel backbone. Perhaps in this incipient campaign Kilpatrick would find a good fit for his military predilictions. "If you have got him you will have to do something this summer for he is a fighting man," a Michigan trooper told his brother, one of Sherman's cavalrymen.[15]

But Kilpatrick's prospects seemed to match Culpeper's sodden war- and winter-stripped landscape. After crossing Mountain Run, his column passed Glen Ella, a plantation house where Major General Gouverneur K. Warren was packing his belongings for a move to new headquarters in Culpeper. Warren, who had temporarily commanded the army's II Corps in Major General Winfield Scott Hancock's absence, had taught Little Kil at West Point.

To understand why the Richmond raid had failed so miserably, it is important to measure the character of its instigator and understand his background, which sheds light on who the man was and why he acted the way he did. Three years earlier, nearly to the day, Cadet Kilpatrick, fired up by the secessionists' attack on Fort Sumter, had petitioned to graduate early from West Point to join the war effort. He thereafter sought a commission in the 5th New York Infantry, popularly known as Duryee's Zouaves. One of the era's fabulously costumed military units, its men dressed in baggy red trousers, dark blue short jackets, and turban headgear. To get his way, Kilpatrick hitched his star to the Davies family of New York City. Judge Henry Davies endorsed Little Kil as captain of Company H. His own son, Henry, Jr., a lawyer, would also be a captain, while a nephew, J. Mansfield Davies was to be the regiment's major. Kilpatrick's West Point mathematics teacher, Warren, would be lieutenant colonel of the 5th New York.[16]

Once at the 5th New York's camp near Fort Monroe on the Virginia Peninsula, Captain Kilpatrick began to make a name for himself. A sergeant vividly remembered the young officer as "popular in the regiment. . . . [H]e was a pony but not a runt. The little fellow was every inch a man, and the man every inch a soldier. Boldness, fearlessness, activity, firmness and confidence were stamped as plainly in his countenance that everybody predicted a successful military career and they were right. . . . He loved excitement and adventure and the whole Confederacy was none too big for him."[17] During this time, Kilpatrick undoubtedly crossed paths with Major General Benjamin F. Butler, who on June 10, 1861, had ordered the 5th New York forward against Confederate forces entrenched near Big Bethel. During this attack, Kilpatrick took a bullet in the upper thigh, becoming the first regular-army officer wounded in combat.[18]

While recuperating in New York City, Kilpatrick got wind of a new cavalry regiment being raised under the auspices of Senator Ira Harris. Again the Davies family stepped up, helping the young officer land an assignment as lieutenant colonel in the 2nd New York Cavalry, popularly known as the Harris Light Cavalry in honor of its benefactor. The Davies cousins came along with Kilpatrick: J. Mansfield ostensibly commanded the regiment but was often absent; Henry, Jr., served as major.

Neither of the Davies was a West Pointer, so Little Kil often found himself training and leading the Harris Light, a role he used to great advantage. His brigade commander, Brigadier General George Bayard, took note of Kilpatrick's ability. After Mansfield Davies resigned in December 1862, Kilpatrick was promoted to colonel and commander of the regiment. Still a colonel the following spring, he nonetheless was leading a brigade; by June 1863 he had won his first star. On the eve of the Gettysburg Campaign, Kilpatrick was given a division in the Army of the Potomac's expanded Cavalry Corps. But now here he was, three brief years later, on a muddy Culpeper County road with barely the traction to keep his mount and his career moving forward.

Toward evening the previous day General Kilpatrick stepped out onto the small portico of his headquarters, a stately Greek Revival structure of two-and-a-half stories dubbed Rose Hill by its owners, the Alfred Ashby family. The requisitioned residence, a white-pine plantation house that dated to about 1810, stood a quarter mile south of Stevensburg. Prior to Kilpatrick's commandeering the house, a cannonball had hit the roof, furrowing through the ceiling of an upstairs bedroom and leaving a hole that the Ashbys had stuffed with newspapers. War often makes strange partnerships. The family was relegated to the cellar during the general's occupancy, but at least got to stay in their home. Throughout the Union army's winter encampment, they had enjoyed or endured the byproduct of their tenant's notoriety as politicians and persons of influence, real or imagined, crossed the threshold into the white plastered rooms for meetings, parties, and shenanigans. Legend has the general riding his horse through the front doorway, down the center hallway, out the rear door, and back again just to demonstrate his equestrian skill. As one officer recalled long after the incident, "Kilpatrick rode like a Commache."[19]

Despite the wet weather, the general stepped off the porch; he owed his regiments a last farewell. As he approached, the hard-bitten troopers shuffled into ranks in the muddy fields nearby and gathered around in a "drenching rain." Kilpatrick removed his now-famous slouched hat, distinctively worn cocked to the left side of his head. Holding his right shoulder lower than his left as always and partially closing his "china blue eyes," he began to speak. "His voice had a peculiar, piercing quality, though it was not unmusical in sound," remembered a Michigan Brigade officer. A corporal in the 2nd New York wrote a day later that he felt Kilpatrick expressed himself with the "tenderness of a woman—in that peculiar magnetic, love inspiring voice—clear & musical despite his emotion." The general stiffened as he called them "comrades & soldiers." He told stories of battlefields they had ridden, recalling how their valor not only had won him promotion but also had given them a claim to history. One horse soldier later scribbled in a letter that Kilpatrick was "the type of a cavalry officer who though a 'Star' ornaments the shoulder still holds and treats his men as men." Another New Yorker felt truly sorry to see his commander depart.[20]

The men seemed unified in their feelings. A Michigander echoed similar sentiments when he wrote home that Kilpatrick had "made us a speech that brought tears to everyone's eyes and it was the joy, the pleasure, and the sadness at losing so good a man and so good a soldier that made us cry." This trooper was sure none of them would forget Little Kil, who along with Custer had brought the Michigan Brigade glory.[21] "Kilpatrick had many traits that commended him to soldiers," another Wolverine said, "and it was not without regret we saw him go away."[22] Likewise, a veteran of the 1st Vermont felt that his commander showed real leadership ability: "Never was there a general who inspired his men with more confidence than did Gen. Kilpatrick, and never did men love and respect their general more than did the soldiers of Kilpatrick's division." It was this horse soldier's pledge to critics that "we will endeavor to show to our country that we are men who have been led by Kilpatrick."[23]

These troopers knew very well that the recent raid had been a failure, but their commander's impending departure surprised some of them. A Vermonter's immediate reaction was that the sudden "change was an unexpected one; and while it may be 'all for the best,' many cannot see it in that light." He regretted the departure of the "gallant and dashing" Kilpatrick but wished him the best in his new command under Sherman.[24] Perhaps the most evenhanded assessment came from a man in the Harris Light Cavalry. This trooper asserted that the general had "done some rash things all must acknowledge—but that he has done much to give a name to the cavalry of the Union Army must also be acknowledged—and when History shall fill her scroll among the brightest names besides her Murat she will be proud to write the name[s] of Buford and Kilpatrick."[25]

As Kilpatrick reminisced with his men, he first recalled the unwavering courage of his soldiers. He hoped that the westerners he would soon command would measure up to the brave fighters of the Third Cavalry Division. The general also left the impression that he was not happy about the transfer. As one Wolverine told his diary, "He don't like to leave his old Division." At length Kilpatrick brought up his nickname "Kill-Cavalry" during his farewell. The general objected to this cognomen, claiming that it was unjustly applied to him; his men's welfare had always been uppermost in his mind. He felt that if his regiments' losses had been unusual, it was because the "exigencies of the service" had required his brigades to fight more frequently than others of the Cavalry Corps. In fact, he added, "his division was now larger than either of the other two." No one in the ranks challenged the general on his facts. In closing, Kilpatrick assured his men that he looked forward to reading about their future successful exploits under a new commander, trusting that Grant's selection to replace him would be as conscientious in his consideration of their welfare as he had been.[26]

The man slated to succeed Kilpatrick was Brigadier General James Harrison Wilson, considered one of Grant's "pets" by some veterans of the cavalry. As one trooper put it, "Gen Wilson assumes command of this Div today and replaces Gen Kilpatrick much to the dissatisfaction of the whole Div men & officers."[27] Some speculated that their new general could never be his predecessor's "superior in pluck, skill and dash." Others thought the removal of Little Kil took the "soul," "vim," and "fire" out of the division. Wilson "could not gain the love of this division, for Kilpatrick had borne away its heart."[28]

To some extent Wilson agreed with the troopers who stood in the rain the evening of April 16 about their commander. He remembered Kilpatrick quite favorably, writing after the war, "During his entire service, it is safe to say that no other officer could have been personally present at more engagements and have been more frequently in danger of sudden death than the ubiquitous and fearless Kilpatrick." As an upperclassman at West Point, Wilson had admired Little Kil's "energy, ability, and patriotism" as well as his talent as "a brilliant orator." He also noted that it could not be said that Kilpatrick was always successful, but no one ever charged him with being a "laggard" during a campaign or on the battlefield. The new division commander felt his predecessor always bore himself "with conspicuous gallantry. . . . No enterprise was too dangerous to appall him, and . . . there was no position in the army to which he did not aspire."[29] But Kilpatrick was not the solipsist that some modern-day critics like to portray.

As ever, the army did not say why the general was heading west, only that he was heading there. It would have been a surprise if the raid had not been hung on Kilpatrick, though it may have been hung on others too. Major General Alfred Pleasonton, the Cavalry Corps commander, was also relieved and transferred west afterward. Clearing the command structure offered Grant a chance to promote Major General Philip H. Sheridan and General Wilson to leadership roles within the Army of the Potomac's cavalry.

But for all the varied opinions his betters, his peers, and his troops held of him, Judson Kilpatrick was nothing if not a professional warrior. After his last night at Rose Hill, he awoke, dressed, mounted up, and prepared to leave for Brandy Station to board the train, a first step toward joining Sherman's army. He had good company for that brief ride and long journey in the form of three trusted staff officers, Captain Llewellyn Garrish Estes and Lieutenants Theodore Northrop and Henry Wilson, who would continue to serve him to war's end. The general was leaving behind good times as well as the onus of the failed Richmond raid. Custer, the Michigan Brigade's commander, also accompanied Kilpatrick, though only for the ride to Brandy Station. What Custer was thinking that day remains unrecorded, but he probably did not effuse the same tears as the troopers had the previous evening, these boy generals having not always seen things eye to eye. But he and fifty other officers fell into line behind Little Kil and his trio of favorite aides.[30]

After all the sad goodbyes, Kilpatrick must have reflected on the happenstance that had brought him to this pass. Only six weeks earlier he had embarked on a spectacular cavalry raid against Richmond. He had been confident of its success as was President Lincoln, the man who had sanctioned it. But the run at Richmond, which Kilpatrick himself had proposed, had not gone well and had wound up in the tangle of controversy. Someone in a position of influence must have blamed him, the general probably thought, for the intelligence failures and mistakes by subordinates that to some extent he could not have controlled. It was not the first cavalry raid of the war to fail, but it was his failed raid and his alone.

Kilpatrick also surely thought of his beloved wife, Alice, and their son, Judson, both dead by the end of 1863. Had those untimely deaths rocked him more than even he had realized? Regardless, others had noticed. Word of their deaths had floated through the ranks, one officer noting in his diary that he had heard that Little Kil was "gloomy and desperate; just in the state to try something wild."[31] More likely the general, rather than going wild, had grown more cautious, more restrained, when what the operation had most needed was the brimstone and brashness he had displayed earlier in the war.

Kilpatrick's raid on Richmond had its origins in the very purpose of cavalry in war. Over the conflict's nearly three years of fighting to that point, both armies had developed and expanded the use of the mounted arm. Confederate cavaliers had garnered explosive newspaper headlines for their daring exploits. There was great renown to be gained by a successful cavalry raid, particularly one that would operate so deep behind enemy lines. Kilpatrick would not be outdone by the boldness of his Southern counterparts and had developed a plan that would catapult himself to the highest recognition in the land. The story of his 1864 raid against the Confederate capital displays the essence of Civil War cavalry operations, designed to accomplish results nearly beyond belief, though only if it was successful.

CHAPTER 2

"Nothing So Delights a Cavalryman As . . . a Raid"

By late 1863, raiding had become one of the primary functions of both the Union and Confederate cavalry. Federal horse soldiers were as likely as their Southern counterparts to execute a raid on some unsuspecting target. None would have argued with the Pennsylvania officer who later wrote that "nothing so delights the heart of a cavalryman as to go on a scout or a raid." In fact, it was much easier to get a trooper up for a raid than to get him to groom an extra horse.[1] Judson Kilpatrick would not disappoint his horsemen when he decided to take Richmond in February 1864.

Military thinking on the best use of cavalry was evolving in the decade before the war. Union brigadier general William Woods Averell described the mounted arm's historic role as being able to provide "[r]eliable information of the enemy's position or movements, which is absolutely necessary to the commander of an army to successfully conduct a campaign." This West Pointer, a horseman himself, pointed out that in camp, cavalry "furnishes outposts, vedettes and scouts. In battle, it attacks the enemy's flanks and rear, and above all other duties in battle it secures the fruits of victory by vigorous and unrelenting pursuit." After describing some more mundane activities such as guard duty, Averell concluded that effective cavalry "improves topographical maps, destroys and builds bridges, obstructs and opens communications, and obtains or destroys forage and supplies." As the war progressed, Federal cavalry leaders came to see raids that destroyed infrastructure and supplies as a prime responsibility. So did Southern horsemen, who also excelled in intelligence gathering, embodied by Confederate general Robert E. Lee's cavalry under Major General James Ewell Brown "Jeb" Stuart.[2]

As Averell noted, the Civil War changed cavalry doctrine. Horse soldiers were the perfect weapon for disrupting the enemy's lines of communication and supply—principally railroads' tracks, rolling stock, depots, water towers, wood piles, and telegraphic lines as well as factories producing war materiel. It was commonplace for Federal raids to have these primary objectives. But until February 1864, neither side had thought seriously of sending cavalry to seize and hold a major population center like Richmond, even if temporarily.[3]

Cavalry always made headlines. In the eastern theater Stuart's fabled "Ride around McClellan" in June 1862 dazzled reporters and editors above and below the Mason-Dixon Line. This "brilliant exploit" set the stage for future raids on both sides. The operation began as an intelligence-gathering mission ordered by Lee, who only recently had assumed command of the brigades he would call the Army of Northern Virginia. The swashbuckling Stuart, ferreting out information about Union troop deployments near Mechanicsville, Virginia, beat a 150-mile path completely around Major General George B. McClellan's 100,000-man army. Along the way he wrecked considerable Federal war materiel, took Union prisoners, and only lost one man, the gallant Captain William Latane. Lee hailed his bold thirty-year-old subordinate in a congratulatory order to his entire army.

The flamboyant Stuart had critics, even among his own ranks. At least one of his officers was not convinced such raids were worth the cost. Asked cavalryman Robert T. Hubbard, Jr., who rode with Stuart, "was it really a great exploit?" The young man felt the ride around McClellan had "burnt some wagons and stores, sunk a steamer, took some prisoners, and broke down [Stuart's] command on the eve of a great pitched battle that was to decide the fate of Richmond!" Hubbard derided the foray as "a daring adventure which built up Stuart, broke down his horses, and did the country no great service."

This sentiment was echoed later by a Federal general who expressed his open distain for such cavalry capers. Jacob D. Cox, a crusty infantry commander, characterized his rather dour opinion of all cavalry raiding by using Stuart's first exploit as an example. "The use of cavalry in 'raids,' which were the fashion, was an amusement that was very costly to both sides," Cox wrote. "Since Stuart's ride around McClellan's army in 1862, every cavalry commander, National and Confederate, burned to distinguish himself by some such excursion deep into the enemy's country," he concluded. In his opinion cavalry leaders "chafed at the comparatively obscure but useful work of learning the detailed positions and movements of the opposing army by incessant outpost and patrol work in the more restricted theatre of operations of the campaign." But Lee clearly disagreed with such critics. The Confederate leader continued to sanction Stuart's raids until they had damaged the Southern stock of horseflesh nearly to the point of irreversibility.[4]

Stuart set the standard for cavalry raids for the remainder of the war. He continued to surprise his Northern opponents with follow-up raids. In August 1862 Stuart hit Catlett's Station, headquarters for Union major general John Pope's Army of Virginia. One reason for his strike was personal—the week before a Yankee cavalry sortie had cost Stuart his plumed hat, cloak, and a staff officer. Seeking revenge, he asked the indulgent Lee for permission to raid behind Federal lines, ostensibly to wreck Pope's railroad connections, but more likely to assuage his bruised ego. Whatever the motivation, Stuart succeeded enormously. He rode sixty miles in twenty-six hours, capturing 300 prisoners along with General Pope's personal baggage, dispatches and papers, horses, several staff officers, and a large sum of greenbacks. The captured documents proved helpful to Lee in planning his movements against Pope, which ultimately resulted in a smashing Confederate victory at Second Manassas.[5]

Later in 1862, burnishing an already established reputation, Stuart acquired more admirers, especially in the Richmond press, by raiding Chambersburg, Pennsylvania. Again the plumed cavalier circled McClellan's army, this time in Maryland. After a feint toward Hagerstown, Maryland, which proved too heavily defended, Stuart and 1,800 hardy troopers reached Chambersburg on October 9. While there the Rebels destroyed nearly a million dollars in public property, including a machine shop, and took some 1,200 horses, valuable for use as remounts. The four-day foray took Stuart and his troopers 126 miles. The Confederates suffered few losses but returned exhausted, having galloped the last 80 miles in only twenty-seven hours.[6]

Federal cavalrymen simply could not catch the Rebels as they pulled off more raids. As winter closed in, Lee's army took up defensive positions at Fredericksburg while Stuart's horsemen hit enemy communication lines four times. The always reliable Brigadier General Wade Hampton personally led the first three raids. None of these operations seriously unsettled the enemy, only capturing small numbers of Yankees and several wagon trains with supplies while temporarily cutting communications with Washington.

Stuart himself led the fourth and final raid, known as the Dumfries Raid. The day after Christmas, with 1,800 troopers and four guns, he crossed the Rappahannock River at Kelly's Ford. At first the column met with minor success, striking the Telegraph Road in three places and capturing prisoners and supplies, but found Dumfries too strongly held. Instead, Stuart moved north of the Occoquan River, where he skirmished heavily with two Pennsylvania cavalry regiments. Staying on the move in cold windy weather, his brigades destroyed Union camps near the Occoquan. The Confederates extended their stay in northern Virginia after seizing the telegraph office at Burke Station in Fairfax County.

Now Stuart had access to military messages coming to and from the Federal capital. Ever the wit, he found a trooper able to work a telegraph key. Soon a message was sent to Brigadier General Montgomery C. Meigs, the Union quartermaster general in Washington, in which Stuart taunted him about the quality of army mules. The Confederate commander reportedly complained that the inferior beasts had broken down as he was absconding with captured government wagons, though some accounts claim that he thanked the Union general for the mules he was using to take his booty. Whatever words were used, Stuart's audacious display enlarged his legend. From Burke Station the gray troopers rode four miles to Fairfax Court House, where Federal cavalry outside the town forced the raiders back. From there Stuart headed to Culpeper Court House, which he reached on New Year's Eve. The next day he celebrated the start of 1863 with Lee back in Fredericksburg as his wagons pulled into camp with some much needed Yankee provisions for the hard-pressed army. For all the talk it generated and all the Federal embarrassment it engendered, though, the Dumfries Raid was a minor sideshow.[7]

Stuart's grandest excursion, of course, came in June 1863 during Lee's second invasion of the North when he again rode around the Army of the Potomac. Snagging some 125 supply wagons near Rockville, Maryland, Stuart was not able to rejoin the Army of Northern Virginia until the second day of the battle at Gettysburg. His actions during this campaign, still hotly debated, affected the outcome of the climatic engagement in Pennsylvania.[8]

In the end Stuart's raids were designed to wreak havoc on enemy supply depots and lines of communication, gain intelligence, and protect the movements of Lee's army. As the notable historian of the

Army of Northern Virginia Douglas Southall Freeman so eloquently states, "Spectacular raids, in fact, are becoming his specialty, but he continues to learn the arts of reconnaissance, observation and military intelligence." Despite his reputation during and after the war as a great cavalry raider, Stuart never sought to capture any significant population centers like Washington, D.C., much less kidnap the president of the United States.[9]

Yankee commanders could claim to emulate Stuart's exploits in concept, if not in execution. In July 1862 the pompous, blustery Pope planned a sophisticated raid, ordering Major General Nathaniel P. Banks to dispatch some 2,000 horsemen under forty-year-old Brigadier General John Porter Hatch to break the Virginia Central Railroad. Hatch was to ride west to Gordonsville, then make for Charlottesville, wrecking the railroad as he moved. Pope expected the cavalry to destroy the Virginia Central between Charlottesville and Lynchburg, then strike the James River and Kanawha Canal twenty-one miles farther south.[10] In Pope's grand scheme such aggressive raiding would force the evacuation of Richmond. Of course, expediency was paramount to success. But Hatch, a plodding dragoon who had fought in the Mexican War, let down his commander by leaving late. By the time Hatch's troopers were ready to move, most of Lee's army was between Richmond and the Yankees. Having paralyzed McClellan's army on the Peninsula and saved the Confederate capital, Lee had started his army north on a foray across the Potomac. A disgusted Pope fired Hatch, transferring him to the infantry. His replacement as chief of Banks's cavalry was Brigadier General John Buford, whose promotion would serve the Federal mounted arm very well.[11]

Following Pope's defeat at Second Manassas in August 1862, McClellan's return from the Peninsula, and Lee's September invasion of Maryland that culminated in the Battle of Antietam, there was little activity by the Federal cavalry. Shortly after Lee's retreat across the Potomac, save for chasing after Stuart, who was riding rings around McClellan again, Yankee horse soldiers had little to write home that was noteworthy. In the meantime Lincoln relieved "Little Mac" as commander of the Army of the Potomac. His replacement, Major General Ambrose Burnside, did little to enhance the effectiveness of the mounted arm. Stuart and his troopers continued to garner headlines, while the Union cavalry struggled to keep up with their praiseworthy foes.

In late December 1862, about two weeks after the bloody Union debacle at Fredericksburg, General Averell sought an audience with Burnside. The thirty-year-old New Yorker, who was a rising star in the Union cavalry, proposed a raid in the direction of Richmond but did not explicitly mention the Rebel capital as a target. Nevertheless, Averell was quite precise about the units he wanted to use: detachments from the 1st, 2nd, 4th, and 5th U.S. Cavalry plus contingents from the 8th New York, 3rd and 4th Pennsylvania, 1st Rhode Island, and 1st Massachusetts. Two sections (four guns) from Lieutenant Alexander C. M. Pennington's Battery M, 2nd U.S. Artillery, would provide artillery support for the horsemen. Averell's plan involved about 1,000 picked men and thirty-six officers from the nine different regiments, some from outside his own brigade. The general never explained this configuration, but he seems to have put more thought into quality horseflesh than into potential command-and-control issues.[12] Averell had sketched a detailed route that delineated each river, ford, village, and town, but beyond mentioning the destruction of "bridges, culverts, telegraph wires, &c.," the objectives were fuzzy. He did not expect the raiders to retrace their route and return to the army at Falmouth on the Rappahannock River, instead riding on to Union lines at Suffolk, southeast of Petersburg. If the roads to Suffolk were blocked, their alternative would be to ride east and south, perhaps as far as Major General John G. Foster's department on the North Carolina coast.[13]

But the raid never took place. Two days after Averell sent Burnside his detailed plan, the army commander's chief of staff hurried a note back stating that information from Washington required postponing his proposed movement. A disappointed Averell would have other opportunities to damage the Confederate war effort, but he would never see the spires of Richmond.[14]

Within a month Burnside was relieved as commander of the Army of the Potomac and replaced by Major General Joseph Hooker on January 26, 1863. The popular "Fighting Joe" Hooker would not only reorganize the army's cavalry into a united corps-size fighting force, under the command of Major General George P. Stoneman, but also send it at nearly full strength on its first major raid. As one historian has concluded, "Whatever the limitations of the florid, pleasant, but rather blustery Major General who took up his Headquarters at Falmouth in the early spring, he did fine things for the morale and organization of his army, and he, more than any other man, built a real Cavalry force for the Army of the Potomac."[15]

Hooker's grand strategic plan for his newly christened Cavalry Corps involved sending Stoneman, a forty-year-old New Yorker, on a wide-ranging sortie behind the entrenched Army of Northern Virginia. But Stoneman did not seem to have the aptitude for such an operation. Granted, he had a solid record, built in the old army as a dragoon fighting Indians and Mexicans, but since Fort Sumter his performance had been lackluster. An able administrator who could shuffle army paperwork efficiently, Stoneman up to this point had failed to show the devil-may-care brassiness of a successful cavalry leader. He might never lose a plumed hat to the foe, but neither did he seem to have the requisite dash and swagger to effectively damage the enemy. Partly this might have stemmed from circumstance. During the Peninsula Campaign, when Stoneman served as McClellan's chief of cavalry, Union horsemen rarely fought in concentrations greater than regimental strength. By December 1862 Stoneman had quit the mounted arm to head an infantry division. Nevertheless, Hooker tapped Stoneman to reorganize and revitalize the Federal cavalry as "Fighting Joe" imagined it.[16]

Hooker's instructions to his new cavalry commander for the coming campaign focused on operating behind enemy lines. At nearly full strength, the Cavalry Corps would embark on one momentous raid, a maneuver never before untaken by Union horse soldiers. Mobility and massive numbers, Hooker reasoned, would allow his mounted warriors to do maximum damage to Confederate supply and communication lines. With Lee distracted by disruptions in his rear, Hooker could move half his main army around the Confederates' left, leaving the remainder to press the Rebels entrenched at Fredericksburg. It was grand strategy—if all went well.

Unfortunately, raids that looked great on paper inevitably took a different form in reality, often devolving into chaotic improvisation demanded by the weather, the enemy's response, lapses in communication, and other conditions. Stoneman's operation was no exception. Hooker had ordered him to leave the Falmouth area fully two weeks before the main army started its turning movement. Two weeks would give the cavalry ample time to wreck Lee's supply depots and communication lines, primarily along the Virginia Central and the Richmond, Fredericksburg, and Potomac Railroad's. Hooker posited that this would spur Lee to pull troops away from Fredericksburg, allowing him to smash the Rebel army with his overwhelming numbers. But the weather failed to cooperate. Stoneman's column, having left only a brigade under Brigadier General Alfred Pleasonton with the army, numbered some 10,000 troopers and four batteries of horse artillery. The force left on time, but before the Federals could cross the Rappahannock, storms struck, swelling the river and turning the roads into mud. The two weeks Stoneman was to have spent wreaking havoc turned into a sodden encampment on the wrong side of the river. By the time the old dragoon's men did cross, Hooker had started his turning movement, shifting the Army of the Potomac across the Rappahannock downriver at Kelly's Ford.[17]

Once across the river, Stoneman split his command per orders, sending General Averell's 3,500-man division, plus Colonel Benjamin F. "Grimes" Davis's brigade, to chase two small Confederate cavalry brigades under Brigadier Generals W. H. F. "Rooney" Lee and his cousin Fitzhugh Lee. Averell botched his assignment, though, wasting so much valuable time stalled in front of Rooney Lee's meager ranks that a frustrated Hooker recalled and relieved him. Meanwhile, Stoneman sent the rest of his command, Brigadier General David McMutrie Gregg's division and General Buford's Reserve Brigade, at a rapid clip on a mission to destroy railroads.[18]

After burning supplies and tearing up track near Louisa Court House, Stoneman pushed on to the South Anna River, crossed it, and then rode to Thompson's Cross Roads. The general gathered his subordinate commanders together, giving them additional instructions for the remainder of the raid. "We had dropped in that region of the country like a shell," Stoneman wrote later. "I intended to burst it in every direction, expecting each piece or fragment would do as much harm and create nearly as much terror as would result from sending the whole shell, and thus magnify our small force into overwhelming numbers."[19]

As planned, Stoneman divided his command into five independent forces. Colonel Percy Wyndham took two regiments toward Columbia in a bid to destroy locks on the James River and Kanawha Canal. Colonel Hasbrouck Davis's 12th Illinois rode to Ashland and Atlee's Station to wreck more track. General Gregg was to lay waste to bridges and track along the South Anna. Stoneman authorized one of his more competent staff officers, Captain Wesley Merritt, to take a detachment from the 1st Maryland to demolish whatever Southern infrastructure he could. And Colonel Kilpatrick was to take his own 2nd New York, riding to the southeast toward Richmond, to hit telegraph lines, railroads, and supply depots. Stoneman himself remained with Buford's brigade to act as a floating reserve in case any of the "shell fragments" needed help.[20]

After doing various amounts of damage, Wyndham, Merritt, and Gregg all made it back to Stoneman and Buford. En route home, Davis found his return path to Thompson's Cross Roads blocked by Confederate reinforcements arriving by train from Richmond. He decided to attack—a grave mistake. The Southerners forced the Illinoisans to abandon their intended route, instead escaping down the Peninsula to Gloucester Point. As for the brazen Kilpatrick, rather than rallying on Stoneman, he had taken the dangerous path to the Brook Turnpike south of Yellow Tavern. This brought him to the gates of Richmond, where the lightly defended outer fortifications of the city tempted the overconfident young colonel. Leading his Harris Light Cavalry through the outer works, he captured fifteen men of the Confederate Provost Marshal, who afterward sneered that their captor might soon be a prisoner himself. Kilpatrick quickly retorted that he meant "to do a mighty deal of mischief first!" But he was no fool. All too aware that he had stayed too long in Richmond's outer precincts, he made for the Chickahominy River, crossed the Meadow Bridges, and burned them. With Confederates on his heels, the colonel found a black guide in the nick of time and rode hard for Hanovertown. There the regiment crossed the Pamunkey River on flatboats that they afterward burned. On May 7 the 2nd New York finally arrived at Gloucester Point inside Federal lines.[21]

Kilpatrick's part in Stoneman's operation matters less for his exploits than for the fact of how much closer he got to Richmond than any of his fellow raiders. Learning afterward of Little Kil's daring sally, President Lincoln clearly recognized how vulnerable the Rebel capital was. Writing to Hooker shortly afterward, the president, who also had information from an exchanged prisoner of war, said he believed that "there was not a sound pair of legs in Richmond, and that our men, had they known it, could have safely gone in and burned everything and brought in Jeff. Davis." His confidence was bolstered a few days later when he received an intelligence report from the Army of the Potomac that claimed there were only 2,700 troops guarding Richmond. If that were true and Kilpatrick had known it, he could have ridden into the heart of the city and perhaps grabbed Davis. It was an idea that would stick in

Lincoln's mind. A Northern newspaper editor wrote that the raiders could "have gone into Richmond, and snaked Jeff. Davis from his bed—such a dash upon that city has been the dream of our enterprising cavalry officers." Ten months later Kilpatrick's daring would pay off when Lincoln sought an adventurous officer to lead a raid to free starving Yankee POWs held in the Confederate capital—and perhaps even to snatch Davis.[22]

For Stoneman, the raid proved less than fruitful. In his own mind the general thought the operation "achieved a strategic success of grand proportions." But Hooker needed a scapegoat for his defeat at the hands of R. E. Lee at Chancellorsville while the cavalry played the exploding shell behind enemy lines. He reasoned that Stoneman's lengthy absence from the main army allowed Lieutenant General Stonewall Jackson's flank attack to develop undetected and ultimately succeed. Stoneman subsequently gave way as Cavalry Corps commander to another rising star in Hooker's galaxy, Alfred Pleasonton (now a major general).[23]

In addition, the raid had no major effect on Lee's army or the Confederacy. Within days the Southerners had rebuilt wrecked bridges, replaced torn-up tracks, and restrung severed telegraph wires. By May 5, trains were running again on the Richmond, Fredericksburg, and Potomac and on the Virginia Central three days later.[24] One thing was certain, however, although it went unnoticed by commanders on either side at the time: cavalry raids on enemy lines of communications simply used up horseflesh and men without permanently damaging the foe. The need for speed limited the equipment troopers could carry, prohibiting such essential items as picks, axes, and black powder for explosives. Only properly equipped infantry could significantly destroy enemy infrastructure.[25]

Under Pleasonton, Federal cavalry raids waned through the remaining months of 1863. Blue-coated troopers instead focused on running Stuart and his cavalrymen to ground and forcing them to fight. Pleasonton's first foray at that task was fairly successful. On June 9 his mounted divisions caught Stuart's horsemen by surprise near Brandy Station. The resulting standup fight lasted most of the day. As charging troopers, riding stirrup to stirrup, swept at one another near St. James Church and Fleetwood Hill, the Union horse soldiers gave a good account of themselves.

This embarrassing surprise seems to have spurred Stuart into another ride around the Union army as Lee again invaded the

North. Crossing the Potomac River at Rowser's Ford, Stuart's ride through Maryland and Pennsylvania resulted in the most controversial action of his military career. Trying to link up with Lee's army in Pennsylvania, his troopers rode to Hanover, where Kilpatrick, recently promoted to brigadier general and command of the Third Cavalry Division, stopped the Rebel raiders cold. Thanks to this delaying action, Stuart required two extra days in getting back to the Army of Northern Virginia—days during which Lee's army was locked in bloody combat with Army of the Potomac, now commanded by Major General George G. Meade, near Gettysburg. Sparking controversy at the time, Stuart's actions still provoke debate whenever the Battle of Gettysburg is discussed.

During the climactic three-day battle, Southerners several times tested the Union horse soldiers' fighting trim. Generally, the Federals prevailed, as in Buford's dismounted delaying action on the battle's first day or David Gregg's massed regiments, augmented by Custer's brigade, attacking Stuart's worn-down troopers east of Gettysburg on the contest's final day. An exception to this excellent Union performance was Kilpatrick's failure on July 3 to roll up the Confederate right south of town. The lapse cost him personally; his young brigadier Elon Farnsworth was killed in the fighting.

In the weeks after Gettysburg, Lee's retreat to Virginia saw multiple cavalry actions but little raiding. From August 1863 until the end of the year, Union and Confederate horse soldiers battled across the fields of central Virginia at such places as Jack's Shop, James City, again at Brandy Station, and at Buckland Mills—energetic fights peripheral to the maneuverings of the two great armies in Culpeper and Fauquier Counties—culminating on October 14 in a bloody engagement at Bristoe Station in western Prince William County. Lee finally had to retreat once more, this time to the south side of the Rappahannock River. That autumn's nearly constant mounted fighting stifled the raiding impulse on either side. Raids were tough on the troopers and their horses, but so were the hard riding, saber charges, and close combat of the recent months, especially on Stuart's bedraggled brigades. As winter neared and forage grew scarce, Lee's cavalry commander was forced to spread his horses across Virginia and other parts of the South. With Stuart thus neutralized by necessity, Federal commanders once again could plot raids.[26]

In December 1863 the ill-starred General Averell got a chance to buff his tarnished reputation by leading a cavalry raid to destroy the

Virginia and Tennessee Railroad. On the three-week foray, which originated with Brigadier General Benjamin Kelley's Department of West Virginia, Averell surprised his opponents, but amid heavy rain and snow, the Confederates managed to regain the initiative. Acting out the scenario of many a Federal raid, his men wrecked railroad equipment at Salem, Virginia—within three or four days the trains were running again. The result was another Union cavalry raid that had used up blood, treasure, and horseflesh without significant results. But planning such strikes, especially in the direction of Richmond, did not stop. Like Averell's operation, these raids would not always originate with the Army of the Potomac's cavalry commanders.

The next raid targeting the Confederate capital came from the direction of the lower Peninsula, where a general who was arguably the Union army's cleverest politician—perhaps with an eye toward his civilian prospects as a presidential candidate—made a calculated decision to hit the city. The results would provide intelligence that would influence Kilpatrick as he struggled to forget devastating personal losses.[27]

CHAPTER 3

BUTLER'S RAID TO
GRAB JEFF DAVIS

When the war's first battles overcrowded Richmond's city jails,
captured Yankees were housed in former warehouses or on an
island located in the swift-flowing James River. Union officers were
held at Libby Prison, a former ship chandlers' warehouse adjacent to
the James River and Kanawha Canal, while enlisted men were put
on Belle Isle across the river from the Tredegar Iron Works. The barren fifty-four-acre island had a makeshift prison hospital and a few
tents and shacks, with rifle pits and artillery posted on a small hill to
deter potential escapees. Southern political prisoners were incarcerated at Castle Thunder, a former tobacco warehouse. By 1863, prisoner exchanges between the North and South had slowed for political
reasons, which quickly led to overcrowding at Libby and Belle Isle.[1]

In August 1863 Union colonel Abel Streight of the 51st Indiana
Infantry took it upon himself to send a letter of protest to the
Confederate secretary of war, James A. Seddon, outlining the ghastly
conditions facing those held in Libby Prison. "About 600 of us are
confined here with an average space of nearly twenty-eight square
feet each, which includes our room for cooking, eating, washing,
bathing, and sleeping," reported Streight. The officer went on to
describe the minuscule amounts of poor beef, meager bread, rice,
and beans provided by the Confederate government. In his concluding opinion about conditions, the colonel observed, "Even criminals
guilty of the blackest crimes are not, among civilized people, confined for any length of time on insufficient food." Streight was able
to convey a copy of his letter to the U.S. Army's commissioner for
the exchange of prisoners, Brigadier General S. A. Meredith, which
surely made its way to President Lincoln.[2]

If the situation for officers at Libby Prison was bad, that of the
enlisted men held on Belle Isle was atrocious. In an area sufficient
for 3,000 men, the Confederates now crammed almost 10,000 captives. To guard against escapes, prisoners were not permitted to use

latrines after dark. "These deposits of excrement have been made in the streets [of the prisoners' camp] and [in] small vacant spaces between the tents." A Union surgeon found the camp conditions "putrid," a breeding ground for diarrhea and dysentery. A paucity of fuel wood added to the men's suffering during January and February. In the latter month alone, 590 men died while being treated in the island's hospital. One escaped officer referred to Belle Isle as "that rebel hell" in a letter addressed directly to the president. He went on to describe how prisoners had frozen to death or simply died of starvation at a rate he estimated to be twenty men per day. Likewise, another Union army surgeon found words inadequate to describe the condition of recently exchanged prisoners from the island in November 1863: "[M]any had no hats or shoes, but few had a whole garment. . . . [S]ome had no underclothing. Their hair was disheveled, their beards long and matted with dirt, their skin blackened and caked with the most loathsome filth, and their bodies and clothing covered with vermin." His report continued with vivid descriptions of the most vile, cadaveric conditions human beings could tolerate and still be alive.[3]

In October 1863 a general food shortage forced Confederate officials to halve the daily ration for prisoners to half a loaf of cornbread each, a few ounces of rancid meat, and some bean soup when available. Word of these and other deprivations spread to the North through both formal and informal channels. From his bunk at Libby Prison, Brigadier General Neal Dow sent a letter directly to Secretary of War Edwin Stanton explaining the sad plight of his fellow prisoners. Soon Northern newspapers were carrying stories by those freed in the now-rare prisoner exchanges. While the bad press stung, Confederate officials worried more about what would happen if the ragged, half-starved prisoners, abetted by Union infiltrators, rose up. "No force under my command can prove adequate to the control of 13,000 hungry prisoners," warned Brigadier General John Winder, the man charged with guarding Richmond's POW population. Worse, such an event could prompt the Yankees to attack the city's weakened defenses.[4]

Even General Lee was concerned about a potential raid to free Union prisoners when he informed Major General Arnold Elzey, commander of the Department of Richmond, on October 9 that since "Colonel [Samuel] Spear is transferring his cavalry to the Peninsula that he designs making a raid in that quarter." Lee's anxiety was probably superfluous because Spear's movement to the Peninsula had nothing to do with a strike on Richmond. Major General John G. Foster, commanding at Fort Monroe, was acting on a recommendation from Brigadier General Isaac Wistar, who requested more cavalry to chase Rebel guerrillas threatening the countryside. Although Foster was implicated by the Richmond press as a person "undoubtedly aware of the existence of such a plot, and gave it aid and countenance," it appears from Federal records that he was adhering to a request from a subordinate for assistance to crush guerrilla activity in his sector rather than mount a raid to free Yankee prisoners.[5]

The *Richmond Daily Examiner* reported on November 23 the foiling of a plot to liberate POWs held in the capital. Without naming names, the paper laid out how Rebel authorities had thwarted a scheme revealed in "intercepted correspondence." On a prearranged night the inmates at Libby, Castle Thunder, and Belle Isle "were to rise en masse at the tolling of the midnight hour, overpower the comparatively few sentinels," seize weapons, and move at the "double quick" toward Williamsburg and Yorktown, some fifty miles away, met halfway by Federal cavalry under Colonel Spear. To facilitate the prison break, unnamed coconspirators would torch Richmond until it was "a pillar of fire by night, a cloud of smoke by day." The plot promised the destruction of "arsenals, Government works, the important bridges across the James, and the gunboats at the navy yard at Rocketts [Landing]."[6]

This prisoner uprising had been brewing for some time before Confederate authorities took it seriously. Newspaper reports claimed that information about it came to light on October 27, followed by more revelations on the thirty-first. After sifting through intelligence, officials added more prison guards, paraded the local militia near the jails, and emplaced more cannon on the heights of Belle Isle. As the papers were reporting on the escape plot, they also were covering discussions for a relocation of the same prisoners to Georgia and elsewhere. Vexed by the Federals' refusal to exchange prisoners, Lee and others saw this dispersal as eminently logical. Sending the prisoners south would ease the burden on Richmond, make it more difficult for them to escape, and would prevent them from communicating with Union sympathizers. Maintaining a large POW contingent at the Confederate capital made it a "great point of attack of the enemy in the eastern portion of the Confederacy, and the emergency might arise in which it would be exceedingly inconvenient to have Federal prisoners within its limits," as Lee maintained.[7] In his usual measured language, the general suggested that Richmond lacked the forces to deal with 13,000 escaped prisoners, arguing that if those men were scattered across the Deep South, their compatriots would have less impetus to try to free them. On the Federal side, the same implicit awareness made some think the time was ripe to make a move on Richmond.

In November 1863 two events occurred that would change Judson Kilpatrick's life. One would affect the general very personally. The other, while indirect, would create circumstances that would influence his actions as an enterprising cavalry commander.

On November 23 Little Kil received a telegram that broke his heart. He was needed at West Point, New York, where his wife, Alice, and infant son, Judson, were living. Although the general hurried north, his beloved wife of less than three years died before he could reach her side; she had been in "delicate health" for some time, but no one attending her condition believed her death eminent. The tragedy was the first of what would be a double blow for the devoted husband, who had a yellow streamer bearing Alice's name fastened atop his battle flag. The following month their only child, just a year old, also died.[8]

Two weeks before Alice's death, the War Department had relieved General Foster as commander of the Department of Virginia and North Carolina, a post he had held since July 1863. It was not that Foster merited removal, but more the case that Lincoln needed to find a spot for his replacement, Major General Benjamin Butler, who had been relieved from his New Orleans command the previous December.[9] Butler's new assignment would be inextricability linked to Kilpatrick's fortunes in the months ahead.

Butler had been at Fort Monroe early in the hostilities. A War Democrat from Massachusetts, where he had served in the state legislature, Butler first came to note when public opinion credited him with saving Washington shortly after the firing on Fort Sumter. With bellicose Marylanders blockading the entrance to the nation's capital, he boldly landed his Massachusetts soldiers at Annapolis, a flourish that broke the "siege" of Washington. As the war progressed, Butler continued to enlarge his reputation, though not always in a positive way.[10]

In May 1861 Butler's military bravado and political clout led Lincoln to appoint him the Union army's first major general of volunteers. Based at Fort Monroe, his troops lost a fight at nearby Big Bethel in June, but at the same time their leader, using his legal skills, guaranteed his place in American history. Vexed by the question of how to classify and what to do with slaves who had fled their masters or were captured by Federal troops, the general labeled them "contraband of war"—a martial term historically applied to captured weapons and materiel. Turning the Rebel concept of humans as chattel upside down, Butler reasoned that as Confederate property, slaves who crossed the lines became "contraband" to be treated as one might seize cannon, rifles, and other munitions. Welcoming former slaves into Union territory by any means necessary would reduce the labor force that kept the South going. Butler's impeccable and perverse logic maddened slaveowners but made the general popular up North.

Shortly thereafter his political influence with the Lincoln administration won the general command of the land forces accompanying a Union fleet under Admiral David G. Farragut in a combined operation against New Orleans. The subsequent capture of the Confederacy's largest city gave the North control of the mouth of the Mississippi River—and gave Butler, in his capacity as military governor, another chance to outrage Rebels. The general issued a police order that basically tagged white women in the Crescent City, many of whom had taken to insulting his soldiers in the streets, as prostitutes if they continued the practice. Residents soon dubbed their bluecoat overlord "Beast Butler," a sobriquet that stuck for life and had some basis in fact. Not only was Butler cross eyed but, as an Army of the Potomac staff officer described him, "an astounding figure on a horse! Short, fat, shapeless; no neck, squinting, and very bald headed, and, above all, that singular, half defiant look!"[11]

No stranger to making money on his military connections, especially in a city as loose as New Orleans, Butler lined his pockets and those of his friends and family with ill-gotten spoils from cotton smuggling and other nefarious pursuits. The aroma of corruption was so obvious and the resentment of it so ubiquitous that in December 1862 Lincoln had to remove Butler. But the general's intimidating political power required that the president find another assignment for the forty-five-year-old or risk facing him as an opponent in 1864. By assigning him again to Fort Monroe, Lincoln meant to stow Butler where he could not shine but with a promotion as a department commander. He probably intended it as a first step toward Butler's eventual obscurity, but such would not be the case.[12]

The general reached the Hampton Roads area in early November 1863, greeted with admiration by General Wistar, his new chief subordinate. Wistar would soon write to his new commander, thanking him for all his "manifold kindness and consideration" since coming under his authority. As Wistar put it, "A thousand false impressions have been removed from my mind, and it shall be a business of my life to assist friends in doing what you will not—do for yourself, viz. remove similar ones from the minds of others." The general seems to have regarded his new commander as a victim of army and civilian politics, a fate with which he too was familiar, having been assigned to the backwater department principally due to his personal politics. He and Butler had much in common.[13]

Isaac Wistar, a thirty-six-year-old Philadelphia lawyer and former gold miner, had entered the war as a captain in the 71st Pennsylvania Infantry, the so-called California Regiment. This unit had been raised by former California senator and Lincoln ally Colonel Edward D. Baker. In October 1861 Wistar commanded the regiment as its lieutenant colonel at Ball's Bluff, a battle in which Baker led a brigade and was killed. The brief but harsh Union debacle cost Wistar three wounds, the last paralyzing his right arm for life. Succeeding Baker as colonel of the 71st Pennsylvania, he took part in the Peninsula Campaign. He took another severe wound, this time in the left arm, at Antietam, where a young Confederate lieutenant came to his aid. John S. Mosby, not yet famous as a partisan commander, adjusted the Union officer's makeshift tourniquet and gave him a much needed drink of water. After the war Wistar learned the identity of his Samaritan; he and Mosby would be linked again.[14]

After Antietam Wistar had to leave the service for about eight months to recuperate in Philadelphia. In May 1863 he accepted promotion to brigadier general but was reassigned from the Army of the Potomac. Washington officials stowed him away in Suffolk, Virginia, a sleepy backwater post, "[f]or political reasons, it was said[; for] not agreeing with some of the policies of the predominant party, more than for the alleged disability caused by his wound, he had been consigned to comparative retirement and inactivity at Yorktown," one observer noted. Whether Wistar was truly important enough politically for the Lincoln administration to worry about is questionable. But generals with Democratic Party affiliations, in addition to being wounded war heroes from powerful states, were numerous enough within the Army of the Potomac to cause concern. A fellow

Philadelphian felt Wistar had "brains and zeal and true devotedness in the good cause. . . . He is brave as a lion and a good disciplinarian [but] from this cause has some enemies who may seek to injure him." Putting Wistar in the Hampton Roads area would keep him out of the limelight. He would remain there into 1864.[15]

In November 1863 Wistar and Butler met at Fort Monroe as fellow veterans and aggrieved political allies. Their Democratic Party affiliation offered a common bond from which an excellent relationship would develop. When a railroad executive praised Wistar to Butler, the general scoffed at the compliment. "I do not need it to know my man," he said. Wistar felt so comfortable with his new commander that he immediately shared a stratagem concocted by one of his subordinates that potentially could win Butler the presidency in 1864. Most likely Butler was already hearing such rumblings among admirers who felt that he had the "necessary qualifications" of "consummate wisdom, pure patriotism and unyielding firmness" to challenge Lincoln. Although he did not always pay close attention to such fawning, the general did listen to Wistar's purloined idea.[16]

Dated November 24, Wistar's proposal for a raid on Richmond had originated with Colonel Robert M. West, one of his subordinates, commanding at Williamsburg. West, a twenty-nine-year-old New Jersey native, had enlisted in the regular army in peacetime as a private in the Mounted Rifles, winning a commission in a Pennsylvania artillery unit after Fort Sumter. He served as the chief of artillery for Major General Erasmus D. Keyes's IV Corps during the Peninsula Campaign, fighting at Yorktown, Williamsburg, Seven Pines, and the Seven Days' Battles around Richmond. When the Army of the Potomac headed back to northern Virginia, West stayed behind, later transferring to the 5th Pennsylvania Cavalry as its colonel. His eighteen months' service on the Peninsula had given him an intimate knowledge of the main roads, back paths, terrain, enemy picket posts, and local inhabitants from Yorktown to the Chickahominy River. Wistar described the colonel as "an accomplished soldier of great prudence and judgment."[17]

West's motive in presenting his plan to Wistar seems to have been noble. He grieved for his comrades held prisoner in Richmond and wanted badly to free them. The colonel did not care who commanded the raid, declaring to Wistar that he was not proposing the action with the intent to lead it. "Not at all," he wrote. "I will further it with all the resources of my mind and of the means under my control."[18] Whether the rescue operation was his own inspiration or if he was influenced by what he had read in Richmond newspapers or heard through a grapevine of Union sympathizers West did not reveal.

The colonel based his plan on careful study and told the general that he had been developing it for over a year. West tallied nearly 1,400 enemy soldiers occupying positions between Williamsburg and Richmond, most of them in Brigadier General Eppa Hunton's 800-strong brigade encamped at Chaffin's Farm. Two smaller mounted units of about 250 men each were located at Bottom's Bridge and Charles City Court House.[19] West recommended marching all available cavalry to Williamsburg under cover of darkness and hiding the men and their mounts on a farm out of sight from the main road. Infantry scouts would take the point, capturing all Rebel pickets and courier posts between that town and Richmond. The main body of cavalry would leave Williamsburg by night, timing its departure to arrive at Bottom's Bridge by 3:00 A.M. If the span was out, they could use a nearby ford to cross the Chickahominy, then rout the Holcombe Legion, a South Carolina unit guarding the bridge on the south side. That would leave a straight ride of only twelve miles into Richmond, and West knew every challenge along the way. Once through a gantlet of outer works, the Federals would encounter no other fortifications.

Richmond had "never been before so entirely helpless for defense," West noted. Positing an easy run for his cavalrymen, "the best troops in the world could scarcely recover from such a surprise in time to make an effectual resistance," the colonel maintained. The location of the prisons was well known. West expected "terror" roused by the raiders to "inspire" the POWs to escape and break into the city arsenal for arms and ammunition. The freed soldiers would be organized and led by the escaped officers, pressing into service carriages and ambulances to carry comrades unable to march. West left the decision about holding the city to be made based on circumstances once his men were inside the capital. West's plan seemed foolproof and to guarantee success.[20]

West had nothing but disdain for the Rebel forces guarding the city. "The garrison of Richmond at present is of the most ineffective troops of the so-called Confederacy," he said. "They would be overwhelmed completely with the shock of alarm." Whether Secretary of War Stanton eventually received word of West's opinion from General Butler is unknown. The colonel warned Wistar against communicating the scheme using "telegraphic communication" for fear of detection until the proposal was "consummated or abandoned."[21]

Wistar clearly liked West's thinking; he immediately forwarded the plan to Butler, enthusiastically endorsing it and adding his own comments about Richmond's local defense forces and possible reinforcements available from Petersburg. Once inside the city, he suggested, "parties of picked men, selected from exchanged prisoners and others locally acquainted, might be detached to fire public buildings, including, if possible, the Tredegar Iron Works." The raiders could call on Wistar's infantry to assist the fleeing prisoners, he noted, once they reached Bottom's Bridge. In addition, the crippled general thought it would be helpful to have a small gunboat steam up the lower Chickahominy River to support the operation. While Wistar saw merit in West's scheme, he wanted to grab the glory. He suggested to Butler that the colonel was qualified only to command the cavalry, while he himself would be happy "to assume responsibility and conduct of the enterprise."[22]

West had warned of his proposal, "if it is to be done, it should be done quickly." But his well-intentioned scheme fell into the headquarters morass, and an opportunity to save the longsuffering Union prisoners was lost. Why Ben Butler failed to implement this plan to raid Richmond is not clear. Surely the venture would have appealed to the politically savvy general. Perhaps he may not have felt sufficiently established in his new command, having only been in the post two weeks. The press may have gotten wind of the idea and thus compromised its chances for success. In his diary a Confederate War Department clerk noted that "it was predicted in the Northern papers that Richmond would be taken in some mysterious manner, and that there was a plan for the prisoners of war to seize it by a *coup de main.*"[23]

To test his subordinates in a less ambitious exercise, Butler authorized an expedition coordinated by Wistar and commanded by West. The mission, a combined cavalry and infantry operation, was to root out enemy troops holding a position near Charles City Court House, about thirty-nine miles west of Williamsburg. The Confederates made little or no resistance. The men in Wistar's command showed here that they had the mettle for a longer foray, perhaps as far as Richmond. A proud Colonel West told Butler that his cavalry had covered seventy-six miles in forty-four hours and his foot soldiers had marched sixty-seven miles in fifty-four hours. Wistar touted his subordinate's performance as field commander. A pleased Butler wrote back to the general, "[West's] action brings him up to the standard of his reputation." Even the *Richmond Examiner* called the operation "a brilliant affair."[24]

During his early days as departmental commander, official dispatches show Butler was busy with a number of military activities occurring in North Carolina as well as Virginia. He sought to expand his territorial authority by requesting the subjoining of Maryland's St. Mary's County and Northampton and Accomack Counties in Virginia to his department. Butler's correspondence shows he was dealing with Secretary of State William Seward about tobacco-ownership issues involving foreign counties, an initial move to organize a black cavalry regiment, tracking Rebel spies in Alexandria, a horrific fire in Yorktown, and distributing a smallpox vaccine to POWs in Richmond. His letters also illustrate that he was trying to either repair his sullied reputation or curry favor with the War Department by providing Stanton with intelligence reports obtained from Richmond newspapers. He wrote nearly every day to the secretary of war, and by early December 1863 they were on closer terms. Stanton candidly shared with Butler his mild annoyance with the Army of the Potomac's commander when he tersely wrote, "Meade is on the back track again without a fight." As part of his intelligence gathering, Butler was trying to locate a map of Richmond from a fellow general headquartered in Baltimore. He feared to buy one because he felt it "would cause remark."[25] Amid this cascade of responsibilities and finagling, Wistar's raid proposal would have to wait, though not for long.

West's and Wistar's success near Charles City Court House may have prompted Butler to strengthen his ties with Elizabeth Van Lew, a well-to-do Richmond woman who was anxious to cultivate the relationship. The forty-five-year-old spinster was an ardent Union sympathizer and wily spymaster who had been providing Federal authorities with occasional intelligence. In the guise of assisting Yankee POWs for two years, Van Lew coursed through the Confederate capital's streets in shabby clothing singing to herself, leading some residents to mockingly refer to her as "Crazy Bet." But through her deception, Van Lew was fine tuning her spy craft, even managing to place one of her loyal black servants in the president's residence to soak up information about the Davis family. Butler appreciated the risks she was willing to take for the Union cause. As one of her biographers put it, the "infamous Beast would be a sort of patron saint for Elizabeth Van Lew."[26]

But Van Lew was not alone, for in the shadows and behind closed doors, others in Richmond also embraced the Federal cause. In mid-December 1863 the city's Union underground helped two POWs escape, a breakout that seems to have prompted Butler to reach out to a friend he and Van Lew had in common to ascertain her sincerity. On December 19 the general wrote confidentially to topographical engineer Charles O. Boutelle of the U.S. Coast Survey in Washington. Butler had gotten to know Boutelle as commander of the steamer *Chancellor Bibb*, part of the Federal fleet sent against New Orleans, and recalled that he and Van Lew had some distant linkage, however unclear. The general wrote that he had received by messenger a letter from Van Lew, apparently "a true union woman as true as steel" and a friend of the engineer's, in which she described Richmond's widespread network of Union sympathizers. Butler wanted a Richmond contact able to keep his headquarters informed about events in the Confederate capital and asked if Van Lew might be trustworthy and capable in that role. The general said that he was willing to pay her in cash but hesitated to mention money for fear of offending her patriotic sensibilities. Boutelle vouched for Van Lew.[27]

It seems likely that Butler already was putting together the pieces for a Richmond raid, which may have included kidnapping Jefferson Davis, before he connected with Van Lew.[28] Around January 19, 1864, while in Washington, Butler met with Major General Henry Halleck, Secretary of War Stanton, and perhaps President Lincoln. Halleck resisted whatever scheme Butler floated, but Stanton and Lincoln apparently overruled him.

Encouraged by Boutelle, Butler began recruiting Van Lew and another Union sympathizer in the capital, William Rowley, for his spy network. The general stated that he easily could arrange to receive coded intelligence from them via the flag-of-truce boat that made regular runs up and down the James River delivering mail and civilians between Richmond and Fort Monroe. He would use the alias "James Ap Jones, Norfolk" for an address. Van Lew agreed to send him letters that would look like family correspondence but whose real contents would be encrypted messages written in invisible ink. On January 30 she sent her first communiqué to her "Uncle," delivered by a young boy whom Butler never named in his correspondence but who may have been Merritt Rowley, the son of William Rowley. The dispatch reported yesterday's news: namely, the well-known Confederate plan to move Union prisoners to Georgia, noting that butchers and bakers, essential to feed the POWs in their new location, were preparing to go south at once. Van Lew learned this from the Richmond papers and from a fellow operative, codenamed "Quaker," who may have been William Rowley. The eccentric Van Lew went on to suggest that Butler might have multiple sources for obtaining covert information at his headquarters and provided a warning. "Beware of new and rash council [*sic*]! Beware!" she wrote. "This I send you by direction of all your friends." Van Lew went on to recommend against any raid "made with less than 30,000 cavalry, from 10,000 to 15,000 infantry to support them, amounting in all to 40,000 or 45,000 troops. *Do not underrate their strength and desperation*" (italics added).[29]

Besides reading Van Lew's written message, Butler questioned the young courier. The boy provided more information than the letter did, including advice from Quaker. According to the youth, the operative strongly recommended using a large force to have any hope of capturing Richmond. Quaker suggested a feint toward Petersburg, a simultaneous movement by Meade against Lee on the Rapidan River, and another maneuver by about 300 men from the northeast side of Richmond—mostly likely from Rooney Lee's plantation, White House—to divert Confederate attention. Butler should "then have 10,000 cavalry . . . go up in the evening [from Yorktown], and then rush into Richmond the next morning."[30]

Butler probably dismissed as nonsensical Van Lew's estimate that it would take 40,000 men to raid Richmond. The general never commented directly, but neither he nor Meade could muster so many troops, much less 30,000 of them on horseback. Indeed, there were far fewer than 40,000 men in Butler's entire two-state department. Neither did he comment on the validity of Quaker's lower estimate of 10,000 riders required for a strike on Richmond. But Butler did think the raid practicable. According to Captain David Edward Cronin of the 1st New York Mounted Rifles, stationed on the Peninsula, "The most enthusiastic believer in the feasibility of such an enterprise was Gen. Butler." A skeptical Wistar came around to the idea, according to Cronin. "While not so sanguine of success, Gen. Wistar was also persuaded that a well planned and carefully executed surprise was worth undertaking," he noted, "even as a forlorn hope—the results on the event of triumph being of such magnitude and of great national importance."[31] Unquestionably, Butler was ready to try. On February 2 he telegraphed Wistar asking obliquely about conditions on the Chickahominy. "How is the water at Bottom's Bridge?" he inquired, aware that cavalry could ford efficiently only if the river was low enough.[32]

Several days after Butler received Van Lew's letter, he passed on her report and a transcript of his conversation with the courier to the secretary of war. The dispatch carried the marking "private and immediate" to ensure its direct delivery into Stanton's hands. In the accompanying cover letter, Butler pressed for more troops, estimating that with 40,000 men he could take and hold Richmond, a feat he could not manage with his department's present effective strength of fewer than 37,000 men. Even without reinforcements, Butler apparently was ready to act, using the plan originally proposed by Wistar and West two months earlier. "Now, or never, is the time to strike," he told Stanton, declaring himself ready, if need be, to "make a dash with 6,000 men, all I have that can possibly be spared. If we win, it will pay the cost; if we fail, it will at least be in an attempt to do our duty and rescue our friends."[33]

Butler here was clearly thinking politically rather than militarily. The Confederates had cut into their forces near Richmond to abet an advance by Major General George Pickett (of Gettysburg fame) into North Carolina. The eastern part of that state was a Confederate pantry, supplying herds and foodstuffs to feed Rebel troops in Virginia and the West. Pickett, poised at Kinston with a substantial force, reasoned that taking New Bern, on the Neuse River, would fend off Yankee incursions deeper into the state. Confederate authorities figured that Butler would have his hands full with Pickett, thus diminishing any Federal threat to Richmond. Their Northern counterparts assumed that an attack on Lee's Rapidan River line would draw reinforcements from Richmond because the Army of Northern Virginia had been weakened the previous September by the deployment of Lieutenant General James Longstreet's corps (less Pickett's Division) to the western theater. With a coordinated feint by the Army of the Potomac, Butler could swoop down on the lightly defended capital with a lightning strike of cavalry, free the POWs, destroy various installations, and perhaps grab Jefferson Davis as a coup de grace. The plan had merit—if all the pieces fell into place.[34]

Prior to filing his urgent request with Stanton, Butler had been busy lining up support for his Richmond raid with army brass. Crucial to the scheme was cooperation from the Army of the Potomac, now temporarily commanded by Major General John Sedgwick due to Meade's bout with pneumonia. As Butler saw it, the army should make a series of diversionary attacks and maneuvers at key fords along the Rapidan, which would tie down Lee's army for as long as it took the raiders to advance on Richmond. These feints would also relieve pressure on New Bern, to which Butler felt Lee was also sending troops. But the chore of getting Meade to cooperate was wearing on him. As he impatiently put it in a dispatch to Halleck on February 3, "Why can't Meade move on Friday [February 5]," unaware of the army commander's illness. The cautious Sedgwick may not have wanted to put his neck on the line for Beast Butler, who had not attended West Point and whose unsavory reputation was widely known among fellow officers. But for reasons he did not explain, Halleck refused to help from Washington, forcing Butler to deal directly with Sedgwick.

Later on February 3, telegrams flew between Halleck, Sedgwick, Butler, and Stanton. Within ninety minutes of hearing from Washington in the form of identical messages from Stanton and Halleck, Butler was on the wire to Sedgwick trying to work a deal. The rationale Butler offered the VI Corps commander was that a movement by the Army of the Potomac would relieve pressure on New Bern and allow another "movement I desire to make." Before contacting Sedgwick, however, he fired off a single telegram to both Stanton and Halleck, urgently asserting: "Now is the time, if ever, for General Meade to move; the roads are practicable. That will relieve North Carolina at once *and leave a movement for me of which I spoke to you*" (italics added).

At first Sedgwick stalled. He explained to Butler that Lee's army was indeed in his front, but inclement weather and bad roads prevented a flank movement. Plus, he said, the Rapidan line was "so strongly entrenched that a demonstration upon it would not disturb Lee's army." His stance did not surprise Butler, who had felt for a long time that he had no friends in the Army of the Potomac. But after receiving an order from Halleck around noon on February 5 to give Butler "such co-operation as you can, and communicate with him directly," Sedgwick reluctantly acquiesced. Acting as much a politician himself, he had covered all his bases earlier that day by telling the secretary of war that he would cooperate with the department commander. Butler earlier had complained, "I can get no co-operation from Sedgwick," but soon had to backpedal and admit to Stanton that the general had come aboard. Sedgwick confirmed to Butler that, weather permitting, he would make an effort on Sunday, the seventh. "Uncle John" Sedgwick still was not going to flank Lee's army, but he would attack the Rapidan line. Butler continued to urge action sooner rather than later, telling Sedgwick not to let weather stand in his way. Frustrated, he closed his dispatch to Stanton in veiled sarcasm: "So we may get some co-operation. All the better. We will do our duty." At 9:00 P.M. on Friday the fifth, Sedgwick finally confirmed to Butler that on Sunday the Army of the Potomac would fulfill his request.[35]

Committed to a demonstration against the Army of Northern Virginia that at the least discomfited him and at the worst disgusted him, Sedgwick began issuing orders on Saturday to get part of the army into action. According to one of Meade's staff officers, "Old Sedgwick and Gen. Humphreys [Meade's chief of staff] are cross at the whole thing, looking on it as childish." Nevertheless, the troops got word that evening to prepare to march at seven o'clock the next morning. Two infantry corps and most of the Cavalry Corps would take part in the probes along the Rapidan. The two infantry-corps commanders, Major Generals John Newton (I Corps) and Gouverneur K. Warren (II Corps), were ordered to "communicate, co-operate, and support each other" as necessary. In turn, Newton would be supported by two infantry divisions from Major General David B. Birney's III Corps. His objective was Raccoon Ford; Warren's was Morton's Ford, about three miles downstream from Newton. Once across Morton's Ford, if Warren's men could not hold their position on the south bank, they were to withdraw. If they held that ground with not too great a loss, however, Warren had the authority to press the initiative. The footsloggers took three days' rations but brought no wagons with them, only ambulances and pontoons. Brigadier General David McMutrie Gregg, temporarily commanding the Cavalry Corps, was ordered to send Brigadier General Wesley Merritt's First Cavalry Division over Barnett's Ford, about twelve miles upstream from Newton, while Kilpatrick's Third Cavalry Division was sent to Culpeper Mine Ford, about fourteen miles downstream from Morton's Ford. They were to use their "best mounted men." Little Kil also was to detach some troopers to cross at Ely's Ford and at Germanna Ford, crossings east and west, respectively, of Culpeper Mine.[36]

Meanwhile, awaiting confirmation of the Army of the Potomac's diversionary movement and with Confederate pressure subsiding around New Bern, Butler's arrangements rushed forward for a raid on Richmond. The officer entrusted to lead the operation was Butler's senior subordinate and loyal factotum, Isaac Wistar, commanding at Yorktown. Wistar would have at his disposal 2,200 cavalry and 4,000 infantry along with two six-gun batteries. He would accompany the foot soldiers. The cavalry would consist of detachments from five regiments brigaded under Colonel Spear, the forty-nine-year-old former commander of the 11th Pennsylvania Cavalry. A Mexican War veteran, he had served as a first sergeant in the famed 2nd U.S. Cavalry before Fort Sumter. One soldier described the colonel as "a bronzed old regular, familiar with the Peninsula and distinguished for dash and daring on many fields." Wistar's infantry was evenly divided among three white regiments commanded by Colonel West and three "colored" regiments brigaded under Colonel Samuel A. Duncan. West, of course, brought the experience of a former regular seasoned by over a year's service on the Peninsula. Among his regiments was the 139th New York Infantry. Duncan was a twenty-seven-year-old Dartmouth College graduate, a former schoolteacher, and a veteran of the 14th New Hampshire Infantry before obtaining a coveted colonelcy in a U.S. Colored Troops regiment. Wistar's two batteries (also commanded by West) were Captain James Belger's Battery F, 1st Rhode Island Light Artillery, and Lieutenant John S. Hunt's Battery L, 4th U.S. Artillery. These units gathered at Williamsburg after dark on February 5 as Butler waited until after 9:00 P.M. for confirmation from Sedgwick that he would demonstrate against Lee the next day.[37]

Sunday morning in Culpeper County was "foggy & warm with some drizzle, from time to time." The II Corps's soldiers rose early, but illness kept General Warren from marching with them. He may have been dealing with a migraine headache such as had confined him to camp before. Brigadier General John C. Caldwell, commanding in Warren's absence, advanced a small force across Morton's Ford. Nasty roads had kept the bluecoats from bringing along pontoons and also hampered some artillery batteries' movements due to washed-out farm lanes. But by 10:00 A.M. "cannonading commenced very loud though not very rapid," according to a Union chaplain. Two regiments from Brigadier General Alexander Hays's

Third Division plunged across the cold, fast-running river through waist-deep water. Not standing on rank, Hays himself grabbed an ax to help his men clear away the enemy's obstructions at the ford. The dripping-wet infantrymen surprised the Rebels, taking some outposts, capturing about thirty men from the famous Stonewall Brigade, and then advancing about three quarters of a mile to a ridge facing the Southern army's main works. Caldwell pushed across Brigadier General Joshua Owen's brigade as support. Hays's midday advance caused a sharp exchange to erupt between the two sides.

R. E. Lee rushed reinforcements to his front. The Yankees on the Rapidan's south bank now became caught on a neck of land where Confederate cannoneers could lay down a concentrated, plunging crossfire. Later in the day General Hays received permission to wade the remainder of his division forward across the river. The general remained mounted as eight bullets ripped into the body of his horse, his staff staying by his side as shrapnel tore their mounts from under them and blew off their hats. A lieutenant in the 126th New York Infantry a few days after the fight recalled how "we held the position till nearly dark, when the Rebels made a grand charge along nearly the whole line with a force at least five to one; but our men stood their ground manfully, contending every inch of ground, till a fresh brigade came to their aid, when the enemy were checked and ourselves saved from annihilation." Meanwhile, Caldwell's own division was stationed in a wood line up from the north bank of the river but did not advance.

Apparently unaware of Sedgwick's overall strategy for a limited demonstration at Morton's Ford, the always aggressive Hays begged Caldwell for support. "If supported by our whole corps I have not the least doubt that we would have been enabled to capture the whole force of rebels, including camp and artillery, with less loss then we have suffered," he later reported. Finally, toward nightfall Brigadier General Alexander S. Webb's Second Division, held in reserve most of the day, was ordered to join Hays, though only to facilitate a withdrawal. Two hours later the Confederates had regained the lost ground, forming a strong defense at Morton's Ford.[38] The fighting throughout the day had provided an open spectacle for observers not directly in combat. A peering officer in Caldwell's inactive division excitedly recorded in his diary, "The field of operations was in full view, and our division lay intently watching the progress of the fight, which like all battles, big or little, was extremely fascinating."[39]

Meanwhile, Kilpatrick crossed the river at Culpeper Mine Ford with one brigade while his other regiments struck upstream at Germanna Ford. Michigan troopers drove in Rebel pickets "with their seven shooters in hot haste after them; they more than made the dust fly." The general sent out scouts in a ten-mile radius but failed to find the enemy in force, by sunset bagging about ten prisoners. He stayed on the south side of the Rapidan until the next morning, returning his men to camp around noon.[40]

On the army's far-right flank, Merritt was the first to cross the Robinson River with his cavalry division, which moved on to cross the Rapidan at Barnett's Ford. After a brisk skirmish with some of Stuart's horsemen, they drove the Confederates back. Eager for a fight, Merritt's troopers scoured the countryside before recrossing the Rapidan on Sunday evening with about ten prisoners.[41]

As darkness descended "the blaze of cannon muzzles could be seen plainly." By 9:30 P.M. most of the artillery firing ceased except for "an occasional report of cannon during most of the night." By 11:45 P.M. a recovered Warren was able to report from the battlefield that his troops had been withdrawn from the river crossings except for 150 infantrymen holding a position on the south bank. His corps had lost about 250 men, mostly casualties in Hays's division. At this time Sedgwick ordered Warren to fully disengage. Between 8:20 and 11:35 P.M., the Union cavalry was ordered back to camp. At Raccoon Ford Newton's demonstration was so incidental that he filed no report. By 3:00 P.M. the next day, both he and Birney were ordered back to their camps as well.[42]

For Sedgwick's offensive to be rated a success, the Confederates had to react in strength and with effort. On both counts the Rapidan exercise failed. In a letter home one of Lee's staff officers called the demonstration "very weak," concluding that it "failed to accomplish the desired result, as it did not deter us from re-enforcing General Elzey" at Richmond. Northerners drew a similar inference. A military newspaper editor wrote that the "result of the reconnaissance does not, however, bear out the theory that Lee's army is partly demoralized or very much depleted."[43]

Back on the Peninsula, General Wistar had dispatched two scouts to cut the telegraph wires between a station at Meadow Bridges and Richmond. One, a Virginian from Gloucester County, was from the 11th Pennsylvania; Spear told the general he could "trust him." Wistar sweetened the assignment by offering each man a $250 reward if they succeeded in cutting the wire, an action he hoped would keep Confederate pickets on the Peninsula from alerting Richmond's defenders about the Federal advance until it was too late. Wistar intended to move on February 6 and be at Bottom's Bridge by 5:00 A.M. the next morning. He wrote confidently to Butler expressing gratitude for the opportunity to lead the raid, saying again how happy he was to be under his command. In the Pennsylvania general's opinion, "[i]f the principal cavalry officers are brave the thing must succeed," declaring that he had not overlooked anything in his planning. He asked his commander to "pray for our country and for me," signing his missive, "Your attached friend." But there was one contingency that Wistar had not envisioned.[44]

At Williamsburg the night before the mission was to start, Spear received very detailed orders from Wistar. The colonel was to march at 11:00 A.M., sending Captain Samuel Hill with Company F, 1st New York Mounted Rifles, riding ahead on picked horses to capture Rebel picket posts at New Kent Court House, Baltimore Crossroads, and Bottom's Bridge. The general expected him to take these positions without firing a shot. At Bottom's, as Wistar described it, Hill would find a twenty-man picket occupying a log house on the left side at the far end of the bridge. Once the span was secured, Spear's brigade would proceed west on the Williamsburg Road toward Richmond after leaving one hundred men from the 1st District of Columbia Cavalry to guard the crossing until the infantry arrived. The colonel was to disregard the 250 Confederates of the Holcombe Legion who were camped nearby the Williamsburg Road unless they attacked. The column would move as quickly as possible past Battery No. 2 in the city's defensive line, either capturing or avoiding the battery as circumstances dictated. Spear's primary objective was to enter the Rebel capital as quickly as possible, not seize and secure positions along the way. Wistar estimated that the cavalry would have ninety minutes to get to Richmond before the enemy knew what was happening. Though concerned about the York River telegraph line, the general resolved in his mind that he could not "accomplish anything worthwhile without some risk."[45]

Very specific orders detailed the work cut out for Spear's subordinates once in the city. Major Franklin A. Stratton and 250 troopers from the 11th Pennsylvania would destroy the navy yard at Rocketts Landing. The 3rd New York Cavalry under Lieutenant Colonel George B. Lewis would break from the column to the left,

free the inmates at Libby Prison, and torch specific public buildings. Lewis's cavalrymen would then ride across the James at Mayo's
Bridge, dashing along the river's south side to the bridge linking
Belle Isle with the mainland. There the New Yorkers would free the
enlisted POWs held on the island, shepherd them across the Mayo
Bridge back into the city, then return to the Mayo Bridge, burning
it and the Petersburg railroad bridge. Meanwhile, Colonel Benjamin
F. Onderdonk and 250 men from the 1st New York Mounted Rifles
would destroy the Virginia Central Railroad depot at the corner of
Broad and Sixteenth Streets, after which they would proceed to the
Richmond, Fredericksburg, and Potomac Railroad depot at Broad
and Eighth and put it to the torch. Onderdonk was cautioned to cut
all telegraph lines as soon as he saw them.[46]

The raid's most critical mission was reserved for Major James
N. Wheelan, who with another 300 troopers from the 1st New York
Mounted Rifles was to turn right at Twelfth Street and gallop up
Marshall Street to President Davis's doorstep. The orders were specific: they were to "capture Jeff Davis at his residence." Since it
would be a Sunday morning, the president probably would be home
working in his office. To help locate Davis, Wheelan had with him
the president's former gardener, who had earlier escaped to Union
lines. At the same time, Lieutenant Colonel William Lewis and
his 5th Pennsylvania Cavalry would trot up Main Street to Eighth,
cooperate with the 3rd New York's attack at Belle Isle, and then
"destroy the Tredegar Iron Works and numerous public buildings, factories, and store-houses adjacent." Spear himself would
take the remainder of the 11th Pennsylvania and 1st District of
Columbia Cavalry and establish a reserve post at Capitol Square
to support the other detachments. Each of the various commands
would report back to Spear once they had accomplished their mis-
sions except Wheelan, who was to spirit Davis as quickly as possible to Bottom's Bridge, where waiting infantry would provide
stronger security for their valuable prisoner. Wistar assured Spear
that his men would have at least two, perhaps three, hours to carry
out their assignments in the city before having to contend with
Confederate defenders.[47]

In a sense the whole plan looked similar to Stoneman's May
1863 raid. While Wistar's strike would be on a much smaller scale
within Richmond's city limits, with crisp objectives, it also was
designed to surprise the enemy. Unsuspecting Confederates, charged

with reacting to the situation, would be in shock, not knowing which way to turn.

Apparently, Butler had gotten his hands on a good map of Richmond, and Wistar had used it well. But even after a century and a half, two things about the plan remain a mystery. In so detailed an undertaking, Wistar never issued orders about what to do with the freed POWs, especially since a number of them would be feeble or injured from their captivity, once they were across the Mayo Bridge. Perhaps he had in mind West's November 1863 outline, which recommended commandeering all available wagons and ambulances, but never put it in writing. Another oddity is Wistar's enigmatic concluding remark to Spear: "Other instructions have been given you verbally."[48] What these puzzling words meant was never revealed. If a melee erupted and the raid went sour, was Spear authorized to kill Davis? Butler had sold his proposal to Stanton, Halleck, and Lincoln by emphasizing that its proper execution would free the Richmond POWs, but maybe he was thinking less of the men behind bars than of one man at a grand house, whose capture would shower glory on anyone who ran him back to Fort Monroe in irons. Years later Butler claimed that Wistar's only objectives were to free the prisoners, to hold Richmond until Butler himself could torch the city, and to "capture the Confederate Cabinet and Mr. Jefferson Davis"; there was no mention of killing them. Of course the general was free to put any spin he wanted on the operation nearly fifty years afterward.[49] Unlike written instructions carried on another raid three weeks later, Butler's subordinates would leave no controversial fingerprints if things did not go according to plan.

At 9:00 A.M. on February 6, West's and Duncan's brigades marched from Williamsburg, with each soldier carrying six days' rations and seventy rounds of ammunition. Two hours later Spear's troopers trotted out of town, soon passing the foot soldiers slogging along the same road. By 10:30 A.M. the artillery was rolling. As the infantry marched along the country roads leading west, a Massachusetts man recalled that his company commander started whistling "Rally 'Round the Flag," but by evening the troops "were getting pretty well played out" by the grueling pace of the march. Up along the Rapidan River, Sedgwick's divisions had started their advance as well.[50]

The first problem for Wistar was the weather. The evening of February 6 was cloudy and rainy, which prevented the picked horsemen under Captain Hill from securing the Rebel pickets at Baltimore

Crossroads. But the rest of Spear's cavalrymen remained on schedule, reaching Bottom's Bridge, some fifty miles from Williamsburg, ten minutes early. Unfortunately, the colonel found the enemy at the bridge to be in force—not only infantry but also cavalry and artillery—with reinforcements still arriving. The Confederates had pulled the bridge's planking, obstructed the two fords above and below the span, and had thrown up new entrenchments and rifle pits on the western side of the Chickahominy. A perplexed Spear immediately began to round up men, women, children, and slaves on his side of the river in an attempt to learn who had tipped off the Rebels. Each told basically the same story: the Confederates had gotten word of the impending raid about sixteen hours before the Federals had arrived. Deprived of the advantage of surprise, Spear decided to wait until daylight to take the fortified bridge.[51]

As the sun rose behind them, Major Wheelan and the troopers from the 1st New York Mounted Rifles assigned to capture Davis dashed toward the bridge. As the Yankees galloped up a causeway approaching the span itself, the Confederates opened with canister and musket fire, knocking nine riders from their saddles and killing ten horses. Wheelan's attack was checked; penned in by marshy ground on either side of the causeway, the New Yorkers fell back. On the Confederate side only a South Carolinian in Colonel W. Pinkney Shingler's Holcombe Legion was slightly wounded. Thwarted, Spear had the river reconnoitered several miles above and below the bridge, but scouts reported that the Rebels had fortified every possible crossing. The colonel counted four artillery batteries and at least three regiments of infantry disputing his crossing. Soon a heavy gun was brought into action, but its shells harmlessly overshot the Federal position.[52]

In Richmond bells had tolled at midnight Saturday, alerting the Local Defense Troops to assemble. Some citizens raced through the streets like latter day Paul Reveres crying, "To arms! To Arms! The Yankees are coming!" Intense commotion arose everywhere as residents scrambled to hide in safety. Home-guard units tramped through the streets as their companies assembled. Morning brought no abatement to the commotion. Officials distributed arms to noncombatants to supplement the prison guards. Skyrockets shot off in the clear winter night, signaling the danger and catching the attention of Wistar's approaching column. As one Richmonder later described it, "There was considerable excitement here last Sunday, all the Malitia [sic] & local companies were called out, and were under arms all day expecting orders every moment to march to the Yankees being reported in large force marching on the City." The high anxiety fizzled into scenes of bored men milling in the cold, stomping their feet trying to keep warm, with the "officers blowing on their nails" as the various local units waited for orders that never came. The Local Defense Troops remained under arms until 8:00 P.M. Sunday evening before being disbanded with orders to report again early the next morning.[53]

At the Confederate War Department, telegraph wires connected to the Army of Northern Virginia's headquarters ran hot as General Elzey flooded the lines with anxious requests for reinforcements, which Lee detached so quickly that the men marched without dressing for the cold weather. On the Peninsula Wistar, who at daybreak Sunday was marching with his infantry, heard the "plainly audible" sound of combat coming from the direction of Bottom's Bridge. His soldiers had trudged thirty-three miles, arriving about 2:00 A.M. on February 7 at New Kent Court House, where they rested for about three hours, some with blistered feet from the grueling march. The general's perfect plan was going awry. Mounting his horse, he urged his troops back onto the road, marching to the sound of the guns "with the incessant beating of drums." While approaching Bottom's Bridge, Wistar realized that his plan had failed. Even if his troops forced the Rebels from their defenses here, which he believed his infantry could achieve, the precious element of surprise, so important to the enterprise, had been lost. He sent orders for Spear to withdraw from the bridge, meeting the head of the retreating column at noontime about seven miles east of Bottom's Bridge. A foot soldier thought the passing troopers looked "sad, disappointed, [and] dejected." The colonel reported to Wistar, who reluctantly decided that the risks did not outweigh the hazards. The general ordered his entire command to reverse direction, Spear's mounted troops leading the way back to Williamsburg and 300 men from the 3rd New York Cavalry acting as a rear guard.[54]

Confederate troops chased the retreating Yankees, catching up to them near Baltimore Crossroads, where Wistar had Belger's battery unlimber two guns that easily dispersed the Rebels. The general eventually halted his infantry at New Kent, where the men bivouacked near the courthouse Sunday night; the cavalry, desperate for forage, continued on to Williamsburg. At 10:00 P.M. Wistar sent a preliminary report of the failed operation, giving Butler details about the action at Bottom's Bridge. The next day the infantry marched to Burnt Ordinary (present-day Toano), where they again camped for the night. Wistar galloped ahead the last fifteen miles to Williamsburg, with his staff trailing, to provide more information to Butler. By Tuesday the foot soldiers were back in camp, having marched more than a hundred miles in four days "with alacrity and cheerfulness, and almost without straggling, the colored troops being in this respect, as usual, remarkable." Some cavalry had displayed "a little looseness of discipline," Wistar observed. He immediately began looking for excuses as to why the operation failed. In a brief dispatch to Butler from Williamsburg, the general at first claimed that the cavalry could have displayed more "éclat" when attacking the bridge; whether he was blaming Spear or himself is unclear. Wistar enumerated a host of other factors, including distance from his base, lack of available reinforcements, Rebel readiness, and "above all, the entire defeat of the real object." He felt that he made a better decision by withdrawing but continued to second guess himself. "Was I right?" he asked Butler.[55]

Meanwhile, at noon on Monday, February 8, a signal officer on Garnett's Mountain in Culpeper County advised General Newton: "All quiet. Enemy's pickets [are] in old position. Artillery [is] gone from [the] railroad bridge. No other change." Sedgwick's weary infantry and horse soldiers returned to their original camps with little to show for their efforts along the Rapidan.[56]

Despite the obvious failure of the raid, Butler was ecstatic. "The operation was skillfully and brilliantly done," he declared after reading Wistar's report. "It gives the commanding general renewed confidence in General Wistar as a commander of a division." How he could arrive at this assessment is mindboggling. Other than a commendable march by his highly motivated men, what had Wistar accomplished? If nothing else, he may have influenced Kilpatrick, who was still riding along the Rapidan as Wistar was penning his report. In it the general concluded: "The whole result of the expedition . . . is the obvious fact that a small force in this vicinity, actively handled, can and should hold a much superior force of the enemy in the immediate vicinity of Richmond inactive except for its defense."[57] Whether Kilpatrick ever read Wistar's actual report is unknown. Yet Little Kil surely would have read with enthusiasm newspaper accounts of the operation and calculated that a coordinated move by Butler's forces against Richmond could aid his own future designs of a raid on the city from the north.

Besides a lack of decisiveness on Wistar's part, this strike at the Confederate capital may have failed because Confederate authorities had been preparing for it. An unsigned document dated January 8 alerted Rebel authorities that Butler was in Washington "organizing a large cavalry force to move from Yorktown on Richmond by way of the Peninsula." This intelligence even suspected that black troops were being transferred to join the operation. The enigmatic dispatch's contents were corroborated by a January 11 letter to Davis from Lee three days later informing the president that "[t]here may be some foundation for the report [of January 8], or it may have originated in General Butler's proposition for volunteers to liberate the prisoners in Richmond." Lee urged moving the POWs "far into the interior." About two weeks later, seemingly responding to false information from Elzey, Lee confirmed for him that three black Union regiments had recently landed at Yorktown, a white cavalry regiment had disembarked at Gloucester Point opposite the town, and there was no Federal threat from south of the James. He admonished Elzey, nicknamed "Mr. Excitable" by one of Lee's staff officers, telling him, "You must keep men right in the front of the enemy, never losing sight of them, if you wish to know what they are doing." The general cautioned the Richmond commander to be vigilant for Butler's arrival. On January 30 Lee reiterated his concerns to Davis, predicting emphatically that Butler was preparing a move. Lee wanted all sectors to be on the alert for Yankee mischief, especially emanating from Yorktown.[58]

Butler soon found another reason for Wistar's failure that would not reflect ill on either of them. During the winter of 1863–64, President Lincoln decided to show mercy to Union soldiers convicted of capital crimes. This reprieve aided Private William T. Boyle of the 1st New York Mounted Rifles. Boyle had been convicted in a court-martial of willfully murdering an officer. The episode began when Boyle was absent without official leave for five hours at Dillard's Farm, North Carolina. He was arrested and returned to camp but resisted confinement. The private then burst into his commander's quarters, shouting at Lieutenant William W. Disosway that he "was not going to be guarded by a lot of Dutch hounds." Brandishing a blade, the enraged Irishman swore, "I will bury this knife in the breast of the first man who lays hands on me." Disosway approached. "I will bury this in your heart," Boyle shouted before making good on his threat in front of witnesses. In minutes the lieutenant was dead. Boyle was convicted and sentenced to be shot, a decision Butler approved. To his dismay, however, Lincoln commuted the death sentence, a move the general called an "unwise clemency of the President." Boyle took advantage of his stay of execution. Conning his guard, Private Thomas Abraham of the 139th New York Infantry, Boyle escaped from Fort Magruder four days before Wistar departed on his raid. The wily Irishman headed west toward Richmond, where he was again arrested, this time by Confederate authorities. To save his skin, Boyle used information he had learned from his guard about a troop buildup near Yorktown and convinced Southern officials that a Yankee horde was coming. He evidently saved his own life this time with a tale that soon came true. Boyle's military file soon reinstated his death sentence, but the man was never heard from again. But within a month of the raid's failure and forty-eight hours after his own trial, Private Abraham faced a firing squad, convicted on four of the eight capital charges against him.[59]

Boyle's defection was a minor blow to the secret raid. Confederate military commanders and government officials had undoubtedly been watching all points east of New Kent Court House for a move by Butler well beforehand. Even a Yankee captain felt that Southerners were preparing to repulse a raid from the Peninsula. Boyle merely confirmed the obvious for them, corroborating what officials already suspected. But the fugitive did present Wistar and Butler with a whipping boy. The *New York World*, a daily unfriendly to the administration, quickly seized on the story as an excuse Butler was using to escape censure. "The story that the rebels were warned of their fate by a Yankee deserter is an afterthought, to excuse the failure," the editors wrote. Accusing fingers pointed in all directions as exhausted soldiers returned to their winter quarters on the Peninsula and in Culpeper County.[60]

Lincoln's pardon of Boyle rankled Butler well after the war. When he published his autobiography nearly thirty years after the raid, Butler described his intention to capture Jefferson Davis with a sarcastic jab at Lincoln's policy. Davis "would be taken on a ride to Fortress Monroe to greet an old friend of his who would have taken special care to keep him there, certainly as long as the telegraph wires would not work between there and Washington so that the

President's pardon could not reach him." Clearly, Butler was convinced that Lincoln had scotched his shot at fame and glory.[61]

Reactions to the raid's failure varied. General Sedgwick was not pleased, of course. He wrote to Halleck immediately afterward that cooperating with Butler had "spoiled the best chance we had for a successful attack on the Rapidan." Lincoln's reaction was not officially recorded, but a partisan newspaper editorialized that the president was probably "gratified that Butler is not the conqueror of Richmond." Another correspondent claimed that Lincoln "laughed at Butler's propositions to take Richmond." The general's presidential aspirations definitely suffered as a result of his failure to grab Davis. But Stanton sided with the department commander. In consoling his friend, the war secretary said that he believed "failure, through the treacherous disclosure of a deserter, could not be effectually guarded against, and, while regretting the want of success, I am glad the enterprise has not suffered disaster." For good reason Stanton felt more concern about military calamities than a general's political catastrophe. Evidently, he was willing to leave the door open to the possibility of another run at Richmond: "Perhaps there will be better luck next time." But insiders at the War Department were telling the press a different story. The *Army Navy Journal*, a widely read military paper, raked the operation hard. Its editor wrote: "we find no proof of the necessary dash in the officer to whom the execution of General Butler's plan was entrusted. . . . It is reported from Washington that the War Department is not at all satisfied with the result of the raid on the Peninsula, and that it is to be investigated by a Court of Inquiry." The anti-Lincoln *New York World* called Butler's raid "the most unmilitary and sorry exploit of the war." The editors claimed that the attempt had the nod from Lincoln and Stanton but not Halleck, an obvious slap at the non–West Pointer and politician Butler.[62]

Even General Hunton, who commanded a Confederate brigade camped at Chaffin's Farm about eleven miles southwest of Bottom's Bridge, was astonished at the Federals' decision to break off their attack: "I am at a loss to understand why the enemy has retired for the small repulsed received. Have they abandoned the object of the expedition?"[63] Judging from this Southerner's reaction, the Federals' half-hearted stab at Richmond may betray the true motive of the operation. If its major purpose had been to free the prisoners, the force clearly should have numbered more than 6,200 men. But if the real objective was to bring Davis back in irons, Wistar's decision to withdraw upon recognizing the loss of surprise was an easy one.

The Army of the Potomac's winter encampment buzzed with talk of Butler's failure. A soldier in the Vermont Brigade wrote home, claiming that Wistar "lacked the requisite energy and skill to overcome the slightest opposition the rebels were able to offer." This man apparently spoke for comrades when he declared, "The opinion here is, that if Gen. Kilpatrick had been in command, he would have gone through, captured the city and liberated our prisoners." Less than a month later, Kill-Cavalry would get his chance, without being fettered by Butler's political aspirations.[64]

CHAPTER 4

THE WINTER ENCAMPMENT

T hree shadowy figures dismounted their horses and moved carefully through the woods of Culpeper County on a chilly, cloudy night in early 1864. As the trio picked their way toward the Rapidan River about a mile above Ely's Ford, one of them, Jake Swisher, had the unenviable task of keeping quiet a pack mule hauling a collapsible rubber boat. The men moved in silence, hoping not to alert enemy pickets on the far bank. Any sound could provoke a rattle of gunfire from Confederate patrols looking to pick off gallivanting Yankees like these three scouts from Army of the Potomac headquarters.

Swisher's job was to row James Wood and Martin Hogan across the Rapidan, return, and be there to retrieve them. The river crossing was only one stage of a dangerous mission that occupied Wood and Hogan that winter. The Rapidan was a boundary between Culpeper and Spotsylvania Counties. Once on the Spotsylvania shore, the scouts used a pocket compass to hike another seventeen miles to the farm of a Union sympathizer named McCamack. By prearranged signal Wood and Hogan would wait in the woods near the house until daybreak to see if McCamack emerged and walked around his well looking skyward—the all-clear sign. If the planter failed to show, the scouts knew something was afoul but were prepared to spend that day and another chilly night outside until the danger passed. If and when McCamack gave a nod, the two men would scurry into the house, spending the day cramped in an upstairs room, always vigilant for roaming Confederates.

While Wood and Hogan kept watch, McCamack traveled to Frederick's Hall, a small depot on the Virginia Central Railroad, ostensibly to sell his farm products. His real purpose was to meet a fellow Union sympathizer named Robert Orrick, who had property near the railway depot, a solid cover for being in the area. McCamack swapped eggs and Federal greenbacks with Orrick for Southern-army rumors, idle gossip, Richmond newspapers, and hopefully shreds of useful information that McCamack could bring back to the waiting scouts.

Upon returning to his home, McCamack would recite what he had heard, not risking being caught with written notes. The scouts would memorize his intelligence report, then anxious to return to army headquarters but mindful of prowling Rebel cavalry, would carefully pick their way back to the Rapidan. One of them would signal Swisher by leaning out from the riverbank, holding his hat over a match, and striking it so that the light shined only on the water. Swisher's only response would be to cross. Hogan and Wood would nervously listen for the light splashing of his pole. Once safely across the river, the three men would gallop to Major General Meade's headquarters, where staff officers would analyze their report and forward a fair copy of it to the War Department. The scouts' nerve-wracking routine was part of the so-called middle line of communication between the Federal army's winter encampment in Culpeper and the semiorganized band of Union sympathizers in and around Richmond chiefly led by Elizabeth Van Lew.[1]

Many years later Wood claimed that the information provided by Orrick and his Richmond compatriots at this time served as an incentive for the raid undertaken by Judson Kilpatrick in February 1864.[2] It is not clear what Kilpatrick knew about the intelligence generated by this "middle line of communication." But an officer in the 5th Michigan noted in his field book that by early February 1864 Kilpatrick had "received intelligence of the condition of affairs in and around Richmond, which led him to believe the city was in a weak condition of defense." Furthermore, the general was given to understand that in a "sudden emergency" the city could only muster "local militia and inexperienced citizens."[3] An Ohio captain who commanded the general's headquarters guard said years later that "Kilpatrick conceived the idea that Richmond might be taken and burned by a sudden dash on it by a cavalry column" because "from spies it was ascertained that it was almost stripped of troops."[4]

Kilpatrick was surely aware of Wistar's failed raid in early February from the part his own command played in the Army of the Potomac's diversionary movement along the Rapidan fords. Perhaps he sought out unpublished information at army headquarters with the notion that it might lead to a spectacular adventure. The young general had just lost his wife and only child and was apparently in a mood to try something as crazy as a cavalry raid on the heavily fortified, though apparently not strongly manned, enemy capital.[5]

Whatever his mental state, the New Jersey general had cultivated enough political capital among senators and congressmen to advance his own agenda. Kilpatrick's resourceful mind might well have conjured up a raid in the direction of Richmond as a remedy for his blues without regard to the consequences if things flummoxed.

Camp talk buoyed such speculation. A soldier in the Vermont Brigade wrote home shortly after Wistar's aborted raid that his comrades felt that Kilpatrick could have captured the Confederate capital and liberated the prisoners if he had been in charge.[6] At any rate, the army's winter encampment provided an excellent venue for the ambitious young cavalry commander to try his hand at career advancement.

Things returned to normal in the Third Cavalry Division's camps near Stevensburg following the demonstrations south of the Rapidan in early February. The troopers enjoyed "good log huts" with cozy, chimnied fireplaces, leading one cavalryman to comment that some of the cabins were "nicely built."[7] Spirits were high among the men. The division had returned from the latest foray without casualties, recrossing the Rapidan unmolested. Its commander glowingly wrote that his horse soldiers had scoured a large area south of the river without finding any significant Confederate cavalry force; at this time many Johnnies lacked horses and arms.[8]

While his blue-coated troopers settled into daily camp routines following the demonstration, Kilpatrick himself was anything but idle. Twice he sent Captain Edward Whitaker, his aide-de-camp, to Washington "on business for the Gen'l." The twenty-two-year-old Connecticut native was a trusted staff officer who had served in the Harris Light Cavalry since the unit was mustered in 1861. Whitaker kept his business for the general in the nation's capital confidential, though in a letter to his sister late in 1863 he confided, "We are bound to release these starving prisoners in Richmond"—a prescient comment by an officer closely associated with the Third Cavalry Division's headquarters.[9]

The bait for garnering an independent command, especially a hazardous operation behind enemy lines, would be the chance to free the longsuffering Union officers housed in Libby Prison and the enlisted men languishing on Belle Isle. Conditions were horrific. In Libby the prisoners had no blankets, bunks, or chairs, but were forced to sit and sleep on the floor. Basement cells were rife with rats, mice, and "loathsome filthiness." The prison's windows were open to the elements except for pieces of canvas provided in December 1863. Moreover, on Belle Isle there were no tents, and the enlisted men held there wore ragged uniforms without shoes or overcoats. As one Federal officer noted: "During the winter of 1863–64 While the army of the Potomac was Lying round Brandy Station & Culpepper on the Orange & Alexandria RR in Va there would occasionally come into the North statements of the suffering of our prisoners in the hands of the Rebels that would make the blood of every True soldier and patriot boil with indignation."[10]

Fueled by rumors in Richmond that easily made their way across Federal lines, word spread about the potential relocation of Yankee prisoners farther south. If this happened, fewer opportunities to escape or to be rescued would be available to POWs. Indeed, Confederate chief of ordinance Josiah Gorgas recorded in his diary in mid-February that the "prisoners on Belle Isle are being sent to Americus, Ga., at the rate of four hundred a day."[11] An enterprise to free the languishing prisoners while they remained within reach surely would appeal to Lincoln's angst over the miserable conditions he had heard about firsthand from Libby escapees.

Kilpatrick's timing was ripe for gaining the administration's approval of a raid on Richmond to rescue the POWs. And the general had cultivated all the right channels to help his proposal. The president summoned Kilpatrick only days after Benjamin Butler's scheme to free the prisoners, destroy the Confederate capital, and grab Jefferson Davis had failed miserably. Washington insiders were chattering about the War Department's ire over this operation. The administration and certain politicians were concerned as well. Kilpatrick's proposal was "brought to the attention of men prominent in political circles in Washington by whom it was presented to and urged upon the President to whose humanity and kind feelings it strongly appealed," according to Brigadier General Henry E. Davies, Jr., a loyal subordinate who had followed in Kilpatrick's footsteps to command of a brigade in the Third Cavalry Division. Years later in a memoir, Libbie Custer wrote that Little Kil "used all his political influence, and also enlisting the women in his family, his State Senators, and Congressmen for the same purpose, had overridden the commander of the great army, and [had] gained from the War Department permission to organize a raid into Richmond in February 1864, ostensibly to release the Libby prisoners, in reality for his own aggrandizement."[12]

Surely Kilpatrick was searching for an enterprise that promised maximum national attention. Wistar's failure, the prisoners' misery, and reports of weaknesses in Richmond's defenses all collided in mid-February 1864 to endorse action, and Kilpatrick was a man of action. A Maine trooper told his diary that the general "never lets an opportunity to fight pass unimproved; even if he knows he will accomplish nothing." Hearing rumblings about a possible Richmond sortie, this same man observed, "I understand it was got up at Kilpatrick's solicitation and was probably another attempt of his to win another star." From serving under Kill-Cavalry, he could confidently state: "If he lives he will have another star. I'll bet my life."[13]

Less than seventy-two hours after Butler telegraphed Lincoln news of Wistar's failure, John Sedgwick, still standing in for the pneumonia-plagued Meade, confirmed receipt of a message beckoning Kilpatrick to meet with Lincoln, which had arrived at army headquarters shortly after 9:00 P.M. on February 11. All the general could glean from the cryptic telegram indicated that Kilpatrick alone was needed, and only for two or three days. The possibilities had Sedgwick's headquarters speculating with anticipation. Sedgwick forwarded the order to Major General Alfred Pleasonton at Cavalry Corps headquarters since he was Kilpatrick's immediate superior. During this time Meade rose from his sickbed. Somewhat better, the commanding general headed to Washington to take part in a congressional inquiry into his actions during the Gettysburg Campaign. Nevertheless, Lincoln did not request his presence at the session with Kilpatrick. According to Meade's chief of staff, Major General A. A. Humphreys, Secretary of War Edwin M. Stanton told Meade the president had sent for Kilpatrick to discuss an idea for using Federal cavalry to distribute an amnesty proclamation aimed at Southerners fighting against the Union; Meade need not be involved in the meeting. Nor would Kilpatrick's immediate superior, Pleasonton, be invited to the Executive Mansion, though he may have been left out of the loop because he had just returned from a leave of absence himself on February 11. As one historian has observed, such behavior was typical of Lincoln's idiosyncratic management style.[14]

It is unknown exactly how much time elapsed between Kilpatrick's initial overture to his friends on Capitol Hill and his invitation to Washington, but the Butler fiasco seems to have spurred Lincoln to look for a commander who could get the job done. The president may not have minded the cavalryman jumping the chain

of command, but neither Meade nor Pleasonton would have coun-
tenanced it. Not only were they out of the loop but so was Major
General Henry W. Halleck, commander of all Union armies. Little
Kil probably did not give a fig who bristled at his machinations.[15]

Kilpatrick immediately accepted Lincoln's invitation. Third
Cavalry Division headquarters near Stevensburg must have vibrated
with excitement as the general read the order from the Army of the
Potomac's chief of staff to Pleasonton, directing Kilpatrick to meet
personally with the president. But Lincoln's telegram seems to have
been vague about the reason for so urgent a summons. Though its
intent was veiled, the message did not stay a secret for long and soon
became fodder for campfire jawing. An ordnance sergeant detached
to division headquarters from the Michigan Brigade thought he had
the inside track on the gossip when he speculated that Little Kil was
in line "to get his other star (Major General!) . . . [though] others [say]
that it is to consult him about another raid."[16] That star was further
off—fifteen months—but anyone who bet on a raid happening soon
would have collected.

The general's mind must have raced as he most likely donned
his finest uniform for his visit with the president. February 12 was
windy but unseasonably warm as his horse was saddled and waited
by the front porch at Rose Hill. Kilpatrick swung a leg over his
mount, grasped the reins, and spurred the animal onto the dusty road
that meandered through the treeless countryside, past the camps of
the II Corps. Little Kil knew well the four-and-a-half-mile ride from
Rose Hill to Brandy Station, the railhead where he would catch a
train like any other soldier traveling between the winter encampment and the capital. By noon he was on a military train chugging
north toward Alexandria.[17]

The coach he rode in rocked more than a little, despite the
hasty improvements army engineers had made to the Orange and
Alexandria Railroad track bed. Doubtless as he swayed the young
brigadier must have reviewed again and again the plan he would
present to the president, assuming Lincoln wanted to see him about
a cavalry raid. In any event, the general would be prepared. He might
have thought of Stoneman, who had said the previous May, "To take
the enemy by surprise and penetrate his country was easy enough."
That was the same bill of goods Kilpatrick had to sell Lincoln. Yet
did Little Kil remember the rest of the sentence in Stoneman's
report: "to withdraw from [enemy territory] was a more difficult

matter."[18] Even if he had read the report thoroughly, Kilpatrick's self-confidence would prevent the older soldier's warning from dissuading him. He was ready with a positive solution to the POW problem in Richmond and confident that his plan would appeal to a president desperate to save the suffering troops.[19]

Kilpatrick soon arrived in Alexandria, a city firmly in Federal hands since the outbreak of hostilities. He probably had to borrow a horse from a local livery for the final leg of his journey to the Executive Mansion. As he strode up to the entrance, his trademark "consequential walk" marked him as a man as ready to see Lincoln as perhaps the president was to see him.

The initial introductions must have bordered on caricature, with the six-foot-four-inch president towering over his uniformed guest. With his large, bony right hand extended to the diminutive five-foot-seven-inch young cavalry officer, the fifty-five-year-old president's winning smile instantly exuded an air of confidence, keen intelligence, genuine kindness, and friendly demeanor. Well known himself for his own unwavering good nature and ready repartee among his peers, Little Kil finally may have been left speechless.[20]

Kilpatrick's audience with Lincoln was brief, for he was also scheduled to meet that day with Secretary Stanton, a former trial lawyer and Lincoln's principal advisor at the War Department. The discussion with Lincoln was not recorded, but the president probably emphasized his desire to distribute an amnesty proclamation he hoped would persuade Southerners to abandon their cause and return to the Union. Two days prior to Kilpatrick's visit, another politically connected Michigan officer from the Third Cavalry Division had visited, specifically at the president's invitation, to discuss the amnesty proclamation, indicating the importance of its distribution to the president; Stanton also took part in the conversation.[21] Lincoln also may have mentioned to the general a recent article in the *New York Times* commenting on the frequency with which Confederate deserters coming into Federal lines expressed ignorance of the amnesty policy because "not a single copy, it is believed, has been seen in Lee's army."[22] Kilpatrick's favorite journalist, E. A. Paul, who often had ridden with Little Kil and his men, had written the piece, so the cavalryman might have been aware of its contents and used that familiarity to make points with Lincoln.

Kilpatrick probably had time to pitch, however briefly, his plan for a cavalry raid similar to Butler's but promising better results.

Lincoln probably embraced the idea quickly; a cabinet member confided to his diary about this time that the president had a penchant for "secret movements." Once his meeting with Lincoln concluded, the general proceeded a half city block to the War Department at the corner of Pennsylvania Avenue and Seventeenth Street NW, where Secretary Stanton was waiting to hear more details about his scheme to penetrate Richmond.[23]

The physical mismatch between Lincoln and Kilpatrick was apparent. But when Little Kil entered the cabinet official's office, it was the cavalry officer's starkly different personality that would straightaway become evident. The outgoing manner that ingratiated the general to his officers and men was severely lacking in the fifty-nine-year-old Stanton's puritanical temperament. One historian has characterized Lincoln's secretary of war as having a "natural reserve, piety, temperance, and lack of humor [that] made for uneasy relationships. Even his stately proportions and fastidious dress worked against social intimacy."[24] A Union general who worked closely with the secretary in a War Department bureau later described Stanton as "a cantankerous man, filled with an exalted ego," who "felt that he was the dominant intellect to those about him, . . . had not the politeness to conceal it," and "seemed to get the idea that he was the whole thing."[25] The two men could not have been more different in demeanor. Nevertheless, Stanton and Kilpatrick shared an unbending love for the Union, deep distain for the Southern rebellion, and an abhorrence of slavery.[26] These commonalities, not their disparities, prevailed as they got down to the business at hand.

At length Kilpatrick's plan met with the bespectacled cabinet officer's approval. On the surface the proposal seemed tailored to the president's goal and to cover most contingencies. The official objective would be to distribute copies of Lincoln's amnesty proclamation not only to Confederate troops along the Rapidan but also to civilians living around Richmond. At the same time, Kilpatrick thought that his horse soldiers could destroy enemy communications and free Yankee prisoners held in Richmond; no recorded mention was made of any more-sinister goals. Kilpatrick submitted a detailed layout, including his proposed routes, required troop strengths, and an explanation of how he would accomplish his mission.[27]

To achieve his objectives, Little Kil calculated that he needed 4,000 cavalrymen on good mounts, a six-gun battery, and five days' rations; forage for the horses would be scoured along the way.

Kilpatrick's notion was to live off Southern farmers as his troopers rode through central Virginia. Perhaps he reminded Stanton of Lieutenant Colonel Charles Sawtelle's report following Stoneman's raid. Sawtelle, chief quartermaster of the Cavalry Corps at the time, bragged in detail about how the Federals had "subsisted entirely off the country through which [they] passed. . . . [T]here was no suffering on the part of men or horses for food. . . . We found bacon, corn meal, flour, corn, and frequently hay or fodder, in sufficient quantities to supply the whole command."[28]

But by the time Kilpatrick and Stanton met, the bountiful conditions Sawtelle described no longer existed. That very month General Lee was telling Confederate secretary of war James Seddon of his concern over food shortages. Furthermore, he complained, such shortages were sapping morale and discipline.[29] Whether Stanton questioned Little Kil about the current state of Virginia's succor is not known. But it appears the demands of war had reduced subsistence for both men and horses in the ten months since Stoneman's bluecoats had ravaged the countryside south of the Rapidan.[30]

Nonetheless, Kilpatrick assumed that he would not have a long supply train, as he explained to Stanton. His column would cross the Rapidan at Ely's Ford and quickly advance to Spotsylvania Court House, where he would divide his force. Some five hundred men would divert to the southwest, crossing the North Anna River and moving swiftly to Frederick's Hall, where they would do whatever mischief they could, including pulling down telegraph lines and wrecking the Virginia Central Railroad's track. After leaving Frederick's Hall, these horsemen would then cross the South Anna River, galloping due south through Goochland County to the James River. There, this smaller force would destroy part of the James River and Kanawha Canal above Richmond, then cross the river, approaching the Rebel capital from the south. In their path on the south side of the James, the blue-coated cavalrymen would find and torch Bellona Arsenal, rip up another railroad line, and then "act as circumstances may require."[31]

The main body, under Kilpatrick, after fording the Rapidan at Ely's, also would gallop through Spotsylvania Court House, veering toward Mount Carmel Church. They too would cross the North Anna River, then proceed down Brook Turnpike, hitting the Confederate capital directly from the north. At Guinea Station another detachment from the main force would destroy the Richmond, Fredericksburg, and Potomac Railroad, rejoining Kilpatrick before he reached the capital's outer works. The next step would be to free the Union prisoners at Libby Prison and Belle Isle "in conjunction with troops sent from the direction of West Point" on the Peninsula. The only Federal troops near West Point would have been Butler's men. These soldiers, marching on the capital from the southeast as they had in February, would distract the city's defenders as Kilpatrick punched in from the north.[32]

Butler's participation was crucial. No doubt Kilpatrick wanted him to draw defenders away from the city's northern entrenchments. Butler's role in this operation has been largely overlooked by commentators who scoff at Kilpatrick's failure to capture Richmond. Even men in the ranks knew the importance of this partnership. An Indiana trooper who was not on the raid wrote home during the operation that Kilpatrick would be assisted by "a force under Gen. Butler coming up the Peninsula from Fortress Monroe in capturing Richmond."[33]

Some elements of Kilpatrick's plan resembled those in a proposal made nine months earlier to Major General Joseph Hooker by Captain Ulric Dahlgren. The young staff officer's scheme, far smaller in scope than Kilpatrick's blueprint, included crossing the James River in Goochland County and destroying Bellona Arsenal. The arsenal, named for the Roman goddess of war, dated to the aftermath of the War of 1812, when the federal government, stung by the ease with which the British had attacked the U.S. coast with impunity, went on a fort- and arsenal-building spree. Operated by the U.S. Navy, Bellona stood in Chesterfield County on land owned by John Clarke. The facility was a quadrangle of buildings, surrounded by seventeen-foot-high stone walls, overlooking the James. Inside the perimeter were a three-story main arsenal, a one-story frame structure housing technicians and soldiers, two brick workshops, and an officers' quarters. Outside the walls were a stable and a stone gunpowder magazine. It was shut down in 1832, not only for logistical and financial reasons but also because some Virginians feared that rebellious slaves could seize the complex and use it as a base for an uprising, and reverted to private hands. In April 1861 the owners leased the buildings to the Confederate government. During the war, Bellona ranked second only to Richmond's Tredegar Ironworks as Virginia's leading manufacturer of arms. Perhaps Dahlgren had inside information that made the arsenal worth hitting—surely his naval-officer father, an ordnance expert, would have known the place. Hooker never entertained the notion of a Richmond raid, so the idea lay dormant in young Dahlgren's mind.[34]

Kilpatrick's plan eventually added another major diversionary movement, though that element might not have come up when he met with Stanton. This addition would include a column of 1,500 horse soldiers led by Kilpatrick's other brigadier, George Armstrong Custer, supported by two infantry divisions. Custer's force would head for Charlottesville, passing Lee's left flank. The hope was to entice Jeb Stuart's Confederate cavalry into chasing Custer's command, thus freeing Kilpatrick's column to gallop around Lee's right and ride directly south toward Richmond without harassment.[35]

Kilpatrick and Custer had history, not always happy, because they were born competitors both on and off the battlefield. Since late June 1863 Custer had commanded the Second Brigade in Kilpatrick's division, but he was not destined to play a major part in the main event unfolding at Kill-Cavalry's headquarters in February 1864. Instead, his role would be as a supporting actor in the operation, one that would have little effect on the ultimate outcome. Why Custer was not with the Yankee raiders who left Stevensburg is not exactly clear. It may have had its origin several months earlier, well before Kilpatrick's plan to enter Richmond was even conceived. In fact, its roots probably took hold shortly after the two egotistical officers were shunted together in the Third Cavalry Division.

George Armstrong Custer was barley twenty-five years old in February 1864. His meteoric rise within the Cavalry Corps was attributed to General Pleasonton, a patron to several brash young cavalry officers. After Pleasonton succeeded Stoneman as Cavalry Corps chief, it was his brainchild to bring in fresh, youthful, hot-blooded officers to lead his troopers. Up to this point in the war, Stuart's incredibly successful gray horsemen had literally run rings around their blue counterparts. Custer was part of the "boy generals" cadre Pleasonton promoted during June 1863. Along with Elon Farnsworth and Wesley Merritt, he formed a triumvirate of youths who jumped from company-grade officer to brigadier general in one day. All three burgeoning but inexperienced commanders would distinguish themselves in one way or another, with Farnsworth's brief but heroic career lasting only five short days. Custer and Merritt would end the war as major generals and have memorable postwar military careers. Pleasonton also should be credited with promoting

Kilpatrick to brigadier general two weeks prior to the other three young officers. He went one step further with Little Kil by giving him command of a cavalry division, with Custer and Farnsworth as his subordinates.[36]

An acerbic officer on Meade's staff made several unflattering comments in describing Custer, who was "a sight to behold, looking like a crazy circus rider! He has a faded velvet suit, with tarnished lace trimmings, a little gray felt hat and long boots. His head is garnished with short flaxen curls, and he had a devil-may-care blue eye, very appropriate to his style."[37]

A native Ohioan who grew up in Monroe, Michigan, Custer had a penchant for acquiring nicknames like "Autie," "Fanny" and "Curly" during his early days. He distinguished himself at West Point with his accumulation of demerits and a class standing of dead last. A year behind Kilpatrick, Custer's class graduated a year early, in June 1861. With Washington hectically raising thousands of volunteers for the war effort, officers with at least a modicum of military schooling were desperately needed to train and lead the raw recruits. Early graduation was a blessing for Custer because chances were slim he would have lasted through his final regulation year at West Point.

The newly commissioned second lieutenant served as a staff officer with the brevet rank of captain under Major General George McClellan, making a name for himself as a daredevil. By 1863 he had moved over to a staff position in the Cavalry Corps, where Pleasonton looked on him as a rising star in the mounted arm. On June 9, 1863, at Brandy Station "Curly" showed his pluck in a charge with the 8th New York Cavalry that drew his commander's notice; Captain Ulric Dahlgren displayed similar feats of bravery on another part of the field. As a result of the courage Custer demonstrated that day, Pleasonton used his clout to place him in command of a brigade. The regiments assigned to the new brigadier were all from his adopted Michigan. Custer would take these troopers and whip them into one of the finest and hardest-fighting units in the Union cavalry, the Michigan Brigade.

On June 30 near Hanover, Pennsylvania, against Stuart's brigades Custer proved that he would not shirk under fire. Again two days later at Hunterstown and then in an open field east of Gettysburg on July 3, Custer proved his mettle. The young general established a reputation as the beau ideal of a cavalry leader: bold and aggressive with nerves of steel. At Gettysburg Custer gained enduring glory by riding at the head of his Michigan Brigade yelling, "Come on, you Wolverines!" But his actions were miles from Kilpatrick's eye and did not endear himself to his division commander by his independent showmanship. Kilpatrick expected his subordinate to support the rest of the division on the south end of the battlefield, where Farnsworth's brigade assaulted Confederate infantry and artillery alone.[38]

Custer rejoined the division during the pursuit of Lee's beaten army, fighting at little-known places like Monterey Pass, Smithsburg, Boonsboro, Funkstown, and Falling Waters. In September 1863 "Custer's luck" temporarily ran out when he received a minor leg wound in a fight near Culpeper Court House. This temporary setback proved fortuitous when Autie cleverly used his medical leave to return to Michigan. Back in his hometown, he "audaciously courted Monroe's most beautiful belle, the 22-year old, Libbie Bacon." Following this brief respite, Custer returned to Virginia the next month, leading his brigade at the second battle of Brandy Station. His Wolverines were less successful at Buckland Mills, forever coined as the "Buckland Races" by jeering Confederates, when Kilpatrick's brigades were whipped by Stuart's horsemen. This debacle solidified an ongoing riff between Custer and his commander, causing the former to write, "Yesterday, October 19th, was the most disastrous this Division ever passed through." In another letter about Buckland, he wrote: "All would have been well had General K. been content to let well enough alone. . . . My consolation is that I am in no way responsible for the mishap, but on the contrary urged General K. not to take the step which brought it upon us, and the only success gained by us was gained by me." Custer's anger was understandable. His headquarters wagon was captured by the Rebels along with his official and personal papers, some of which were printed in a Richmond newspaper.[39]

As the 1863 campaigning season began to wane, Custer saw an opportunity to journey back to Monroe as a war hero. He convinced Judge Daniel Bacon and Libbie that he was the right man for her. The two lovers exchanged vows on February 9, 1864, just about the time Kilpatrick was hearing reports of Butler's failed raid on Richmond. After spending most of their honeymoon traveling (with stops in Buffalo, West Point, New York City, and Washington), visiting relatives, dancing, and partying, Autie was summoned back to his command in Stevensburg.[40]

Most modern historians credit Custer with high marks as a combat officer and cavalry leader during the Civil War. One biographer wrote: "A soldier's duty merged with a personal quest for glory that made Custer a superb cavalry commander and a dashing, unmistakable hero. . . . He was perhaps the war's last knight." Another historian, who wrote only on Custer's Civil War career, concluded that "George Armstrong Custer's brand of leadership was distinctly personal. He was truly a charismatic chieftain. He was in a class all by himself. He could not be copied or replaced. In short, he was an indispensable man." Another writer stated, "Incontestably, Custer was a superb cavalry officer."[41]

During the war, officers and men who served under Custer or were his superiors held similar opinions. Major James Kidd, who served in the Michigan Brigade, said: "Custer was a fighting man, through and through, but wary and wily as brave. . . . There was in him an indescribable something—call it caution, call it sagacity, call it the real military instinct—it may have been genius—by whatever name entitled, it nearly always impelled him to do the right thing." Another officer felt that "Custer's conduct in battle was characteristic. He never ordered his men to go where he would not lead, and he never led them where he did not expect his men to follow." Pleasonton declared: "Custer is the best cavalry general in the world. . . . Custer has met my highest expectations."[42] Wartime letters, battle reports, and postwar reminiscences praised the young officer, at least as a general in the Union army.

Such contemporary praise for Custer probably was not lost on Kilpatrick, his division commander. Their correspondingly explosive personalities were bound to cross swords, if not literally, at least in heated verbal and written exchanges. Between August and November 1863, Kilpatrick sent numerous reprimands to Custer through the division's assistant adjutant general, Captain Llewellyn Estes. These directives criticized the brigadier for his failure to provide monthly and trimonthly reports in a timely manner, an infraction that kept him in camp until they were completed. He also was ordered not to under any "circumstances forward an official communication to Maj. Gen. Pleasonton except through" division headquarters. Apparently, the Second Brigade commander had been violating the chain of command. But Custer owned his star to Pleasonton, not Kilpatrick, which may have justified his actions in his own mind.[43]

Custer was also admonished for not sending "all scouts and persons with valuable information" directly to his immediate commander. Throughout the fall of 1863, Estes was busy quoting chapter and verse of army circulars and regulations that Custer seemed to ignore. Kilpatrick was not satisfied with his subordinate's handling of a disciplinary action against a Michigan Brigade officer either. The brigadier had been ordered to investigate an infraction by the junior officer but instead gave his opinion on the matter "in a manner most disgraceful to your commanding officer." Custer, through his communications with headquarters, was displaying "some feeling" toward Kilpatrick that was interpreted as offensive. Finally, Little Kil claimed in a communication, "it is impossible for me to command the Division without the willing support of my Brigade commanders," an obvious dig at Custer since the other brigade commander, Henry Davies, Jr., always gave Kilpatrick unwavering loyalty. It appears that thousands of men willingly, almost blindly, followed Kill-Cavalry into battle, but he had trouble getting Custer to comply with simple army paperwork and follow the chain of command, tasks that should have been routine for any West Pointer.[44]

Beyond professional-performance disagreements, a dispute arose between the two young generals about a certain female frequenting Custer's headquarters during the fall of 1863. Annie Jones, a teenager with a questionable past, liked the company of general officers. She frequented the headquarters of Major General Franz Sigel and also claimed to have served on Major General Julius Stahel's staff as an honorary major; some evidence points to a liaison with Major General Gouverneur Warren too. Jones's passion for army brass eventually brought her to Custer's camp. Kilpatrick suspected that she was a Rebel spy, ordering Custer to get rid of her, though she claimed that he was "jealous of Gen. Custer's attention." When the eighteen-year-old was finally arrested on charges of spying, she implored the brigadier for help because she had gone to the front "as the friend and companion of Gen. Custer." Meade and Pleasonton initiated an official inquiry. Custer defended himself in writing, claiming that Jones had come to his tent offering her services but only as a nurse. When the controversy heated up at Third Cavalry Division headquarters, Custer finally ordered her out of camp. Whatever the true nature of her expectations—or Custer's for that matter—a rift between the two young generals erupted. The actual story of Custer's relationship with Jones, and perhaps Kilpatrick's alleged jealousy, cannot be definitively explained from existing records. It is only clear that Jones was in the cavalry camps, Kilpatrick was not happy about it, and Custer did what he thought necessary for damage control. Regardless, the Annie Jones "affair" further damaged the already strained relationship between Custer and Kilpatrick.[45]

The bad blood between the generals is obvious from official army documents, including the Annie Jones incident. The conflict also exposed itself in personal correspondence. Custer's comment to his wife's friend following the Buckland Mills fiasco reflected a schism with his commander. What was privately said between the two young generals is anyone's guess. But this deepening animosity between the two generals has gone unremarked in previous studies of Custer, Kilpatrick, or the raid on Richmond. If his proposed operation generated any glory for its leaders, Kilpatrick was not going to allow Custer a share in it. This hostility may have been a major factor in Kilpatrick's decision to accept, or at least not dispute, the inclusion of Ulric Dahlgren as his subordinate rather than Custer.

To get the secretary of war on board, Kilpatrick did not fail to boast about his own "thorough knowledge of the country" through which his troopers would ride. Perhaps he mentioned his part in Stoneman's raid, when his brigade rode the same Brooke Turnpike he now had in his plan to within two miles of Richmond's intermediate defenses without a serious challenge. He could even describe a ready-made exit route over the Meadow Bridges northeast of Richmond, across the Pamunkey River at the Hanovertown Ferry, across the Mattaponi River at Aylett's Ferry, and after traversing King and Queen County, winding up at Gloucester Point. Stanton, a seasoned defense attorney, likely would have appreciated the case Kilpatrick made and the thoroughness with which he had addressed every contingency.[46]

By the time Kilpatrick left the secretary of war's office, he had a deal. His plan would be unstoppable no matter what his superiors in the Army of the Potomac thought of it. Indeed, Kilpatrick's scheme may have been part of a larger personal strategy to gain command of the Cavalry Corps, if the Richmond raid was successful. At the very least he was angling for promotion to major general, according to one published report.[47] As an officer in the Michigan Brigade wrote home shortly after Little Kil returned from Washington: "The program now is [for] Kilpatrick to have the cavalry corps. The infantry and artillery to be put in three columns called the right, left and center columns; Sedgwick to command the right, Hancock the left and Pleasonton the center. Custer [is] to take Buford's old Div and Genl Davies this one."[48] Now it was time for the man of the hour to solidify his success with the administration by gaining the support of Washington's political elite.

Four days after returning to Stevensburg, Kilpatrick telegraphed the powerful Michigan congressman Francis W. Kellogg, inviting him and his friends to the army's winter encampment for a fete honoring George Washington. Kellogg, considered by some to be the "Father of the Michigan Cavalry," was just the type of kindred spirit Little Kil would want on his side.[49] But others were on the general's guest list as well. A senator's son wrote of Kilpatrick: "In order to ingratiate himself with the senators, he extended a large number of invitations to them and their families to pay his headquarters a visit and witness a general review of the Second Army Corps."[50] It would be a multiday affair of speechmaking, horse racing, military reviews, mock tactical exercises, and a grand ball. State and national dignitaries would attend, bringing along their wives, daughters, and in some cases "other ladies" with "very romantic names" who were granted special passes by the War Department. General Kilpatrick was very much in the thick of preparations, acting as "manager" of the "grand theatricals" being planned.[51]

Two days before the Washington's Birthday celebration, Kilpatrick drew a large crowd of politicians, their guests, and fellow officers to an old tavern he had outfitted as the Third Cavalry Division's "theater." The spacious hall was decorated brilliantly in red, white, and blue draperies along with the battle flags of General Kilpatrick and his two brigade commanders, Davies and Custer, and the division's regimental standards. "The Division Band was present to discourse sweet music." On one side of a makeshift fifteen-by-eighteen-foot stage hung a full-length portrait of Little Kil, with one of the Goddess of Liberty on the opposite side, "pretty well executed for the materials" that were available. When the program commenced, the stage was packed with army brass in the "glitter of rich uniforms." Also present were Senators Jacob Howard and Zachariah Chandler of Michigan, Morton S. Wilkinson and Alexander Ramsey of Minnesota, Congressman William Higby of California, and of course, Congressman Kellogg.[52]

The program allotted each senator and congressman time to discourse on his enthusiasm for the war effort, each to resounding cheers from the audience. The final speaker, of course, was Judson Kilpatrick, who "demonstrated that he was no less an orator than a fighter." In his own uniquely eloquent didactic style, he plied his political guests with perfect patronizing words to puff up their egos. He railed against the secessionists and their Copperhead supporters for their efforts to destroy the Union. As one diarist observed, "the Gen[eral] is a splendid speaker and brought down the house in some glowing nuances made to the ladies of whom many were present." Another officer later remarked that Kilpatrick's "speech was the gem of the evening and stirred up no end of enthusiasm." Exacting precisely the response he wanted, Little Kil sat down to thundering applause as the band struck up "Hail to the Chief," a song used to honor presidents since 1829. Following a minstrel show "caricaturing the negro in fine style . . . , the invited guests repaired to Gen. K's headquarters to partake of the entertainment for the inner man." With all the skill of a modern-day Washington lobbyist, the general worked expertly to ensure that his name would be remembered in a positive light by some of the nation's most powerful men in 1864. Gradually the guests covered the quarter mile to Rose Hill, where a profusion of "wines, liquors, and eatables" flowed. "Kilpatrick was happy, and as active as a flea and almost as ubiquitous," and his "hospitality was unbounded," a guest remembered.[53]

Later, after a roundly celebratory evening but now with the sound of taps echoing in the camps, several young staff officers with a newfound civilian friend withdrew to Rose Hill's attic to share a couple of mattresses on the planked floor. A cannonball had hit the house earlier in the war, furrowing through the ceiling of an upstairs bedroom and leaving a hole now stuffed with newspapers. Hearing youthful female voices below them, the randy officers took turns wetting the newsprint with their fingers to form a spyhole. The aperture was unsubtle enough that one of the girls, described as "a noted beauty of New York City in a white, open-necked nightrobe" with a "lovely face, bosom, and falling mass of golden hair," spotted it. She and her companions went at the flimsy barrier with broom handles, causing the blue-coated gentlemen to sue for peace, secured only when the staff officers lowered down on a rope a "half dozen bottles of Pommery Sec."[54] What the general was doing during these high jinx is not recorded, though he probably was in a smoke-filled first-floor room cosseting his political allies, actual and potential.

But he undoubtedly would have enjoyed hearing about the "Battle of the Rose Hill Attic" the next morning.

The next day Kilpatrick's staff busied themselves with amusing more than fifty guests. There were horseback rides (for the ladies) within sight of enemy picket lines, reviews of the troops, and important preparations for the grand ball, not to mention horseracing between the cavalrymen and horsemen from the II Corps. To the general's chagrin, a private in the 1st Michigan Cavalry lost by two lengths to a II Corps rider, with the wager-minded cavalrymen losing three thousand dollars. On Sunday Kilpatrick again entertained his patrons and their companions with a review of his division in the pastures near Rose Hill. There was even a skirmish drill by Company H, 5th New York Cavalry ,which much delighted Congressman Kellogg.[55]

On Monday evening the main event of the four-day extravaganza, a Washington's Birthday ball hosted by the army's famed II Corps, took place. Tickets, at ten dollars each, were in great demand. Soldiers had built a rough pinewood hall more than ninety feet long and almost fifty feet wide, roofed with canvas and decorated with regimental battle flags and evergreen wreaths. The stage was set with drums, bugles, stacked arms, and two highly polished brass Napoleon cannons. As night fell a thousand tapers lit the gathering. Politicians who had reveled at the general's headquarters two nights before were joined in the rustic setting by Andrew Curtin, Pennsylvania's governor, and his wife and their daughter. Miss Curtin "attracted universal attention" with her "dignified, sweet and graceful . . . demeanor." She and a "bevy of beauties" she brought with her from Philadelphia, however, had pulchritudinous competition from twenty-four-year-old Kate Chase Sprague, who some "acknowledged as the handsomest woman in America." Kate, the daughter of Treasury Secretary Salmon P. Chase, was accompanied by her husband, William, the governor of Rhode Island. Other notables were Vice President Hannibal Hamlin; his daughter, Sarah, "a most agreeable young lady"; Senator John Hale's wife and daughters; U.S. Supreme Court Justice Samuel Miller and his wife; and a large party from the British embassy. Sprinkled among the crowd were also several "ladies" with "very romantic names," according to one guest.[56]

There was no shortage of general officers mixing with dignitaries and female guests—no less than five major or brigadier generals, according to a sharp-eyed junior officer. Army of the Potomac commander George Meade spent time with the II Corps commander, Major General Winfield Scott Hancock, who was still nursing a nasty wound from Gettysburg. The acting commander of Hancock's corps, Gouverneur Warren, stood near Cavalry Corps leader Pleasonton and his veteran Second Cavalry Division subordinate, Brigadier General David McMutrie Gregg. Of course as expected, Kilpatrick was mingling everywhere, trailing rumors and gossip in his wake. Unfortunately, the chatter mostly involved information better kept secret. But during his bravura two nights previous, "Hints were thrown out of an indefinite something that was going to happen." A chagrined civilian observed ladies at the gala "discussing freely and talking enthusiastically about the projected expedition of Gen[eral] Kilpatrick . . . , giving openly the details of the plan."[57]

As hoop-skirted young damsels danced away the night with their boyish officer-escorts to music provided by the combined bands of the 57th New York and 14th Connecticut Infantry Regiments, one handsome officer did not take the floor. His striking good looks, with "manners as soft as a cat's," would appeal to many of the evening's belles. But there would be no waltz or reel that night for the twenty-one-year-old, one-legged colonel who leaned against the rough wood wall, a crutch under one arm for support.[58]

The next day another highlight event for the visiting dignitaries was scheduled, a grand review of Hancock's II Corps and, not surprisingly, Kilpatrick's cavalry. With sunshine warmly drenching the fields of the army's encampment, nearly two hundred ladies adorned on horseback joined General Meade and his staff as the reviewing party. One civilian observer later recalled seeing Colonel Dahlgren mounted on a "magnificent coal-black stallion" despite the loss of "his right leg below the knee."[59]

Reaction to the military display was mixed. A junior officer later remembered that "the men looked well" passing in review. A curmudgeon on Meade's staff said the "cavalry looked Gipsey as usual. . . . The infantry were unequal, some . . . excellent, others marching & looking indifferently." Once the foot soldiers tramped past Meade and a mock artillery demonstration concluded, it was time for Little Kil to put on a show. Bugles sounded. About five hundred blue-coated cavalrymen drew sabers that flashed in the sun. The horse soldiers then stepped off at a walk, with mounted skirmishers out in front and at flank. Advancing to a trot, the troopers picked up speed as thundering hooves shook the ground. With a shout, every man rose in his stirrups as General Kilpatrick galloped across the plain, leading his men in a grand charge to an awestruck crowd's merriment. The spectacle left a lasting impression on one Washington civilian, who later recalled, "It seems as if nothing could stop those reckless, brave, death-dealing troopers and their horses."[60] On the grimy plains inside friendly lines, such confidence came at no cost. Charging Richmond's menacing fortifications would prove more challenging.

The day ended at Rose Hill with a collation for the general's special guests. Later that evening a reserved train transported most of the visitors back to Washington, leaving soldiers and civilians alike with lasting memories. For that they had Judson Kilpatrick to thank. He hoped they would do so in ways he appreciated.[61]

CHAPTER 5

KILPATRICK'S RAID BEGINS

Five days after Kilpatrick's return to Rose Hill from his visit with President Lincoln, he encountered young Ulric Dahlgren, who would figure dramatically in his plans to raid Richmond. Standing together, the two officers were truly an odd couple. Kilpatrick was short, with scraggily whiskers, a foul mouth, and a common-man demeanor, while Dahlgren was "a boyish looking young man, of middle height, thin and with light hair, moustache and imperial." A Confederate officer described the colonel as handsome and dashing, with a manicured goatee and "manners as soft as a cat's."[1]

The last time the two had seen combat together was eight months earlier. The Army of Northern Virginia was retreating after its defeat at Gettysburg. Kilpatrick's cavalry division was doggedly pursuing Stuart's horse soldiers through southern Pennsylvania and the Maryland countryside as Lee's army sought safety on the Virginia side of the Potomac River. On July 6, 1863, near Hagerstown, Maryland, then-Captain Dahlgren volunteered to fight with the Third Cavalry Division as the general's aide after the remnants of his own command had dissolved. Kilpatrick's task was to attack the gray cavalry occupying the town, and he ordered a squadron from the 18th Pennsylvania forward. An aggressive Dahlgren fell in with the lead company, assuming command of the attack. The captain charged into Hagerstown and, showing great tenacity, pushed a strong force of Rebel horsemen back to the main square. Pinned down but quickly amassing reinforcements, the Southerners held their position. Dahlgren galloped back for help and rapidly returned with twenty troopers from Company D, 18th Pennsylvania. He ordered an advance on foot. As the Yankees moved down both sidewalks toward the enemy positions, the redoubtable captain remained mounted, riding down the middle of the street.

The Federals had come within three hundred yards of the square when the Confederates poured on a hot dose of gunfire. Almost miraculously, Dahlgren, with bullets whizzing about him, remained untouched. Unfazed by the flying lead, the impromptu

74

leader cried out, "Now, boys, give it to them!" The Pennsylvanians responded, opening up with a volley from their Burnside carbines that broke the Rebels' ranks. The enemy retreated to the town's Dutch Reformed Church, where they crouched behind headstones in the adjacent graveyard. They garnered support from a horse-artillery battery situated on a small knoll behind them. Still mounted, Dahlgren turned to meet a flank attack on his right, presenting a tempting target to the Confederates at the church. He felt a sting as a bullet smashed into his booted right foot. The ball had struck the ankle bone and passed out through the top of his foot. He cried to a nearby war correspondent, E. A. Paul, who was covering the action for the *New York Times*, "Paul, I have got it at last!" Even so, Dahlgren remained in the saddle half an hour more until pain and loss of blood drove him to withdraw. Still, he gave his wound short shrift. Riding back to Kilpatrick, he gave a report without dismounting or mentioning his wound. Not realizing that his aide had been shot, Little Kil gave the captain further orders. Suddenly, Dahlgren blurted out, "General, I am hit," and pointed to his shattered foot. As he dismounted to lie down on the ground, he passed out.[2] This show of raw courage and unflagging stamina prompted a captain in Kilpatrick's escort to later write that Dahlgren was "one of the most chivalrous and knightly men that ever rode at the head of embattled squadrons."[3]

Born on April 3, 1842, outside Philadelphia in Bucks County, Pennsylvania, Ulric Dahlgren was a child of fortune. His father, John A. Dahlgren, was the son of a Swedish trade consul, a prominent U.S. naval officer, and a patent holder on a technologically advanced piece of naval ordnance known as the Dahlgren gun. The senior Dahlgren's rank and ingenuity brought the family stability, status, and financial security. At five years old "Ully," as his father called him, moved with the family to the nation's capital when the elder Dahlgren was assigned to the Washington Navy Yard. Varina Davis, whose husband, Jefferson, then was representing Mississippi in the U.S. Senate, recalled meeting the "faired-haired boy" looking "pretty . . . in his black velvet suit and Vandyke collar." Later, by virtue of his family's prominence, Ulric attended a private academy in the capital, where he studied the classics and mathematics and was "expert with the pencil." His privileged status also provided entrée to the Washington social scene, where Mrs. Davis and her husband claimed to be "intimate with his parents."[4]

In his teens Ulric came to work with his father, wandering the navy yard shops. Intrigued by the machinery, he thought he might become an engineer or a lawyer. Athletic, with a bent for swimming and rowing, he had a particular fondness for "horses which remained to the last." An accomplished horseman, he was described as "not surpassed, but [he] was a bold, practiced and elegant rider." But status was no safeguard against ill fortune. By the time he was fifteen, Ully had lost two brothers and a sister in their infancy as well as his beloved mother to a debilitating but undiagnosed disease in 1855.[5]

At seventeen Dahlgren set aside his studies and struck out in early 1859 for an uncle's plantation in Natchez, Mississippi, hoping to gain some practical experience and to see the country. His route took him through Richmond, Virginia, where he might have seen some of the landmarks he later described to support his qualifications for Kilpatrick's provocative mission.[6] His uncle, Charles Dahlgren, was in a position to mentor a nephew on the cusp of adulthood. A native Philadelphian, Charles was a successful banker and cotton planter who had amassed over seven thousand acres and more than two hundred slaves.[7]

The Dahlgren birthright carried with it some flatulent character attributes. One biographer of the Nordic clan has observed, "The Dahlgrens were virile and impetuous glory seekers who played dangerous games for the sport." John Dahlgren's younger brother, William, used "deceit and cunning" to enrich his mercenary career while serving the Italian revolutionary Giuseppe Garibaldi. John and William came literally to physical blows while serving together in the navy, which caused John to have his younger brother arrested; they never reconciled. All three brothers "courted danger—from street fights and duels in Natchez to rebellions in Italy, from filibuster campaigns in Central and South America to the Atlantic blockade against the South." Moreover, John was a stickler for protocol, sensitive to insults, and ready to duel when merely left off a dinner's guest list. The naval officer was also known for a superiority complex, which did not add to his popularity among his sailors.[8]

Lincoln's navy secretary, Gideon Welles, who had close dealings with John Dahlgren, described him as "proud and very sensitive and the strictures of the press he would feel keenly." Undoubtedly, it was the secretary's polite way of saying that the elder Dahlgren was thin skinned. Welles felt that he had a "cold, selfish and ambitious nature . . . , but he is neither a fool or insane." The secretary knew the naval officer's subordinates liked him even less than did the reporters who dealt with him. Some collegial disaffection among his "professional brethren" could be blamed on Dahlgren's rapid advancement in rank, but probably it resulted from his own personality flaws.[9]

Ulric seemed to have inherited aspects of his father's temperament. He could be warm but also "resolute and quick to resent a real insult."[10] During the teen's Mississippi visit, a young friend of the family took note of his risibility. A favorite family escape from the Natchez humidity was Beersheba Springs, a resort five hundred miles away in Tennessee. While there with cousins and friends, Ully remarked that a young local woman had beautiful eyes, which unfortunately were wasted on a backcountry mountain girl. His causal condescension so irritated a companion, Lucy Virginia French, that she recorded it in her diary, terming Dahlgren "an arrogant young man with patronizing ways."[11] This penchant for hubris and "feeling superior" to others, traits akin to his father's demeanor, have gone unremarked in previous accounts of Ulric Dahlgren's character. Yet it casts a different and penetrating light on some of the young man's reckless decisions during his career as an army officer.

After about a year in Mississippi, in September 1860 Ulric returned to Philadelphia, where he began to study law at the office of another uncle, James W. Paul. By then the clouds of sectional conflict were gathering around the contentious presidential election of 1860. When Southerners fired on Fort Sumter, Dahlgren, nineteen, joined a Philadelphia home-guard unit as a lieutenant. During the first year of the war, he caromed between Philadelphia and Washington. But his father, commanding the Washington Navy Yard, was well positioned to help his son land a plum commission anywhere he wanted.[12]

Shortly after taking over at the navy yard, John Dahlgren, who despite his bluster had a reputation for straight talk, humor, and an ability to listen, became close friends with President Lincoln. For Lincoln, who valued men not inclined to palaver and willing to hold their tongues and open their minds, the relationship would last as long as he lived. "Lincoln and Dahlgren became close enough for the President to confide in him to a degree that he did with few others, including old friends from Illinois," one commentator observed.[13] Lincoln liked to visit the navy yard, but also invited the naval officer to the Executive Mansion on numerous occasions. In fact, it was not unusual for Dahlgren to drop by to visit the president without an appointment.[14] Perhaps it was his "witty and wise sailor-talk" that the garrulous Lincoln enjoyed.[15] As Dahlgren commented, "The President often comes to see the Yard, and treats me without reserve." This intimacy brought him into the circle of cabinet members, senators, and congressmen.[16] Dahlgren's son rode his father's coattails into that era's edition of the power elite, and he too developed a rapport with the commander in chief.

Lincoln may have had a deeper bond with the naval officer than other members of the government. "When I am depressed, I like to talk with Dahlgren," he confided to a friend early in the war. "I learn something of the preparations for defense, and I get from him consolation and courage." Perhaps the president was thinking of the Bull Run debacle, when Dahlgren dispatched five hundred sailors and marines to defend an artillery battery in Alexandria until army replacements showed up.[17] Whatever the root of his father's and Lincoln's friendship, Ulric enjoyed entrée to the most powerful man in the North.

The young Dahlgren did not give up his law books and quit his home-guard unit until May 1862. He was barely twenty, but circumstances easily afforded him an officer's commission, courtesy of a note signed by Lincoln requesting the appointment from the secretary of war. Stanton went the president one better, making the young Dahlgren an army captain, albeit one with no command—yet.[18]

Captain Dahlgren, six feet tall in his new uniform, first joined the staff of Major General Franz Sigel in the Shenandoah Valley. A native of Baden, Germany, Sigel was a revolutionary in the 1848 disturbances, coming to America in 1852. He was a political general cultivated by the Lincoln administration for his ability to recruit immigrant Germans to the Union cause. Dahlgren saw action at Cedar Mountain and during the Second Manassas Campaign in August 1862, but by the fall, when Lee invaded Maryland, he was running messages back and forth between Sigel's headquarters in Fairfax Court House and Washington. The general, impressed with the young officer, recommended him for promotion to major in September 1862 because he saw in him "a young officer of merit and usefulness . . . who has already distinguished himself and reflected much credit on the service."[19] The War Department never acted on Sigel's recommendation.

In November 1862, while still serving on Sigel's XI Corps staff as an aide-de-camp, Dahlgren was allowed to make a scout across the Rappahannock River near Fredericksburg to gather intelligence in preparation for the Army of the Potomac's next move. Leading a small contingent of less than two hundred troopers on a reckless three-day operation, Dahlgren captured some thirty Confederate prisoners after a sharp fight with sabers and clubbed carbines in the streets of the city.

Revealingly, en route to Fredericksburg Dahlgren got lost several times. According to his father's version of the tale, his son, to escape detection during a snowy night, "avoided the main road as much as possible, and, in consequence, lost the right direction," which "bore most heavily on the jaded troopers and their horses." Thanks to miserable weather and "repeatedly missing the road," the younger Dahlgren was "four hours" later than he had expected to be in reaching a ford, his father said. The captain himself admitted in a report that when he finally reached the Rappahannock, "I found the river too high to ford at the regular fording-places." This forced his men to cross at a shallow rocky passage only wide enough for one horse at a time. Once across the stream, the Federals charged into the town, where they had a short but hot encounter with some Confederate cavalrymen who nearly cut off their retreat. In addition, it appears that part of the command disregarded his orders to hold the intended ford once the tide went out. Luckily for Dahlgren, the Rebels failed to seize the ford either, so he and his men crossed back without resistance.[20]

Once on the north bank of the Rappahannock, Dahlgren sent most of his force back to Sigel's headquarters with the prisoners. He then proceeded to Aquia Creek with a twelve-man detachment. Finding the railroad bridge there in "tolerable condition," he continued on, burning bridges over the Potomac and Accokeek Creeks. In fact, the rookie raider burned too many bridges. "The captain's indiscretion would cause serious headaches for the U.S. Military Railroads later on," one historian noted.[21] But Sigel ignored his subordinate's missteps. Instead, the general complimented Dahlgren for carrying out "one of the most brilliant and daring" operations "since the breaking out of the war" and for "his soldierly and manly qualities." Of course, Sigel was considered a "fourth-rate" general by at least one Union officer and an outright failure by some historians for his military performance, so his praise came with caveats, though not that Captain Dahlgren cared.[22]

During the Fredericksburg "raid," Sigel heard that Dahlgren might have been captured. Ever the politician, the general quickly reported this rumor to the captain's father, knowing well what could befall a man who lost the son of one of Lincoln's closest confidants. No doubt Sigel sighed in relief when not only the captain but also his men, tired to the bone, dragged back into camp at Gainesville. General Halleck counseled Sigel not to send his aide on any raids in the immediate future.[23]

Undaunted and perhaps exhilarated by the fracas in Fredericksburg, Dahlgren, by happy accident or canny intent, showed up at a choice moment at Army of the Potomac headquarters. Hours after the captain had left on his raid, Lincoln, weary of McClellan's feckless posturing, had tapped Major General Ambrose Burnside to take command of the army. Dahlgren arrived at Burnside's head-quarters on December 11, 1862, as the new commander was about to launch a massive attack against Lee's army. The Confederates had fortified Fredericksburg's streets and were strongly entrenched on heights west of it. Crews in pontoon boats rowed Union infan-try across the icy Rappahannock with orders to seize the town and eliminate pesky Rebel sharpshooters. Captain Dahlgren climbed aboard one boat. Mentioned in dispatches, this gutsy act perhaps earned him a temporary spot on the commanding general's staff, but by mid-January 1863 he was back with Sigel.[24]

The Fredericksburg assault failed, a bloody mess further soiled by the Army of the Potomac's January 1863 "Mud March." After this Burnside, upon his own request, was relieved of command. In his place the brave but brash Major General Joseph Hooker was appointed by Lincoln, who thought that he could whip some steel into the demoralized army. In the shakeup that followed, Sigel lost his command, freeing Dahlgren to join Hooker's staff as an aide-de-camp. He could have earned the post on merit, but a personal letter from his father cemented the appointment.[25]

Hooker reorganized the entire army, reemploying the corps structure, including the newly formed Cavalry Corps. For the spring offensive, he conceived a strategy to outflank the Army of Northern Virginia with his force by crossing the Rappahannock above Fredericksburg. The new commander also sent his massed cavalry brigades under Major General George Stoneman on a circu-itous raid that would place Union horse soldiers at the rear of the Southern army. Dahlgren remained at Hooker's headquarters, but he was constantly in the saddle, carrying orders to field command-ers and reporting his observations of Confederate movements back to the general.[26]

Not even the Union defeat at Chancellorsville could dampen Dahlgren's exuberance. He might have cribbed some notions from reports about Stoneman's raid as fodder for actions he might like to pursue. His family ties and position at army headquarters trumped his callow age and relatively low rank, opening lines of communications closed to his counterparts. As a result, by the end of May, Dahlgren had confected a fairly detailed plan for a raid on Richmond and its environs. Writing formally of it in a letter to General Hooker on May 23, the captain theorized that Jeb Stuart's cavalry was itching to find a gap in the Federal lines to exploit with a raid, as the gray cavalier had successfully done before. If the Confederates attempted such a movement, Dahlgren proposed responding by moving rapidly with a small body of cavalry, specifically the 6th U.S. Regulars, against Richmond. His plan specifically recommended the destruction of the Bellona Arsenal and selected bridges near the capital. He laid out a scheme that had his force crossing the James River in Goochland County west of Richmond and entering the city as well as the railroad hub at Petersburg to the south. Once there, though, the young officer did not say what his troopers were to do.[27]

Dahlgren was not the only Yankee officer convinced the Rebels were spoiling for a raid. Three days before the captain wrote to Hooker, Major General Samuel Heintzelman, commanding the Washington defenses, scribbled in his diary that intelligence supplied by a Federal operative on the Peninsula claimed that Confederates were also contemplating a raid. The unnamed spy reported seeing "a large number of coats, cleaned and on the line to dry," in Richmond; the coats, he claimed, were blue. The agent insisted that 1,500 picked cavalrymen would wear these false uniforms in a raid on Washington, gaining entry by using a countersign provided by an unnamed "disloyal colonel," and seize Lincoln, Stanton, and Secretary of State William Seward. Whether or not the president was aware of the potential kidnapping is unknown, but if so perhaps it fostered the idea in his mind to reverse the situation on Davis the following February.[28]

Hooker might have spoken immediately to his aide about the raid, but he did not respond in writing. Dahlgren recorded in a memorandum book, "Hooker thought it too desperate." Nor is it known how much, if any, attention the War Department or the administration paid the proposal. John Dahlgren noted that three days after floating the idea, his son accompanied Hooker to Washington but never mentioned a possible Richmond raid.[29]

Following Lee's great victory at Chancellorsville, the Army of Northern Virginia prepared to invade the North again, this time in hopes of marching beyond the Mason-Dixon Line. In anticipation Stuart's cavalry began to assemble south of the Rappahannock fords near Brandy Station in Culpeper County. At the same time, Major General Alfred Pleasonton, who had replaced Stoneman as commander of the Cavalry Corps because Hooker was displeased with the latter's performance during the Chancellorsville Campaign, was also preparing to move. The Union cavalry was to cross the Rappahannock to hit Stuart's massed brigades, which Pleasonton believed were at Culpeper Court House; the Rebel camps were actually about seven miles closer to the river. With his usual exquisite timing, as the operation was to commence, Captain Dahlgren found a slot for himself in the vanguard as an acting aide-de-camp to Pleasonton.

The early morning hours of June 9 found Dahlgren astride his mount with Brigadier General John Buford's cavalry division waiting his turn to splash across Beverly's Ford. When Yankee troopers met initial resistance from the Rebels near St. James Church, Buford ordered a charge by the 6th Pennsylvania Cavalry (also known as Rush's Lancers for the antiquated weapons they originally carried to war in 1861). Perhaps out of Keystone State kinship, Dahlgren joined the Lancers' attack, riding bravely alongside their commander, Major Robert Morris, Jr. Charging with sabers drawn, the Pennsylvanians took heavy losses, including Morris, who was wounded and captured. Untouched by the rounds zipping past, Dahlgren stepped in to rally the troopers. A sergeant in the regiment wrote home six days later, "it was Capt Dalgrean [*sic*] who rallied our men on their Collors, and Charging the Enemy cut their way out again."[30]

Pleasonton, a political if not military wizard, noted in his report that "Captain Dahlgren was among the first to cross the river and charged with the first troops. . . . [H]is horse was shot four times. His dashing bravery and cool intelligence are only equaled by his varied accomplishments. . . . [He was] frequently under the hottest fire . . . in conveying my orders."[31] Probably after having a word with Dahlgren, a war correspondent echoed the general: "Captain Dahlgren, of General Hooker's staff, a model of cool and dauntless bravery, charged with the regiment, and his horse was shot in two places. He describes the charge as one of the finest of the war."[32] Whatever reputation Dahlgren had built on the battlefield and at headquarters, it was beginning to spread to the public at large.

By now John Dahlgren had made rear admiral. He had suffered the loss of two sons and a daughter and did not want to lose another child, even to patriotic glory. The admiral wrote to General Hooker on June 15, stating that he had need of "some competent person . . . to take charge of business and papers of a confidential character" and suggested his son would be the most "suitable for the purpose." He assured him that neither the navy nor the War Department would object to the reassignment if the general concurred. Hooker, no political neophyte, acceded to the request, making a point of mentioning the obvious loss to his own headquarters. He said he could not "too highly commend the zeal, efficiency and gallantry which have characterized the performance of [Dahlgren's] duties while a member of my staff." But the transfer did not occur; whether because Hooker reneged, Ulric refused, or the son changed his father's mind is not known.[33]

After the great cavalry battle at Brandy Station, the Army of Northern Virginia began a steady march north toward Pennsylvania. At the Army of the Potomac's headquarters, Ulric Dahlgren, having escaped the safety of his father's embrace, pressed his superiors for more-active duties, declaring that he knew the countryside through which Lee's army was marching.[34] His value at headquarters was made clear when he remained on the staff even after Hooker was relieved and replaced by Major General George Gordon Meade. At this time Dahlgren's excessive self-regard reared its obnoxious head. Meade took command on June 28, knowing something big was up and scrambling to establish himself, but he had to contend with this arrogant stripling son of an admiral yammering about his self-serving ideas of scouting and raiding behind enemy lines. With his new commander struggling to get a handle on where Lee was, Dahlgren proposed "to take some men and operate on the rebel rear." Meade, known among his subordinates as the "old snapping turtle," finally relented, directing Pleasonton to get the youth some men for the mission he proposed. Eventually, ten men along with four scouts from the Bureau of Military Information rode with Dahlgren on a jaunt behind Lee's lines of communication.[35]

Arriving at Greencastle, Pennsylvania, on July 2, midway through the bloody slugfest at Gettysburg about thirty miles to the east, Captain Dahlgren and his men stumbled into a situation that would become a legend of the campaign. With sabers drawn, the little band of Yankee troopers rode into town and managed to capture two dozen Rebels, including two couriers bound for Lee's army with letters from Jefferson Davis and Adjutant General Samuel Cooper. In those dispatches Davis and Cooper confirmed that Lee could expect no reinforcements from elsewhere in the Confederacy. Instantly recognizing the letters' significance, Dahlgren left his men and galloped alone some thirty miles, through the path of the Confederate army, to Meade's headquarters, set up in a house owned by a Mrs. Leister, arriving early the next morning.[36] While this intelligence had some strategic and tactical value to the army commander, the real value of it had expired. Meade and his generals had already decided to maintain the army's position along Cemetery Ridge during their council of war on the evening of July 2. It appears that Dahlgren arrived too late to interject his news into these deliberations.

It is generally believed by historians that any importance now attached to the captured dispatches is "based upon fact, fancy, and fiction which is a perfect example of history by innuendo." One unequivocally states that "Dahlgren's intelligence, comforting as it may have been, had no bearing on Meade's decision to stand and fight at Gettysburg."[37] What may be more circumspect—and unmentioned by these writers—is the fact that the captain deserted his tiny command in order to gain whatever singular glory might accrue from delivering the letters directly into the hands of General Meade. Surely, several of the accompanying scouts were capable of riding through or around the enemy's lines. Nevertheless, Dahlgren abandoned his men near Greencastle, knowing elements of the Confederate army were at hand. His likely motivation was to promote his own ambitious military career over any basic understanding of good leadership.

Notwithstanding Dahlgren's grand but pointless gesture, Meade's army finally defeated Lee's battered ranks on July 3. The Confederate chieftain began his retreat to Virginia soon thereafter. The captain, as if remembering his stranded men in Greencastle, sought another command in hopes of rejoining his original unit and hindering Lee's withdrawal. Pleasonton ordered Brigadier General Wesley Merritt to detail one hundred picked men and some officers to accompany Dahlgren. Merritt selected troopers from the 6th Pennsylvania Cavalry under Captain Charles Treichel. A skeptical Pennsylvania officer was not convinced that Dahlgren's next adventure was worth the risk when he later wrote, "soon the fine detachment . . . was thrashing around the enemy's rear, on the wrong side of the mountains for safety and comfort, without any reasonable hope of accomplishing with such a small party, anything to compensate for the risk they ran."[38]

Dahlgren's little band managed to twice hit the Confederates' wagon train of wounded and Pennsylvania plunder, destroying several hundred wagons loaded with supplies and capturing some prisoners, many of whom eventually escaped. During three days in the saddle, his force showed relentless stamina, driving the Southern cavalry out of Greencastle and saving Waynesboro, Pennsylvania, from the Rebel torch. But the regimental historian of the 6th Pennsylvania Cavalry credited that showing to their actual leader, Captain Treichel, rather than Dahlgren. The action exhausted the Keystoners, who scattered, some taking refuge with locals, others returning to their regiment. By July 6 Dahlgren was pretty much on his own. He may have held himself in singular esteem, but he needed an outfit, so outside Hagerstown he tendered his services to General Kilpatrick.[39] That decision would cost him his right leg.

Kilpatrick appreciated what Dahlgren had done and saw what he might be able to do. As one Michigan officer put it, the captain had "established a reputation for extraordinary dash and daring." Brave and courageous in battle, yet he was at the same time reckless and careless as a military leader, traits he clearly demonstrated during his 1862 Fredericksburg raid and again in the actions around Greencastle. A month after the skirmish of July 6, Kilpatrick cited his volunteer aide, who now was out of action for what would be seven months, for "gallantry that came under my observation" in "leading a daring charge through the streets of Hagerstown."[40] Another observer called this same action "[b]rave almost to rashness."[41]

Three days after Hagerstown, Dahlgren arrived at his family's home in Washington, his left leg a stinking mass of inflammation. But he found his father gone. After years of running the Washington Navy Yard, the admiral had been assigned to command the South Atlantic Blockading Squadron off the coast of Charleston, South Carolina. The young man had to content himself with the comfort of a procession of officials, including his commander in chief. "Among the first to sit by his bedside, with kindly words of heart-felt sympathy, is Mr. Lincoln," one account mentions. Other visitors included Secretary of War Stanton accompanied by General Hooker. Navy Secretary Welles came out of fear the young man was at death's door; Ulric would later repay this courtesy by visiting Welles at the Navy

Department in October to demonstrate how well he was doing on his crutches. Lincoln must have been moved by the weakened condition of his friend's son. Shortly after his visit, the president penned a note in which he expressed his opinion, "I really think Capt. Dahlgren is entitled to the promotion asked."[42]

That promotion, originally suggested by Assistant Secretary of the Navy G. V. Fox, advanced the wounded hero three grades to colonel of volunteers. With the young man's parentage no less in mind than his record, Fox proposed a promotion to the rank of "captain of Cavalry or Artillery in the Regular Army." He detailed his reasons for the request with a narrative of Dahlgren's accomplishments and sent it directly to Lincoln, who endorsed it and then, perhaps thinking the captain might die, amended the recommendation. Stanton's letter to the young hero justified his decision to jump ranks: "Your gallant and meritorious service has, I think, entitled you to this distinction, although it is a departure from general usage, which is only justified by distinguished merit such as yours." In accepting the promotion to colonel, Dahlgren specifically thanked the president. The original order from Stanton "through some oversight was omitted to be enclosed at the time of its issue" in Dahlgren's military record. His acceptance of the commission is well documented, however, but the original order of appointment remains missing.[43]

Doctors monitored Dahlgren's wounded leg for several weeks as he continued to weaken. His surgeon eventually decided that amputation was the only alternative. "An attempt was made to save the foot which put his life in danger," so "amputation was required." On July 21 he removed the young man's right leg below the knee. The lifesaving procedure left the proud Dahlgren hobbled and dependent on assistance to dress and, before he got the hang of crutches, to walk.[44]

It would be a long convalescence period, necessitating a series of requests to the War Department for leave to recover. Optimistic as young men are, he asked for a leave of absence in August 1863 to visit his uncle at the seashore near Newport, Rhode Island, so he might dodge "the extreme heat prevailing" in Washington. Army bureaucrats were asked to treat his request as "a special case from the Sec[retar]y of War." From the shore Dahlgren went to Philadelphia for a week, but by September he was back in the nation's capital. There he spent time lobbying for a friend to be named lieutenant colonel of the regiment he intended to raise once his leg healed enough for him to return to active duty. During October, he spent about a week in Harrisburg, Pennsylvania, visiting friends, again retreating afterward to his father's house in Washington. In November he boarded a supply ship bound for the admiral's station off the South Carolina coast. At the end of that month, on the ground in South Carolina, he hazarded his first horseback ride since the fight at Hagerstown. Dahlgren's recuperation proceeded, but in January 1864 he was still on a leave, though well enough to alternate between his father's flagship, observing the South Atlantic Blockading Squadron off Morris Island, South Carolina, and spending time ashore to work on his rehabilitation exercise. Shortly before the young officer left his father's station, the admiral remembered seeing that Ully could ride a horse "as well as ever, and gets about in odd places surprisingly" well. By way of Philadelphia, Ulric returned to Washington on January 26.[45]

The same day that he returned to Washington, the young colonel met E. A. Paul, the newspaperman who had been with him when he was shot in Hagerstown. Paul was a frequent hanger on at Kilpatrick's headquarters and thus could provide high-level scuttlebutt to anyone who would listen. Dahlgren expressed to the journalist an interest in returning to active service. Paul in response might have mentioned Kilpatrick's ideas for a raid on Richmond.[46]

But Dahlgren may have found out about these plans through another of his myriad connections. Feeling fit after his sea journey, he made the rounds of social gatherings and called on officials, including Lincoln, though on his first try a busy schedule kept the president from seeing him. Undaunted, Dahlgren attended a January 30 Saturday "White House Matinee." During the crowded event, Lincoln told him to expect a private meeting. Dahlgren wrote to his father that he meant "to call every day [on the president] until I find him in."[47]

A diarist remembered the handsome, tragic young colonel on crutches at a "dancing party" in the National Hotel, where a "sweet-faced young woman said: 'He used to be such a beautiful waltzer!'" Between his good looks and his highly advertised injury, Dahlgren was like a magnet to the daughters of politicians, judges, generals, and naval officers. "He is splendid!" one debutante declared. Perhaps it was at this hotel affair that he overheard rumors of Kilpatrick's grand scheme. According to the admiral, his son heard of the "project of an expedition to rescue the Union soldiers from the horrible dungeons of Richmond, where they were immured." Such a leak was not surprising, for even a Washington haut monde with no direct ties to the army knew of rumors flying about the capital's streets regarding "a cavalry ride thro Virginia," which gave "due notice to the enemy to be ready to defeat its object." Within the army, one of Meade's staff officers observed that a "secret expedition with us is got up like a picnic, with everybody blabbing and yelping." By the middle of February, this same officer felt that "[a]ll Willard's chatters of it. . . . Some confidential friend finds out a part, tells another confidential friend, swearing him to secrecy, etc., etc."[48] By whatever means, Dahlgren sniffed out the hint of a Richmond raid, and once he did, *he could no longer be restrained*" (italics added).[49]

Finally, the colonel met personally with Lincoln as the president's barber trimmed his hair. Dahlgren's correspondence about this meeting leaves out any talk of raids, dealing instead with his father's blockade work. It was also characteristic of the younger Dahlgren to share many details of his own activities with his father.[50] Later that month, however, his letters would be much more animated about his chances of being part of a raid on Richmond. If Dahlgren and Lincoln spoke about his prospects of participating in an upcoming raid, or if the president wanted the young colonel to play a special role at his request, there is no evidence in Ulric's correspondence to prove it. The letter does reveal a certain amount of familiarity with the chief executive when the young man refers to the president as "Old Abe." It is likely Dahlgren would have confided to his father if Lincoln had betrayed a desire for the colonel to carry out any special instructions.

On February 18 Dahlgren rode the train from Washington to Brandy Station. Disembarking with some difficulty—he still was not accustomed to his new prosthesis—he tried to maintain his composure as he fumbled with his crutches. Aided by an enlisted man, the colonel mounted a horse and rode five miles straight to Third Cavalry Division headquarters near Stevensburg. How Dahlgren was greeted by General Kilpatrick is unrecorded. By this time the division commander's operational preparations were well underway, with or without the handicapped colonel's participation. An unnamed source said later that he tried in vain to dissuade the admiral's son, claiming that "he was urged, by his best friends, to remain in camp, not only because of the utopian character of the proposed enterprise, but because of his own physical disability to withstand the fatigue which it necessarily imposed on him." Dahlgren did not seem combat ready or entirely recovered from his wound to a newspaper reporter who visited Kilpatrick's headquarters. Much later Admiral Dahlgren remembered, "Every one was aware that he was in no condition to take the field just then. . . . [T]he wound was not perfectly healed; he still was weak and could only move on crutches." But Colonel Dahlgren had long since committed himself to a "holy war," and according to one acquaintance, "He felt it was glorious to die for one's country."[51]

Little Kil's plan required subordinates who would operate independently of the main body to attack Richmond from the south side of the James River. Dahlgren would soon be entrusted with this critical responsibility. How he garnered such an important assignment, with seemingly little affiliation with the general except for the brief episode at Hagerstown, is unclear. Kilpatrick never publicly commented on Dahlgren's intrusion on his mission, but years later an army scout posited this lingering question: "Does any soldier who knew or served under General Kilpatrick believe, had the selection been left to him, he would have gone outside his old Third Cavalry Division for a leader?"[52]

Perhaps the president or the War Department had a hand in determining Kilpatrick's command structure. Lincoln, based on his intimate relationship with Admiral Dahlgren and his son, through an intermediary may have strongly suggested that the colonel be included on the expedition after the two met on February 12. It was known by at least one army officer that the recovering officer was a "personal friend" of Secretary of War Stanton, who surely could have pulled strings to get Dahlgren the assignment. But it is mere speculation to conclude that Lincoln personally interceded on behalf of his young friend. Admiral Dahlgren, who may have known more about the situation than most, later wrote of his son, "No sooner was he apprised of what was contemplated than he sought to join the enterprise," and "the reluctant consent of the authorities was at last yielded to his earnest entreaties."[53] A civilian observer who was visiting the army's winter encampment at the time Dahlgren arrived claimed that the colonel "sought and obtained permission to lead an attack . . . upon Richmond, being confident he, alone . . . could capture that city which had already baffled the attempts of older soldiers."[54] This commentary again illustrates the hubris of the young man who seemed determined to gain glory for himself.

Nine months after the Richmond raid, a newspaper report alluded to his physical incapacity and wondered how he ended up with so important a command. The article concluded, "He was scarcely convalescent when he started upon the great cavalry raid, and it was only by his most urgent request that he was allowed to accompany General Kilpatrick."[55] But if the admiral is to be believed as well as other contemporary observations, there was no clandestine intervention by Lincoln to place the crippled colonel with Kilpatrick. Barely twenty-one years old and overly zealous, perhaps Dahlgren just wanted to be part of a grand scheme to make history and secured his position through his own persistence. Apparently, Little Kil in this instance allowed good judgment to be overshadowed by political expediency, if he indeed had any say in the matter.

Colonel Dahlgren arrived at Kilpatrick's headquarters on February 18. That same day an unidentified officer was dispatched to Washington with orders to select horses for the planned operation. "These animals, it was cautioned, must be the very best, well-shod and able to take the strain of days and nights of hard, merciless riding."[56] Led by a man nicknamed "Kill-Cavalry," this reads like a subtle understatement.

The ten days following Dahlgren's arrival saw incessant preparations for the raid, irking Kilpatrick's superiors. The seemingly unstoppable scheme found no friend in Pleasonton, who voiced grave reservations about the mission to his superior, Meade. Excluded from Kilpatrick's sessions with Lincoln and then Stanton, the cavalry commander bristled. He foresaw losses in horseflesh at least as heavy as those Stoneman took the previous May. More an administrator than a dashing, cavalry leader, Pleasonton thought that his corps could not support such equine losses with the spring campaign only weeks away. Furthermore, he thought that surprise was essential but not attainable. Even though the Army of Northern Virginia was virtually inactive at this time, not all telegraph lines to the Confederate capital could reasonably be cut before the raiders dashed off from Stevensburg. Finally, Pleasonton believed that sufficient copies of Lincoln's amnesty proclamation were already out and about the Virginia countryside. All these reasons underpinned his curt comment that the enterprise was "not feasible at this time."[57]

Meade, likewise, saw little merit in the operation, but he was a realist who surely overheard the jabber among congressmen and senators at Kilpatrick's Washington's Birthday celebration. The army commander knew a lost cause when he saw one, so he gave tacit, if reluctant, support. His son and aide, George G. Meade, Jr., later said his father "did not wholly approve of it tho[ugh] there is nothing in the record to show this & of course after it was ordered he did all that could be done to make it a success." Besides, the general seems to have thought the scheme had a scintilla of succeeding. He regarded Richmond as lightly enough defended to be taken by a coup de main, the prisoners released, and with their saviors be on the highway before enemy reinforcements from Petersburg or Lee's army could disrupt the operation. Meade "thought it possible by a secret, rapid, and bold movement conducted with judgment" that this could all occur.[58] But no matter the generals' personal biases, "strong pressure from Washington" forced both Pleasonton and Meade to cooperate, according to a trusted Kilpatrick subordinate.[59]

One of Meade's staff officers was less optimistic about the raid's outcome. Lieutenant Colonel Theodore Lyman believed that it would surely fail for several reasons. Lyman deemed Kilpatrick "an incompetent officer for such a thing; he is a great talker & manager, but has no head or skill, so far as proved." Next, the Harvard-educated officer thought that "[g]eographical difficulties, & rivers, and roads bad or hard to find" would impede the Federal horsemen. And finally, there were "[m]ilitary difficulties": the "home-guards must be poor indeed if, behind some breastwork or stone wall, they fail to drive off our cavalry," he said. Lyman had other objections but failed to enumerate them in writing.[60] Captain James Biddle, another member of Meade's staff and who had known about the plan for a few days, was not quite as pessimistic as Lyman: "It is a very bold undertaking and Kilpatrick will make a great name for himself if only successful."[61]

After meeting with Pleasonton, perhaps to mollify him, Meade ordered the Third Cavalry Division reinforced to a strength of 4,000 officers and men along with a battery of horse artillery. At the same time, Meade's chief of staff, Major General Andrew A. Humphreys, after being "enveloped in mystery," finally issued Kilpatrick orders mentioning the raid's only goal as the release of prisoners.

A "congregation of high mandarins," including Generals Kil-patrick, Sedgwick, Warren, Newton, and Merritt, convened on Saturday, February 27, at Meade's headquarters near Brandy Station. Custer who was to play an important role by making a diversionary attack on Lee's left, was absent. In addition, there is no mention of

Dahlgren being at this meeting, even though the raiders would be riding out the next day. Two days later, with the bluecoats en route, one of Meade's staff officers knew the "idea is to dash into the city (which is supposed to be feebly defended by home guards and a few regulars), liberate the prisoners, grab all the M.C.'s possible and then make the best of their way to the nearest, and safest, part of our lines."[62] The timing of this observation matters because this officer, who in his letter mentions the generals' meeting, only refers to capturing, not killing, Confederate officials.

On February 26 Dahlgren penned a poignant letter to his father, which he sent in care of his aunt, Martha Matilda "Patty" Dahlgren, to safeguard in case "I do not return." He assured her in an accompanying note that the mission would succeed, and "it will the grandest thing on record." He reserved for his father a son's eloquence, explaining that he had not returned to the admiral's fleet despite a standing invitation "because there is a grand raid to be made & I am to have a very important command. If successful it will be the grandest thing on record & if it fails many of us will 'go up.'" Obviously understanding that the stakes were high, the excited staff officer turned raider continued, "I may be captured or I may be 'tumbled over' but it is an undertaking that if I was not in it I should be ashamed to show my face again, with such an important command. . . . [I]f we do not return there is no better place to 'give up the Ghost.'" He closed on a cheery note, predicting a "successful although a desperate undertaking."[63]

As the deadline ticked closer, Kilpatrick, Dahlgren, and other senior commanders in the Third Cavalry Division squared away the welter of details associated with the upcoming expedition. General Davies, Kilpatrick's senior subordinate during the operation, was supposed to participate in court-martial proceedings but begged off until his return. The rank and file sensed that something eventful was up too. Great excitement was in the air as rumors flew about the cavalry camps near Rose Hill. "Rumor says that our Div[ision] is soon to go somewhere," a Vermont officer wrote to his wife. "I guess to Butler, overland, perhaps try our hand at Richmond. You must not say anything about it, as coming from me. We may not go for a month & perhaps not at all & perhaps we may be off sooner. I am not well posted."[64]

Such opinion was commonplace among other officers as well. With a day left before riding out, a lieutenant colonel from

Michigan wrote home: "[I]t is all guesswork. I suppose it to be one of Kilpatrick's tears as they are called here, a drive behind Lee's army as far as we can get committing deprecations upon all kinds of rebel property perhaps to Richmond as prisoners or victors, perhaps to the Peninsula." This officer did his best to dodge the assignment, "a desperate undertaking," he called it, but he could not delegate it to the regiment's next-senior officer. "I may come out with honor or never come out. God only knows," he concluded.[65] But a major in the Michigan Brigade appeared better informed when he boasted assuredly after the war that "the secret [about the raid] was an open one." He remembered "the rumor of the projected movement had been for some time flying about from ear to ear, and from camp to camp."[66] The harshest indictment about lack of discretion came from Kilpatrick's most trusted subordinate, Henry Davies. The brigade commander blamed Kilpatrick himself because he "made no secret of his plans which became a subject of common talk about the Camps and the important element of secrecy so essential on such an enterprise was entirely disregarded."[67]

One officer speculated that recent orders to prepare five days' rations of hardtack, sugar, coffee, and salt—but no meat—appeared "extremely raidish," though "it would certainly be more than an ordinary raid." A Vermont newspaper reported shortly after the raid's conclusion why the division was lightly supplied: "They carried with them only two or three feeds each for their horses and about as many days rations for the men, the General being determined that for once the celebrated order, 'subsist on the enemy's country' should be faithfully executed." One man in the Michigan Brigade "knew for some time before we stated that we were to make a raid but did not know in what direction." Most of the Yankee horsemen did not know their next assignment; even so, the monotony of winter quarters had them itching for action. "A winter of tents, engaged in daily drills, guard-mountings, and parades is monotonous; even card-playing, horse-racing, and kindred intellectual amusements became 'stale and unprofitable' when made a steady occupation," another horse soldier complained.[68] For cavalrymen, a raid was always preferred to the everyday drudgery of picket duty and drill. And for at least 3,500 Yankee horse soldiers, the next two weeks would prove anything but dull.

Scouts assigned to Meade's headquarters had an inside track for participation; in fact, some were already on the job. On February 20, five scouts were sent to hide out within Confederate lines. Their mission was to cut all the telegraph wires connecting Richmond with Lee's army on the night of February 28. "Each scout performed the duty assigned him and all wires connecting General Lee's army and Richmond were severed," remembered one of these men after the war.[69] Orders also went to the Signal Corps to make ready for a cavalry raid. On February 26, signal officers were assigned to the commands forming at Kilpatrick's headquarters. Color-coded rockets would link the main body and the diversionary strike force splitting off to cross the James River. Captain Joseph Gloskowski, who would accompany the main column, and Lieutenant Reuben Bartley, assigned to Dahlgren's smaller force, agreed on a secret code for the "parachute rockets," using various combinations of red, white, and green.[70]

Meanwhile in the Confederate capital, a Richmond newspaperman observed President Davis, accompanied by Generals Lee and Braxton Bragg, inspecting the city's defenses. He later reported that the men traveled by carriage "without attendants or an escort of any kind," demonstrating an apparent atmosphere of complacency among the Southern high command.[71]

Back north of the Rapidan, elements of the Union operation crystallized on February 27. After the meeting of the "high mandarins" at Meade's headquarters, the army commander issued Kilpatrick official orders through his chief of staff to proceed with the expedition. Again, Meade implied his tacit understanding of the political circumstances by the rather brusque instructions he provided. He would give "no detailed instructions . . . [s]ince the plan of your operations has been proposed by yourself, with the sanction of the President and the Secretary of War, and has been so far adopted by him that he considers success possible with secrecy, good management and utmost expedition." If Meade had any cause for hope, it was because his own scouts had reported "almost no troops around Richmond and the prisoners . . . but lightly guarded." In a letter dated immediately after the raid ended, though, the general betrayed his true feelings when he confided, "I did not expect much from it."[72]

Horses and men began to assemble near Kilpatrick's headquarters on the twenty-seventh, though not all were from the Third Cavalry Division. Captain Nehemiah Mann of the 4th New York Cavalry received orders to report with a hundred troopers to brigade headquarters by 4:00 P.M. There he joined picked men and horses from his brigade for the march to Kilpatrick's camps. In a "confidential" message that day, Pleasonton ordered five hundred men from the Second Cavalry Division and seven hundred more from the First Cavalry Division, with a proper complement of officers, to report to Kilpatrick by 8:00 P.M.[73]

Furloughs and lack of serviceable mounts had left the Third Cavalry Division shorthanded. Some 370 veterans in the 1st Michigan went home on furlough as a reward for reenlisting for the war's duration. Other troopers in the Michigan Brigade were likewise absent from camp. The furlough option had been extended at Meade's request when he figured out back in December that the enlistments of 21,000 soldiers in his army would soon expire. The general mentioned to Halleck that half these men probably would reenlist if provided a thirty-day furlough. Another 5,000 cavalrymen would stay if offered the same terms.[74]

Mounts were a different matter. "Horses were very scarce and there were quite a large number of unmounted men in camp," a Maine trooper said. "About two hundred of our regiment had enlisted for three years more and had gone home on thirty days furlough," he added. Poor performance and health issues had taken out some officers over the winter. On paper the division showed an aggregate strength of 3,653 officers and men, nearly the number Kilpatrick needed for his plan. The other two cavalry divisions were much smaller. Deducting troopers on special detached duty, sick, on leave, or under arrest, Kill-Cavalry's division dropped to 2,309 present. He overcame this impediment by arranging to have units, individual companies, and parts of companies detached from the other two divisions. In all, at least fifteen different regiments from the Army of the Potomac's three cavalry divisions would ride for Richmond.[75] This agglomeration gave Kilpatrick his required number to achieve his goals; it remained to be seen if reality would wreak havoc on his command structure when the operation's more complex aspects unfolded during the heat of action.

The wheel was in spin. Units from the First and Second Cavalry Divisions began to march to Stevensburg. At 6:00 A.M. a detachment of three hundred men from the 1st Maine under Major Constantine Taylor reported to brigade headquarters at Brandy Station, receiving orders to move immediately to Kilpatrick's camps.[76] The Maine boys, part of Gregg's Second Cavalry Division, were among Kilpatrick's favorite regiments. He may have even requested the

Pine Tree State troopers himself, being familiar with their tenacity from leading them in a charge up Fleetwood Hill during the June
battle near Brandy Station and crediting their showing that day with
winning him his brigadier's star. "This detachment was composed
of the flower of the regiment," according to the regimental historian,
"and was mounted on its best horses." The men carried three days'
rations, one day's forage, and "were poorly prepared for the work
before them, especially at that inclement season." Also arriving
were two squadrons of one hundred cavalrymen each from the 4th
Pennsylvania and 16th Pennsylvania, making good on Pleasonton's
promise to send five hundred men from the Second Cavalry Division.
Riding in at about 4:00 P.M., they were assigned to General Davies's
command.[77] The next morning a comrade who had been left behind
in camp was somewhat melancholy about the Pennsylvanians' leaving, though upbeat too: "Seems very lonely so many of our Boys
gone—but it means liveliness for them, and maybe a good deal more
both for them and The Johnies."[78]

Men of the First Cavalry Division joining the expedition left
their camps just west of Culpeper Court House. In a pattern typical of this operation, "a detail of fifty picked men and horses from
the several companies . . . with light saddles and two days' rations"
from the 9th New York rode east to Stevensburg. A hint of the command complexities ahead showed in the fact that while a line officer from the regiment commanded the unit's men, they came from
various companies within the regiment. It was the same situation
with the 17th Pennsylvania, in which "ten men from each company
were detailed with four officers to report" to Kilpatrick. This contingent of "the best men and horses" was augmented to about two
hundred troopers total from the regiment. Most of the First Division
men came from the Second Brigade.[79]

The Third Cavalry Division's camps were soon humming.
Officers winnowed units of men incapable of the ride to Richmond.
One trooper recalled when he wrote home, "we got orders to get
five days hard tack no meat but plenty of salt" plus "our blankets"
and "one day's forage for our horses." Fortunately or not, the writer
did not have a healthy mount and so was forced to remain behind,
although he very much wanted to go. But he had no doubts about the
raid's outcome because the men riding out "were led by the bravest
of the brave Gen Kilpaterick [sic]." He further believed "that if any
man can go into Richmond that Kilpatrick can."[80]

One Michigan officer selected men to go on the raid because he wanted "to get some fighting out of them," a motivation speaking volumes about the experience of those selected to go with Kilpatrick and Dahlgren. Most troopers were picked because they and their horses were healthy and fit, not necessarily their time in action. Accounts vary whether only veteran cavalrymen went on the raid or that less experienced recruits were included too. A Vermonter remembered, "None but veterans were to go, so we did not consider this would a pleasure party by any means." But a New Yorker reported that from his regiment, "Most all the green boys went." "A large number of the men under my command were new recruits," a captain from Maine observed. "They were made veterans in a single week." One thing was certain: "a more savage insulting swaggering set of wretches" was never seen except marching under Kilpatrick's banner.[81]

February 28 was warm but cloudy, with a hard wind blowing, according to one trooper who recorded the day's conditions. Typical of Virginia's mercurial weather at that time of year, the late winter days had been sunny, almost "beautiful" in one staff officer's opinion, but it soon became cloudy. By the time the horse soldiers were ready to leave that evening, it was "cold, cheerless with drizzling rain." Such ominous signs were not going to slow down an operation personally approved by the nation's commander in chief, however.[82]

Once the First and Second Cavalry Division detachments arrived at Stevensburg, they drew additional rations and were assigned to the various commanders. An army chaplain recalled, "Many and some larger sum[s] of money were left with me to express and [to] keep till their return." Ten scouts from Meade's headquarters also rode in to participate in the raid. A quartermaster sergeant inventoried torpedoes and rat-tailed files along with turpentine, oakum, and other inflammables. The torpedoes, gunpowder-filled artillery shells with percussion fuses, were for destroying bridges and the James River and Kanawha Canal locks. The raiders would use the oakum to torch buildings. Six ambulances, each pulled by a six-mule team and loaded with assorted ammunition, lined up, as did three wagons carrying forage for the horses as well as explosives and incendiaries. Horse-artillery support would be provided by Captain Duncan Ransom's Battery C, 3rd U.S. Artillery, with six three-inch ordnance rifles and eight caissons.

All was in order. The road to Ely's Ford on the Rapidan River had been scouted and found in excellent condition. A cavalry captain reported, "The mud caused by the rain did not extend but a few inches below the surface, and could not, in my opinion, impede the passage of artillery or wagons over the good, hard bed found underneath." The auguries were good. According to Kilpatrick himself, he mounted 3,582 men for his operation against Richmond.[83]

Between 2:00 and 3:00 o'clock that afternoon, a forty-man detachment from the 5th New York under Lieutenant Henry Merritt and three army scouts cantered out of Stevensburg headed to Ely's Ford. Their mission was to secure the crossing undetected by the enemy for the use of the advancing column. The army scouts—Martin Hogan, James Wood, and Jake Swisher—had been down this road before, going behind enemy lines and returning all winter.[84]

About an hour later Colonel Dahlgren left Stevensburg with his remaining 420-man contingent. These troopers were from five different regiments: the 2nd New York, 1st Vermont, 5th Michigan, the balance of the 5th New York, and about 150 men from Companies D, F, H, K, and M, 1st Maine, under Captain John Myrick. Tucked in among the front ranks was a black man dressed in field-hand clothes. He had been sent to Dahlgren only hours before by Captain John Babcock, an intelligence officer at Meade's headquarters. Babcock included a cryptic message, which noted that the man might be useful as a guide but his credentials were sketchy at best. Some thought they had heard him called Martin Roberson, but the man's identity would remain a mystery until the raiders reached the James River.[85]

Major Edwin F. Cooke, twenty-eight and a close friend of Kilpatrick, would serve as Dahlgren's second in command.[86] Members of the 2nd New York admired Cooke and believed that he would be an asset for the one-legged colonel. An army scout described him as "brave, gallant, [and] genial. . . . He was beloved by all who knew him, particularly the members of his old regiment—the Harris Light Cavalry." A captain in that regiment found him a "deservedly popular officer." Moreover, "no officer in the regiment had a greater number of warm personal friends than he." With Cooke would be Captain John F. B. Mitchell, also from the 2nd New York. Both men "were selected for their well-known and daring invincibility in desperate circumstances." It proved fortunate that both officers were with Dahlgren.[87]

Drawn up in a column of fours, Dahlgren's command passed under Kilpatrick's approving eye near Rose Hill. The colonel rode in an ambulance, crutches alongside him, because he "was still so feeble as to require to be helped into his saddle." As the troopers passed, a curious exchange took place. Kilpatrick shouted to Cooke, "Good-bye Major, do this thing up clean for me, and then ask anything you like." Riding by, Cooke replied, "You will find it all right General, depend on me."[88] Soon the column passed down the sloppy road leading to Ely's Ford before the main body was ready to move out.

Around sunset troopers in overcoats with sabers and revolvers hanging from their belts walked up and down the camp's company streets, "talking in low tones." At 5:00 P.M. bugles sounded "Boots and Saddles," and all that were going hustled to saddle up. Officers nervously barked orders: "Lead into line! Right dress! Number by fours! By fours! Right wheel! Forward march!" An hour later Kilpatrick's entire column was ready to move. One participant summed up the cavalrymen's enthusiasm: "old Kill Cav (as he is familiarly called by us) rode along the lines," and "the boys felt a thrill of pleasure through them for they knew they were to have some exciting scenes before we returned & so it proved." A New Yorker heard the general say, "Butler wouldn't have the fun of taking it alone."

Nearly four thousand troopers, led by "the dashing and intrepid cavalry leader, General Judson Kilpatrick, rode out of the Union lines, their horses' hoofs ringing on the icy ground, their equipments clinking in the frosty air." General Davies, "a gallant officer" with "some fine officers and regiments with him," led with his brigade, followed by Ransom's battery. Most likely, the amalgamated units from the First and Second Cavalry Divisions followed the artillery. "To Colonel Sawyer with the Vermont and Michigan men fell the irksome duty of bringing up the rear of the column, the chief care being to keep up the pace, not losing sight of the front, of which for a good part of the night there was much danger," a Michigan officer grumbled. Sandwiched in between Davies's and Sawyer's troopers was a sixteen-piece mounted brass band that Kilpatrick had appropriated from Custer's brigade. By the time the 1st Vermont, bringing up the rear guard, finally left Stevensburg about 7:00 P.M., the sky was black but for a dim rim of light at the western horizon.[89]

Brigadier General Judson Kilpatrick. From the author's
collection.

Colonel Ulric Dahlgren. From the author's
collection.

Brigadier General Isaac Wistar. Courtesy the Wistar Institute, Wistar Archive Collections, Philadelphia, Pennsylvania.

General Kilpatrick and staff at Rose Hill, Stevensburg, Virginia (1864). Courtesy Library of Congress Prints and Photographs Division, LC-B817-7516 Lot 4186 K.

Rose Hill, Kilpatrick's headquarters, Culpeper County. Courtesy Dave Roth, *Blue & Gray* magazine.

Major General George Armstrong Custer (January 1865). Courtesy Library of Congress Prints and Photographs Division, LC-DIG-cwpb-05340.

Dover Plantation, Goochland County. Courtesy Goochland County Historical Society.

Eastwood Plantation, Goochland County. Courtesy Goochland County Historical Society.

Sabot Hill Plantation, Goochland County. Courtesy Goochland County Historical Society.

Sallie Seddon. Courtesy Goochland County Historical Society.

Libby Prison, Richmond, Virginia (April 1865). Photograph by Andrew J. Russell. Courtesy Library of Congress Prints and Photographs Division, 11486A, no. 2.

Brigadier General Henry E. Davies, Jr. Courtesy U.S. Army Heritage and Education Center, Carlisle, Pennsylvania.

Major General Wade Hampton, C.S.A. (ca. 1860–1870). Courtesy Library of Congress Prints and Photographs Division LC-B813-6770B, Lot 4213.

Major Edwin F. Cooke. From the author's collection, courtesy the Keller family, Franklin, N.J.

Kilpatrick and his wife, Alice. Courtesy U.S. Army Heritage and Education Center, Carlisle, Pennsylvania.

CHAPTER 6

CUSTER'S SIDE SHOW

Brigadier General George A. Custer, who had married a few weeks earlier, returned to the Army of the Potomac's winter encampment fresh from his honeymoon. To get to his brigade headquarters, he had only to ride from the Brandy Station depot to Clover Hill, a Revolutionary-era house remade in the fussier gingerbread style of the day, where he as well as his new wife, Libbie, would live. But he arrived there to find orders to take his troopers into the field.

In much the same way that the army had staged a feint early in February to facilitate Wistar's ill-fated raid on Richmond, now three weeks later Custer was to create a diversion toward Charlottesville. His objective was to draw the attention of the Army of Northern Virginia to the west as Kilpatrick moved out to the south and east on his sortie against the Confederate capital. By riding around Lee's left flank while supported by several infantry divisions, Kilpatrick hoped that Custer would make the Confederate commander think that the whole Union army was flanking him, thus tying down his forces while Kilpatrick rode unmolested for Richmond.

Custer was to take 1,500 troopers with him. These men would come from the Cavalry Corps's Reserve Brigade of Wesley Merritt's First Cavalry Division and two regiments from David Gregg's Second Cavalry Division. The force would consist of mounted detachments of about one hundred men each from the 1st, 2nd, and 5th U.S. Cavalry, the 19th New York (also known as the 1st Dragoons), and the 6th Pennsylvania, numbering in all about five hundred men. Major William P. C. Treichel would command the regulars, New Yorkers, and Pennsylvanians. Lieutenant Colonel William Stedman, a forty-nine-year-old Ohio merchant and farmer, would serve as Custer's second in command leading one thousand troopers selected from the Second Cavalry Division's First Brigade along with detachments from the 1st New Jersey and 6th Ohio. The young general would also take along a two-gun section of Battery E, 1st U.S. Artillery, commanded by Lieutenant Essex Porter.[1]

Late on the afternoon of February 26, John Sedgwick, now back commanding his own VI Corps, was ordered to support Custer by moving two divisions to Madison Court House by Sunday evening, February 28. The fifty-one-year-old general was further ordered to establish a signal station on Thoroughfare Mountain several miles south of James City. His men would take six days' rations, forty rounds of ammunition, and some entrenching tools. Three artillery batteries, commanded by Colonel Charles H. Tompkins, would accompany the divisions. The general was cautioned that "secrecy" was essential to the operation's success but also was authorized to use force as necessary against the enemy to assure Custer's safe return. Major General David B. Birney's division of the III Corps would cooperate with Sedgwick, who would be the infantry's overall commander.[2]

On February 27 Sedgwick's First Division, under Brigadier General David A. Russell, marched about thirteen miles from its winter camps at Welford's Ford on the Rappahannock River, passing through Culpeper Court House, to James City, where the men bivouacked for the night. A keen-eyed soldier in the Vermont Brigade noted the spectacle of the VI Corps's march in a letter home: "Long lines of infantry with their gleaming bayonets and handsome regimental colors, with now and then a battery of artillery, then infantry again, and occasionally a white-topped supply wagon." The following day Russell's troops advanced another nine miles to Madison Court House after crossing the Robinson River around noon at Russell's Ford and brushing away some Confederate mounted pickets. Arriving at 4:30 P.M. on the twenty-eighth, Russell placed most of his division in front of Madison Court House on either side of the road, where the men remained the following day. One brigade remained behind to guard the river ford two miles to the north and to build a bridge over the Robinson on the chance that a sudden storm might cause the water to rise.

Sedgwick's Third Division, under Brigadier General Henry L. Eustis, followed the same route as Russell. The troops reached Madison Court House on February 28 amid regimental bands playing "their liveliest airs." Birney's men did not leave their camps until February 28 due to his orders not arriving at III Corps headquarters until the morning of the twenty-seventh. The general then marched with his division and two artillery batteries as far as James City, where they bivouacked.[3]

On February 27 Custer assembled his column in the fields near Pony Mountain, a well-known signal station west of Stevensburg and convenient to Clover Hill. The weather was "as bright and beautiful as ever winter saw," a Rhode Island infantryman wrote home. "The roads were in splendid condition, the men in good trim and all was propitious." Custer had picked an excellent assembly point, wide and flat, with plenty of room for his men to camp. Stedman's Ohioans and New Jerseyans left their camps at Warrenton Junction on the Orange and Alexandria Railroad and marched most of the day, arriving near Pony Mountain late, some after midnight. To reach the rendezvous, units from the Reserve Brigade, camped near Mitchell's Station to the south, had to ride only two hours. The regulars and Pennsylvanians reported to the general at 9:00 P.M., just as the weather began to get "very blustery and cold."[4]

Near Pony Mountain the next morning, Custer briefed his subordinate officers, explaining the diversionary intent of their enterprise and noting that they would operate in the direction of Charlottesville "in order to facilitate other movements of the army." He was authorized to advance far enough toward that city to enable his troopers to destroy the Virginia Central Railroad bridge over the Rivanna River. By burning that span and cutting telegraph lines, Custer would sever an indirect line of communication between Lee's army and Richmond. Combined with the army scouts' work of cutting telegraph lines elsewhere, Lee could be potentially isolated from information. The general also knew that his infantry support would not march beyond Madison Court House, Pleasonton having warned him not to let Rebel cavalry or infantry get between him and Sedgwick's brigades at that location. Ending the meeting with his subordinates, Custer returned to Clover Hill for the night.

Starting at midday Sunday, February 28, as Colonel Dahlgren's advance force was riding east toward Ely's Ford, Custer started his regulars, Pennsylvanians, Ohioans, and New Jerseyans on the road southwest toward Charlottesville. By 6:00 P.M. Custer's mounted force was in the vicinity of Madison Court House, mingling with the advance elements of Sedgwick's infantry. As he passed the VI Corps's camp, Custer took the opportunity to ask "Uncle John" Sedgwick more about his mission, having been left out of the meeting of "high mandarins" at Meade's headquarters the previous day. The young brigadier was nervous about reports that Rebel infantry was guarding the railroad bridge at Charlottesville. Reports also

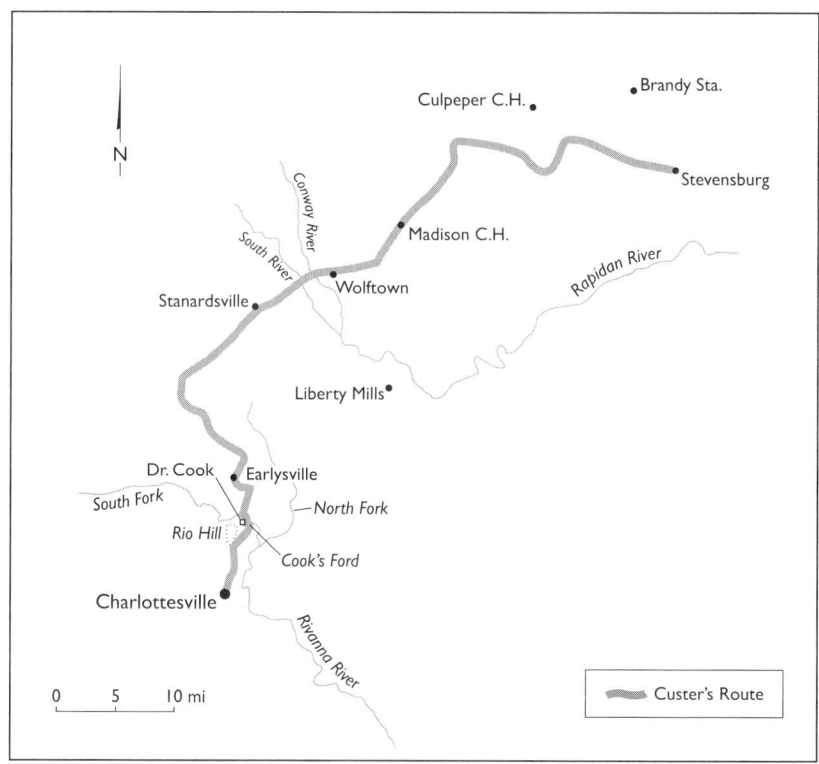

Culpeper C.H.

Brandy Sta.

Stevensburg

Madison C.H.

Conway River

South River

Rapidan River

N

Wolftown

Stanardsville

Liberty Mills

Dr. Cook   Earlysville

South Fork   North Fork

Rio Hill

Cook's Ford

Charlottesville

Rivanna River

0   5   10 mi

Custer's Route

Custer's Raid to Charlottesville. Map by Bill Nelson. *Copyright © 2016 by the University of Oklahoma Press.*

placed an exaggerated number of 5,000 Confederate cavalrymen, under his former West Point classmate Brigadier Thomas L. Rosser, nearby. Sedgwick assured him that the generals at Meade's meeting had weighed all these matters. Custer was not convinced. "Well, then, I may have to do one of two things: either strike boldly across Lee's rear and try to reach Kilpatrick, or else start with all the men I can keep together and try to join Sherman in the south-west," he reportedly told the older officer.[5]

As darkness fell that day, Custer's horse soldiers camped about three miles from Madison Court House, enjoying only a few hours' rest before reveille sounded at midnight. The men had two hours to gnash some hardtack, washing it down with hot coffee from tin cups, and prepare their mounts for a bleary-eyed but fast-gaited ride to Wolftown, the 6th Pennsylvania in the lead. There they found Confederates picketing the road, and swapped a few carbine shots.

A charge by the Keystoners quickly dispersed the Rebels, who abandoned two wagonloads of flour. By 5:00 A.M. Custer's column was splashing across the Rapidan River at Banks's Mill Ford en route to Stanardsville. The Federals were traversing Virginia's Piedmont, a farming region—"well-cultivated and high-rail-fenced fields," a Pennsylvanian remembered—of low mountains descending into rolling hills, dense woodlots, twisting country roads, and mostly small streams. They forded the Conway River and the South River, tributaries of the Rapidan. Around 8:15 A.M. at Standardsville they encountered and brushed aside another scanty enemy picket. From there the column gained speed and proceeded to Earlysville "at a rapid rate for the next Three or Four Hours without anything of interest occurring." By 2:00 P.M. Custer and his command were at the Rivanna River, about five miles north of Charlottesville. On the north side of this larger river, the Yankees encountered another cavalry picket. "We never Halted. We charged right through their camp, and they fled to the Woods in every direction," wrote home a Pennsylvania trooper, "which proved that they were taken completely by surprise and that they never drempt [sic] that there were any Yanks within 60 miles of them." The bluecoats had been in the saddle for fourteen hours by this time, and their horses were "completely fagged out."[6]

Charlottesville, named for King George III's wife in 1762, when it became the seat for Albermarle County, sits in the shadows of the Blue Ridge amid rich lands that produce oats, corn, tobacco, wheat, and livestock. Its most famous resident, Thomas Jefferson, had founded its most famous institution, the University of Virginia. Before 1861 the bustling market town was home to 3,000 residents, "a small piece of city dropped there among the foothills of the Blue Ridge," with merchants selling everything from dry goods, jewelry, pipes, soaps, and sewing machines to hats and bonnets, boots, shoes, and carriages. Among its service providers were a photographer, a surgeon and dentist, and a gunsmith. The town also boasted several banks, an insurance company, and a newspaper. The university and the railroad depot supported several hotels, boarding houses, restaurants, and saloons. War brought construction of eight large hospitals there to care for Confederate sick and wounded. Nestled in the picturesque Piedmont region, nearly a hundred miles from the main axis of war running north to south from Richmond to Washington, Charlottesville was an ideal place for Confederate soldiers to encamp during the winter months to refresh and refit.[7]

At the end of February 1864, members of Major General Fitzhugh Lee's staff were in town, but Jeb Stuart's Horse Artillery Battalion made up most of its military population. The broken-down horses were making the most of the oats, hay, and wheat available while also grazing on the grassy hillocks. Likewise the men of these batteries were at ease, rebuilding their strength and stamina for the coming campaign season. They had been in the vicinity since just before Christmas, occupying a camp of log huts and horse sheds they had built about a mile south of the Rio Bridge on the Charlottesville–Earlysville Road four miles from town. The units assigned to the area were Ashby's Battery, commanded by Captain Robert Preston Chew; the 1st Stuart Horse Artillery Battery, led by Captain James Breathed; Captain William H. McGregor's 2nd Stuart Horse Artillery; and the Lynchburg Battery, commanded by Captain Marcellus Moorman. In the absence of Major Robert F. Beckham, Moorman was the acting battalion commander.[8]

About 10:00 A.M. a Confederate horseman galloped into the Horse Artillery Battalion's camp. Described by an officer as "an amateur courier," the excited rider declared that Yankee cavalry were only six miles away and advancing rapidly toward Rio Hill. This unexpected news brought a laugh from the scoffing gunners, "as no one thought it could be possible." Horses were grazing the fields; the guns were stationed in an artillery park. Minutes later another anxious trooper, perhaps a former picket from the Rapidan ford, reined in his lathered mount to say the same thing. A furloughed cannoneer who was on his way to the train station in town later recalled, "This was hard for me to believe as everything was perfectly quiet when I left camp and thought it almost impossible for the enemy to come so far so suddenly upon us without some notice." Finally, at around one o'clock that afternoon, the skeptics were converted when the 1st Virginia Cavalry's Lieutenant James N. Cunningham, who had been shadowing Custer's command since it left Madison Court House, arrived and reported that the Yankees were crossing the Rivanna, probably not more than a mile and a half away. Captain Moorman, who had just returned to camp, believed him.[9]

Moorman had been joined by Privates Marcellus Fuqua and Littleton Moorman, his brother, who had gone to town to pick up mail. When they returned, Captain Moorman decided their mud-splattered horses needed a scrubbing and ordered the two to take their horses to the river. The captain decided to accompany the men since his own mount needed a wash. As the three men rode toward the river, their commander suddenly pulled up his horse, telling Fuqua and his brother that he had forgotten something at camp, and galloped back; attending to his horse's appearance would have to wait until later. Ten minutes later the two privates, who had continued on to the river, were grabbed by Yankee cavalrymen. Captain Moorman's memory lapse thus had saved his skin.[10]

After Cunningham alerted Captain Moorman, chaos ensued, with officers shouting orders and men and horses running in all directions. Soldiers herded mounts from the fields, hitched them to the artillery pieces, and rushed away. Moorman had no infantry support, so while his men were limbering their pieces, he organized a few gunners, armed only with pistols, to act as skirmishers. He sent a few men beyond the Rio Mills Bridge to confront the Federals, who swept them aside. The Yankee cavalry galloped across the long wooden bridge without much problem, soon reaching Crawford's farm about three miles from Charlottesville. Custer ordered a squadron of the 1st U.S. Cavalry to reconnoiter upriver and sent a squadron of the 5th U.S. Cavalry downstream on the search for Rebels. He apparently did not know that he had four batteries of enemy horse artillery right in front of him, totally confused and ripe for the taking. As Moorman oversaw his unit's hasty evacuation, some caissons were left behind so the guns could be saved. Pistol shots rang out, alerting the captain to the impending danger to his camp.[11]

Charlottesville itself was also in chaos. Authorities assembled all citizens capable of bearing arms, hustling them into a local-defense unit. "All the stores were closed . . . boys, old men, Alderman of the town, the Methodist clergymen, [and] farmers . . . were all animated with the same spirit," reported a Lynchburg newspaper. Fitzhugh Lee's wintering staff quickly organized the armed civilians, placing them at key points throughout town. Charlottesville would not be given up to the Yankee onslaught without heroic resistance. As one Rebel horse artilleryman observed, "Even the ladies showed fight, and at one of the boarding schools they armed themselves with dinner cutlery, and stood boldly on the defensive."[12]

Once Custer crossed the Rio Mills Bridge, however, his attack stumbled. He sent about sixty-five volunteers under Captain Joseph P. Ash of the 5th U.S. Cavalry on a road through the woods to find the Confederate right flank. As Ash's men crossed the river at

Cooke's Ford and probed for the enemy's right, Custer, unable to see much due to the uneven topography, convinced himself that he faced a heavy concentration of enemy cavalry, four batteries of artillery, and a strong force of infantry. He might have imagined it or might have been fed a line by the captured privates, Fuqua and Moorman. Custer had questioned both men as well as a servant of a Dr. Cooke, who told him that the enemy had "six pieces of artillery and that our soldiers were camped from Dr. Cooke's farm all the way to Charlottesville." The general continued to hear significant cannon fire, yet he knew that he had only brought along two guns; several shells also burst near where he was questioning his prisoners and the slave. Custer drew the faulty conclusion that he was facing a substantial number of artillery pieces in his front. Hearing train whistles blowing beyond his immediate front further added to his paranoia as he imagined Rebel reinforcements detraining by brigades at the Charlottesville station. In reality, this was probably the regular passenger train the furloughed cannoneer had intended to take, not a military train full of reinforcements. With his back to the river and a perceived overwhelming enemy force to his front, Custer decided that he was in no position to receive a Rebel counterattack. His hesitation allowed Captain Moorman the necessary time to form what defense his men could offer.[13]

Captain Ash and his regulars encountered Moorman's improvised skirmishers, brushed them aside, and charged the artillery camp, firing pistols and brandishing sabers. The Federals captured six caissons filled with ammunition, two forges, and piles of valuable harness equipment, meanwhile burning the huts and sheds. On Rio Hill the remaining Confederates watched the flames flicker and the Yankees make off with their gear. More men from the 1st U.S. Cavalry joined Ash, but he abandoned the fight.

Moorman's stopgap resistance stymied Custer, and the Federals failed to exploit their advantage. In the lapse Rebel gunners hitched up their frenzied horses and saved their guns. Either Moorman or one of his subordinates ordered some cannon wheeled into battery by hand, allowing the dismounted artillerymen to blast away at the faltering Union cavalrymen in front of their camp, while others were fired from their parked position; one Yankee trooper counted thirty rounds screeching overhead in rapid succession. The sudden discharge of artillery had a demoralizing effect on the mounted Yankees, who trotted back out of range.

This fugacious wincing allowed Moorman the respite he needed to gallop the remainder of his guns to Charlottesville and out of danger. With four guns left on Rio Hill, four hundred yards from his wrecked camp, the captain kept up the fight, firing on the Yankees as they regrouped for another charge. Those artillerymen who were not servicing the pieces he placed on horseback, armed only with pistols and "three sabers" among them, under Captains Preston Chew and James Breathed; an "old Confederate battle flag" flew over the mounted artillerists. Unarmed men carried "sticks and clubs" as well as "fence rails" to give the appearance of being well armed. Moorman's makeshift force supported his cannon and protected his flanks. They may have received some negligible support from furloughed and dismounted men commanded by a cavalry brigade quartermaster, Major Robert Franklin Mason, who was in Charlottesville, although the captain never mentions his presence in his report. Moreover, Chew yelled out for Colonel Richard H. Dulany and his 7th Virginia Cavalry to come up and join the fight. "Tell Colonel Dulany to bring up the Seventh Regiment," he screamed out, which may have been within earshot of some Yankees. But this was mere theatrics; Dulany's regiment was nowhere near Rio Hill, the closest Confederate cavalry regiment perhaps eighteen miles away at Liberty Mills. The combination of these Fabianlike tactics saved Moorman's battalion.[14]

Moorman's ruse worked. Though he did not have more than two hundred mounted men, Custer thought he was facing Brigadier General Williams Wickham's cavalry brigade. When one of Chew's abandoned caissons exploded, Custer concluded that more Rebel artillery had come into play, and Confederate prisoners might have hornswoggled him into thinking that Major General Jubal A. Early's infantry division was in the vicinity. One Yankee trooper shouted, "By—, the Secesh have been reinforced, let's go back." A Union officer thought that Confederate "troops from Gordonsville—a few thousand—were in waiting to give a warm reception" with "about one hundred guns and a few thousand small arms." The blue-coated cavalrymen "concluded not to pass their five infantry lines, drawn up in style to meet us."

Against all odds, Moorman had miraculously held off a much larger force of enemy cavalry, a feat compounded when another contingent of Custer's troopers mistakenly opened fire on Ash's men as they looted the Rebel artillery's camp. When that happened, both units fled; a development understandably absent from subsequent Federal reports. With about twenty mounted men, Breathed charged into the confused Yankees. "The order was given us to charge them with a [Rebel] 'yell' which we did and routed them completely, they running like devils," one artillerist wrote home. "By bold riding and terrible shouting, they drove the enemy from our camps," another of Moorman's men wrote. Breathed's men chased the Federals across the Rivanna, where a sharp firefight occurred. Custer's men pushed back long enough to torch the turnpike bridge and Rio Mills. Porter unlimbered one gun, which after a few rounds took the bravado out of the pursuing Rebels, who returned to camp. The fight at Rio Hill had lasted about an hour. Despite heavy cannon firing from the Confederate horse artillery and intense small-arms shooting on both sides, casualties were light. Union losses were one man wounded; the Confederates lost two men, seven horses, and two mules.[15]

Custer began a retreat in the same direction he had come, back up the Stanardsville Road. One horse artillerist claimed that the Confederates chased the Federals some twenty miles, tagging on their rear like "annoying hornets." At about 9:00 P.M. Custer called a halt about eight miles south of Standardsville to rest and feed his weary horses and troopers. A storm blew in, first a pounding rain, then sleet. "It was Raining very Hard, and Dark as the Devil. . . . [I]t continued to Rain very hard all night," a Pennsylvania trooper recalled. After a ninety-minute rest, the exhausted blue-clad troopers remounted and rode on, soaking wet. The weary battery horses had a great deal of trouble pulling Porter's guns along the wooded, muddy, root-choked country lanes. Colonel Stedman's advance party of about five hundred men became separated from the main column, itself getting lost on soggy, unfamiliar roads until Custer called a halt so the troopers could close up, giving their guides a chance to regain their bearings. The men spent an uncomfortable night lying on the wet ground without shelter or fire. The officers wanted to ditch Porter's troublesome guns, but Custer refused. Aides went out to find Stedman but were unable to locate his command. During the night, the colonel's column had passed through Stanardsville, taking the road to Banks's Mill Ford. Custer dismounted his remaining troopers until daylight.[16]

While Custer's men slowly made their way back to the Rapidan, Moorman's command gathered about four miles south of Charlottesville on the Scottsville Road to spend the night. The next day the Horse Artillery Battalion returned to its wrecked winter quarters, there to remain for three weeks before moving to Gordonsville. In gratitude for the unit's heroic performance, women in Charlottesville raised five hundred dollars for a splendid silk flag, whose left-hand corner displayed the traditional Confederate battle flag while the right bore the inscription "From The Ladies of Charlottesville To Stuart's Horse Artillery, Our Brave Defenders," along with crossed cannon barrels. Chew's Battery carried the banner until Appomattox, and rather than surrender the men disbanded, the flag never furled.[17]

Late on the afternoon of February 29, hearing of Moorman's repulse of Custer, Jeb Stuart sent Wickham and his brigade, then between Orange Court House and Liberty Mills, after the retreating Yankee column. The Confederate cavalry arrived near Stanardsville just after Stedman's detachment passed through the town.[18]

Early on Tuesday morning, March 1, scarcely refreshed, Custer's column resumed its retreat to Madison Court House, occasionally drawing Rebel sniper fire. A squadron of Captain Edward H. Leib's 5th U.S. Cavalry now replaced Stedman as the advanced guard. A mile out of Stanardsville, the regulars prepared to enter the town with the order "advance carbines," followed by a squadron with sabers drawn; Custer followed the lead squadron. "They fixed their hair up, pulled on their caps tightly, and then the trot, then the gallop, through the town, the people in our front leading off at full speed," Leib wrote later. At first the squadron found no Southern horsemen, so the captain dismounted his men for a quick breakfast. Once they had eaten, the men continued their search for Rebels. About two miles from Stanardsville, Leib's men ran into Confederate cavalry that had been following Stedman's strayed column. Stuart's troopers may have mistaken the regulars for a rear guard of the column they were following. At that moment Leib's troopers were in a deep cut in the road. From high ground near a fork in the road, the Southerners, led by Stuart himself, immediately charged, pushing Leib's men back into Custer's main body. Stuart ordered a charge by Company K, 1st Virginia, that sent the Federals reeling. He then summoned the 2nd Virginia, which came up at a gallop.[19]

Custer had massed his main force in a hidden ravine out of sight. As Leib's fleeing Yankees entered the position, the general ordered a charge by the remainder of the 5th U.S. Cavalry, under Captain Abraham K. Arnold along with Captain Ash. "Officers and men moved forward in magnificent style, charging desperately upon the enemy, driving them back in confusion," reported Lieutenant George W. Yates, a Pleasonton staff officer who accompanied the expedition. Arnold's charge hit the 1st Virginians hard, the Federals only reining in their horses when they saw Stuart and the 2nd Virginia. "The range of hills in our front was literally swarming with Yankee cavalry, which deployed right and left on either side of the road," one of Stuart's staff officers recalled. "The Yankees were now getting ready to dash upon us, and in another moment they commenced a charge." The attackers "came within easy pistol shot of Gen. Stuart," who observed that a fence stood between him and the bluecoats, whereupon he "cantered along down the lane rather too leisurely, turning every now and then to his ordnance officer and saying, 'Shoot that fellow, Grattan! Shoot him!' as he pointed to a Yankee who was firing away at both of them." Sensing success, without giving the enemy time to rally, Custer immediately ordered the rest of his command to attack, leading them himself. Stuart knew he was whipped and fell back.[20]

From a few captured Confederates, Custer learned that he was up against Stuart. He quickly positioned his two guns on a hill to the right of the ravine, where Lieutenant Porter laid down fire on the Southern horsemen, who just as quickly withdrew out of range. However ineffective Porter's rounds might have been, they put on a great show "crashing among the frost-bound limbs of the [nearby] forest," a Pennsylvanian said. A scattering of Confederate horsemen rode for Banks's Mill Ford, though the majority headed down the road leading to Burton's Ford on the Rapidan. Custer's troopers pressed the second group for about two miles, then realized that they could be riding toward enemy infantry. The general ordered his men back to the fork in the road, where they took the left path to Banks's Mill Ford. The Rebels followed the Yankees at a comfortable distance so as not to renew the fight.[21]

On the way to the river the Federals burned a large flour mill, and at the crossing they destroyed Banks's Mill, which contained flour and cornmeal. About five miles south of Madison Court House, the errant Colonel Stedman came galloping up with his five-hundred-man detachment, having heard Porter's guns barking. Stedman had reached Wolftown about daybreak, then made for Burton's Ford, where his Ohioans skirmished briefly with the enemy on the north bank of the river. The colonel withdrew, instead marching back toward Madison Court House, where he ran into Custer's returning column. Before dark the reunited command reached the courthouse, amid a heavy snow and sleet storm, where Sedgwick and his officers welcomed them "like lost children." The raiders brought in five hundred horses captured along their route and about sixty prisoners, mostly private citizens. Hundreds of slaves took advantage of the circumstances and had followed the Yankees to their camps. Custer's command had suffered about six men slightly wounded; estimates held that three of the enemy had been killed and several wounded.[22]

In his preliminary report made directly to Cavalry Corps head-quarters, which he drafted while his men were eating, Custer began with excuses for failing to burn the railroad bridge over the Rivanna. He claimed to have found "four batteries of artillery, two brigades of cavalry, and a very large force of infantry" at Charlottesville. The general then inventoried what his men had captured in exchange for wearing out fifteen hundred horses and riders.[23]

The mission completed, Custer's cavalry and Sedgwick's infantry began a retrograde movement back to Culpeper County. The horse soldiers arrived late on March 1 "thoroughly soaked" from the unrelenting snowstorm, which had continued all night during their march. Sedgwick's infantry crossed the Robinson River and bivouacked about three-quarters of a mile from it. Breaking camp at 7:00 A.M., the troops marched to their various winter quarters at Brandy Station, Welford's Ford, or near Culpeper Court House. Perhaps an unintended consequence of the operation was the free-ing of hundreds of slaves in Madison and surrounding counties. "Hundreds of contrabands returned along with us, men, women, and children, on horseback, in all conceivable sorts of vehicles . . . , or on foot where no conveyance offered," wrote a Rhode Island soldier. A Lynchburg newspaper noted how the Federal cavalry brought away slaves owned by various landowners along its route of march. On March 2 Custer's various detachments returned to their respective winter quarters near Mitchell's Station and Warrenton Junction. Captain Leib wrote a letter to a friend, telling him the raid "was the hardest that I have yet been through" but was also "the most exciting I was ever in." Missing from Custer's official report was the tally of "chickens, Turkeys, Ducks, Geese, Hams, &c." that came back to quarters hung from saddles and stuck into haversacks.[24]

Back at Clover Hill Custer reviewed the action and, in a follow-up report dated March 3, provided more details about the fight
at Rio Hill and his run in with Stuart's cavalry near Stanardsville.
This second report added his assumption that Fitzhugh Lee's cavalry
division was camped near Charlottesville and identified the infantry he faced as being from Early's Division. Portraying himself as
facing overwhelming enemy numbers at his front, Custer claimed
that he deployed his regulars to gain more information about the
enemy's strength; contenting himself that they were vastly superior, he retreated. He noted that en route back to Union lines, his
men destroyed "a quantity of Government stores, consisting of bags,
caps, saddles, leather, muskets, flour, and whisky." (The last item
might have been denied the enemy by consumption rather than
destruction.) The young general judged his fight with Stuart a fair
success. Finally, he had covered about 150 miles and not lost a man.
Custer, in whom the phrase "self-confidence" found its apotheosis,
was pretty proud of himself. So was his corps commander and the
press. Two weeks after General Pleasonton sincerely congratulated
the young officer, the cover of *Harper's Weekly* featured an Alfred
Waud sketch of Custer charging the enemy at Charlottesville.[25]

While Custer had failed at a major goal of the operation by not
burning the railroad bridge, he had wrecked the artillery camp,
burned some mills and materiel, taken some prisoners, freed no small
number of slaves, and had drawn Stuart's cavalry to his command
like a moth to a match. But another entry to Custer's discredit was
his failure to destroy or capture one of the most precious commodities in the Confederacy—sixteen field pieces of artillery. If instead
of imagining himself outnumbered Custer had pressed his advantage, he would have been able to grab Moorman's guns, significantly
damaging Stuart's horse artillery for many months. And the victory
at Rio Hill that evaporated due to Moorman's Fabian tactics would
have allowed the boy general to continue east through Goochland
County, where he could have linked up with Dahlgren en route to
Richmond. The colonel was definitely aware of the possibility of
Custer joining him as indicated by the contents of his papers captured later.[26] But Custer, who should have demonstrated the traits
of a cavalry leader—rashness, daring, and élan—instead decided to
play it safe, thus forfeiting prizes that were within his grasp; this
would not come to light until years later, though, when Moorman's
report became available. Yet Custer's men thought no less of him for

his decisions under fire at Rio Hill. "Gen Custer you know distinguished himself as he always does," a Michigan trooper wrote.[27]

In actuality, Custer had not "distinguished himself" as an independent cavalry commander. If he thought that Fitzhugh Lee's brigades were near Charlottesville, his intelligence was sadly outdated. These troopers had taken up winter quarters near the town the previous December but were called up by R. E. Lee to serve under Jubal Early when his infantry was sent to Staunton to intercept William Averell's raiders in western Virginia. When he returned to the Charlottesville area in mid-January, Fitzhugh Lee disbanded a major portion of his division, including whole regiments, for the remainder of the winter. A February 20 field return for Stuart's corps notes, "Lee's brigade not reported; Lomax's brigade all absent; total present, Lee's division, consists of Second and parts of First and Fourth Virginia Cavalry; remainder absent recruiting." One historian of the Army of Northern Virginia's cavalry has concluded: "Wickham's and Lomax's brigades virtually ceased to exist for two months or longer. [Fitzhugh] Lee did this not only to force his men to subsist themselves, but also so they might recruit for their units." It was practically impossible for Custer to have faced Lee's cavalry at Rio Hill. Besides, the general himself was in Richmond at the time Custer approached Charlottesville. While Major Mason, F. Lee's quartermaster, was in Charlottesville, the number of furloughed or dismounted men he could gather up was negligible.

Captain Moorman made no mention of cavalry or infantry support during his defense of Rio Hill. The elements of Wickham's Brigade that assembled near Stanardsville under Stuart must have been woefully understrength. Custer's reference to facing Early's infantry division illustrates the boy general's propensity to believe rumors rather than reality, for on February 29 Early's men were on picket duty along the army's Rapidan River line in Orange County nowhere near Charlottesville.[28] While there are many examples of where Custer performed admirably on the battlefield, even gallantly as a subordinate commander, when given an independent command like the Charlottesville raid, he opted for caution (at least at this point in his career), envisioning Rebels where they did not exist.[29]

Meanwhile, as Custer was providing a limited distraction for Lee and Stuart on the western end of the Confederate line, Kilpatrick and Dahlgren were embarking on their long-awaited raid on Richmond around the eastern end of the Army of Northern Virginia.

RIDING TO RICHMOND

Two hours before Dahlgren's command left Stevensburg, a detachment of forty troopers and two officers from the 5th New York along with two army scouts—Martin Hogan and James Wood—galloped off from the Third Cavalry Division's camps. This advance party proceeded through the inky night to a blind crossing about two miles above Ely's Ford, which they reached about 9:00 P.M.

Lieutenant Henry Merritt led fifteen dismounted volunteers and the scouts to the blind ford, which they crossed, maintaining strict orders against "superfluous talking." The cavalrymen plunged into the cold water up to their armpits, carrying their revolvers and cartridge belts above their heads to keep them dry. "It was a cold wade, and the icy water was nearly up to my chin most of the way," one scout wrote later. Crossing in a single file to the south bank, the chilled volunteers stopped just long enough to empty their knee-high boots and wring out their stockings before pressing on.[1]

Guided by the scouts, the marauders silently picked their way through a ravine to the road that led to the picket post at Ely's Ford. Hogan, twenty-three, a "tall and lithe Irishman," captured the mounted guards, members of Cobb's Legion. To keep from alerting them, he had left most of the volunteers in a ravine near the road, proceeding to the ford with only himself, Wood, and Sergeant David Schofield. Approaching the Georgians from behind, the Yankees found themselves properly challenged. The quick-witted Irishman barked back as if he were an officer of the guard, slowly advancing and demanding to know why no one had ordered him to halt farther back. A sheepish vidette, one of the two on duty, muttered an apology. By this time Hogan was near enough to grab one picket's reins and shove the barrel of his revolver under the man's nose, promising to blow his head off if he made a sound. In a blink the ambushers had subdued the Georgians; Schofield disarmed them.[2]

The crossing was now in Union hands, but the advance party had to capture the picket reserve if the oncoming column was to get behind enemy lines unnoticed. The more blustery of the two Rebels was brought back to the volunteers in the ravine while Hogan took the timid one and, "under threats of instant death," compelled him to point out the reserve headquarters, which sat "some distance back from the river." Hogan and his comrades crept toward the structure, "a large square house, with a piazza all around," situated on the left side of the road leading up from the river. The picket reserve had tied its horses to fences and trees all around the property, but carelessly, no guard stood watch. A fire burned in the parlor fireplace, surrounded by gray-coated cavalrymen sleeping on the floor. Wood silently approached the front of the house while Hogan went to the rear. "Hogan jumped through the window, carrying slivered glass and sash with him," Wood later wrote. "We immediately made such a terrific noise, discharging our revolvers into the floor, that the Confederates thought the whole army had surrounded the house." The stunned Rebels raising their hands included Captain W. B. Young, a second officer, and about fifteen Georgians. As one participant later recalled, "you should have heard the Confederate captain swear when he learned he had surrendered to 13 of us." Wood remembered, "He denounced it as a d—d Yankee trick, and wanted to fight me with or without arms."[3]

With the ford secured and its defenders captured, Hogan lit a match to signal Lieutenant Robert Black and the New Yorkers waiting on the far side of the Rapidan that it was safe to cross. By this time Colonel Dahlgren had arrived with the bulk of his command. After pausing at the river to water their mounts, he and his men set off at a trot for Spotsylvania Court House, though not before Dahlgren made an extraordinary statement. Gathering his men, he explained their mission's goal, adding that he was offering permission "to anyone to return to camp that had not the courage to go on." Dahlgren read aloud from a paper he held, telling the men that after freeing their brothers in arms from the Confederate prisons, they were "to destroy and burn the hateful city" and not allow "the rebel leader Davis and his traitorous crew to escape." But he had not told them everything he knew about their objectives. Not a man turned back, and the column "started . . . at a brisk trot."[4]

For its flawless performance at the ford, Dahlgren rewarded the 5th New York with the honor of leading the advance. They set a pace so fast that the column had trouble staying together. The Federals "pushed on at a lively pace through the woods until we struck the Plank Road" near Chancellorsville, a Vermonter recalled. Another

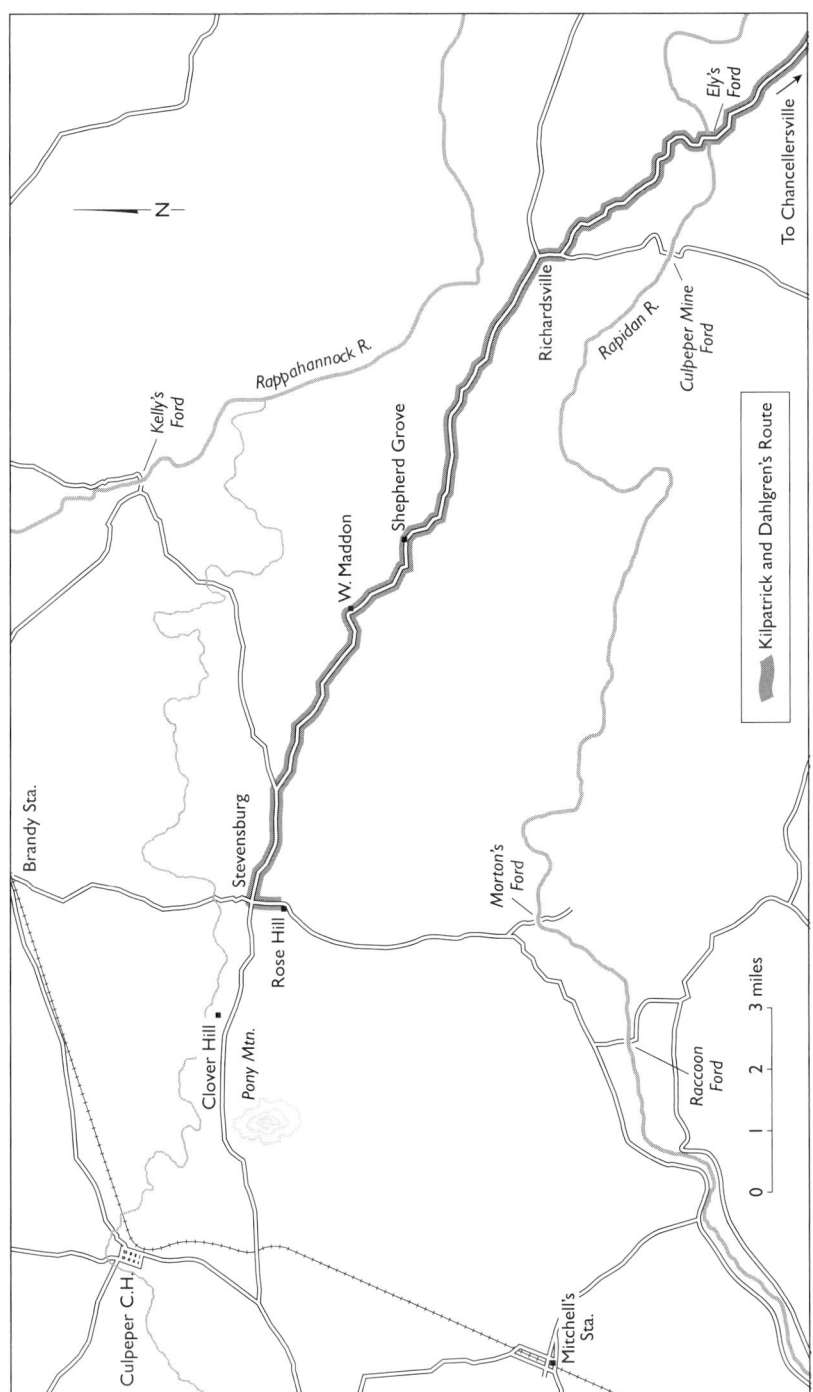

-N-

Kelly's
Ford

Rappahannock R.

Shepherd Grove

W. Maddon

Ely's
Ford

To Chancellersville

Richardsville

Rapidan R.

Culpeper Mine
Ford

Brandy Sta.

Stevensburg

Culpeper C.H.

Clover Hill

Pony Mtn.

Rose Hill

Morton's
Ford

Raccoon
Ford

Mitchell's
Sta.

▬▬ Kilpatrick and Dahlgren's Route

0   1   2   3 miles

Start of the Raid on Richmond. Map by Bill Nelson. *Copyright © 2016 by the University of Oklahoma Press.*

trooper said the cavalrymen went "most of the way on the gallop." The steep climb up Ely's Ford Road had to have taken a toll on the horses and riders, in particular the gaunt Dahlgren, who already was showing signs of stress. He "was much emaciated, his wooden leg seemed to annoy him during the march, and in mounting he needed assistance," a Wolverine officer observed.[5]

Kilpatrick and the main body arrived at Ely's Ford near midnight but waited about ninety minutes for the men to rustle up a local guide to show the way to Spotsylvania Court House—an odd turn blamed on an army scout who absconded en route to the ford. The impatient general paced back and forth near the ford waiting for a guide, but he was able to salvage a bit of humor. Sidling up to the captured pickets from Cobb's Legion, he asked them if they knew the Yankee general Kilpatrick. "No," the prisoners answered, "Have we got him?" Kilpatrick chortled. "No . . . by god," he cried, "he has got you."[6]

During this interlude, Kilpatrick's troopers got the word of their mission: freeing the prisoners in Richmond and Butler's third-prong sally. No detailed record exists of how it was disseminated or what was said. The reaction among Kil's horse soldiers was the same as Dahlgren's, according to a Vermonter: "The men at once entered into the plan as one worthy of all efforts."[7]

When a guide was finally secured, Kilpatrick got his column moving again. Once across the ford, he sent a message back to Cavalry Corps headquarters, at around 1:00 A.M., reporting in a positive tone the facile capture of the crossing and picket reserve. "It was a complete surprise," he boasted, adding that Dahlgren already had reached Chancellorsville. "The start was thus auspicious," a Wolverine officer agreed. "The enemy does not anticipate our movement," Kilpatrick concluded, which reassured General Meade. The army commander wrote home the next day, saying, "My cavalry expedition for Richmond got off last night, and at 2 A.M., the last I heard from them, they were getting on famously . . . , not . . . discovered by the enemy." Meade spoke with a bit more enthusiasm for Kilpatrick's plan when he said, "I trust they will be successful; it will be the greatest feat of the war, if they succeed, and will immortalize them all." He did not say in detail what that feat might be. "Young Dahlgren, with his one leg, went along with them," he added, not illuminating the young colonel's role. But Kilpatrick's exuberance and Meade's confidence would prove misplaced.[8]

The evening the Yankee raiders were leaving Stevensburg, Judson McKnight, a Union army scout, crossed the Rapidan between Jacob's Ford and Germanna Ford. Riding with him was James McCamack, the son of the Virginia farmer linked in the "middle line of communication." The scout had orders to wait at McCamack's house near Old Verdieville, observe Lee's response to news of the incursion, and report back what he saw. McKnight watched the road all of Monday, February 29, from McCamack's second-story window. At some point he spotted a gray-clad cavalryman riding down the road and sent McCamack out to query him. "5000 Yankees at Waller's Tavern by sun-up this morning," the rider exclaimed. The farmer hastened to Orange Court House near Lee's headquarters to learn more, returning to tell McKnight that Major General Wade Hampton, one of Jeb Stuart's division commanders, had been ordered to Ely's Ford. McKnight immediately made for the Rapidan, crossed, and galloped on to the Army of the Potomac's headquarters, where he conveyed the news to Colonel George H. Sharpe, the army's chief intelligence officer.[9] McKnight's information was not entirely accurate but did alert the Federals to the possibility that the Confederates knew of Kilpatrick's operation and were taking countermeasures. Of course, they had no way to pass this along to Kilpatrick or Dahlgren.

Back at Ely's Ford, Kilpatrick's cavalrymen were making ready to ride. "The first night of our march was beautiful," a Union signal officer wrote. "Myriads of stars twinkled in the heaven . . . , the moon threw its silvery light upon the Rapidan waters when we forded it, and it seemed as if the Almighty Judge was looking silently upon our doings." Another officer paid more heed to their pace, "a fast walk" that had the rear elements scrambling to keep up and "going most of the way [to Spotsylvania] on the gallop." Riding in darkness, the Yankee troopers could only keep their ears attuned to the hoof beats ahead to stay in column. "Often it was necessary to take the trot, sometimes the gallop, and even then the leaders were out of sight or out of hearing," one man commented. A Vermonter told his diary that they "rode all night . . . most of the time on a trot or gallop," not stopping until 10:00 A.M. the next morning. Exhausted horses were shot, with new mounts grabbed from farms and plantations along the route. Kilpatrick's signal officer, Captain Gloskowski, had a tough time setting off rockets and keeping up. "The march was not only rapid but it was continuous," he remarked. Kilpatrick was moving with "an air of undue haste—a precipitancy and rush not at all reassuring."[10]

Up ahead with Dahlgren's column, army scouts Wood and Hogan, to relieve themselves of their wet blue uniforms, stopped at the house of a prosperous planter. There Wood secured a Rebel artillery uniform and Hogan "found a swallow-tail coat with brass buttons and a tall hat." Hats and clothing were not the only items usurped by the Yankees that morning. In addition, Dahlgren's raiders appropriated many "blooded animals" during their trek behind enemy lines, where most Southerners surely thought their livestock was safe for the winter. The colonel insisted that his men make such accruals in silence. For instance, one trooper carelessly discharged his carbine before the column reached Spotsylvania. This random imprudence offended Dahlgren, causing him to exact a harsh punishment. Another of the scouts, A. B. Carney of the 5th U.S. Cavalry, tried to intervene on the transgressor's behalf, but the colonel insisted that "such carelessness ought not to be overlooked." The man was forced to dismount and walk his horse for the next three hours.[11]

With Dahlgren's command hours ahead of them, Kilpatrick's column needed a safeguard against enemy cavalry that might attack from either side. The general sent a complement of about two hundred men to ride a few hundred yards ahead of the main body, assigning a staff officer named E. P. Roe to keep them close. Roe would slow the van until Kilpatrick and his staff caught up. The tension of the ride through that night proved fatal to an officer who broke protocol. He "had ridden carelessly into the woods" and out again just as the main body neared. Failing to identify himself immediately, the wayward rider drew a bullet from his unsuspecting comrades and died on the spot.[12] Moving through "flat, low and wooded" country, that portion of the 1st Vermont not with Dahlgren's force provided cover to the rear of the column. Twenty-five picked men served as a rear guard a mile or two back, watching for trailing Confederates, with the rest supporting them.[13]

The Vermonters failed to keep a sharp watch, though. Just before the tail of the main column finished crossing the river, two of Hampton's famed "Iron Scouts" infiltrated the Union ranks on the north bank. These members of the 2nd South Carolina Cavalry got their nickname from their foes "because they recovered so quickly after being wounded and seemed to be free from capture." Seeing so many Federals in the vicinity of Ely's Ford, the South Carolinians decided to collect a few. Walking alongside the rear of the main body, several Iron Scouts led out two horses and took their sleepy riders prisoner, holding them in the woods while two of the Southerners, Dan Tanner and Hugh Scott, mounted the Yankees' horses. Tanner and Scott fell in line with the blue-coated cavalry, crossing the Rapidan with them. Once they realized that Kilpatrick's men were riding toward Spotsylvania Court House, the bold horse thieves bolted the column, riding hard for General Hampton's camp near Fredericksburg, about a dozen miles away. By 11:00 A.M. Tanner and Scott were telling their burly commander that the Yankees had taken the ford and were heading for Spotsylvania. Hampton had received similar news from Brigadier General Pierce M. B. Young, who had queried several local citizens and his own scouts.[14]

Wade Hampton reacted quickly. Reputed to be the wealthiest man in the Confederacy, he commanded one of Stuart's two far-flung cavalry divisions. During 1863 his command had lost many mounts, and the troopers who still had horses returned home to rest and refit them. But Hampton was ready to ride with the meager forces remaining if Stuart gave the order. By noon on February 29, the barrel-chested general had telegraphed his commander what he knew, following up shortly thereafter with a second wire noting that Yankees had been spotted at Mount Pleasant. Stuart did not answer; Hampton had no way of knowing that the Virginian then was engaging Custer outside Charlottesville. Hampton stayed put, sending a third wire that evening.[15]

All the intact telegraph wires were hot with messages about the Yankee raiders. Confederate colonel Bradley T. Johnson led the Maryland Line, a small mixed brigade of cavalry, infantry, and artillery wintering at Hanover Junction. Major General Arnold Elzey, commander of the Department of Richmond, sent a dispatch alerting Johnson, who had orders to protect the junction's depot and the railroad bridges over the North and South Anna Rivers.[16] Less than twenty-four hours after Ely's Ford was captured, the Federal operation against Richmond was anything but a secret.

Knowing none of this, Dahlgren forged ahead with his detachment, reaching Spotsylvania Court House at about 2:00 A.M., February 29. The men and horses rested until daybreak, when the head of Kilpatrick's column began to arrive.[17] The main body was still strung out two miles beyond Chancellorsville. From a "Negro direct from Guinea's Station," an army scout learned that Hampton feared an attack on his rear. This information led a Union intelligence officer to erroneously conclude that Kilpatrick was "well assured of success."[18] Kilpatrick's column stopped only briefly at Spotsylvania, perhaps as little as twenty minutes, time enough for the men to eat and to feed and water their weary mounts at the Po River. Locals goggled at the sight of so many Federals, behaving as if they were seeing "men come up out of the tombs" as they rode through the mist, a Michigander remembered.[19] During the break, Kilpatrick wrote at least one more encouraging message, informing Pleasonton, with whom he had apparently made a wager, that he was still bound as planned: "Twenty miles nearer Richmond—Am all right. Will double my bet of $5,000 that I enter Richmond." A scout took the boastful message back to headquarters.[20]

The column spent most the morning clearing the village, during which time the Federals emptied local larders. One old woman tagged the raiders "nothing but nasty dirty Yankees after all." Kilpatrick had brought provisions, but Private William Pollard, an Englishman serving in the 7th Michigan and in charge of the general's headquarters wagon, had given two dismounted men from his brigade a lift. The Wolverines, ravenous as their namesake, cleared out Little Kil's cupboard.[21]

This was the last time the two commands would be as one. Dahlgren led the way out of Spotsylvania Court House to a point at or near Mount Pleasant, where the Federals split. Dahlgren's detachment stood mounted in column of fours, waiting for his two ambulances to slowly cross a stream. The one-legged officer rode along his line—the first time since Stevensburg that many of the men had gotten a look at him. He did his best to maintain an air of confidence despite the hard ride. With the wheeled-vehicles finally across the creek, he and his men headed southwest for Frederick's Hall on the Virginia Central Railroad, while Kilpatrick's force diverged toward the same railroad's main yard at Beaver Dam Station as a "chicken, a goose, a ham or a side dangled from every saddle." The men were in excellent spirits, gleeful at the successful foraging and disappointed only that there was "not enough time to eat it."[22]

No official reports, letters, diaries, or reminiscences say where Dahlgren's column crossed the North Anna River. In 1864 the men could have used either of two bridges, most likely Carr's Bridge rather than Davenport's Bridge, which is too close to New Market (present-day Partlow) and nearer the route Kilpatrick took when he crossed the North Anna at Anderson's Bridge. Carr's Bridge put Dahlgren closer to Waller's Tavern, a location mentioned by Confederates stalking the raiders. In May 1863 Stoneman had labeled Carr's as the likeliest crossing point on the North Anna River from Frederick's Hall Station. The way to that bridge was "the main road leading from Spotsylvania to Goochland, on the James River, . . . one of the principal highways," the general had written in his report, which was familiar to the staff officers who planned Dahlgren's route to the James through Goochland County.[23]

Frederick's Hall, a Virginia Central Railroad depot, was the winter encampment of the artillery train of the Army of Northern Virginia's Second Corps, commanded by Lieutenant General Richard S. Ewell. The artillery units were spending a quiet winter, far in the rear of the army, so their horses could rest and feed. Never expecting Yankees so far behind their lines, the Confederates did not closely guard Frederick's Hall. A quintet of Yankees surprised a Southern artillery sergeant and about fifteen other men who were inspecting a picket line. The Federals asked the sergeant to give up his sword, which a horse had stepped on. "No effort could pull it from its scabbard," recalled one of them. "As it was not good to anyone, the Confederate compromised matters by throwing the whole outfit into a ditch." The wily Rebel later told Dahlgren that at least a full infantry regiment guarded the artillery reserve.

When the colonel's troopers reined in their mounts near the Virginia Central's tracks between 11:00 A.M. and noon on February 29, they were a mere three hundred yards from Ewell's eighty-three guns. The captured sergeant and a black man Dahlgren had encountered two miles from the depot led him to think that the field pieces were guarded by "a small brigade." A Union veteran later wrote, "Ten of his troopers could have scattered the Confederate guard at a dash, as most of them were no better armed than the sergeant." More than one Confederate memoirist said the same. A Maine officer later lamented that "timid counsels prevailed and the undertaking was abandoned." The colonel had his men veer southeast to avoid the phantom hazard. Guided by another escaped slave, his column took farm roads toward Bumpass Station, another stop on the Virginia Central.[24]

By timing rather than timidity, Dahlgren narrowly missed a chance at a prize far more valuable than Ewell's artillery. About an hour before the Yankee horse soldiers arrived near Frederick's Hall, a train bearing Robert E. Lee had passed the depot en route from Richmond, where the general had been conferring with Davis and other Confederate officials. It was the last to pass this way for many days.[25]

With Lee absent from army headquarters until the afternoon of February 29, Confederate forces lagged in answering the Federal thrust, even though they knew about it early Monday morning. Upon leaving for Richmond, the general seems to have turned technical command of the army over to Ewell, his ranking subordinate. But Ewell, known as "Old Baldy," was camped fifteen miles from army headquarters at the Rodgers farm near Orange Court House. To stay informed on the situation while away, Lee relied on two staff officers, Brigadier General Robert H. Chilton and Lieutenant Colonel Walter H. Taylor, to telegraph him about developments. The night the Union raiders departed, Federal scouts had cut most of the lines between Richmond and the Confederate army, so "little" was done about the invasion until Lee returned. Even as far north as Culpeper County, Federal observers could see that the Southern army was not taking action. Reporting on the twenty-ninth to Army of the Potomac headquarters, the Garrett Mountain signal post noted, "No change in the enemy's position in our front—the enemy seem[s] to be ignorant of the move as they are all very quiet." The signalmen reported that some regiments spent the entire day drilling.[26]

Once Lee was back at his desk in Orange County, however, things started to happen (though not fast enough for one staff officer, Colonel Taylor, who thought his chief indecisive in "little affairs" demanding quick action and longed for Stonewall Jackson's intuitive, decision making). First, using a circuitous loop of intact telegraph lines, he alerted General Samuel Cooper in Richmond that Federal cavalry was moving to the army's right near Frederick's Hall and to its left toward Charlottesville. Next, he had Taylor notify Genera Elzey of a reported cut in the railroad line near Frederick's Hall, adding that Federal cavalry were in Louisa County, probably Richmond-bound, with more Yankee horsemen spotted riding through Spotsylvania. If their target was Richmond, Elzey would be the man charged with defending the city. Finally, two days later Lee ordered Major General Edward Johnson's division of Ewell's corps to march east toward the Wilderness to "intercept" Kilpatrick's command should the Union cavalry return in that direction. Meanwhile,

Elzey was ordered to contact Bradley Johnson to get the colonel's help in thwarting the raiders. This message set in motion Johnson's crucial work of destroying boats and ferries along the Pamunkey between Hanover Court House and White House Landing.[27]

In other ways, though, Yankee luck held. The columns rode right past Confederate camps, a stroke of boldness that "took away all suspicion." Seeing the distant riders' dusty, mud-caked uniforms and thinking them comrade cavalrymen, Southern gunners at one site stopped firing practice artillery rounds. But when word came of the invasion, it electrified everyone. A surprised Rebel artillery-man was in a "female's parlor" when a neighbor burst in, breath-lessly announcing, "Yankee cavalry are scouring the country . . . and will be here any moment." This fellow felt that this Northern auda-ciousness was a "rude awakening" for his side. One unit of gray artil-lerymen ran their guns into an open field, formed a hollow square assisted by 120 sharpshooters, and waited for a mounted attack that never came. The captain of the Charlottesville Battery prepared his men to pursue the Yankees along with some of his comrades, but no "stirring event" ensued, and the weary gunners returned to camp.[28]

About three miles east of Frederick's Hall, Dahlgren's column had passed around a low hill when the cavalrymen spied a small log house bustling with activity, with horses tied up at the rails and a team of four hitched to a wagon full of firewood.[29] Lieutenant Merritt led the charge on the cabin, with cover from Cooke and a squadron from the Harris Light Cavalry. The attackers soon discovered that they had interrupted a court-martial presided over by Lieutenant Colonel Hilary P. Jones, an artillery-battalion commander.[30] The Southerners at the hearing were shocked. "Running to the windows and doors of the house and looking out they saw a number of Yankee cavalry galloping toward the house firing their pistols and shouting as they came . . . , pointing their large pistols into the windows."[31] The demand for surrender was made "in no polite terms." Since the Confederates carried no sidearms, Jones ordered the surrender of all present, about thirty soldiers and "six or eight girls." He was "rather morose" after his capture and attempted to play the "game of supe-riority" with his captors, which irked the Yankees. The captured officers and enlisted men were led away on "mules without saddles and on some jaded horses that our men had traded for better." A trooper controlled each prisoner's mount. Dumping the firewood, the Federals ordered the Confederates into a wagon, whereupon the prisoners broke into a chorus of "Wait for the Wagon," a popular wartime tune. Dahlgren joked that since the court-martial had ended, all charges were dropped. On the other hand, another Yankee "wag remarked, as the court prisoners, and witnesses were all present, the trial might go on and the proceedings might be sent to General Long [the Second Corps artillery commander] from Point Lookout or Fort Delaware," two well-known POW camps up North. Later, former prisoner William Fendley Dement, at the time a captain in the 1st Maryland Artillery, said he found Dahlgren "a most agreeable and charming villain" who was "very civil to the prisoners, shared his food" with the captain, and "on several occasions invited him to take a nip of whiskey with him."[32]

In another action near Frederick's Hall, the raiders bagged William G. Richardson, unburdening the Virginia Central Railroad "roadmaster" of "a splendid gold watch and chain, about $100 in gold, and $1000 in Confederate notes" before releasing him.[33]

Near Bumpass the raiders put their blue-clad shoulders to the task of wrecking several hundred feet of track and cutting telegraph lines, though they lacked the proper tools for real destruction. Midway through their labors, a Virginia Central train approached from the north, but the engineer saw heavy black smoke from the burning ties in time to throw his locomotive into reverse and save his train. As at the cabin, troopers kept an eye out for fresh mounts whenever they passed a farm with horses—and this part of Virginia was dense with blooded mares and stallions sequestered there by their owners to prevent exactly this occurrence. The dusty blue-coated boys took the fresh horses, shooting the disabled ones.[34]

Once the track wreakers finished as best they could, they remounted, heading south toward Goochland County with their prisoners. One, a corpulent major, was too heavy for his mount to bear. When he lagged behind, his captors poked the straining animal with their sabers. Dahlgren asked the Rebel officer what his problem was, to which the portly major responded that he was plagued by "Job's Comforters." The colonel, who knew a thing or two about discomfort, allowed the man to continue his journey in an ambulance.[35]

Soon after marching out of Bumpass Station and still some thirty miles from his next objective, the James River, Dahlgren behaved exactly as a gentleman should and exactly as a commanding officer should not. One prisoner, Hilary Jones, asked to visit his wife, Elizabeth, who was a guest at Chantilly, Dr. George Fleming's plantation located in western Hanover County, with their baby son. Perhaps Jones desired to check on the boy, who was only three and a half months old, though the specific reason for the stop is unknown. Dahlgren allowed the family visit, delaying the march by an unrecorded period of time.[36]

As the grimy Yankee troopers left Chantilly, the weather changed. "A storm which had been threatening came upon us, and we rode in a drenching rain till after midnight," recalled Captain John Myrick, a former lawyer from Maine. The column rode "through dense woods and swamps . . . until two o'clock the next morning, when a short halt was made, and the men got what sleep they could." Though soaked, most riders were able to nap as their equally weary animals plodded Hanover County's mud-swollen roads. One officer admitted that he "slept soundly at least half the night while marching," adding that some horses would join their "tired riders in mutual slumbers." But sleeping in the saddle carried a price. "The command suffered heavily in stragglers by the horses carrying our sleeping troopers off in the darkness, unobserved by their comrades, where they, on awakening, frequently found themselves left too far behind to rejoin the command, or lost in the woods of the enemy's country," a Michigan captain wrote.[37] But marching in such dismal weather had its advantages for men operating in enemy territory. "It was with the greatest difficulty that the column could be kept together; everything had to be done by sound, and it was unsafe to make any noise for we were now entirely cut off from any support and liable at any moment to be attacked, but our very boldness saved us," Dahlgren's signal officer said.[38] Marching in wet silence, straggling and struggling to catch up, the men endured a grim night, summed up by a school teacher from Maine turned cavalry private. Traversing Hanover County's dense woods and swampy lowlands "was like marching in a tomb and the heavy door closed behind," he said in stark counterpoint to an officer's opinion that being so deep in enemy territory was "intensely exciting." Eventually, the hard-driving rain let up, replaced by heavy fog, creating a ghostly tableau of slumped riders atop weaving, half-sleeping horses.[39]

It was also during this grueling trek to the South Anna River that Dahlgren's column was temporarily assisted by the black servant of a Confederate officer. Toward nightfall, having been "struggling through the mud holes of the miserable swamp roads," the raiders came to an intersection where no one, not even the veteran scouts, knew the roads. The advance guard captured a Rebel signal officer who had with him "a mulatto servant who was about twenty-five years old" named William, who apparently had never been in bondage. The captain and William, his valet, claimed to have been home on furlough. As the conversation meandered, Martin Hogan recognized the valet's knowledge of the region. The scout claimed that he himself knew Richmond "like a bog," having once been a prisoner there, but in the swampy backcountry of Louisa and Hanover Counties, he did not mind calling on local talent. After a "long conference" in which William displayed familiarity with plantations the column had passed, Dahlgren became convinced of the valet's worth and offered him a liberal reward to serve as a guide, warning that any lies would get him strung up. Hogan's fellow scout, James Wood, said later that he saw no nefarious conversations between the Confederate officer and William. Another account, written only a day after the raid ended, described how an unnamed black man came up to the lost Yankees and offered to guide them. The Maine trooper credited this fellow with leading the men through swamps, over fields, and across rivers.[40]

During the rainy evening of February 29, the blue-clad horsemen and their numerous captives, crossed the South Anna by torchlight at Turkey Creek Ford. The horses stumbled over the rocky bed, distracting the men guarding the prisoners and providing several a chance to escape. Lieutenant Giles Courtney, a battery commander and by this time on foot, fled into the bushes and dove into a ditch, remaining motionless in the cold, muddy water while the rest of the Yankee column passed. Courtney found a house, whose occupants welcomed him, fed him breakfast, and washed his uniform. One by one, most of the men grabbed near Frederick's Hall got away, an eventuality the Federals looked on with mixed emotions. "We were unable to guard them properly," an officer admitted, "and, in fact, Colonel Dahlgren did not care to be troubled with them." Dahlgren seems to have facilitated, if not encouraged, the escapes by telling his signal officer, Lieutenant Reuben Bartley, that he felt the prisoners could complicate their efforts. Taking the colonel's meaning, Bartley offhandedly mentioned to the one of the captive officers that it would not be too tough to make a break for it, a broad hint greeted with thanks and a quick change of the subject. In time even the newly taken signal officer absconded, though his valet remained with the Yankees. Whether Dahlgren weighed the potential consequences of these escapes is unrecorded.[41]

To wait for fifty-some stragglers, Dahlgren halted the column at about 3:00 A.M. on March 1 near a cluster of houses with a store nearby. His men, appreciating their leader's grit and his disability after thirty-six hours in the saddle, made him "a bed of fence rails, stretching across them a rubber blanket, [and] covered him with woolen blankets." Their sentiment was deep and real. "Who could complain of weariness when he looked at the colonel, still weak from his wound, riding along quietly, uncomplainingly, ever vigilantly watching every incident of the march?" a man told Admiral Dahlgren much later. As loyal as his troopers were, they also must have recognized that their young commander was weakened and perhaps disoriented by the ordeal they had all endured, a fact confirmed when dawn revealed that the column had been traveling in circles, three times passing the same plantation. The colonel made no indication to his subordinate officers that he was willing to turn back or, better yet, relinquish his command to Major Cooke, a more seasoned officer.[42]

Meanwhile, some twelve miles away, Kilpatrick was playing havoc with the Virginia Central Railroad, "probably the most important railroad in the state," according to one historian of Lee's army.[43] After an hour's stop by the Po River south of Spotsylvania Court House, Little Kil was able to close up his attenuated column. He and his 3,000 troopers marched southeasterly at a swift pace bound for another depot on the Virginia Central. To reach Beaver Dam Station, according to a 7th Michigan man writing home immediately after the raid, meant "travelling at a gallop. . . . It was in fact a regular charge for 75 miles." Eating hardtack as they rode, men struggled to keep up with the general who long since had earned his murderous sobriquet.[44]

With General Davies's brigade in the lead, the Federals moved rapidly from Mount Pleasant to New Market, then on to Chilesburg in Caroline County. South of Chilesburg at midday, the cavalrymen crossed the North Anna River at Anderson's Ford. After burning Mrs. Anderson's mill, they reached Beaver Dam Station between three and four o'clock on the afternoon of February 29. Captain Llewellyn Estes, Kilpatrick's assistant adjutant general and devoted factotum, immediately dashed into the telegraph office with a squad of men, capturing the telegraph operator before he could tap out any warnings. The destruction soon commenced, as Kilpatrick detached parties up and down the line to demolish track, engines, and rolling stock. One Vermonter counted about five miles of track wrecked. Virginia Central president Edmund Fontaine, who lived nearby, fled his home amid carbine shots as his company's property went up in flames.[45]

"The railroad depot, water tanks, store house, etc., were destroyed, the switches, turn-outs, and track pulled up and burned, the telegraph cut, and the poles taken down for a considerable distance," General Davies reported. "The air became full of smoke as we neared Beaver Dam Station, which was all in flames, with a train of cars, hundreds of cords of wood, and everything of value consigned to the flames," wrote a quartermaster sergeant. Captain Gloskowski reported, "Twenty wooden buildings were at once set on fire, forming one sheet of flame, rising high above the surrounding woods, and the black forms of our soldiers jumping around it seemed from a distance like demons on some hellish sport." The inferno engulfed a large, new, brick freight house 125 feet long, an engine house, and the telegraph office. The raiders freed three slaves, including Renty, who had been Fontaine's property. A soldier cursed not acquiring "a nice Virginia cured ham," later beaming to see that two comrades had snagged some for their mess. "These hams were sure good compared to the salt pork we had been eating for the previous fifteen months," he declared. For Beaver Dam Station, sacked before and to be sacked again in the future, it was just another day in worn-torn Virginia.[46]

But Kilpatrick's perfect destruction of the Virginia Central Railroad's property did not sustain a sublime conflagration for long. Two potential problems caught the general's attention. First, a train approached the station from the direction of Richmond until the conductor, alerted by the fiery sky, ordered the engine thrown into reverse, eluding capture. Its complement of twenty-five Confederate guards jumped off, putting up a brief fight, and firing a volley at Davies's advance guard, driving back pickets from the 1st Maine. Momentarily, the regiment's commander, Major Constantine Taylor, arrived with the remainder of the 1st Maine and supports from the 4th Pennsylvania. The new arrivals formed up on a skirmish line as the 16th Pennsylvania formed into line of battle in the road. The Northerners' vigorous attack sent the Rebels fleeing into the woods at the cost of two 1st Maine men wounded.[47]

A second problem was the nasty weather, which had turned to rain while Kilpatrick's men burned the depot; it was also plaguing Dahlgren's smaller column. As the Federals trotted out of Beaver Dam Station, the storm's volume and intensity accelerated. Cold, raw, and rainy, conditions soon worsened as a sharp wind drove sleet at the cavalrymen, forcing them to ride with their eyes shut. A Wolverine officer accustomed to Michigan's brutal winters wrote: "On and on for hours and hours, facing the biting storm, feeling the pelting rain, staring with straining eyes into the black night, striving to see when nothing was visible to the keenest vision, listening with pricked up ears for the sound of the well-shod hoofs which with rhythmical thread signaled the way." But they were no longer riding unobserved. Since the destruction at the station, a company of twenty men under Captain George W. Emack of the 1st Maryland Cavalry had been shadowing Kilpatrick's column. Emack sent back intelligence to Colonel Johnson near Hanover Junction, keeping his commander informed of the raiders' movements. The dogged Marylanders would follow the Yankees throughout the night and into the next day.[48]

The weather's ferocity, however, could not defeat the hardy veterans, for even the newcomers were now steeled with experience after twenty-four hours in the saddle with virtually no rest and little nourishment. Kilpatrick's troopers rode on with "cheerful fortitude." Though they did not complain, it was a hard march. One Michigan trooper observed: "Now to sleep on horseback one needs long legs, but no backbone. A spinal column . . . is a stiff torment to a drowsy horseman." Another comrade found "the night intensely dark, and it was extremely difficult to follow the column, as many of the men fell asleep and let their horses carry them whither they would." The night took its toll as the slumbering men unwittingly straggled off. It was a long and wearisome trek, "requiring almost superhuman efforts on the part of both officers and men" to keep up. After riding about six to eight miles from Beaver Dam Station, the raiders halted to feed their horses, make coffee, and await stragglers.[49]

Kilpatrick had expected his force to cross the South Anna River at Ground Squirrel Bridge. The storm's severity apparently confused his black guide, a boy perhaps no older than ten, who lost his bearings and took the column off course. Robbed of valuable time, the troopers "depended on the instinct of their horses." In desperation, the general sent up two signal rockets coded to tell Dahlgren where his command was but to no avail, given cloud cover and other conditions. At 8:00 P.M. he ordered a halt, but that did not mean any rest for the men, who were kept busy going plantation to plantation demanding the proprietors "to pay tribute to the Yanks according to their stock," as a Michigan sergeant put it. "We come down on them like 'June bugs,' cleaning them out of everything of value." But this plundering did not go unnoticed, Captain Emack and his Marylanders watching from the shadows.[50]

During the evening of the twenty-ninth, Kilpatrick's men captured a small wagon train loaded with corn and bound for Richmond. The raiders' horses consequently had a good supper, with enough forage left over for the next day. The men also roasted corn for themselves, providing some semblance of warm food. The mischievous bluecoats allegedly also came across a barrel of peach brandy in a tavern's cellar, according to one of Kilpatrick's scouts. Confiscated as contraband of war, about half of it went into canteens before the general learned about the violation and ordered two kegs from one of the ambulances filled with the liquor.[51]

As midnight neared under horrendous weather conditions, boundless fatigue, and the perils of marching off course, Kilpatrick ordered Major William Hall of the 6th New York to pull 450 men from the main force to move out and destroy the Richmond, Fredericksburg, and Potomac Railroad bridge over the South Anna near Taylorsville. Hall's command, with the 17th Pennsylvania leading the way, included detachments from the 4th, 6th, and 9th New York as well as ten men from the 3rd Indiana. They rode away from Kilpatrick's main force in "a cold, drizzling rain" on a night as "dark as Egypt."

Initially, Hall encountered only a Confederate picket post not far from the railroad. He ordered Captain John Q. Brown of the 9th New York to dismount his men and drive off the Rebels. Forming a ragged skirmish line, Brown's men advanced into a thicket, firing their carbines and yelling wildly as the captain, a seasoned thirty-four-year-old, cursed at his younger troopers to keep quiet lest they betray the paucity of their numbers. The New Yorkers' bansheelike screams trumped his caution but unnerved the Rebels, who cried out, "Don't shoot, we surrender." Hall's expeditionary force continued on a very narrow road until about 3:00 A.M., harassed constantly by snipers firing from behind makeshift barricades of felled trees that blocked the road. As the Federals approached to within "ten feet" of one such obstruction, they noticed a fence on one side and woods on the other, causing them to feel "entrapped." Their foes opened up with such a hot fire that it silhouetted the Rebels, triggering a brief but brisk exchange of carbine and musketry fire. About a dozen Pennsylvanians under Lieutenant Martin Reinhold gained the barricade to the left, flanking the remaining defenders. Hall then rushed up reinforcements under Lieutenant P. A. English to complete the job. The Federals captured ten Rebel enlisted men and two officers. Two Northerners were hit during this action; one died two hours later, the other lost his arm the next day.

Following this fight, the Yankees abandoned their quest for the railroad bridge. Hall heard that a Confederate infantry brigade, supported by artillery, was guarding it. An Indiana veteran claimed to have seen the Rebel camp in a valley between the oncoming raiders and the bridge. The Confederates, he reported, had cavalry, infantry, and artillery, with guns posted by the latter unit to command the road on which the Union troopers were advancing. As Hall withdrew, the Indianan was proven correct. As the detachment fell back, the Southerners opened up with artillery. "We were in rather uncomfortable quarters and did not fancy our surroundings," wrote the 17th Pennsylvania's regimental historian. The withdrawal stalled when an ambulance had to turn around in the narrow road so that the advance now had to fight as a rear guard, fending off some 200 gray-clad cavalrymen. Several Federals went down in the melee, but the rest of Hall's troopers found Beech Tree Ford, splashing across the South Anna early in the morning of March 1 in search of Kilpatrick. Along the way the major's men captured several Southern soldiers home on furlough; thinking like Dahlgren, he quickly paroled them. Hall also destroyed a wood train, deepening the Virginia Central's ill luck.[52]

By the evening of February 29, despite not knowing in detail what the Federals had in mind, Confederate commanders were ready to counter them on several fronts. From his Richmond headquarters, General Elzey ordered Colonel Walter H. Stevens, who commanded the city's defenses, to move light-artillery units up to key road intersections along the intermediate line of the Confederate works, expecting them to be in place by early the next morning. Guards were doubled along the line as well. Captain Linnaeus B. Anderson of the North Anna Home Guards stayed in touch with his immediate contact at Hanover Junction, Colonel Johnson, relaying word

of the Yankees' movements as they passed along Trinity Church
Road. Anderson had been stealthily moving "through woods, plantations, etc., avoiding all roads," until he spotted the enemy campfires. Johnson was busy making sure that boats at important river
crossings were going up in flames. General Hampton, who had not
yet heard from Jeb Stuart since sending his earlier messages, now
informed his commander of Beaver Dam Station's total destruction. He then moved the 1st and 2nd North Carolina Cavalry—300-
odd men—along with a two-gun section of Captain James Hart's
South Carolina horse-artillery battery to Mount Carmel Church in
Caroline County.[53]

After tangling with Custer near Stanardsville, Stuart turned his
attention to Kilpatrick and his raiders. He ordered General Rosser
to pursue the Yankees. Rosser's Laurel Brigade moved out so rapidly that the men left their overcoats in camp, riding unprotected
to the east, for Charlottesville, into the same northeaster plaguing Dahlgren and Kilpatrick. A "sheet of ice" soon enveloped each
Confederate and his horse, giving them a "weird and ghostlike"
appearance beneath a wintry moon. "Hat, coat, equipments, hair,
and beard covered with ice, furnished a complete disguise," the unit
historian wrote. "The horses, too, were masked in glittering white,
and shivering with cold the men moved on in profound silence,
nothing being heard but the steady tramp of the column." An all-
night ride brought the frozen troopers to Charlottesville for a fleet-
ing respite in camp before setting out again after the raiders. Rosser
never caught Kilpatrick's cavalry on a trek that, along with several
others that winter, eventually wore out his brigade.[54]

Shortly before midnight on February 29, Captain Gloskowski
sent up two more rockets to signal to Dahlgren to move forward for
a simultaneous attack on Richmond at ten o'clock the next morning. General Davies's command, still leading the main body, moved
out of their makeshift camp and "took the road to Richmond."[55]

DAHLGREN INVADES GOOCHLAND COUNTY

Three aged mules hitched to a single towrope slowly walked in tandem along the towpath late on the morning of February 29, 1864. A black man carrying a tin horn to signal the animals led them as they pulled the canal boat *Packet*. If its passengers were lucky, the rickety vessel made four miles an hour. The same storm-laden clouds seen by Dahlgren's Yankee troopers near Frederick's Hall were also threatening to open up on the *Packet*'s passengers. The old boat, which made the journey along the James River and Kanawha Canal from Richmond to Buchanan, Virginia, the canal's terminus, had seen better days.

The James River Company, which formed in 1785 under George Washington, was thought by 1808 to have exerted "one of the most successful internal improvements in the country." In its heyday between 1850 and 1860, the renamed James River and Kanawha Canal Company hauled corn, wheat, tobacco, timber, and iron ore from the western hinterlands of the state to Richmond. Reversing their route out of the city, keelboats like the *Packet* brought man-ufactured goods as well as passengers bound for the plantations of Goochland, Fluvanna, and other interior counties. After Fort Sumter, the waterway was used to transport troops and military supplies. The stagnant ditchwater of the canal was a breeding ground for snakes, bullfrogs, and insects. Lily pads floated below willow trees which lined the canal's banks. Two passengers on board the *Packet* on this particular trip from Richmond had no idea what was in store for them when they disembarked near Sabot Hill plantation that cloudy February day.[1]

One of these was former Virginia governor Henry A. Wise, wear-ing the gray uniform of a Confederate brigadier general, in company with his nineteen-year-old daughter, Ellen Mayo, and a fellow sol-dier who lived in western Goochland County. Wise, fifty-seven, was heading for Eastwood, another daughter's home, to enjoy a reunion

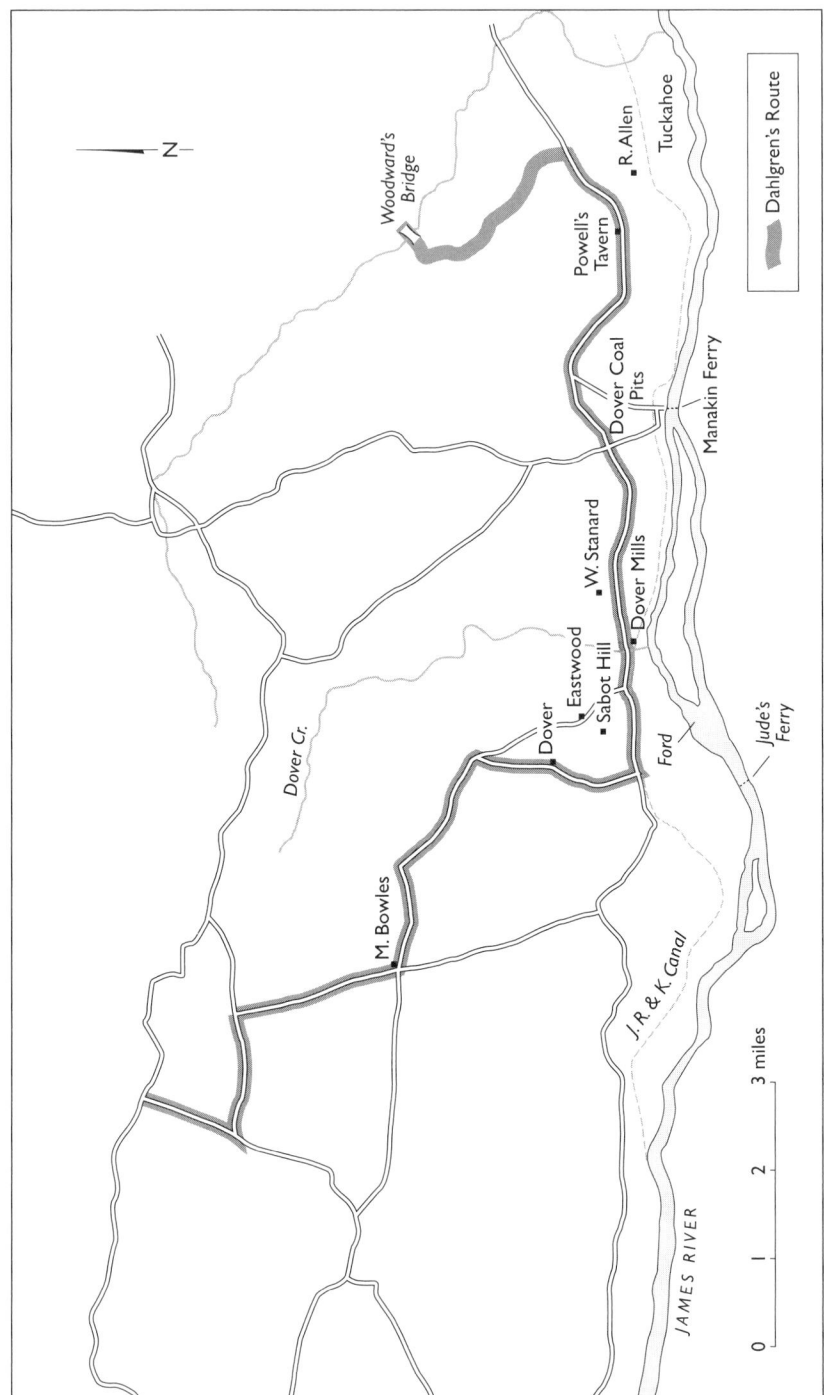

Dahlgren's Movements in Goochland County. Map by Bill Nelson. Copyright © 2016 by the University of Oklahoma Press.

with family and friends and a winter furlough from military service. A lawyer, he had entered politics early, serving as a Democrat in the U.S. Congress during Andrew Jackson's administration and briefly as minister to Brazil, but had switched party affiliation several times. As Virginia's governor from 1856 to 1860, Wise could claim the distinction of hanging the rabid abolitionist John Brown in 1859 after his infamous, ill-fated attempt at triggering a slave rebellion. The uprising, if you could call it that, ended in bloodshed at Harpers Ferry when a detachment of U.S. Marines under U.S. Army lieutenant colonel Robert E. Lee, supported by Virginia militiamen, stormed an engine house that Brown and his followers had seized and fortified. Wise had no military experience but strong family ties to Pennsylvania; George Meade was Wise's brother-in-law.[2] Jefferson Davis made him a general after Sumter. Wise served in western Virginia, then in North Carolina at the Battle of Roanoke Island, where he saw one of his sons killed. He had come home now from Charleston, South Carolina, where he was serving under General P. G. T. Beauregard.[3]

The gathering of the family at Eastwood promised to be a grand revel. The house was constructed in the 1850s by Wise's son-in-law Plumer Hobson, a prominent local landowner who was prevented by poor health from entering Confederate service. One of rural Goochland County's Italianate mansions, Eastwood stood in a grove of oaks, its doors and windows opening onto a wide lawn that faced the James. The house and its dependencies reflected the way of life associated with the needs of Virginia's planter class—stables, quarters for the household slaves and an overseer, housing for field workers, barns for livestock, and hundreds of acres of cropland. The farm bustled with horses, cattle, sheep, and hogs, tended by thirty-eight slaves toiling in the fields and working in the master's house.

The general's wife, Mary Elizabeth, had preceded them to the Hobson home. When Wise and his daughter arrived at the plantation wharf at Dover Mills, they were met by a trusted servant named Uncle Ephriam, who loaded a carriage with their luggage and quickly drove them the mile between the landing and the plantation house. Uncle Ephriam turned off the public way alongside the canal and, passing through the plantation's outer gate, onto the private path that rose toward the house, affording the trio a look into an odd distant glow in the evening sky. At first they thought they were seeing the aurora borealis, a strange celestial phenomenon that to unsophisticated adherents portended unusual happenings. Giving scant notice to the peculiar appearance, the general entered his son-in-law's house, receiving cordial greetings from family and friends alike. Warm fireplaces burning stout logs cut by the plantation's slaves greeted the weary travelers. A sumptuous feast, despite wartime privations, awaited the visiting family as they celebrated with genuine coffee, sugar, and sorghum. After dinner Wise retreated to his assigned bedroom to rest his tired bones "on snowy pillows . . . with linen, lavender-scented sheets, and warm, soft blankets," a blessed relief from his stoic military mess. For her part, Ellen Mayo enjoyed the evening as well, but she paid closer attention to the shimmer at the horizon.[4]

As Wise and his daughter landed at Dover Mills, Dahlgren and his men were trying to recover from their fit of misdirection. It seemed a good augury that their advance guard was able to spot a Rebel wagon train's campfires. Immediately a charge was ordered. Just as quickly, six forage wagons bound for Lee's army fell into the raiders' hands. At first the Southern teamsters took the sudden attack as a "huge joke," never suspecting Yankees in the neighborhood. Their grins vanished when the industrious cavalrymen grabbed axes to destroy wagon spokes and rip open grain sacks. There was more than enough corn to feed themselves and their mounts, and the teamsters provided valuable information that the Federals were only six miles from Dover Mills. By the time Eastwood's proprietors and their guests had bedded down and the big house had gone quiet on that wet, cold night, Dahlgren's column was only three miles north of Hobson's house. The one-legged colonel called a halt well after midnight, perhaps at 2:00 or 3:00 A.M. He and his bone-weary horse soldiers were almost out of Hanover and nearly into Goochland County, not at all where Dahlgren had expected to be at this hour on March 1, a Tuesday. He gave his troopers about two and a half hours to rest and wait for stragglers before resuming their march. Dahlgren took advantage of the pause to rest his own aching body. Unknown to the colonel, Sergeant John Gathright, a local member of the Goochland Troop, 4th Virginia Cavalry, was home on furlough when the Yankees first entered the county—a fortunate thing for General Wise.[5]

Soon after Dahlgren awoke, he and his men were punching on at "a rapid pace," arriving about six miles northeast of Goochland Court House about 7:00 A.M. but still some twenty miles from their objective. He became a little unsure of his command's direction, which was left to his black guide, Martin Roberson, employed for the specific purpose of getting the bluecoats over the James, having replaced William as Dahlgren's principal guide. But "Dahlgren had ridden in the advance with the scouts and the colored man, of whom he had become very suspicious," an army scout later recalled. He had good reason to be nervous. His column should have been at least twenty miles closer to the Confederate capital by this time, Kilpatrick's plan calling for simultaneous attacks against Richmond that morning.[6]

Near present-day Cardwell, Dahlgren halted again to feed his horses and allow his tired troopers to eat. He also divided his small command, sending Captain John F. B. Mitchell and one hundred men from the 2nd New York due south, along with ambulances; the remaining prisoners from the disrupted court-martial, Captain Dement and Lieutenant Blair; captured horses; and plenty of torpedoes, turpentine, and oakum. Mitchell was to ride along the canal's towpath on the north side of the James, destroying as much property as possible. The captain ordered Lieutenant Alfred Randolph, with twenty men and the ambulances, to take the river road while he and the remainder of his command took the towpath; the two were to converge at Manakin's Bend. Mitchell was to rejoin Dahlgren in Richmond after the colonel had crossed the river and rode along the south side to the vicinity of Belle Isle, opposite the city. If this plan failed, Mitchell was to make for Hungary Station, about six miles northwest of Richmond, there to rendezvous with Kilpatrick's main force. On the first leg of his assignment, the New Yorker excelled, wrecking numerous business and agricultural enterprises. Meanwhile, Dahlgren's reduced column was similarly busy, destroying several flourmills, a small factory, a gristmill, and a steam plant; sinking or burning about fifteen canal boats; and commandeering at least twenty sorely needed fresh mounts. "We captured a large number of fine horses," a Union officer recalled. "Our command had been able to keep well mounted from the number of horses secured up to this time." Dahlgren also had a following of about five hundred runaway slaves who had fled plantations, some reported to be "mounted and armed."[7]

Among the first large Goochland County plantations that the Yankee raiders hit on March 1 was Dover, owned by James M. Morson. Besides his tracts in Goochland County, the Richmond lawyer owned sugar and cotton plantations in Louisiana and

Mississippi, with some eight hundred slaves working his holdings. Morson had married well and done better. In 1843 he married Ellen Bruce, whose father, James Bruce, was said to the third richest man in the United States. Ellen's sister Sarah, called "Sallie," had married James A. Seddon two years later, another attorney and who would become Confederate secretary of war. The Bruce sisters were known throughout antebellum Richmond's social circles for their beauty and talent. Sallie, now forty-two, was "an accomplished heiress . . . , beautiful in person and in character, and thoroughly educated" in Northern finishing schools. Her voice was "one of the sweetest that ever sang," and "she was an admirable performer on the piano." Unfortunately, Ellen Morson died in 1862 while visiting her husband in New Orleans. By the time of Dahlgren's raid, Sallie Seddon was taking care of Ellen's four children as well as her own nine at her home south of Dover, her brother-in-law remaining in the Deep South on business.[8]

James Morson's plantation house was enlarged in 1845 from an original eighteenth-century eight-room brick structure. Once completed, it was considered "the stateliest home in Virginia," with lavish Corinthian columns in front, a large ballroom, and Carrara and Florentine mantles moved from his Richmond home. As at other plantations, the main house was the gem in a crown studded with dependencies—stables, barns, gardens, orchards, sheds, and slave quarters.

But that was before Dahlgren and his men arrived in the early morning hours of March 1. The raiders had developed a pattern and a rhythm, and no sooner had they come upon Dover than they automatically went into action. "The straw barn, farm barn and stable were utterly destroyed, with all appurtenances," one Southern observer later wrote. "One mule was burnt & nearly all the horses and mules carried off—The meat house was emptied, and not a pound of bacon, nor an ounce of flour, nor a grain of corn" remained. The cavalrymen filled four wagons with staples. In two hours the Northern ruffians "broke down the outer and several of the inner doors, smashed up the china and glass, stole the plate and a great deal of clothing." By this account the troopers invited Morson's slaves to help themselves, then inquiring as to whether any young ladies of the plantation were available. Not a one, the slaves said. Denied sex, the men made do with violence, torching a stone barn valued at $65,000 as well as three more stables. Another Southern account claims that the raiders burned Morson's horses in the stables—hardly an action that would be taken by a cavalry unit on the run behind enemy lines and needing every horse it could steal. The same hyperbolic writer may have been the source of a report describing Dahlgren's men cavorting in the front yard in "fancy dress" apparel and "costly feminine costumes." A third, more believable witness stated, "The Federal soldiers regaled themselves on Mr. Morson's fine wine, drinking it from his silver goblets, and, as mementoes of the feast, carried off the goblets with them."[9]

Whatever accuracy these reports convey, they reflect badly on Dahlgren as a commander not in control of his troops at a crucial hour, although a New York officer later blamed the destruction at Morson's plantation on his own slaves. Most of the plunder, he claimed, was done by the women: "Pantries and closets were thoroughly ransacked, judging from the appearance of the ground outside the house." The slaves felt justified in rioting because "they were nearly starved, overworked, and cruelly beaten without cause." Most postwar accounts praise the bondsmen for loyalty to their masters during the Goochland rampage, but slavery had its price, usually paid in chaos. But the Federals were not without blame. A Michigan lieutenant later recalled a woman at Dover, whom he mistook for Mrs. Seddon, begging him to stop the soldiers from smashing her furniture. He shouted back: "Madam, they are not my men. If they were they would come out of there or I would shoot them." The officer referred her to Dahlgren but failed to record his colonel's reaction, though he did note that he took "a fine full-blooded Kentucky horse" for himself. A 5th New York officer later confirmed, "Some excesses were committed."[10] But the Federals mostly left the Morson mansion alone, apparently believing a claim that a very sick person lay inside. Fear of smallpox or the like thus convinced the men to stay clear of the stately building.[11]

During the melee word probably came to Dahlgren that General Wise was nearby at Eastwood. In his fervency for the Union cause, the colonel naturally would have champed at the bit to capture the man who had hanged John Brown. Dahlgren might have swooped in and surprised Wise and his relatives but for the daring Sergeant Gathright, who rode hard to Eastwood with the news that Yankee raiders were only three miles away. At daybreak the Hobsons and the Wises assembled in the plantation-house library, reviewing the situation and quickly deciding to leave the women to deal with the

Yankees while the general and Plumer Hobson, who was more than willing to make up for his hated noncombatant status, rode to Richmond to sound the alarm. Uncle Ephraim and another slave named Tom ran to the stables to retrieve a mount for Wise, returning with Pulaski, a blind warhorse ridden by the general's late son, Captain O. Jennings Wise. Hobson mounted his own thoroughbred mare, Lucy Washington. The men dug their spurs hard, driving their mounts across the great lawn and down the hill to the river road, which they could ride straight to the capital. No sooner had they disappeared into the morning mist than slaves from the next plantation over came running toward the house, shouting to Annie Hobson that Dover's yard was "black with men" in blue uniforms.[12]

The women of Eastwood, who had just bidden their men farewell, were starting to absorb that news when Sergeant David H. Schofield from Company K, 5th New York, dashed up to the front door, purportedly with his pistol drawn.[13] "Where is the man that hanged John Brown?" he shouted. By now Ellen Mayo was on the porch and answered truthfully that her father was not at the house—though out of the corner of her eye she could see her father and brother-in-law four hundred yards off, specks galloping toward a woodlot that would hide them until they reached the river road. Schofield followed her glance, though, and he and another trooper spurred their mounts after the men, who soon outdistanced the New Yorkers.[14]

Despite harboring the accursed former governor, Eastwood and its owners suffered nothing like the fate visited on Dover. In fact, the raiders who visited this plantation disturbed little or nothing, asking only for some food for their empty bellies. Amid this rumpus Dahlgren, vexed at not finding Wise at Dover or Eastwood, rode to the next plantation in search of him.[15]

Sabot Hill was another large estate, 946 acres, with a fine Italianate-style mansion built about 1851 at a cost of $64,000. The decade before it had been one of James Morson's real-estate deals, having sold it to his cousin, James Seddon. Less ostentatious than Dover but still tallying twenty-six rooms, Sabot Hill was meant to accommodate Seddon; his wife, Sallie; and their nine children. The space came in handy after Morson's four children joined the Seddon clan in 1862. Sturdy oak front doors opened into a hallway whose centerpiece was a spiral staircase beneath a stained-glass skylight. Appropriately for the home of a civilian in charge of making war,

Seddon had fitted the house with bulletproof interior shutters made of steel.[16]

A scion of a well-to-do family in Falmouth, Virginia, Seddon was born in 1815, one of eight children. A sickly fellow, he spent part of his late adolescence in Louisiana and Mississippi speculating in sugar lands, then returned home to read the law at the University of Virginia. He set up a practice in Richmond, where talk of states' rights drew him into Virginia politics and a hotly contested 1844 run for Congress that he won by a "handsome majority." Seddon continued that winning streak when, soon after the election, he wed the beautiful heiress Sarah "Sallie" Bruce of Halifax County—a triumph astounding in its own way, given that Seddon was described as humorless, "gaunt and emaciated, with a sallow and cadaverous [look], resembling an exhumed corpse after a month's interment." Doubtless the sprightly Sallie fell less for the outer man than for the inner, who a contemporary painted as "courtly, widely read, and a clever conversationalist." While the couple started their family, Seddon served three terms in the U.S. House of Representatives until 1851, when health problems attributable to neuralgia forced him to leave office. But in 1860 the secession crisis—he was a staunch states' rights man in the mold of his hero, John C. Calhoun—hauled him back into the fray, serving in the Provisional Congress of the new Confederacy. In November 1862 President Davis named him secretary of war, making use of his skills as "a practical and clear-eyed administrator . . . [who contributed] a large measure of common sense and efficiency in the day-to-day conduct of the war."[17]

Thwarted in his pursuit of Wise, Dahlgren would have been happy with Seddon as a consolation prize. He might have taken him too, but March 1, 1864, was a Tuesday, and as on most weekdays, Seddon was in Richmond attending to War Department matters. Late that morning the colonel rode the half mile from Dover to Sabot Hill and into a story that ever since has acquired lapidary richness of detail and a lesser amount of scrutiny about its accuracy.

The tale goes that the weary officer dismounted in the front yard and hitched his horse. Navigating awkwardly on a crutch, he climbed the broad steps to the front door and gave a knock. When Sallie Seddon opened it, her Southern-belle sangfroid was exquisite. She curtsied and said, "Good day, sir." Dahlgren replied, "Good day, ma'am," and introduced himself. "I know that name!" she exclaimed, explaining that while in Philadelphia at finishing school, she had met a John

Dahlgren, whom she termed an "old beau" of hers. Ulric's mother, Mary Clement Bunker Dahlgren, and Sallie had been schoolmates when the future admiral came courting. The implications—but for fate, both their lives might have been quite different—were compelling. Ulric Dahlgren doffed his cap to his late mother's school friend. Apologizing for ignoring the young colonel's disability, the beautiful matron invited him to come in and sit down. He clumped inside, happy to accept her suggestion that he sit with her and have a glass of blackberry wine bottled in 1844. While the colonel enjoyed that moment, his men went to work on the plantation. Sallie Seddon's hospitality saved her home but not one of her barns, which the bluecoats torched. In her kindness she also inadvertently or intentionally distracted Dahlgren while Plumer Hobson and General Wise were beating it up the road to Richmond with news of the Yankee invasion.[18] It is a great and enduring tale, one of many that speckle the war's human side, and integral to any account, especially given locally, of Dahlgren's dalliance in Goochland County.

Sad to say, no accounts from the Northern perspective, either contemporary to the raid or postwar, confirm the story of the admiral's son and the quick-witted chatelaine. The tale itself emerged forty years after the supposed event in a leading Confederate journal of reminiscences.[19]

The indict testimony of Seddon herself may cast the interlude into the dustbin of fable. After the war Nanie R. Johnson, a grandniece of James Seddon, produced a letter in Sallie's handwriting describing the Yankee's dirty work that March 1 at Dover, Eastwood, and Sabot Hill. In the missive to her husband dated that very day, Seddon describes in 874 words what the raiders did to the three properties. She says that she was dressing when a slave named Louisa rushed into the house and announced that "strange men were in the stable, seizing horses." The lady of the house looked out the window to see "two monsters" at the back gate "parleying with Jarrett & the other servants, who say that their eloquence saved me a visit." She recounts hiding silver plate, wines, and other valuables in the house slaves' quarters. Yet Seddon never mentions a one-legged Yankee colonel or Dahlgren by name or rank, let alone having a drink with him. But those 874 words might not have been all that Sallie Seddon wrote. The niece claimed that the letter is missing its close, so perhaps she saved the blackberry-wine story for a stunning ending—but probably not. What proud Southern woman would have waited until the letter's end to inform her husband that with her feminine wiles she had snookered a crippled Yankee invader out of defiling their sacred home? More resonant of reality is Seddon's statement, in her own crisp handwriting, "I never thought I hated the Yankees with all my heart before, but the feeling was intensified by this spectacle."[20]

If more ammunition need be aimed at the tale, there is the diary of Anne Hobson, Eastwood's mistress, which makes no mention of the supposed tête-à-tête. Hobson waited until April 3, 1864, to make an entry about the events of March 1, which were dramatic enough at her house, but did not include a handsome one-legged Yankee colonel in the parlor sipping wine—though it is unlikely she dismissed the detail out of jealousy. And in 1896 Hobson's sister, Ellen Wise Mayo, could have told the blackberry-wine story in an article she wrote for *Cosmopolitan* magazine about Dahlgren's depredations— what author would ignore so ripe a piece of narrative fruit as that if it were true? As with Seddon's refined outburst in her letter, there is a greater sense of truth in this Goochland resident's postwar claim to have heard that the Yankees "threatened to burn Mrs. Seddon's house over her head," which may have been an example of horse-soldier hyperbole being uncorked on a civilian, but it also rings truer than the more fabulous blackberry-wine anecdote.[21]

Finally, the numbers do not add up. Sallie Bruce was born in 1822. Mary Clement Bunker was born in 1817 and married John Dahlgren in 1839, when she was twenty-two. John thus would have been thirty years old when Sallie was only seventeen. From a practical point of view, it seems unlikely that John Dahlgren would have been her "beau" during finishing school or that Mary Dahlgren would have been her classmate. Of course, postwar reminiscences do not always let the facts get in the way of a good story.

There is a practical point to discussing the wine-sipping myth. If true, it portrays Dahlgren's judgment and self-control in poor light. Entrusted with a pivotal role in a great military enterprise, he had no business sitting around in the middle of the day talking and drinking with an old flame of his father's. But nothing supports the story, and Dahlgren's firmly documented behavior more than suffices as a record of his flaws, personal and military. The winsome tale thus stands as an example of persistent early twentieth-century romanticism run amok.

The Union troopers stayed about two hours at Sabot Hill, according to one New York officer, an estimate likely accurate for their time at three plantations since elements of the column were scattered among them.[22] As the Yankees were doing their worst, or perhaps less than their worst, an incident occurred that left Goochland County with a genuine Confederate hero.[23]

That winter James Pleasants, nineteen, had been home on furlough like many of his comrades in Stuart's cavalry. Having a season to build up weary mounts for the coming spring campaign also gave their riders a rest. As many had, Pleasants joined up soon after Fort Sumter. He signed on with Company F, 4th Virginia Cavalry, a home-grown unit, known locally as the Goochland Light Dragoons or the Goochland Troop. Whatever Pleasants's reasons for enlisting, it let him substitute for his uncle, James H. Bowles, also a Goochland resident. Three other Pleasants served in the same unit.[24] Though Pleasants had rotated home on furlough, most of his regiment was at work, tangling with Custer near Standardsville. The 4th Virginia did not exactly cover itself with glory in that spat; the Yankee cavalry rode nearly unmolested through the town and back to the safety of Union lines. But the private redeemed his unit's honor back home in Goochland County.[25]

The young man was staying with his uncle, who lived near Cardwell. Among his few possessions was a blue Federal sack coat that he had snatched while on some sally with Stuart or perhaps acquired in a game of poker, at which he excelled along with his carbine. Dahlgren's raiders struck the Bowles place the morning of March 1 but did not search the house; if they had they would have found Pleasants dead asleep upstairs, as any nineteen-year-old of any era would be. He snoozed through the rustling, finally emerging for breakfast to hear his aunt complain that the Yankees had stolen their horses. Incensed, the young man pulled on his souvenir coat, grabbed his carbine, and went looking for the rascals and his family's horses.

However haphazard his disguise, none of the enemy horsemen who saw him thought Pleasants was anything but a fellow raider going on foot—all through the raid, men had had to give up their worn-out mounts. Near Hebron Presbyterian Church, he spied a lone Yankee looking for some breakfast and made quick work of disarming the man and taking his horse, making for Dover with his prisoner walking ahead. Hiding in the bushes, the Confederate cavalryman managed to capture another Union trooper, then started back to Cardwell with his prizes. In a woodlot north of the Morson plantation, and again near his home, the intrepid Virginian bluffed the surrender of several more Federals. One man escaped, but Pleasants, now feeling that he was managing as many men and horses as he could, herded the rest back to Cardwell. At a well the party encountered two more Northerners. One, a mounted officer, answered Pleasants's demand that he give up by yelling, "Surrender, Hell you say!" Bluffed, the young poker player showed his hand, firing his carbine and dropping the officer, inducing his subordinate, on foot, to raise his hands.

In all, James Pleasants bagged thirteen Yankees and sixteen horses. His uncle and Dr. Quintas Snead, a local physician, helped the private conduct the prisoners across the James at Michaux Ferry and into the Powhatan County jail to wait for more-suitable imprisonment. Besides the captured Federals, local residents managed to gather a wagonload of arms from the raiders.[26]

Yankee deprecations at the Morson, Seddon, and Hobson plantations are the most notorious stories associated with Dahlgren's hours in Goochland County, but there were others as well. Edwin DuVal, a prosperous planter and businessman, owned Oak Grove, on Manakin Town Ferry Road a half mile off the river road. Warned about the raiders, he took his horses and slaves into the woods beyond the Federals' main route along the river, leaving his eldest daughter, Lucy, to deal with the Yankees. From the large frame house's front porch, Lucy watched them approach, "silverware, quite a bit of it, strapped to their saddle bags." She nearly had the troopers convinced that Oak Grove offered nothing of value when a slave named Simon appeared. Seeing that Simon had a brass watch, the Federals said that unless he told them where his master was hiding with his valuables, they would take it. In a blink the slave pointed them toward DuVal's hiding place. The landowner had a fast horse and got away, but he had to leave the rest. In time all his slaves save one returned, but he never saw his horses and mules again.[27]

While Dahlgren was wreaking havoc on the river-view plantations, Captain Mitchell and his hundred troopers from the Harris Light Cavalry were doing their destructive part along the canal, making efficient use of the oakum, turpentine, and the crate of torpedoes they hauled along. The New Yorker reported that "six flourishing grist mills, filled with grain and flour, one saw-mill, six canal boats, loaded with grain, the barn (also well filled) on Secretary Seddon's plantation, coal works at Manakin's Ferry and Morgan's Lock" were destroyed. But as his small command was working its mischievous way eastward along the towpath, about ten miles outside Richmond a messenger brought Mitchell an order from Dahlgren "to abandon our work of devastation, and join him without delay at a point *north of the river*" (italics in original), according to Lieutenant William Mattison.[28] The unexpected dispatch put a grim wrinkle in a process that, except for the wretched weather, seemed to be going flawlessly.

As Mitchell and his men were puzzling over his order, Dahlgren was making one of his most bizarre and controversial decisions of the raid's first forty-eight hours. General Kilpatrick's original plan called for Dahlgren's smaller force to cross the James in Goochland County; ride east along the river's south bank, along the way torching Bellona Arsenal; and then free the Union prisoners on Belle Isle, opposite Richmond, before entering the Confederate capital. A river crossing implied access to a ford or a ferry, but the official record makes no mention of any specific crossing the colonel was to use.

From Sabot Hill Dahlgren had several options for crossing the James. About a mile west, near where Genito Creek flows south into the river, was Jude's Ferry, which linked Powhatan County on the south shore with the canal running parallel to the north bank. John Jude originally started the operation as a private venture about 1763 on land once owned by Thomas Jefferson's father, Peter. A landing on the south, or Powhatan County, side saw use during the American Revolution for offloading military stores coming upriver from Richmond for safekeeping when the British invaded Virginia in 1781. By the time of the Civil War, Jude's Ferry was a local landmark whose age doubtless made it familiar beyond the immediate area. Certainly the raid's planners should have known of the ferry, which could have carried Dahlgren's men across in several trips.[29] Southeast of Sabot Hill was an "excellent" river ford near Dover Mills, the canal-boat landing. Locals knew the river there to be "fordable, except at times of freshet." There was also a third possible crossing available three miles below Dover Mills at Manakin Ferry. Finally, ten miles or so west, some officers thought, was a ferry at Columbia Mills, which actually was more than twenty miles away.[30]

However many crossing options they knew of or that otherwise were available, Dahlgren and his scouts lacked details on their locations. After the war one scout on the raid questioned why "some of General Meade's scouts" were not "selected to accompany him, on account of their knowledge of the country between the Rapidan and Richmond." That no one familiar with Goochland County, or at least the general vicinity around Richmond, accompanied the raiders may be traced to the region's remoteness from the general area of action in the eastern theater. Once the column left Frederick's Hall, the Federals were in terra incognita. Dahlgren's scouts were seasoned at their job, just not in this part of Virginia, which had not been reconnoitered since Stoneman's raid. The colonel's signal officer noted, "As soon as we were south of the railroad our old guides were of no more use."[31] Dahlgren badly needed a local guide, and by chance one literally fell into his lap, for better and for much, much worse.

CHAPTER 9

THE MYSTERY OF DAHLGREN'S GUIDE

In Bruce Catton's Pulitzer Prize–winning book, *A Stillness at Appomattox*, the acclaimed writer chose to begin the third and final volume of his Army of the Potomac trilogy with a chapter subtitled "A Boy Called Martin." Referring as it does to an African American, the phrase, so benign in 1953, doubtless would not be published or even drafted today. In his immensely popular history, Catton tells what has become the most famous version of a notorious episode in the Kilpatrick-Dahlgren Raid.

But this is not the only version of the story. Since that pioneering investigation of the incident, in which a black man through treachery, ignorance, or simple bad luck so infuriated Colonel Dahlgren that he hanged the poor fellow, historians and writers have widened and deepened scholarship on the matter. The dead man now has a full name—Martin Robinson—ostensibly sieved from a reminiscence written more than forty years after the raid by a Confederate veteran with no connection to Goochland County or the incident.[1] But that identification is not beyond dispute.

Sources both Northern and Southern hint at other identities for the doomed guide. He could have been named Martin Robinson, a freed bricklayer suddenly grabbed up in Goochland County by Dahlgren to help the Federals find a river crossing. The fellow could have been William, a twenty-five-year-old mulatto freedman and a Confederate signal officer's valet, recognized by Hogan for his knowledge of the area below the South Anna River. Dahlgren's guide could have been one of James Seddon's slaves sent purposefully to deceive the Yankees by leading them into an ambush in exchange for his freedom. Yet another source paints the man as a free black and Confederate sympathizer who "wanted to see Jeff Davis succeed." There is also the possibility that he was a Samaritan who helped a Union man fleeing Libby Prison through Confederate lines, then was presented to Dahlgren as having more

knowledge than he actually possessed about the James River vicinity. One story describes an unnamed "burly" black man the raiders encountered on the Stanard plantation who, for ten dollars in
greenbacks, offered to ferry the Federals across the river. The most
outlandish claim is that a white man in a minstrel's "black face"
makeup deceived the invaders.[2]

The ill-fated guide most definitely was not Thomas Heath, a
thirty-one-year-old free black man from Goochland County said
to have aided Dahlgren. Heath was still alive on March 15, shortly
after the raid ended. By then, though, he was in serious trouble with
Confederate authorities, who had heard accusations that he gave aid
and comfort to the enemy.[3]

The notion that Dahlgren was duped by a white man "dis-
guised, blackened up and the like" was put forth by Edgar P. Sloan
of Company K, 1st Vermont Cavalry. To a regimental comrade,
Horace K. Ide, who was collecting reminiscences for publication in
1872, Sloan stated that he saw a white man hanged. This was, of
course, after the trooper had spent hours in the saddle with scant
rest or nourishment; his eyes—and his brain—might have been
playing tricks on him. If the hanged man was a mulatto, as some
accounts have it, the skin of his chest, made visible when his exe-
cutioners tore open his shirt, might have been lighter than his face,
as sometimes occurs in people of mixed-race heritage. There were
fires aplenty in Goochland County that day, which could have left
his face sooty. If Sloan's tale (through Ide's retelling) was the sole
source describing the confused guide as white, it would be logical
to discount that claim as the ramblings of a an exhausted, confused
witness. But soon after the raid, the *Army Navy Journal* reported
Dahlgren's late guide to have been "a white man, who is now supposed to have been a Rebel spy. . . . The guide and a negro, who was
implicated with him, were immediately hanged to the nearest tree."
This report further tangles the tale by adding a second corpse dangling from a tree in Goochland County. The newspaper account says
Dahlgren expected to find a bridge, an option the plan never mentioned and which simply was not available at the time. No other
source, contemporaneous or subsequent, has the raiders hanging
two men or thinking that they would cross the river via a bridge.
Whatever corroboration the *Army Navy Journal* account offers for
Sloan's recollection, it probably amounts to rumor reworked by a
reporter not present for the events.[4]

"Martin" likely was not a slave Seddon traduced into setting up the Yankees for ambush. In April 1864 the secretary of war, in a report to President Davis on his department's recent operations, devoted considerable space to the Kilpatrick-Dahlgren Raid, specifically mentioning Dahlgren's hanging of a black man. He suggested that the colonel "sought to cover the timidity that shrank from trying a doubtful ford by an act of savage vengeance on his negro guide, who indeed well merited his fate, but not at the hands of the enemy, for his treachery to an indulgent master and his attempted services to a cruel foe." Had Seddon conspired to gull the Yankees, he probably would have put a more benign description of the guide's fate.[5]

Two things are certain: the guide was black, and Dahlgren hanged him. To ascertain the identity of this man, it is necessary to look to the earliest references to him in contemporary sources, an exercise that has heretofore eluded chroniclers of the Kilpatrick-Dahlgren Raid.

On February 9, 1864, 109 Federal officers tunneled out of Libby Prison. One was 1st Lieutenant Godwin Scudamore, thirty-nine, of the 80th Illinois Infantry. The English-born Scudamore had been captured on May 3, 1863, by Confederate brigadier general Nathan Bedford Forrest near Rome, Georgia. Shipped to Libby, he spent "all the time studying to escape" and must have studied well. Only half of the fleeing POWs made it to Union lines, and he was one of them—more than that, he got out of Libby and back to the Federal army without assistance from Richmond's Union sympathizers, including the wily spinster Elizabeth Van Lew. Van Lew herself hid Scudamore's comrade, Colonel Abel Streight, in her home until he could make it safely out of Richmond. Scudamore might have done likewise, but where Streight ran directly for Van Lew's house, he ran the other way—west toward Goochland County—apparently alone. Moving only by dark through slimy swamps in which he lay up all day to avoid his pursuers, Scudamore came down with rheumatism, which wracked him with pain as he waded icy streams and lived without shelter and with little or no food until he collapsed on February 13. Fortunately, "friendly negroes" took him in for nine days, feeding and nursing the fugitive until he could resume his trek with the help of one of them as a guide. The officer and his new comrade continued to move until the Illinoisan's aching joints ground to a halt, forcing a three-day stay at an unnamed location. Scudamore's flight did not end until February 27, when he walked into Union lines near Brandy Station, a feat that even reached General Meade's ears. The commanding general had to talk with the man who had "made his way . . . through the main body of Lee's army and into our lines." But in a letter about that conversation, Meade said nothing about the lieutenant's companion. Scudamore never gave the black man's name either, nor did he name any of the others who helped him or even mention anyone accompanying him to safety.[6]

But a month after the raid, Anne Wise Hobson, owner of Eastwood, recorded in her diary the identification of Dahlgren's guide, describing him as "Martin the vile free negro who absconded to them with the escaped Yankee prisoners one fortnight before the raid, and who led them upon us, to his own wife's house at Dover through hogpaths and byways." In that entry Hobson gives at least three solid pieces of information about the guide: his given name was Martin; his status is a freedman whose wife lived at Dover; and a date that corresponds closely with the timeline of Scudamore's trek.[7]

Two Northern sources corroborate Hobson's account. In a letter written on February 28, 1864, a member of Meade's staff mentions seeing "an officer who had escaped from Libby prison at the same time as Col. Streight and came through the whole of Lee's army into our lines this morning." In another letter the next day, the same man names Lieutenant Scudamore as the officer he identified as the fortunate escapee. Nearly a week and a half later, this same staffer conclusively states that the black man who helped Scudamore was the man Dahlgren took on the raid. Another Meade staff officer provides the most convincing linkage. After the raid Lieutenant Colonel Theodore Lyman made in his private notebook an entry about Dahlgren's guide, stating that Meade's headquarters had provided the individual. "This man was a faithful creature who had protected and nursed for nine days, one of our officers escaped from Libby, (and who was sick) and afterwards brought him safe through our lines passing in the midst of the whole Rebel army." An account written thirteen years afterward by an officer who was on the raid claimed that the guide was "considered faithful and reliable on account of his having just piloted escaped officers from Libby prison into our lines." He further stated that the guide was born near Dover Mills in Goochland County.[8]

Pertinent but less conclusive evidence comes from a former Union private who served in the Bureau of Military Information, which under General Hooker was the intelligence arm of the Army of the Potomac. In a undated message marked "Confidential" from the Provost Marshal General's Department, John C. Babcock, a former architect, an unofficial army "captain," and an amateur cartographer working at Meade's headquarters, wrote to Dahlgren shortly before the raiders departed: "Dear Colonel: At the last moment I have found the man you want; well acquainted with the James River from Richmond up. I send him to you mounted on my own private horse. You will have to furnish him a horse. Question him five minutes, and you will find him the very man you want." In the margin of his message, Babcock added an important detail for the colonel to consider: "He crossed at Rapidan last night, has late information."[9] Evidently Dahlgren, while staying at Kilpatrick's headquarters, had voiced interest in securing a guide familiar with the James River crossings, prompting Babcock's communiqué. While Babcock does not name the party or his race, it is not unreasonable to think that he sent Martin, the freedman who had helped Scudamore escape. More pointedly, a New York officer with Dahlgren simply said, "The man was sent from headquarters."[10]

Neither staff officer's account mentions whether the guide sent was a contraband or a freedman. If the "Martin" in Hobson's diary entry indeed had the last name of Robinson, as a Southern postwar reminiscence holds, there is no contemporaneous evidence saying so.[11] Immediately after the raid, two Richmond newspapers identified Dahlgren's guide, one reporting that he was "a negro belonging to Mr. Weems, whom they had as a pilot," the other described him in a more extensive article two days later as "a boy named Martin, the property of Mr. David Meems of Goochland."[12] The writer of the latter account seems to have mistaken "Meems" to mean David Mimms, a slaveowning Goochlander of the era.[13] In the furor to go to print, "Meems" or "Mimms" easily could have been transmogrified by sloppy penmanship or typographical error into "Weems," a common Virginia name. The second report got the given name right but evidently misspelled the surname. Neither account mentions Martin absconding earlier with an escaped Yankee prisoner.

The guide seems to have been a freedman named Martin, but no proof from that time confirms his last name as Robinson, a claim that appears only in reminiscences by persons lacking firsthand knowledge of the man. One recollection, albeit based on secondhand information related by a raid participant, identifies him as Roberson. In 1898 Dr. William Pilcher interviewed a black man named Jones, formerly from Goochland County and then working at the Naval Gun Shop of the Washington Navy Yard. According to Jones, he joined Dahlgren's command as a cook, was with the column when it reached the ford at Dover Mills, and heard the colonel refer to his black guide as Roberson. Pilcher also interviewed L. C. Clark, a mercantile clerk from Manakin, who said that Roberson's wife, Baker, was a slave on the Morson plantation. This corroborates Anne Hobson's mention in her 1864 diary entry of Martin leading the raiders "to his own wife's house at Dover." Pilcher quotes Clark as saying that Congress voted Roberson's widow a pension, a claim unsubstantiated by a 1940 search of government pension files.[14] While speculative, Pilcher's chronicle calls into question the assumption held by some historians that Dahlgren's guide was named Martin Robinson. Like so many aspects of the raid, Martin's true identity will remain an enigma forever dangling from a noose.

After several hours near Dover Mills, Dahlgren decided to cross the James. Much damage had been done to the plantations of Seddon, Morson, and Hobson, including the destruction of barns, a steam plant, a large gristmill, canal boats, storehouses, and stocks of flour, meal, and grain. Remounting his command, the colonel led the men toward the river with his guide at his side, wearing about his neck a jaunty black silk scarf. Using Jude's Ferry was out of the question; the boat was on the far shore, probably tied there by Powhatan County residents who had spied smoke from the plantation fires. Martin said that they could cross at the nearby Dover Mills Ford, less than a mile to the west by the western end of Sabot Island, he "staked his life on it." The path leading to the crossing was directly in front of Seddon's hilltop mansion but in bottomland, flooded by the heavy rains of the day before. That Dahlgren did not expect this and dismiss Dover Mills is another conundrum, for clearly the river was in spate. A Confederate soldier stationed at Chaffin's Farm near Richmond confirmed the situation in a letter home: "I am told the James was never much higher than it was during the last tremendous freshet."[15]

Martin then piped up with another idea: cross at a point about three miles east. The column wheeled to the left and started down the canal towpath in search of another crossing, then moved up to the river road, pausing along the way for more handiwork: burning a mill and stable on William Stanard's farm, freeing slaves, and capturing Dr. William T. Walker, whom they soon released. The troopers also damaged the Manakin Iron Works and disabled a canal lock at Sampson's. Dahlgren now began to show frustration with his guide; no doubt his stump ached and his body was weary and wracked with pain. From frustration grew suspicion and ire. The colonel warned Martin that his failure to find a crossing was vexing him—and for good reason. Noon had passed and still the column had not yet crossed the James.[16]

At Manakin Ferry the swollen river again thwarted the Yankees. A trooper and his horse drowned, further inflaming their commander. Martin pleaded "piteously" with the colonel, promising to find a usable crossing downstream. He was sure there was a ford "nine miles above Richmond." Dahlgren briefly conferred with his officers and scouts, deciding collectively that it was best to hew the river road in hopes of finding the elusive crossing. A guard was assigned to the guide lest he think about absconding. The column moved on.[17]

The search continued past Tuckahoe plantation, first owned by Thomas Randolph. The main house dated to 1715 and was said to be the oldest frame residence along the James River. Thomas Jefferson began his schooling in a small building that was still standing on the property when the raiders arrived. Tuckahoe figures in another entertaining but unsubstantiated story. Plantation owner Virginia Allen heard that Dahlgren was coming with terror in mind. Wearing her finest dress, she strapped on a brace of pistols and rushed through the north door to confront the Yankees, standing fearlessly on the porch as the colonel, reining in his horse, recognized her as a fellow guest at grand balls they both had attended up North in happier times. "Instead of burning the house, Dahlgren came inside for tea while his men watered their horses," so the story goes.[18] Nothing but air supports this yarn, which has become a thread in the tapestry of legendary feminism, like Sallie Seddon's story, that emerged during the postwar era in the South.

After Tuckahoe the raiders, still on the river road, reached Powell's Tavern. The day by now had tilted into afternoon. Dahlgren, with Martin and his scouts, was riding with the advance guard. They heard cannon fire in the distance—Kilpatrick! It seemed that the attack on Richmond had begun, and Dahlgren had failed to achieve his main objective. The colonel decided to press on for the capital, abandoning any thought of crossing the James. He demanded his ever-more-nervous guide to get them as quickly as possible to Richmond.

As Dahlgren hectored Martin, the column approached a split in the road. Martin pointed to the left fork, and the column took it. But soon Dahlgren became suspicious. Meeting a crowd of male contrabands roaming at large, the colonel asked which way the road they were on led. To Ashland, one man told him—essentially, the Federals were riding north instead of east toward Richmond. The contraband added that their guide should have known better. An infuriated Dahlgren turned to Martin, who stammered that he had made a mistake, and accused him of betraying his trust and jeopardizing his men's lives. Major Cooke seconded these complaints, whereupon Martin admitted that he "had done wrong."

In Stevensburg Martin had bet his life on his guiding skills, hoping to be paid well if he could find a crossing but idly granting that if he could not, the Yankees could do their worst. An army scout who was present remembered years later the guide admitting that he had hoodwinked the raiders, that he had never been a slave but was a Rebel sympathizer who wanted Jeff Davis to succeed and to see Dahlgren's men killed or captured. A man in Dahlgren's command reinforced this view when he wrote home shortly after the raid, "the treacherous negro had intentionally misled us." A day after the raid was thwarted, a Richmond newspaper reported that the plan to release the Union prisoners had "miscarried by the treachery or ignorance of their negro guide." Not so, according to Dahlgren's signal officer, Lieutenant Reuben Bartley. He felt the guide "did not look like he intended to betray us or lead us into a trap, for he could have left us at any time." A Michigan officer concluded that the column's need to keep off the main roads, taking "by-roads and cow paths," confused the fellow. Camp talk after the raid was divided. "Some think the negro misled Dahlgren purposely. Others, that he made a mistake at first and then was frightened, he knew not what he did afterward, which is my opinion," a man in the 1st Maine told his diary. But Bartley's conclusion summed it up best when he said what Martin "did will always remain a mystery." From the moment he swung, however, one thing was certain, according to some horse soldiers, "no good would come of it."[19]

Dahlgren, with his reputation, career, and entire command at stake, decided that Martin's life was forfeit, as per the man's own terms. He told one scout, "Carney, have that niggar hung alongside of the road within 15 minutes." Soldiers bound Martin's hands with a carbine strap and, with Carney accompanying, led him on his horse back to the vicinity of Powell's Tavern, where they found a sturdy-limbed oak. The guide pleaded for mercy as Carney rummaged an ambulance for a length of rope. When he saw a lariat, Martin knew he would receive no mercy. The scout fashioned a noose and looped it around his neck, the men leading his horse to a spot beneath a stout limb. Carney threw the free end of the rope over the limb. Someone slapped Martin's horse, which bolted, and the unlucky guide was sent swinging. In desperation he managed to twist his hands free of the straining leather strap and clutch the rope around his neck, buying a few seconds of breath. But the troopers were relentless. They seized him and pulled his hands away from the noose. One untied the black silk kerchief from his neck and used it as a more efficient bind for his wrists. Once the white men had satisfied themselves that this time he would swing to his death, they let go of Martin and let gravity do its job. After ten minutes of groans and kicking, he went limp on the line. The rear of the column approached and with Union men riding by, Martin dangled there near Powell's Tavern.[20]

"As the column passed along some of the boys threw flour in [the guide's] face saying, 'There, you are a white man, no colored man ever betrayed us,'" a Michigan officer wrote. Another Wolverine officer riding in the rear ranks, moving along with his eyes to the ground, felt something "tapping me on the shoulder as I passed under a tree. Upon looking up I saw our false guide suspended, with a halter strap around his neck, to an overhanging limb. We then knew we were nine miles from Richmond, and that the second ford was also a myth."[21] Lore about the incident blossomed, some of it immediately.

Leaving Manakin Ferry, Captain Mitchell found that his ambulances could not negotiate the towpath. Between the ferry and Tuckahoe plantation, likely as the hanging was taking place, a messenger brought orders to rejoin Dahlgren. Mitchell returned to the river road, mystified to find hoof tracks clearly left by the main column and soon after coming upon an oak limb from which swung a dead black man whose corpse "was yet warm." Mitchell's troopers cut the body down, thinking the man a victim of local bushwhackers. A Confederate prisoner from the court-martial near Frederick's Hall who remained with the raiders later verified that these men cut down the dead guide and left his corpse in the river road. But another Southerner's account claimed that locals "allowed the coal-black corpse to hang there for a week as an object lesson to impress slaves of the vicinage with a new idea of Northern feeling toward the blacks." A veteran of Stuart's Horse Artillery claimed that the Yankees cut off Martin's head and "stuck it on a sharp fence stake, where I saw the ghastly sight several times afterwards when passing that way." There is a distance between folklore and history, and in this instance the distance between what people say happened to Martin Roberson, or "Robinson," and what truly befell him is the arc between these latter accounts and the record of Mitchell's actions on the river road.[22]

With Martin's body cut down and laying in the road, the captain's troopers remounted and trotted down the narrow road in search of their commander. They would not have to ride very far to find him.

CHAPTER 10

KILPATRICK ATTACKS RICHMOND

A t his headquarters General Meade awaited word from Judson Kilpatrick. The last courier from the field had reached the Army of the Potomac on the afternoon of February 29, Kilpatrick reporting that he was thirty miles outside Richmond. Meade hoped that they were working from good intelligence, that the Confederate capital had only a sprinkling of defenses. If so, the Pennsylvanian wrote in a personal letter, Kilpatrick would "have a chance of getting in and liberating all the prisoners, which is the great object of the movement." If he knew of more-sinister plans for the raid, this letter did not reveal it. At first uncomfortable with the operation, he seems to have come around. "God grant [Kilpatrick] may [succeed], for their sakes and his," Meade wrote.[1]

Having shattered the Virginia Central Railroad's headquarters at Beaver Dam Station, Kilpatrick's column ignored the nasty weather and advanced rapidly, with Davies's brigade still in the lead. They "rode all night," a Vermonter wrote in his diary. Not until around 2:00 A.M. did the raiders halt, at which point the hapless private William Pollard, who earlier had taken aboard his wagon the rogues who gobbled the general's personal victuals, again found himself in Dutch. Still driving Kilpatrick's headquarters wagon, he pulled up when the column halted and immediately fell asleep. When the men roused themselves and moved on, he did not. Finally waking to lonely darkness, Pollard whipped his mule team to a froth trying to catch up but only careened the whole shebang into a ditch. Unhurt, the private coaxed the mules up from the water to right the wagon and finally found the Federal column's rear guard.[2]

The night march saw Kilpatrick's entire command match Pollard for ill fortune. The weather disoriented the local black youth the Yankees had recruited as a guide, taking them off course. Kilpatrick had meant to cross the South Anna River at Ground Squirrel Bridge. Instead, the confused youth led the horse soldiers along the Ridge Road toward Ashland, much as the doomed Martin Roberson had misled Dahlgren's column. Kilpatrick pushed on cross-country, finally crossing the South Anna at Blunt's Bridge, about three miles northwest of Ashland, at 6:00 A.M. in drizzle and fog. Crossing the old dilapidated structure was no easy matter. The cavalrymen had to dismount and lead their horses over the trembling span in single file to keep it from collapsing. The tired horse soldiers never noticed that they were crossing under the watchful gaze of a Confederate home-guard unit, commanded by Captain Linnaeus B. Anderson. From the woods the hidden Southerners could see how much trouble the teamsters had getting their ammunition-laden ambulances over the rickety old bridge. The Yankees had to dump twenty-six boxes, perhaps a ton of cartridges, into the swollen South Anna. Once over Blunt's Bridge, the Northerners burned it. As soon as the raiders were gone, Anderson's men scrambled into the icy water, retrieving several hundred rounds for their Burnside carbines, then continued to shadow the Federals as far as Independence Meeting House west of Ashland.[3]

Other Confederate units, under General Hampton and Colonel Johnson, were reacting to the Yankee incursion. Hampton had his men moving all night from Milford Station toward Hanover Junction, while Johnson's troops were traipsing the Pamunkey River, destroying ferry connections. Neither effort paid off immediately, but both bore long-term dividends. Kilpatrick had no problem burning the Richmond, Fredericksburg, and Potomac Railroad depots at Ashland and at Kilby Station (present-day Elmont) while wrecking sheds, water towers, tracks, and culverts. Harassment on the north side of Ashland by Rebels from units of the 1st Maryland Line irked the raiders but did not slow their progress. Kilpatrick moved through Richmond's outer defensives like water through cheesecloth; he would soon not have so easy a time of it.[4]

Major William Hall's force, sent to destroy the railroad bridge over the South Anna River, was missing, though through the night Kilpatrick had heard firing from that direction. Captain John Brown's detachment had done all right, but Hall had faltered. By daylight on March 1, Confederates near the railroad bridge had opened up with artillery and advanced a line of skirmishers. Hall hesitated to attack an unfamiliar enemy position, retreating a bit, then giving up on the bridge. His men crossed the river at Beech Tree Ford, capturing and paroling several Rebel pickets. The major marched all day toward Richmond, hoping to find Kilpatrick, on his way firing a Virginia Central train of fifteen cars and blowing up the engine. Crossing a trestle bridge over the Chickahominy, he burned it afterward by rolling flaming lumps of pitch like bowling balls from hell onto the planks, which quickly spread the conflagration to structural elements. "The timbers burned splendidly," a Pennsylvania officer wrote. While the bridge was going up, some hungry Federals wandered off in search food; Confederate horsemen trailing the column scooped them up. Hall and his men took hours to find Kilpatrick's main body, linking up too late to influence the general's thinking about how to come at Richmond.[5]

After crossing the South Anna River at dawn, Kilpatrick's column paused to close ranks, resuming its movement in what an Ohio officer called "one of the most rapid marches on record." Kilpatrick wanted to be at Richmond's gates by 10:00 A.M., and he "was on time to the minute," according to a Michigan officer. Leaving Kilby Station in flames, the main column turned right and rode directly south on the Brook Turnpike. General Davies's regiments, again in the lead, easily passed an empty first line of works at the fortifications' intersection with the pike. From this high ground the Federals could look down the thoroughfare and count the spires on the churches in the city. "We are going into Richmond sure," an excited officer on Kilpatrick's staff exclaimed. By some means, an intelligence officer traveling with the raiders had been in Richmond a week earlier. This captain stated that no regular Confederate troops were in the city, the only obstacles to them being "the fortifications manned only by Government Clerks and book-keepers."[6]

The Federal force approaching the capital was not the same contingent that had left Stevensburg. Kilpatrick had led nearly 3,600 troopers toward Ely's Ford, but Dahlgren had taken 460 horsemen to Goochland and Hall had taken another 450 men to burn the railroad bridge near Taylorsville. Hall's contingent had not returned, still miles away. After accounting for casualties and stragglers dropping out of General Davies's and Colonel Edward Sawyer's brigades, Kilpatrick was probably leading no more than 2,600 men down the turnpike.[7]

The Federals met no resistance until they were about a mile from Richmond's intermediate lines. But Rebel couriers and riders from the countryside north of the city had been sounding alarms, galvanizing the capital into a city "full of rumors" and scrambling to defend itself. "Kilpatrick's route and the progress made on it were well known . . . so that when he arrived . . . quite a number of people were there to welcome him," a Confederate officer drolly said. Davies, always in front, saw "a second line [of fortifications] which was found to be fully manned and supplied with artillery which at once opened a heavy fire upon the head of the column." A Pennsylvania trooper agreed with the general's assessment, observing both soldiers and citizens running to take positions in the defenses.[8]

One man rushing to the barricades was Colonel Walter H. Stevens. The commander of the Richmond Defenses meant to stand tough. A native New Yorker, the thirty-six-year-old West Point engineer had wed a Louisiana belle before the war; love and rearranged loyalty cemented his allegiance to the Confederacy. After serving with Generals P. G. T. Beauregard and Joseph Johnston early in the war, Stevens gained command of Richmond's fortifications, which he enlarged and strengthened. The colonel claimed to have five hundred men in the Confederate works prior to Kilpatrick's arrival. Until reinforcements arrived, he would thwart the Yankees with skirmishers and field artillery. About 10:30 A.M., after inspecting his works, Stevens ordered Captain J. Henry Rives's 2nd Nelson Light Artillery to deploy where the Brook Turnpike intersected the intermediate lines. Captain James D. Hankins's Surry Light Artillery, supported by heavy artillerymen serving as infantry, ran up its guns to where the lines intersected the Mordecai Mill Road. After placing pickets from Lieutenant Colonel James Howard's Second Division out beyond the fortifications, Stevens galloped downtown to General Elzey's headquarters for more orders. The first Yankee wave drove back the pickets. Howard then ordered two of Rives's guns to open fire, sending "shot and shell down [the road] like a ten pin alley." Rives held his position, supported by Captain Charles S. Harrison's Company D, 10th Battalion of Virginia Heavy Artillery, until casualties forced the battery to retire. Around noon the rest of the Confederate artillery opened on Kilpatrick's forces.[9]

In a little-reported step before the raiders appeared, the Confederates had tightened security at Libby Prison. Ever since Wistar's incursion, officials had worried about the possibility of 13,000 Northerners running wild in their capital. A Richmond editor claimed that residents "slept each night on the crust of a volcano." In response, guards pulled down the building's stairs, watches were increased, and prisoners came under more general scrutiny. One diarist, a government official, wrote that General Winder "ordered that a large amount of powder be placed under [Libby Prison] with instructions to blow it up if the attempt [to free the prisoners] were made." Secretary of War Seddon initially vetoed the measure, but eventually several hundred pounds of black powder were placed at the prison. A POW who said he saw powder kegs being unloaded at Libby's canal dock later recalled speaking with the warden, Major Thomas Turner, who claimed that if the inmates made a peep they "would all be blown to hell." Another Union officer remembered Turner's words more sarcastically when the warden told the prisoners that if the Yankee cavalry assaulted Richmond, the "prisoners [would] go out by way of the roof" to freedom. Confirming the mining of Libby, a March 1864 parolee said he had heard Rebel officers condemned the step as "a most unheard of barbarism."[10]

Back on the Brook Turnpike, according to the plan, once under fire Davies was to dismount half his command on the Union left and "make a brisk attack upon the works in that direction while the rest of the Brigade under cover of the artillery and supported by the Second Brigade would charge down the road." But when Rives opened up with his cannon, Kilpatrick ordered his senior brigadier to first throw out a skirmish line from the 5th New York. Company H, under 1st Lieutenant Elmer Barker, deployed to the right of the road—until the raiders ran into a post-and-rail fence too high to climb easily. Spying a break in the fence line, Barker and his New Yorkers were about to make a run for it when the twenty-one-year-old officer persuaded a scout clad in civilian clothes to ride along the fence waving a white handkerchief. This so startled the Southern artillerymen at the works that the bluecoats were able to squeeze through the gap and deploy in the open field beyond. The Union advance seemed to be regaining momentum but then stalled. Barker sent word to Davies that he thought he could carry the works in his front if permitted. The general ordered the New Yorkers to hold until dark, which they did, awaiting further orders that never came. "Several hours were spent reconnoitering the enemy's works," but no attack was ordered, recalled one army scout.[11]

Davies decided after a firsthand look that "it was impracticable from the nature of the ground to maneuver cavalry on either side of the road except as skirmishers, the fields being very soft and muddy, and intersected with wide and deep ditches." The thousand yards in front of the Confederate works were "open and perfectly level." Mounted men could only be used on the road, "which was wide enough to admit of movement by platoon fronts." The enemy's

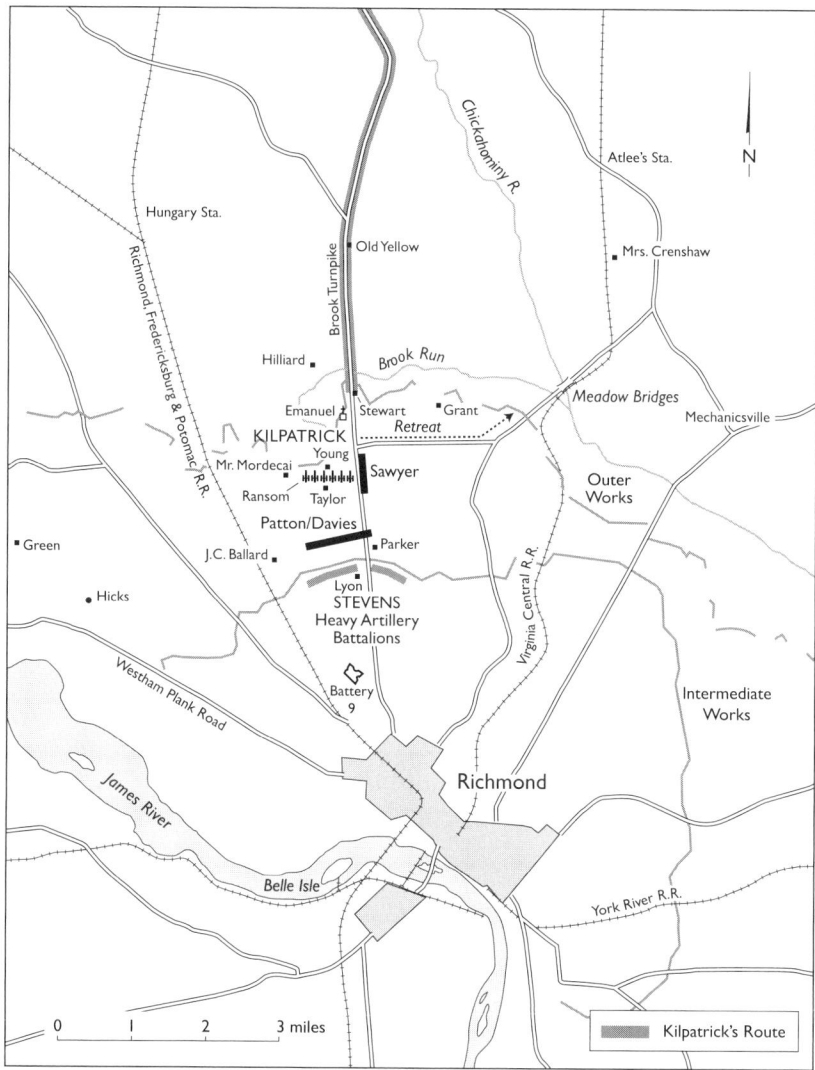

Kilpatrick Attacks Richmond. Map by Bill Nelson. *Copyright © 2016 by the University of Oklahoma Press.*

lines were "fully manned and supplied with artillery which at once opened a heavy fire" upon his men.[12]

Behind Richmond's intermediate works were troops from the 10th, 18th, 19th, and 20th Battalions of Virginia Heavy Artillery. Once the South started conscription, such units filled quickly with men enlisting because they wanted to have a say in their service and thought the heavy artillery less hazardous. Mortality rates bore this out, and gunners often got to barrack in permanent quarters near home. Though drilled initially on large-bore cannon, as the war ground on heavy artillerymen often found themselves armed with muskets and retrained as infantrymen. Most of the artillerists now in Richmond were carrying muskets but were not, as some have written, only old men and young boys. The 10th Battalion's oldest man was 62 and the youngest boy 13, and the unit's median age was 28. The same was basically true of the 18th Battalion, whose grayest beard was on a 63-year-old; its youngest artillerist was age 15. Again, however, the median age in the 18th Battalion reflected a similar statistic of 28 years of age, with the average age being 29.8 years. Two men in the 20th Battalion were 58 years old in contrast to its 15-year-old youngest member; the unit's median age was 26 years, with the average age in the battalion being 28 years. By the time of the raid, many older men in the 19th Battalion had been discharged, but 10-year-old Millard Fillmore Morris was in uniform and on hand. The 19th Battalion had the lowest median age of the four units at 25 years. Clearly, while Dahlgren may have faced units partially composed of old men and young boys on March 1, Kilpatrick, according to these statistics, did not.[13]

To support Davies's dismounted cavalry, Kilpatrick ordered Battery C, 3rd U.S. Artillery, to unlimber at about 1:00 P.M. Two guns were set up in the road, but that location quickly became too hot. The entire battery then moved to the west side of the turnpike onto a plowed field in front of the residence of John B. Young, Henrico County's commonwealth's attorney. "Soon our spunky little batteries were playing into them heavily," a Pennsylvania diarist wrote. Two Yankee shells landed in the front yard of prominent Richmonder James Lyons, who lived about a quarter mile behind the Confederates' intermediate works. Southern gunners returned this fire "with terrible precision" and brought more guns to bear. "The enemy soon appeared in heavy numbers, and showed a large amount of artillery, shoving out 30 or 40 pieces," a Michigan trooper observed. As a tonic for his men, Kilpatrick had his division band play "Yankee Doodle" and other patriotic airs. But as Battery C pounded away at the Confederate line and music skirted above the smoke, the general and his senior officers, according to a Southern account, inexplicably ate a sumptuous dinner prepared by Mrs. Young; some insolent Yankees even helped themselves to the

Youngs' wine cellar. The men responded to the band with enthusiasm as "cheer after cheer rent the air as each successive shell sped on its way." Implicit in the racket of Kilpatrick's counterbattery fire was an invitation, albeit one issued in vain, for Dahlgren and Ben Butler to join his attack on the city.[14]

With the Union guns engaged, Davies developed his plan of attack on the east side of the pike. The 5th New York maintained its skirmish line within 250 yards of the enemy's works. Davies ordered Major William Patton of the 3rd Indiana to prepare five hundred men for an assault on foot. Kilpatrick in a special order had reinforced Patton's command with seventy-five men from the 1st Maine commanded by twenty-one-year-old Lieutenant John A. Heald, "a born leader" with an "iron strength, indomitable good-nature, and [who was] fearless to the last degree." Along with Heald was a newly commissioned lieutenant named Phineas Foster, Jr. This was Foster's first fight, and he was at the front "saying 'Come on boys' while the other officers could be heard saying 'Go ahead boys.'" The 18th Pennsylvania remained mounted on the pike with sabers drawn, ready to charge once Patton's men secured the Rebel battery in their front. But the Federal attack stalled when a "considerable force opened upon [Patton's men] with musketry."[15]

At the same time, some fifty Union carbineers, sheltered by woods and outbuildings, crept toward the house of John A. Parker, a Richmond lawyer. From this position they could concentrate fire more effectively on the entrenched Confederates. Peering over a wall, Major Mark B. Hardin, commander of the 18th Battalion of Virginia Heavy Artillery, was immediately struck by a bullet, though not seriously wounded. Colonel Stevens, now back at the intermediate lines, ordered Howard and Lieutenant Colonel John Atkinson to clean out the Yankee sharpshooters near Parker's house.[16]

William Chaplain, a young lieutenant from Company B, 20th Battalion of Virginia Heavy Artillery, volunteered for the mission. A Norfolk man, he had been court-martialed the year before and may have had something to prove. He and twenty men advanced at the double quick across an open field, supported by men from Harrison's Company D, 10th Battalion. Securing the house, the Confederates found five women, one near seventy years old, huddled in the parlor. Ushering them to the basement as carbine rounds whizzed through the windows, Chaplain next attacked the New York marksmen. Howard, fearing that Chaplain was outnumbered, quickly ordered forward twenty-seven-year-old Captain Winfield S. Griffin with a detachment from the 18th Battalion of Virginia Heavy Artillery. After a Yankee round killed Private Zebulon M. Williams of the 18th Battalion, the New Yorkers made a hasty retreat from the Parker property. When the firing slackened, the women came out of the cellar and were escorted to the Confederate works unharmed. Company B counted six casualties, while Griffin's reinforcements suffered six men wounded in addition to Williams's death.[17]

Major Patton, meanwhile, was developing his attack between the Brook Turnpike and the Mordecai Mill Road. The Indianan and his men spent about two hours fighting for the intermediate works, though at a distance of 250 yards. The taciturn fellows of the 1st Maine agreed that it was the "warmest place they had ever been" as "bullets flew like hail stones." But casualties were light. As the Federals inched closer, some "seven or eight hundred" enemy artillerists wielding muskets generally overshot their intended targets. To mock their lack of marksmanship, Captain Estes, Kilpatrick's ever-faithful assistant adjutant general, rode along the Union line in clear view of the enemy, the red lining of his uniform cape flung out with an air of toreadoran bravado. Estes's "courage was proverbial among the cavalrymen of the Third division," according to one officer. But Rives's guns forced a large contingent of Yankees massed between the turnpike and the road to scatter into a thick woods east of the pike. The Confederates inflicted scant damage, but the troopers never advanced closer than 200 yards after nearly two hours of fighting, though perhaps for good reason since now they were taking casualties. "Our Regt. was dismounted in front of Richmond and charged the Reb batteries and rifle pits, but they were too strongly guarded and our men had to fall back," an Indiana trooper not on the raid but informed by his mates later of what happened wrote home.[18]

Sawyer's Second Brigade, having passed the outer works at about 11:00 A.M., remained on the turnpike near Brook Hill in a column of fours, the men sitting on their horses behind the front line awaiting orders to advance. Their instructions were to charge into Richmond and free all the prisoners they could find, an aide to Sawyer said later. The colonel's men started at a trot toward the Confederate lines when orders came to halt. Perhaps Kilpatrick was hoping to hear from either Dahlgren or his carbines as he joined the fight, but neither messages or the sound of combat came from that side of the city. Sawyer never received an order to join the attack. "It was indeed a trying time to sit there on our horses so long expecting every minute to hear the signal for us to charge and see the works less than a mile away swarming with Johnnies ready to receive us," a Pennsylvanian attached to the brigade told his diary. It was an uneasy time for the men in the ranks. "There was less joking among the boys than I ever knew in the same length of time," the cavalryman observed.[19]

Rebel artillery and small-arms firing "was furious for about four hours—the shells bursting in every direction," according to one Southerner. Jefferson Davis was put in "a bad humor" when he heard the sound of the Yankees' guns coming through his office window. He joined other Confederate brass riding out to observe the fighting, including General Braxton Bragg, Davis's military advisor, General Elzey, and General Fitzhugh Lee. They may not have seen much, the disputed area and its vicinity blanketed by artillery smoke.

As four o'clock neared, Kilpatrick decided to break off his attack. He had a host of matters to consider in making this decision. He had no idea where Dahlgren was or what the one-legged colonel was doing. Butler had failed to come up the Peninsula with a diversionary attack or second front. Moreover, Hall's 450 men were still missing. Finally, "lightly defended" Richmond was putting up a much stiffer and bigger fight than expected in terms of manpower and bulldog determination. All these factors combined to put Kilpatrick into "a moody silence" that matched the grim drizzle soaking the scene, according to one Michigander.[20] Train whistles south of the city signaled impending reinforcements, or at least triggered the fear of them. Bells too were ringing across the city. In the chaos, a Union staff officer remembered, the general entered a "period of hesitancy. . . . The enemy in the meantime had developed quite a strong force . . . , and we could see that the inner works were filled with men and every preparation made to receive us." This was the critical moment—rather than seize it, Judson Kilpatrick withdrew, perhaps for the first time choosing caution over daring. The order to retreat shocked his men. "Kilpatric [sic] never lets an opportunity to fight pass unimproved," a cavalryman wrote. "If they get in and Kilpatrick doesn't have a fight it will be a mystery." But Little Kil was not going to rampage through Richmond, and this demoralized his men. His decision to withdraw

put a "damper on the men," who felt "from that moment good fortune [had] left" them. Nevertheless, with a cold, drizzly rain starting to fall and no sign of Dahlgren or Butler, Kilpatrick "deemed it
prudent to retire."[21]

Some historians blame Kilpatrick for losing his nerve, even displaying rank cowardice. But their conclusions do not stand up when
most accounts of his decision making are considered.[22] In a postwar
memoir a Wolverine officer said, "Kilpatrick who, at the start, was
bold and confident, at the last when quick resolution was indispensable, appeared to be overcome with a strange and fatal irresolution."
This officer, who took up journalism after the war, drew a needling
conclusion when he wrote, "A courage to execute commensurate
to the ability to conceive was presupposed." An Ohio captain who
served with the general's escort detail wrote, "it is still believed by
many who were with [Kilpatrick] that he might have been successful, if he had not lost heart and faith in the enterprise." A Federal
intelligence officer, Captain John McEntee, who accompanied the
raiders was more disgusted with the cavalry's performance. "My
observation of the whole affair shows me that it is not the object of
a cavalry raid to do any more fighting than is absolutely necessary,"
he reported. The captain went on to opine that as he "was with Gen.
Kilpatrick I do not wish to detract any from his credit, but I hardly
think we will ever be able to take Richmond without some fighting." He concluded that the general's failure to hear from his separated commands weighed heavily in his decision to withdraw from
in front of Richmond.[23]

But there are other ways to view Kilpatrick's decision to retreat.
Davies, the senior brigade commander, said that Patton's advancing
dismounted cavalrymen found the enemy "in considerable force"
in Richmond's defensive works. Once his men were deployed, the
major himself returned and told Davies that "the enemy had exhibited a considerable force of infantry when he began his attack." The
subordinate could not say with assurance what was in his front. The
Confederate heavy-artillerymen-turned-infantry were sturdy young
men whose commanders expected them to hold their works against
the raiders, and regular Confederate regiments seem to have joined
the effort during the day.

A Washington newspaper reported soon after the raid that "the
works were defended by a whole brigade of infantry which had been
stationed at Bottoms Bridge to prevent an advance of General Butler

on the rebel capital by that road, but on hearing of General Kilpat-rick's movements, it was moved back to a position where the Union forces found them." Civil War reporting was not notorious for accuracy, but this article is substantiated by reliable sources. As the raid uncoiled, Brigadier General Eppa Hunton's brigade was in the vicinity of Richmond's defenses, encamped near Chaffin's Bluff. Hunton's men were battle-hardened veterans of the Army of Northern Virginia whose experience included Pickett's Charge at Gettysburg, during which the general was wounded. Later Hutton remembered being ordered to help defend Richmond from the raiders. Randall Taylor, a private in the 19th Virginia Infantry, a regiment in Hunton's Brigade, was killed during the action. A Richmond newspaper had the 28th Virginia Infantry, another regiment of Hunton's Brigade, marching to reinforce the Local Defense Troops against Dahlgren's tardy attack but arriving too late to see any fighting. In addition, at the end of February, Brigadier General Seth Barton's brigade of Virginians was camped within five miles of Richmond. At least one company of its 14th Virginia Infantry manned "the works around Richmond to repel the Yankee raiders." Captain E. A. Williams of that regiment was wounded. Other regular companies remained in line of battle in or near the city. Major General George E. Pickett, commanding at Petersburg, specifically ordered Colonel Hector McKethan's 51st North Carolina Infantry of Brigadier General Thomas L. Clingman's brigade to proceed north because "the enemy had approached near Richmond in heavy force." Most likely the train whistles heard signaled the arrival of the North Carolinians. The sight of mounted Yankees would not be enough to persuade veterans such as these to abandon an entrenched position. Kilpatrick was sure that Dahlgren had failed to cross the James, and without him continuing the attack was pointless. "An attempt to enter the city at that point would but end in a bloody failure," he wrote later. "I reluctantly withdrew my command at dark."[24]

Previous studies of the raid are shot through with the fiction that Kilpatrick faced vastly inferior numbers. But what strength could the Southerners muster the day of his attack? Confederate trimonthly returns for the Department of Richmond indicate troop levels on February 10, less than three weeks before the raid, at an "effective total of 5,160 men." This figure included Hunton's Brigade of 1,135 assigned to the department. It also includes 1,589 men listed as the "Richmond Defenses," reflecting the combined strength of the 10th,

18th, 19th, and 20th Battalions of Virginia Heavy Artillery, the units that fought Kilpatrick for several hours. Records dated March 31 show an "effective total" of 7,500 men at Richmond but do not include the Department of Henrico, under Brigadier General John H. Winder, which reported 1,593 effectives on March 10, exclusive of military prison guards. Clearly, more soldiers were available for defending the intermediate lines than the 500 men estimated in Colonel Stevens's report, though he probably was referring to the number of combatants in the lines before or at the beginning of Kilpatrick's attack. It is logical to conclude that as the day passed, many more Southerners reinforced Stevens's position.[25]

Many of the troopers with Kilpatrick during the attack on Richmond believed that the Confederate defenders were more powerful and numerous than expected. One man in the 5th Michigan wrote home shortly after the raid that he knew by 3:00 P.M. that the "rebels were too strong for us [and] we retreated." In a March 1 diary entry, a comrade in the 7th Michigan made a similar observation. A week after the raid, a trooper in the same regiment let the folks back home know that "General Kilpatrick soon discovered that it would be worse than useless, in fact a wholesale slaughter to attempt to charge into the city and with commendable prudence" ordered his men to fall back. Another Wolverine claimed to overhear the general say to Davies, "they have too many guns for me," whereupon a "moody silence" overcame Kilpatrick. A fellow Michigander felt that a desperate effort had been made to capture Richmond, but after hours of fighting and with reinforcements coming up from Petersburg, it seemed like a good idea to retire.

The general had made a similar assessment of the situation. According to one regimental historian, Kilpatrick approached Lieutenant Colonel Allyn C. Litchfield of the 7th Michigan and declared, "they have too many of those d—d guns; they keep opening new ones on us all the time." His observation is supported by a letter written shortly after the raid by a Union intelligence officer who reported that the general found "a large force with too many guns and too strong a position for him to attack." Indeed, the Confederates were using more than field artillery, for a siege gun from Battery No. 9 was belching out solid shot against the Yankees. A Wolverine trooper agreed that the Rebels were "calling out the heaviest ordinance in response" to the Federals' "pepper box batteries." Another chronicler felt that since "Butler had not moved up the Peninsula to attack the city on the east, as was the program, and the civilians opened such a hot fire as to give rise to a suspicion that the defense was full of infantry," the general's decision had some merit. In addition, Captain McEntee reported immediately after the raid: "The main difficulty with Kilpatrick was that the force which he had sent to the R. R. bridge over the South Anna [Major Hall's detachment] had not returned nor had he heard any thing from them neither had he heard a word from Dahlgren who had been instructed to communicate with him a 10 A.M. on Tuesday." "Kilpatrick reluctantly withdrew," as one man saw it. A staff officer in Colonel Sawyer's brigade who later examined the Richmond defenses came to the unequivocal conclusion that "Kilpatrick was wise in recalling the charge. We never could have made it without very heavy loss and maybe not then; his second thought was the best."[26]

Meanwhile, Bradley Johnson had captured Federal couriers who revealed that Kilpatrick was in front of Richmond. Though the colonel had only three score saber-wielding riders from the 1st Maryland Cavalry, he brought his men to Kilpatrick's rear and boldly attacked a picket post held by the 18th Pennsylvania. Johnson's surprise attack worked. No sooner did the Marylanders hit than the Yankee general realized that he was fighting on two fronts, perhaps in danger of being cut off at the rear. Johnson was far too understrength to accomplish that, but his aggressive sortie had an effect far beyond the moment. With Rebel forces surrounding him as far as he knew, Kilpatrick "concluded that it was useless to further attempt entering the rebel stronghold."[27]

The simplest explanation for calling off the attack may be that, in addition to fearing for his men's lives, Kilpatrick was a physically sick man and suddenly was getting much sicker. To this point Little Kil, while showing signs of illness, "had resolutely and skillfully carried out the plan. . . . But now he was 'not in it.' He did not seem himself," according to an army scout. "I know he was feeling unwell before starting on the journey, and complained during the trip. I have always thought his illness the cause of the feeble effort made to enter Richmond," the scout reflected.[28] Whatever the reasons, Kilpatrick made a critical decision to break off the attack on Richmond and start a retreat.

For the suffering POWs in Libby Prison and on Belle Isle, Kilpatrick's decision was a great disappointment. The miserable prisoners spent that March day in fearful suspense. What would be their fate—freedom, indefinite imprisonment, or sudden death by exploding gunpowder? One captive Yankee poetically remembered: "This subject was gold in the morning, silver at noon, nickel by 3 o'clock, and common every day mud, at sunset."[29]

At Kilpatrick's order, the retreat began around 4:00 P.M. Not all the troopers wanted to call it a day. "We went in sight of the City, threw a few shells, skirmished a little and then vamoosed," a Michigan cavalryman wrote. At Richmond's northeastern edge, with the weak late-winter light fading, General Davies, Kilpatrick's trusted subordinate, covered the withdrawal from Richmond. His commander led the demoralized column over the swampy Chickahominy River at the Meadow Bridges, guided by an impressed white Virginian named Algerine Storrs. From batteries nearby Confederate gunners unleashed a surprising but ineffective barrage that had his captors charging Storrs with treachery and threatening to string him up. The Yankees might have been withdrawing, but they still knew how to exact a price from the enemy, sweeping up slaves, horses, mules, carriages, bacon, corn, a gold watch, the mite of a widow named Watson, and pretty much whatever they pleased as they exited the environs of Richmond. To thwart any pursuit, they destroyed both the Virginia Central Railroad and the causeway bridges over the Chickahominy, sparing "neither torpedoes nor turpentine." In the rush to cross the river before these structures went up, some riders splashed into the water, getting several horses mired in the belly-deep mud to be left behind or shot where they wallowed as their riders waded across as best they could. Besides the wear and tear on his ego, Kilpatrick's bleak day at Richmond had cost him sixty men killed and wounded.[30]

During the withdrawal, Major Hall and his men finally arrived, falling in with Davies's rear guard. Both officers and troopers were spent, but Hall might have been worse off from riding all day in frozen clothing, with "feet and hands numb as steak," trying to rejoin the main force. Once Kilpatrick got his horsemen across the Chickahominy, he stopped them for the night near Eliza Crenshaw's farm, about a mile from the bridges and at a discreet distance along the road running between Atlee's Station and Mechanicsville, two miles to the south.[31]

Even with the burned bridges between the Union force and its foes, the raiders enjoyed no respite. "After dark a severe storm of sleet and rain came in which lasted through the night," Davies remembered. "It was raining and freezing so our clothing was ice," an officer in the 5th New York wrote. "Take off our overcoats and they would stand alone." The New Yorker went on to describe how the "roads were a puddle of mud. The night was dark as pitch." Fires were impossible, which meant no coffee for men at the far side of exhaustion. "We were all very sleepy and tired having had no sleep nor rest since we left Stevensburg," a Vermonter told his diary. There was "not a tent in the command" to provide shelter, but that did not stop some weary riders from stretching out on the sodden ground, bridle reins around their wrists, and sleeping. Some more-fortunate troopers were able to start fires and brew coffee. Others balanced on fence rails to keep themselves out of the mud, "wet as drowned rats," as they tried to catch what sleep they could. A few had rubber blankets, a minimal layer of protection against storm and slop. Some officers had the foresight to order only the saddle girths loosened, not the saddles removed with the men slipping their arms through their bridle reins.[32]

Kilpatrick was not thinking about weather, muddy roads, hot coffee, or even a defensive perimeter for his camp, not even posting "a regular picket line, only [guarding] the roads with some picket reserves." He was focusing on how to regain the ground he had lost. Physically, he may not have been feeling any better, but psychologically he was still in the game. Between 9:00 and 10:00 P.M., the general decided to make another run at Richmond. Extrapolating from information scouts and spies provided, he concluded that most of the capital's Confederate troops were concentrated north and west of the city, thus leaving the Mechanicville Road to Richmond barely covered—two picket posts with reserve troops. He drew up a plan calling for Lieutenant Colonel Addison Preston (1st Vermont) and Major Constantine Taylor (1st Maine) to take separate "dismounted" detachments of 500 men each and renew the assault. Each officer had his own objectives: "one was to liberate prisoners confined to Libby, and the other was to *secure* Jeff Davis" (italics added). Kilpatrick, with the remainder of his force and the artillery battery, would hold the area around the burning Meadow Bridges, waiting to cover the escape of the prisoners and the return of Preston's and Taylor's men. He did not say how a horde of weakened POWs were to get across the swollen, wintry river without access to bridges.

However cracked this proposition may have been, Kilpatrick had chosen two solid officers to make it work. The twenty-seven-year-old

Taylor was a veteran of the old army, having served in the 5th U.S. Cavalry before joining the 1st Maine, and Preston had earned plaudits throughout his regiment. "The name of Preston was guarantee that the dash, if made at all, would be bravely led," a Michigan Brigade officer later wrote. "There was no more gallant officer in the whole cavalry corps." A Vermonter remembered Preston as "an officer who makes everything *stir*, and in the right way" [italics in original]. Another Green Mountain cavalryman proclaimed that Preston "is undoubtedly the best fighting Colonel in this Brigade and is everywhere very popular."[33]

Before the units could move out at 2:00 A.M., however, actions elsewhere further eroded Kilpatrick's venture. Near Atlee's Station on the Virginia Central Railroad, Lieutenant Colonel Litchfield had orders to make fires, allow coffee for the men of his 7th Michigan, and establish a ten-man picket post south of the depot. He did as instructed, and not a few of his men seized the opportunity to get their first dismounted sleep in sixty hours. By 9:00 P.M. they were fast asleep, while the regimental commander paced back and forth, dressed in a fine overcoat collared and cuffed in astrakhan fur. Then all hell broke loose.

Whatever precautions the twenty-eight-year-old Massachusetts native took to protect his camp, it did not deter a bold Wade Hampton from launching a surprise attack against the Wolverine pickets about 9:00 P.M. from the direction of Hughes's Crossroads. The South Carolinian and his staff set up headquarters in the Atlee's ticket office, where plans were finalized for the strike. His men approached the Michiganders' line in "pitchy darkness" without making a sound. Two of his Iron Scouts walked point to take down any Union pickets, doing so without firing a shot. Hampton then ordered "the most difficult duty of soldiers—a night attack." The general sent one squadron under Captain J. C. Blair, Companies C and F, 1st North Carolina, into the fight dismounted as skirmishers. The Carolinians came within fifty yards of the Union campfires. "It was dark as an Egyptian night" when the Confederates attacked. A piece from Hart's two-gun section barked as the remainder of Colonel William Cheek's 1st North Carolina attacked with about 120 men, swarming the Federals on foot, while the remainder of Hampton's cavalry stayed mounted in the rear. Raining carbine fire on the sleepy raiders, screaming Carolinians ran headlong for the Union campfires. With Litchfield's hastily organized skirmish line

silhouetted by their own fires, the troopers made fatally easy targets. The sloppy ground kept Lieutenant Edwin Halsey, commanding Hampton's artillery, from using both of his guns, but he fired
the one piece so rapidly that the Federals thought they were in the
sights of several batteries. Halsey's shelling badly punished the raiders' horses. Hitched to trees, they could not run, and several were
wounded while others were captured. The special terror of being the
target of a night attack was the subject of a Michigan man's letter
home a few days later: "It was dark as a stack of black cats, and we
could only see the blaze of their cannon, while the grape and canister and shell came in from all sides. We were almost scared to death,
we were so sleepy, but we had to get out of it horse or no horse, just
as soon as we could." Hampton had achieved a textbook surprise.[34]

Litchfield, described as "gallant and impetuous" by a fellow
officer and with a "keen intellect" by another, had to improvise.
He sent Captain Robert Sproul's company out across both sides of
the road leading from Atlee's Station. To protect Sproul's flank, he
placed twenty men under Lieutenant Hiram Ingersoll in a field,
meanwhile sending Sergeant Major Lucius Carver to find his acting brigade commander, Colonel Sawyer, and deliver a note advis-
ing that he could not hold much longer and asking for orders. Carver
found Sawyer in a blacksmith shop south of Litchfield's position.

Litchfield was asking the wrong man in the wrong place at the
wrong time. Sawyer, a Republican lawyer with political connections
and Machiavellian instincts, had garnered his position in the 1st
Vermont, even gaining rank over more experienced and deserving
officers, not by valor, but by conniving. His gamesmanship had pro-
voked "extreme emotions" within the regiment. In 1863 Sawyer was
investigated for embezzlement and "entertaining lewd women in his
camp" by Captain Wesley Merritt, later a noteworthy major general.
He dodged a court-martial then, but Merritt's findings suggested that
the regiment deserved better in its commanding officer. Sawyer did
not redeem his reputation in battle. After the second battle at Brandy
Station, in October 1863, a Vermont cavalryman wrote, "I saw the
Colonel with his face towards Vermont when we went into that last
charge." His men, who knew Sawyer for what he was, did not have
to change their opinions after the fight with Hampton.[35]

Not getting immediate help from Sawyer, Litchfield decided to
string out a dismounted skirmish line around his entire regiment as
snow began to fall. In the darkness Hampton, whose cannon were

only 150 yards away from the Wolverines, threw shells as Cheek's attacking troopers uncorked the fearsome Rebel yell, a blood-curdling sound one Union officer described as "a mixture of Panther, Wolf, dog, Peacock and Screech owl." One North Carolina captain later recalled, "what we lacked in numbers [had to] be compensated for in noise and rattle." All the Wolverines had to do was aim their Spencers at the flashes of artillery rounds being sent their way. But Confederate bravado, effective small-arms fire, and fourteen rounds from Halsey's gun forced Ingersoll's men to give way, exposing Sproul's flank.[36] During the melee, 1st Lieutenant John Q. Sessions sent Corporal Andrew Pray and four other men across the Atlee Road to hold the regiment's left. Hearing firing toward their rear, the corporal ordered his men to head back to the main camp around the Crenshaw house. After discovering that the Rebels had captured their horses, Pray and his comrades surrendered, though the corporal made a break for it. As he ran down a hill, with Carolinians firing over his head, Pray fell into a pond, then ran smack into a tangle of grapevines, but made it to the Federals' rear guard, mounted a spare horse, and finally returned to his regiment with only his shell jacket, boots, and trousers.[37]

With Ingersoll's line gone, Captain Sproul exhorted his men to "lick the h—l out the blank, blank Rebels." But they had to withdraw as Rebel carbine fire on the 7th Michigan's flank increased. As one man recalled, "The fight was severe, and no other coming to our help, we were obliged to fall back." Horseless, his revolver cylinder empty, Litchfield tried to escape the melee on foot but unexpectedly ran into half a dozen Rebels. He quickly retreated back to Crenshaw's, his makeshift headquarters. There, in his "best Southern tone," Litchfield tried to bluff his way out of his predicament. The six-foot officer, dressed too well in his fur-trimmed overcoat to be a Rebel, drew the gaze of three Tar Heels, who grabbed the colonel as a prisoner. Lieutenant Samuel B. Carll was less lucky. Surrounded, shot through the lungs, and left lying in his rain-soaked uniform all night after his unit fled, Carll was found the next day by Confederate soldiers. The Southerners took him to a house to get him out of the elements but could not get him medical treatment for ten days. The forty-six-year-old officer recovered, though exposure cost him an eye. Litchfield, for his part, landed in Libby Prison with Carll, Ingersoll, and Captain John A. Clarke, incarcerated with black soldiers as punishment for being raiders. Forty-five other men of the 7th Michigan also were captured in the fight.[38]

Only now did Sawyer finally decide to support the 7th Michigan's fight with Hampton. As a Confederate shell smashed through the shake roof of his headquarters at the blacksmith shop "with an awful crash," the colonel ordered 2nd Lieutenant Billy North, twenty-one, of Company K, 5th Michigan, to support the imperiled 7th Michigan's line. North's reinforcements had scarcely advanced before Litchfield's men appeared, "coming helter-skelter down the road in a panic and . . . [running] completely over and through [them], scattering the company so that it did not get together again until the morning." After this Sawyer sent the remainder of Lieutenant Colonel Ebenezer Gould's 5th Michigan to help North, but it was too late. The thirty-minute fight with Hampton had devolved into a rout. The regiment was "retreating on the run the rebs yelling halt you Yankee sons of bitches," a private in the 7th Michigan wrote home, "but I had no particular desire to make their acquaintance."

As Sawyer's units fled to the rear, weary troopers wrapped in rubber blankets popped awake, scarcely knowing where they were. "Men began running to all points of the compass and became completely lost," a veteran recalled. Lieutenant Colonel Preston managed to form up his Vermonters. They fired eight to ten rounds from their Spencers on foot before Preston ordered them to mount up and fall back. Major James Kidd was also able to mount his 6th Michigan troopers without loss. His fortuitous orders to only loosen girths and not unsaddle saved his unit; sleeping with reins in their hands, the men had only to tighten girths and mount up. But another Wolverine, serving on Sawyer's staff, saw less preparation when he described the withdrawal as a "great confusion in our ranks and very little order." Major Kidd said later that Sawyer had left them to fight on their "own hook." Troopers who tried to put up a dismounted fight lost their horses to the Confederates. On this part of Kilpatrick's line, demoralization was "wonderfully and fearfully" rampant. Hampton's surprise attack "was perfect and the result damaging to the raiders."[39]

A few raiders escaped the confusion. "We were mounted and formed in line with as little excitement as though we were falling in for drill," a diarist in the 9th New York observed. General Davies claimed that Sawyer's brigade actually repulsed Hampton's cavalry without his brigade's help, an opinion supported by a trooper in the

5th Michigan who described in a letter home how his comrades jumped for their arms "in a twinkling" and "were in position and charged the Greybacks who ran away."

With Hampton's attack on the 7th Michigan subdued by other troopers from Kilpatrick's command, the order to move out quickly came. An artilleryman who was closer to Third Cavalry Division headquarters remembered that "every order was given and executed as coolly and as quickly as though nothing uncommon happened, but we got out of that place in the shortest time possible." The "men followed the splash of mud in front of them" as staff officers hurried to and fro, carrying the general's orders and directions for the regimental commanders. Another man remembered that their "orders were to follow Kilpatrick's headquarters, and, they did not tarry long on the road." A Vermonter who was probably with Sawyer recorded in his diary, "we traveled on the double quick until five this morn then halted about three hours." Kilpatrick's signal officer reported that "dark and raining as it was, not much confusion ensued" as the two brigades retreated. Major Kidd, a frequent Kilpatrick critic, remembered that the column "was moving at a walk on the road leading to Old Church." Even Hampton credited the Federals with making "a stout resistance for a short time." But that short time quickly came to an end.

"Soon the road and fields were filled with crowding, cursing men each one trying to protect himself," a Vermonter wrote. "Everyone was now making an effort to escape. . . . Away we go on the trot, now gallop, now on the dead run and then come up with a sudden stop against the men ahead. More cursing and crowding and then plunge ahead again; and so on during the night . . . , a disgusted mob of men, without any formation of any kind." The retreating Federals freed their Rebel prisoners, a number put by some at as high as four hundred, though probably an exaggeration. As the column left Mechanicsville, "the men were sleepy, the horses tired and everyone [was] in bad humor"—but not panicky. "Oh no! It was more disgust than fear," a cavalryman remembered. Whatever their emotions, few raiders would forget that night.[40]

About 1:00 A.M., March 2, Kilpatrick's column halted at the intersection of roads leading from Mechanicsville to Old Church and from Hanover Court House to Bottom's Bridge so that the ranks could close up. The Federals then proceeded for several hours, skirmishing briefly with Rebels near dawn. A Pennsylvania trooper scribbled in his diary how the column was harassed "for a mile or two with the rascals in our rear" until the Yankees halted, then charged with a determination that ended the pursuit. This rearguard action was performed by three companies of the 6th Michigan and part of the 1st Vermont. The raiders now moved off in the direction of Old Church, where they regrouped at about four o'clock the next morning. The weary riders then bivouacked until 1:00 P.M. near Old Church Tavern.[41]

The snowy fight with Hampton had lasted less than thirty minutes. A bitter Litchfield later criticized Kilpatrick for not properly picketing his line; allegedly, the general knew by noon of March 1 that Hampton was after his flank. But Davies squarely blamed Sawyer, the acting commander of Custer's brigade, saying that the colonel's "pickets were carelessly posted." Likewise, Kidd, an avowed Custer admirer, also blamed Sawyer for not rushing his entire brigade to Litchfield's defense. This accusation brings up a typical "what if" question to consider. Would Custer's presence on the raid, commanding his own troops rather than serving as a decoy near Charlottesville, have made any difference? Of course, any answer would only be speculative, but it probably would have made little difference. The raid's success was jeopardized more by Dahlgren's mistakes in route to Richmond than anything Kilpatrick or his immediate subordinates did wrong. Plus, Butler's failure to show up as a diversionary spear was a major factor not to be ignored. And finally, Custer and Kilpatrick's mutual intolerance of each other probably would have been starkly evident as their cavalrymen faced resistance from the Confederates ensconced behind the intermediate defenses. Their distain might have erupted into stubborn, raging tempers to the detriment of the men in the ranks. Custer's absence, therefore, was really not a factor relative to the success or failure of the raid. Moreover, Kilpatrick's orders to build fires, while apparently humane in intent, served "as lighthouses to direct the course of the enemy whom he knew to be pushing a vigorous pursuit." It appears that Kilpatrick, Sawyer, and Litchfield should all share blame in allowing three hundred ragged, freezing Southerners the opportunity to disrupt two veteran brigades of Federal cavalry, notwithstanding their wretched condition after three straight days in the saddle.

Years after the war, Wade Hampton, by then a U.S. senator, apparently had a conversation about his attack at Atlee's Station with a still-disgruntled Allyn Litchfield, who considered the ex-Confederate cavalryman "one of the bravest Southern Generals" to have fought in the war. Litchfield's Libby Prison experience had apparently affected his physical as well as his mental health. From a soldier who had been "cool, collected, determined, [and] energetic," he had become "apathetic, listless, woody, unresponsive," and in one doctor's opinion, perhaps "insane." Litchfield had bumped around from job to job during the postwar period due to his "fits of the blues." Broken physically and mentally, his experience in the raid's aftermath provides a well-documented case of post-traumatic stress disorder, a condition prominent today but often overlooked by studies of Civil War soldiers. Nevertheless, Litchfield had recovered his mental faculties sufficiently to buttonhole the former Confederate general one day about his decisions on the evening of March 1. In response to the query, Hampton seemingly said, "I had no idea of fighting that night, but the thing looked so pretty and inviting I thought I would give the boys some fun." Litchfield used the opportunity to invoke the memory of Custer's military prowess. When the former Union officer posited to Hampton that if Custer had been present, things would have been different for the South Carolinian, the senator impassively agreed, saying, "He would have made it more than lively."[42]

Lauding Hampton's singular victory, a Richmond newspaper summed up Kill-Cavalry's accomplishments on March 1 rather disdainfully. The editor took a not unexpected swipe at the Northern general when he wrote that the raid "thus far consisted in robbing hen roosts and stealing negroes." Colonel Cheek, who led the North Carolinians in their wild attack on the 7th Michigan, later felt that the fight at Atlee's Station was more important than the cavalry's other battles at Brandy Station and Trevilian's Station because it saved the Confederate capital from capture. Likewise, the man who defeated Ulric Dahlgren on the west side of Richmond on March 1, Captain John McAnerney, considered the turning back of the Yankees attributable to "obstinacy and good luck." He went on to paint a vicious picture of what the alternative would have been: "Imagine what would have been the result if their plans had succeeded. Thirty thousand federal prisoners, many of the toughs from the great cities [loose]. It would have been a sad night for the homes, women and children of Richmond." But one of Hampton's company commanders had a more intuitive opinion of the success. Captain

J. C. Blair of the 1st North Carolina reasoned that had it not been for Hampton's decisive action, Kilpatrick would have taken Richmond the next day. But Blair's most incisive invective was a backhanded slap at army brass when he opined that the South Carolinian's attack "was the best managed of any fight I was ever in, and yet they think no one can manage troops but a West Pointer."[43]

While Kilpatrick was managing the retreat occasioned by Hampton's deft and splintering attack, Dahlgren, only a few miles away, was about to have his own shattering experience.

CHAPTER 11

RICHMOND'S LOCAL DEFENSE
TROOPS ANSWER THE CALL

Dahlgren's troopers, now all too aware that they were late and still as far as nine miles from Richmond, heard train whistles blowing from the direction of Petersburg, signaling the movement of Confederate reinforcements toward the fight they were missing. They could also "hear Kilpatrick's artillery giving tongue on the north side of the city." These auditory clues could have persuaded the colonel to change direction, moving away from the river.

Around two o'clock the column entered the coal-pits region on the border between Henrico and Goochland Counties. Digging had begun at the pits in the mid-eighteenth century, spurring industrial development such as Tredegar Iron Works. Originally, wagons hauled the coal to the capital, but by 1846 the teamsters had the option of taking it to Hungary Station on the Richmond, Fredericksburg, and Potomac Railroad. The region around the pits was a tangle of narrow roads, and these carried the raiders toward Richmond, along the way playing havoc with mining operations. "We ran the trucks down the incline and set fire to the tipple," Dahlgren's signal officer, Lieutenant Reuben Bartley, recalled. From the coal pits the column turned north, apparently crossing Tuckahoe Creek at Woodward's Bridge. Reaching Quioccasin Road, the column turned again, this time to the east past the Franklin farm near Ridge Baptist Church and coming to a point about a mile from the city's first line of fortifications. By now the sounds of combat to the east was fading.[1]

To ponder his next move, Dahlgren called a halt that lasted several hours, affording the men a chance to brew coffee and feed their weary mounts with recently captured corn. Around 3:30 P.M. Captain John F. B. Mitchell's detachment rejoined the column. At about 5:00 P.M. the colonel sent Lieutenant Bartley and eight men to Hungary Station in Hanover County, taking with them the ambulances containing the signal rockets and other incendiary materials, the prisoners, most of the pack animals, and the remuda of spare horses. As if that was not a big enough retinue, several hundred contrabands who had been tagging after the column came along too. According to the raid plan, Hungary Station was the rendezvous spot for relinking with Kilpatrick, who knew the vicinity, having burned the depot there during Stoneman's Raid. In addition, that area was known to be thick with Union sympathizers. As Bartley's contingent exited, the escaping slaves—some mounted, some on foot, carrying all they owned on their backs—might have been "barefoot and almost naked" but were "all seemingly happy in the conviction that they were free," as one officer remarked. And in yet another of Dahlgren's imprudent moves, he also sent off with his signal officer the maps and compass. With Bartley's departure, the column again moved. Finding only a few pickets holding Richmond's outer works, Dahlgren advanced down Three Chopt Road.[2]

The diminishing sound of cannon fire meant that Kilpatrick was stalled in front of Richmond; perhaps he even had abandoned the mission. In any event, the main force could not support Dahlgren, which seemed to confound the young colonel, who became "more excited than [at] any time previous, as he could not account for the attack being made at daylight." Bartley said later that Dahlgren thought the coordinated attacks were to begin after dark, which contradicts all other sources that indicate the assault on Richmond was to commence the morning of March 1. The colonel sent two couriers galloping in search of Kilpatrick to confirm when "the attack was to be made." With a two-pronged strike on the Confederate capital now out of the question, he still believed that he should attack, apparently thinking to retrieve the sorry situation by conducting a reconnaissance of the western part of the intermediate defensive lines. No matter what his rationale, Dahlgren now embarked on a reckless course that would leave a number of his brave men dead, wounded, or bound for the dreaded prisons in Richmond that he was supposed to break open.[3]

Around 4:00 P.M. on March 1, as his men were drinking their stale coffee and feeding the captured corn to their weary mounts, Dahlgren gathered his officers. He and his subordinates were as tired as any of the horses or men they led, having traveled for more than forty-eight hours with little time for rest or refreshment. The officers knew they were late and on the wrong side of the James. And by now hours had passed since they had last heard Kilpatrick's guns on the north side of Richmond. Dahlgren "substantially" explained the raid's objective, according to a Wolverine officer in attendance. They were to attack the Confederate capital, release the Union prisoners confined on Belle Isle, and "capture the city, its officials and archives, if possible."[4] Even though they were still on the north side of the river, Dahlgren reasoned that they could gain some information of the ground and character of Richmond's western defenses if they proceeded. Major Edwin Cooke, Kilpatrick's surrogate and loyal friend, may have objected to the colonel's decision to head for Richmond rather than trying to link up with the main body on the city's north side. Cooke may have considered abandoning the operation, but Dahlgren was possessed of a "burning desire to win imperishable renown by some unequalled act of daring," according to an early historian of the war, thus a retreat was "ill suited with [Dahlgren's] temper or judgment." The officers stood with their commander, saying they should not retreat without at least trying one attempt to carry out the operation, even if its success was "improbable." As one of his soldiers helped him mount his horse—his prosthetic right leg was of no use in such a move—another man heard Dahlgren say, "We are going on; and if we succeed, I'd gladly lose the other" limb.[5]

With clouds darkening the sky, the raiders took the Three Chopt Road, which led to Richmond's outermost fortifications west of the city. With fifty troopers, Captain Smith H. Hastings of the 5th Michigan charged over the breastworks, drove off a few enemy pickets, and captured three mounted members of the City Battalion, who carried only sabers. The column confidently proceeded uninterrupted for two miles, with the 2nd New York in the lead; Lieutenant Samuel Harris and a contingent from the 5th Michigan brought up the rear. Dahlgren did not take the "usual precaution of throwing out scouts and flankers with the advance," a mistake one officer felt would cost his men dearly—and soon it did.[6]

That morning around ten o'clock, the tolling of the Capitol Square bell had summoned Richmond's Local Defense Troops (LDT), made up of government and factory workers. About an hour earlier, Brigadier General Henry Wise and his son-in-law Plumer Hobson had arrived in the city and rode directly to the War Department, where James Seddon had trouble believing their incredible story of Yankee raiders so near his house in Goochland County. But soon the details and other reports convinced the secretary of war to act. He alerted the military authorities and Jefferson Davis. Soon hundreds of machines that were turning out red-hot rifle barrels and other munitions of war came to a grinding halt. Messengers raced through factory buildings shouting at men to get home, grab their weapons and blankets, don uniforms, fill haversacks, and report back to the armory. Included in the ranks were "soldiers on furlough, convalescents, teamsters, armorers and departmental clerks" under the overall command of Brigadier General George Washington Custis Lee, son of the Army of Northern Virginia's commander and a staff assistant to President Davis. But these men would march without Custis Lee that day because he was "physically incapable" of duty in the field, perhaps suffering from another bout of rheumatoid arthritis, a disease that plagued him for many years. The LDT would march instead with only field-grade and line officers to the intermediate works outside the city limits.[7]

Hastily called out when Wise and Hobson arrived to raise the alarm, the local defenders of the city returned to Capitol Square later that day and waited for officers to form ranks. Once assembled, some marched in casual route step from the square up Franklin Street, while others took Grace Street. All along the streets, crowds of women cheered them on while some male onlookers scoffed with good-natured catcalls. One part-time soldier remembered the "quiet laughter and sly jokes of some of our friends on the streets and along the way." The local units often came in for such razzing; in his diary a War Department clerk remarked that politicians and bureaucrats used these outfits as a haven for their "pets and relatives of fighting age." The companies came together at Fifth Street, then proceeded to Main Street, turning off to take Cary Street near the Westham House, where they shifted to the Westham Plank Road, splashing along the muddy road followed by struggling ammunition wagons as the winter afternoon sky darkened. Later the 28th Virginia Infantry, an Army of Northern Virginia regiment stationed temporarily near Richmond, would follow the local troops but arrive too late to participate in the action. The emergency induced many regular-army officers who happened to be in town to join the ranks as privates. One was General P. G. T. Beauregard's assistant adjutant general, Colonel George W. Brent. Even a member of the Virginia House of Delegates from Augusta County shouldered a musket and fell in with Henley's Battalion.

Despite all its shrill bravado, fear gripped the Confederate capital. The alarm bell continued to ring as exaggerated reports poured in from fugitives, both white and black, who related embellished stories about the raiders. People milled around the government buildings seeking information. Mounted officers and couriers, dashing to and fro, only added to the confusion. Colonel Charles Talcott, superintendent of the Richmond and Danville Railroad, was preparing contingency plans to move government officials out of town. Later in the day an "Officers' Battalion," two companies made up of men on furlough, was formed under Brigadier Generals Evander Law of Alabama and Jerome Robertson of Texas. Many of them were staying at the famous Spotswood Hotel, including Colonel George S. Patton, commander of the 22nd Virginia Infantry. The generals efficiently gathered up both officers and "men found everywhere in the streets and at the hotels." The battalion made plans to sleep rough in the city's defenses, which would muddy their shiny boots and soil their clean white collars.[8]

The LDT marched to the intermediate works on the city's west side near Benjamin Green's farm, known locally as Roselawn, a 492-acre spread stretched along both side of Three Chopt Road. The brick plantation house was built about 1843, its stately style reflecting its owner's powerful and diverse business interests in slaves, coal, manufacturing, horse breeding, land development, rental properties in Richmond, and quarries. By the time of the war, Green was estimated to be worth the equivalent of $20 million. Whether he was home or in Richmond at the time of Dahlgren's arrival is unknown.[9]

First to reach Roselawn was the Armory Battalion (1st Battalion, LDT), originally formed in May 1863, its men outfitted in blue serge pantaloons with shirts trimmed in red, which the workers who formed the ranks paid for themselves, and armed with inferior Austrian-made muskets. Major Charles H. Ford, a six-foot-tall veteran of the British cavalry, commanded the battalion. Three of the unit's companies consisted of armory employees, a fourth of carbine factory workers, and a fifth of the harness shop men. These highly skilled mechanics, numbering no than three hundred, marched five miles in muddy clay along the Westham Plank Road through drizzle. From the opposite direction came hordes of civilians, fleeing for the city as if hellhounds were on their trail. Soon the ammunition train overtook the column. Major Ford ordered a halt so the men could fill cartridge boxes. Company D had bullets, so Captain Henry Fitzgerald, Jr., volunteered his unit to take the point. The remainder of the battalion soon followed, turning northwest onto Three

Chopt Road. Ford, astride his chestnut stallion, posted his amateur soldiers just south of the Green farm between four and five o'clock that cloudy afternoon. The major, however, may have been misreading or exceeding his orders by moving his men so far forward.[10]

Dahlgren was also on the road, coming toward the city and driving ahead of his column the rabble of fleeing noncombatants. He had not reached the Green farm when he paused to assess his situation. "We were . . . in a bad place, led by a boy-soldier; but he was equal to the emergency," one of the army scouts later remembered. Even so, the colonel "was as cool then as when he reviewed his command near General Meade's Headquarters the Sunday afternoon before." But though he looked worn, "there was no excitement or nervousness in his manner." Dahlgren presented himself as a "proud, iron-nerved invalid," an officer recalled. After the halt, the column resumed its march.

Three Chopt Road turned abruptly at the Green property, which at first obscured the Amory Battalion's position astride the road, shielded by the Green house and an adjoining orchard. Soon the Yankees spied some of the defenders, and Dahlgren ordered a charge led by the 2nd New York, sabers drawn. The New Yorkers went forward at a gallop. From his mounted position in the middle of the road, Ford ordered a volley. The Rebel fire shocked the Yankees into deploying dismounted to the right. The surprised Federals quickly sought the shelter of a copse of trees from which they could put their breech-loading carbines to good use. Musket volleys and carbine counterfire soon layered the air with smoke, sporadically lit in the gathering gloom by yellow muzzle flashes.[11]

Incensed at his troopers' apparent timidity, Dahlgren ordered the New Yorkers to throw out skirmishers through the woods. He then instructed his remaining troopers to prepare to fight on foot, with one man in four remaining behind to hold his and his comrades' reins, as was standard practice. The colonel repeated his orders, making "threats and expostulations" to little effect—and unsurprisingly. Dahlgren's remaining prisoner from the Frederick's Hall court-martial, Captain William Dement, later recounted in a Richmond newspaper that the Yankees "were completely fagged out, having lost [two] nights' sleep, and were in no condition to fight." Nevertheless, fifty men dismounted and took up positions on either side of the road in timber and underbrush; the rest remained mounted in columns of eight. The New Yorkers of Kilpatrick's

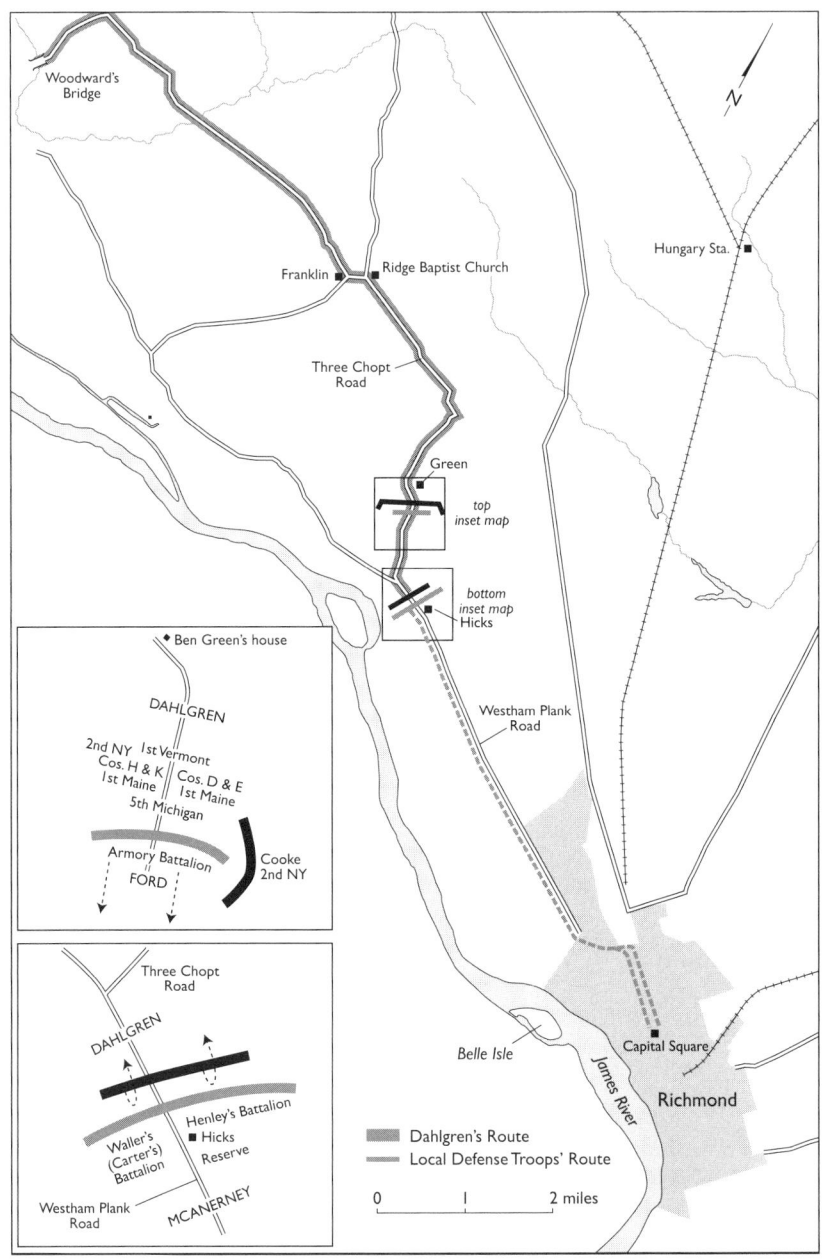

Dahlgren Fights with Local Defense Troops. Map by Bill Nelson. *Copyright © 2016 by the University of Oklahoma Press.*

former regiment ignored Dahlgren, who turned to Captain John D. Myrick, a twenty-nine-year-old lawyer from Augusta, Maine, saying: "Well, then, you go in 1st Maine!" Myrick took control of the attack. He deployed his Maine boys as skirmishers, placing Companies D and F, under 1st Lieutenant William Harris, on the left side of the road, with 1st Lieutenant John R. Andrews and Company H to the right side. Myrick was also on the right, keeping Company K under his own command. Advancing the extreme right of his line to envelop the enemy in a semicircle, the captain pressed forward rapidly. As soon as he noticed the Confederates wavering, Myrick ordered a charge. As the 1st Maine went forward, Lieutenant Robert Haire's 5th Michigan charged down the road, mounted, at the thinly held enemy line. Haire tried to defer to his senior officer, Lieutenant Samuel Harris. But Harris, who had been mostly on staff assignments prior to the raid, wisely realized that Haire knew the men better and demurred. He nevertheless rode alongside Haire but not before ordering a young aide to fall out of ranks and lead away the blooded horse Harris had taken from Seddon's plantation. With a wild charge looming, the lieutenant apparently did not want to sacrifice his valuable new mount.[12]

There is little doubt that Colonel Dahlgren was near the action at Green's farm and apparently regained his composure. He "rode along the line, speaking to the men, so calm, so quiet, so brave, that it seemed to me the veriest coward must needs fight if never before," an officer later wrote in a letter to Admiral Dahlgren.[13]

"Yelling like demons," three dozen Wolverines trotted to support the 1st Maine, with the Harris Light Cavalry cheering them on. They quickly learned why the New Yorkers had faltered. Fences and felled timber impeded their horses, and the armory workers enjoyed a strong fortified position of earth-and-log breastworks. Then there was the unintended consequence of ill-aimed fire from the 2nd New York. The first volley from the Confederates' second-rate muzzleloaders did no damage. While 1st Lieutenant Benjamin Epps, Jr., the battalion's adjutant, rode back to the Westham Plank Road for reinforcements, Rebel officers cautioned their men in tones distinctly heard by the Federals to "keep cool, fire low, don't run." A second barrage was more effective. Corporal Newton Wyman of Company E, 5th Michigan, took a ball in the face that tore off his nose and lodged in the back of his skull. Lieutenant Harris also was wounded, but he had more luck than Wyman. Ten feet ahead of his men, Harris was shot in the left collarbone, the round going through and breaking his shoulder blade. Lieutenant Haire was luckier still. Mounted on a confiscated, unsteady steed that sprang sideways into a ditch, the officer was thrown from his saddle, saving his life if not his dignity. The Yankees fell back, reformed, and started again. The Wolverines quickly accelerated from a march to a trot to a full gallop. To keep up with them, Harris stowed his pistol in his right boot, babying his wounded left side, holding his reins in his right hand, and gritting his teeth against the pain. A Rebel cried out: "Look out there; they are flanking us!"

A flanking maneuver by Major Cooke and two hundred troopers against the Confederate right had worked. Facing mounted Union cavalrymen in the road and dismounted skirmishers rapidly firing carbines, the Armory Battalion gave way. After only two volleys, the Confederates broke and ran. In the looming darkness the muzzle flashes from Yankee revolvers and carbines served like photographer's flash powder to illuminate in staccato poses the fleeing mechanics, making for an open field "like a flock of sheep." There amid fierce enemy fire, officers tried to rally them: Lieutenant Jonathan Sweeney was shot and killed; two other officers were slightly wounded; fifteen-year-old Miles Cary was wounded in the wrist. A few Confederates tried to shoot back from behind walls and a house, but no obstruction deterred the dismounted troopers. The 1st Vermont pounded down the road as the broken defenders heard the Yankees cry, "Shoot the d—d scoundrels." "The sabre properly used proved more than a match for the bayonet," Myrick observed. With the Confederates routed, Harris returned to Dahlgren's side.[14]

While Myrick portrayed himself as a hero in leading the attack against the Armory Battalion in a letter published in a Maine newspaper shortly after the raid, some troopers were skeptical about the captain's performance. A comrade wrote a quarter century later that Myrick was "a good man, a brave soldier, and an accomplished officer" who "was always at his post at the head of his company" but "must have borne a charmed life." Another man in the ranks, however, strongly disagreed with his commander's version of the Green farm fight. Private John P. Sheahan, a schoolteacher in Myrick's company, also wrote home about the action. He claimed that Myrick "lost no horse in the fight but one thing he did lose and that was his reputation as an officer." Sheahan claimed that his captain "gave no commands and if he did he was too far back in the rear to be heard." The private stated that Sergeant William D. Herbert, a tailor by trade, led the Maine boys in the attack and proved himself "superior to Captain Myrick in every way." Sheahan mustered out of the 1st Maine shortly after the raid to accept a commission in an infantry unit.[15]

Myrick ordered his men to "rally on the pike and support the Harris Light, which was already a mile ahead!" Regrouping on the road, the 1st Maine counted seven men killed and wounded and nine more missing. It fell to the Wolverines to gather up prisoners on the Green property, including a company of boys ages fifteen to eighteen attached to the battalion. Lieutenant Harris allowed most of these lads to escape, but his generosity was not repaid. After getting medical care at the Green house, Harris found that his new mount had been shot in the forehead and his young horse holder hit five times, one ball breaking his arm. Myrick estimated that the enemy's loss at upward of twenty men killed and wounded, including several officers, with even more defenders taken prisoner.[16]

The Confederates lost more than ground and dignity at Green's farm; they lost precious expertise. John Jones, whose forte was straightening rifle barrels, lost his life on the Three Chopt Road, a price that immediately cut into the number of weapons the armory produced afterward. Training a replacement would take several months because of "this peculiar and difficult branch of work." The death of Jones shows the two-edged sword of maintaining local-defense forces, which contrasted their value for emergency purposes with the vulnerability their participation in combat raised. The barrel straightener's demise plunged his fellow workers into a slump, prompting Master Armorer Salmon Adams to ask the government to "protect if possible this valuable class of mechanics" in the future if the capital was attacked.[17]

Encouraged by the successful flanking maneuver, Dahlgren pressed on in what one officer called a "scrub race across fields and stone walls . . . with a cheer, a run and a volley from our Spencers." Union troopers pushed their amateur opponents back toward the city line. After pausing near the intersection of the Three Chopt and the Westham Plank Roads, Dahlgren turned his men left and marched them half a mile or so toward a fortified position near Glenburnie, the plantation home of a man named Hicks. Some young skirmishers who had moved forward, led by Captain Alexander Babcock, observed the Yankee horse soldiers, who had some difficulty advancing. First, they had to dismount and tear down a fence. Once that was accomplished, the troopers remounted but quickly found their horses sinking knee deep in the rain-soaked ploughed field beyond, causing more cursing and swearing.[18]

Confederate reinforcements from the 3rd Infantry Battalion, also known as Henley's Battalion, commanded that evening by Captain John H. McAnerney, Jr., and the 2nd Infantry Battalion had arrived near Glenburnie about 3:00 P.M. They would make a last-ditch stand against the raiders at Hicks's plantation.[19]

It was now about 8:00 P.M., "pouring rain—cold and pitch-dark," as the Yankees neared. McAnerny's departmental clerks, along with Lieutenant Colonel John W. Carter's 2nd Infantry Battalion of quartermaster and commissary clerks (also known as Waller's Battalion), formed a line across the Westham Plank Road, with their right resting against a hill sloping into a swampy flat. The departmental troops were generally army veterans who had retired from active duty due to wounds or other disabilities except for Company G, which was "a company of striplings," with an average age of sixteen in 1864. These youngsters carried "cut-off" carbines to match their own physical stature and represented some of the best families in Richmond; another contemporary account called them "able-bodied young clerks." A veteran of Henley's Battalion put the full strength of the two commands at about 800 men. Although documents fail to record an exact count, they probably mustered fewer troops on March 1. A newspaper account put Waller's Battalion at 343 men and Henley's Battalion at about 300 "rank and file." McAnerney positioned Henley's Battalion on the right side of the road, while most of Carter's command took a position to the left. Two companies under Captain Daniel E. Scruggs occupied the roadbed, with the remainder of Carter's men forming a reserve behind the main line. McAnerney formed his men in two ranks, extending into a field about two hundred yards north of the road. He sent Captain Babcock forward with about fifty men to act as skirmishers at a fence at the lower end of Hicks's field near the Three Chopt Road intersection. Babcock had orders to fire one round as the Federals approached, then fall back to the main line. When the captain withdrew per his instructions, Dahlgren was fooled, thinking the Rebels were the remnants of Ford's Armory Battalion scattering down the road. The government workers-turned-soldiers hunkered down to await the oncoming Yankee veterans.[20]

A young boy with Babcock's skirmishers was somehow left behind when the Union attack started. Dahlgren lunged at him with his saber, one swipe cutting his wrist, while another sliced him between his shoulder and elbow. The lad thought that his "bayonet could not have been three feet from [Dahlgren's] chest," but his wet powder prevented a point-blank shot at the ill-fated colonel that night. Whether it was actually Ulric Dahlgren who attacked the young man is speculative, for the story rests on the reminiscences of an old man written more than forty years after the event. If it was the colonel, however, this appears to be the only account that mentions him charging down the Westham Plank Road with his men.[21]

Captain McAnerney slowly and calmly walked down his line as the Federal attack developed. "Don't a man dare fire a shot until he hears my voice," he told his clerks. "Remember, two volleys." The twenty-five-year-old McAnerney was the right man for command in this fight. The son of Irish immigrants who had grown up in Providence, Rhode Island, he was a self-made man. Upon arriving in Columbia, South Carolina, he had befriended General John D. Preston, then later went to New Orleans, where he worked as a clerk and studied law. After Sumter McAnerney stayed with his adopted region, joining the 3rd Alabama Infantry as a sergeant. He was wounded badly enough in the right arm at Seven Pines in May 1862 to be discharged from the regular service but accepted a captain's commission in Company B, 3rd Battalion, LDT, commanding postal-department clerks. His regular-army experience would serve him well as he commanded other veterans who were now working in various governmental departments but serving as part-time soldiers.[22]

At the center of the field between the Three Chopt Road and the enemy's position, Dahlgren halted his command, apparently suspicious. He moved ahead once more, though slowly this time. He halted again. The Yankee troopers were within gunshot range of the Confederate line. Dahlgren then ordered a charge. The Federals pounded forward, firing as they rode down both sides of the Westham Plank Road, sabers rattling, carbines firing, egged on by officers shouting, "Charge the —— rebels! Cut them down! They are nothing but melish!" The scout Martin Hogan, hatless and riding his favorite mount Old John, his red curls flying in the wind, shouted at the top of his lungs, "Come on, boys," as he readied his empty revolver to use as a club. The Confederate clerks remained calm.

The Yankees came on "like maddened fiends," McAnerney said later. The men of his battalions, kneeling with hammers cocked, held their fire, despite the taunts about being only militia, until the horse soldiers reached a hillcrest, rendering them as darker silhouettes against the night sky. One young Confederate recounted shortly after the fight that he "could not see them, and did not know what force they had against us." But he could hear the advancing Yankees "cursing and swearing" at the Rebels. The raiders were soon only fifteen yards away. At this McAnerney shouted, "Rise, attention, first rank, fire!" His soldiers stood, obediently leveled their muskets, and like regulars delivered a "very effective" fusillade. "A perfect hailstorm of bullets whistled past us," a Maine officer recalled. Army scout Anson Carney's horse fell dead, tumbling its rider who feigned death until he could grab a riderless horse. A second salvo finished off the attackers, though not before a good number of boys in Company G suffered saber cuts and other injuries. In the dark confusion several Yankee cavalrymen rode directly through McAnerney's line; four were taken prisoner. After the second volley, the captain ordered his men to reload and "fire at will!" After three minutes the brisk firing on both sides slackened off, according to one Southern officer.[23]

In the melee a Confederate pulled his revolver's trigger five times trying to hit a Union lieutenant. Casting aside the useless pistol, he picked up a stone and hurled it at another Yankee cavalryman, knocking him from his saddle. The dazed trooper was immediately made a prisoner. Other Federals could not seem to control their horses in the chaotic minutes of the fight. One horseman rode directly into an uncovered icehouse on Hicks's property, killing the horse and breaking the rider's leg. A bewildered Confederate who fell into the icehouse simultaneously surrendered to the injured Yankee and vice versa, but it was the bluecoat who ended up in prison. Another Maine trooper was more fortunate. Thomas Gray was riding Little Snap when the horse fell, pinning him. Two unarmed Confederate youngsters tried to capture him, but Gray shook them off, pushing them down in the slippery mud. He grabbed the reins of a riderless horse and escaped.[24]

Near Hicks's farm, Captain Albert Ellery, the sixty-three-year-old commander of the Henley Battalion's Company D and the government's second auditor, "a mild-mannered upright man," was killed when a ball ripped through his right sleeve, passing through his chest and out the left side of his body. R. A. Tompkins, formerly a captain in the Richmond Sharpshooters, a company of the 23rd Virginia Infantry, quickly took Ellery's place only to catch a bullet in the jaw. Trying to keep from being slashed with a saber, fourteen-year-old John Purcell shot his first Yankee that day. The man sprawled off his horse with a crash, and Purcell and comrade George Watt quickly took his spurs and pistol but could not find his carbine or saber.[25]

In the dark dismounted Federals had to scramble madly, straining to find their disorganized detachments among the equally confused Rebels. Waller's Battalion had advanced beyond the battle line and had to be recalled to its original position. The bluecoat charge had left McAnerney's line in shambles and his men unable to pursue the enemy. The Confederates fell back about two hundred yards, where the captain reformed his irregular ranks and encamped the men for the night. The entire fight, which one officer termed "a piece of nonsense . . . mere foolishness," had lasted no more than a half hour in a drizzling rain. Captain Ellery was the only Confederate officer killed in the action. In addition to him, a later account put the defenders' losses at six or seven officers wounded, two or three men killed, and fifteen to twenty men wounded.[26]

Dahlgren concluded that the Confederates' flank could not be turned, unaware that McAnerney's men were now out of cartridges. The pair of well-directed, effective volleys had convinced the colonel that he had encountered a large body of fresh troops. This time doing as Cooke urged, Dahlgren ordered a retreat. His attack had pushed back the Rebels, but in the process his column had shattered, with many men dead, wounded, or taken prisoner. Dahlgren faced his column northwest on the Three Chopt Road, feeling that his men "could do no more" and had gone "far enough." It had become "too hot" for the colonel to continue, one of his officers later wrote. Captain McAnerney saw it differently. He remembered the repulse of the Yankees being attributable to "obstinacy and good luck" as the primary factors. But he also realized that "the backbone of this celebrated raid was broken." A Confederate in the ranks was equally modest when he later wrote, "Our military achievements were not brilliant, but such as they were we are proud of them . . . and had the honor of driving back Dahlgren's raid." But another comrade unabashedly boasted, "We whipped them good" and "saved the city."[27]

Once General Custis Lee heard the musket firing in McAnerney's front, he dispatched his twenty-five-year-old aide, Lieutenant
Clement Sulivane, to assess what was happening. Sulivane reported
that it was "snowing, raining and freezing all at the same time," the
Mississippi native having never seen "a blacker night." On reaching
McAnerney's line, the lieutenant went forward to ascertain the situation on the ground. As he trotted down the Westham Plank Road
in the dark, soaking night, the young aide paused from time to time
to listen for any distant sounds of Yankee horseman, but all seemed
quiet. At one point a voice cried out, "For god's sake, don't shoot;
I surrender." Sulivane found a wounded Federal, took him back to
Confederate lines, and resumed his search for Dahlgren. By the time
he reached Green's farm, Sulivane could finally hear the hoof beats
of blue-clad cavalrymen making their escape. He quickly reported
the results of his reconnaissance to Lee.[28]

With the forlorn Federal column proceeding in "perfect silence
and good order," Dahlgren put Captain Mitchell in charge of the rear
guard. Spurning Cooke's request for that "post of honor," the colonel said that he needed the major at the van to guide the column to
Hungary Station. Cooke reluctantly assented, leaving the remnants
of the Harris Light Cavalry in Mitchell's capable hands.

No Confederate forces pursued the worn-out bluecoats.
Richmond's defenders allowed their foes to retire "leisurely and
without the slightest annoyance," a small consolation given the
numbers of Union dead, wounded, and missing. Sketchy casualty
reports, printed years after the raid, put Dahlgren's losses at twenty-
two killed, twenty-six wounded, and thirty-two captured. Another
report first claimed that forty Yankees were left on the field before
it was amended to eleven killed and thirty to forty wounded. A
Richmond newspaper put the Federal causalities at ten killed, one
mortally wounded, and seventeen others wounded. President Davis
estimated eighteen Yankees were killed and perhaps thirty to forty
wounded, with "many more prisoners." Whatever the actual numbers, Dahlgren's attacks had damaged his command badly. The more
grievously wounded were forced to stay behind in a makeshift hospital set up at the Green house by an assistant surgeon of the 2nd New
York. Reports the next day said eleven severely wounded Yankees
were left in Green's parlor, including Lieutenant Harris's brave
young horse holder. Another report stated that local blacks "peeled"
dead Federals, stripping their corpses of clothing and shoes.[29]

After marching away from Richmond, Dahlgren made his first real attempt to link up with Kilpatrick. He called a brief halt near the Ridge Baptist Church, summoning army scouts Ebenezer Magee and James Wood and ordering them to skirt the city and find the general's column. Still relying on the faulty rockets that had failed to keep Dahlgren and his commander in contact, the colonel told the scouts that if Kilpatrick wanted him to stay in place, he was to send up six rockets, a signal that reinforcements were on the way. But if he was to rejoin the main body by making a detour outside the first line of Richmond's fortifications, Kilpatrick was to fire four rockets. Dahlgren emphasized the importance of their mission as the two men remounted, then galloped into the darkness. Soon after the scouts left, Dahlgren ordered the remainder of his command forward. Dahlgren apparently failed to issue decisive orders, causing one officer to recall that the column started "without any knowledge of our commander's intentions."[30]

Magee and Wood rode along Richmond's outer works until they came to the Brook Turnpike, probably near Yellow Tavern, a prominent landmark, where they picked up evidence of Kilpatrick's main body. Near the road, Wood grabbed a fresh mount from a local doctor and took the lead. He soon spied some horsemen in blue overcoats near a barn. Calling to the mounted riders, Wood was deceived into thinking that he had linked up with the 5th New York, a unit that was with Kilpatrick. As he galloped toward the group of fifteen troopers, they suddenly opened up on Wood with carbine fire that dropped his new horse, pinning the scout underneath the animal. In the rear Magee quickly turned tail and fled, but his worn-out mount soon gave out, forcing the scout to take to the woods on foot. More Confederate shots hit Magee in the hip and side. Both couriers were captured. Magee's wounds proved fatal, and he died shortly after being brought with Wood before a Rebel officer. The man meant to hang them as spies since they were out of uniform. The quick-witted Wood glanced at another officer sitting silently on his horse and made an instant appraisal. The quiet man appeared to have a military bearing absent in the officer holding the noose. Wood immediately appealed to this officer, stating that he was with the 6th U.S. Cavalry. The low-key Confederate questioned him about his unit, indicating that he had some prewar connection with the U.S. cavalry and then, giving Wood the benefit of the doubt, ordered him sent off to Libby

Prison. Like Magee, several other couriers sent from Kilpatrick were killed by deceitfully dressed Rebels.[31]

Confusion, fatigue, and equally rotten weather and morale characterized Dahlgren's retreat. Trying to evade the enemy, the column resorted to "unfrequented wood roads," often blocked by fallen trees that had to be hauled out of the way. Soldiers had "to trace the course with [their] hands—for even the sagacity of the horses [was] often at fault."

Dahlgren had left part of his command near the Hicks farm through his own ineptitude in issuing the order to retreat. A detachment of the 1st Maine that was to the rear during the earlier engagement missed the order to pull back. These men halted on the Three Chopt Road to await further orders. "No order for a general retreat was received," according to the 1st Maine's regimental historian. Dahlgren's inexperience may have caused him to violate a military rule "to post a guide. Especially at night this is indispensible. On this trying occasion this precaution seems to have been eliminated." This evaluation was echoed by a veteran Confederate cavalryman who observed that it was "always a danger to cavalry marching in darkness on unfamiliar roads" that troopers could become separated. A similar claim also appeared in a letter home from Lieutenant William Mattison of the 2nd New York. "Some fifteen minutes passed, and still we remained in the same position," Mattison wrote. "At the request of Capt. Mitchell I rode up the column to ascertain the cause of the delay in moving. To my great surprise I found an officer *faced to the rear.* . . . I found this officer had not received orders to retire, and after investigation that Dahlgren and Cooke, with about a hundred men, had marched on long before" (italics in original). Upon this unsettling discovery, Mitchell assumed command of the entire column, sending scouts out to look for Dahlgren, who had taken a byroad that the scouts and the advance of Mitchell's contingent had missed.[32]

At least two-thirds of Dahlgren's command, now under Mitchell, were separated from the colonel in the darkness somewhere near the Ridge Baptist Church, never to rejoin him. Dahlgren seems to have turned right, while Mitchell went left—a logical move that would take his men near Richmond's outer works. The colonel's father defended his son's reckless actions rather unconvincingly when he later wrote that Ulric had left "pickets on white horses to mark the course taken" by his column. After more than fifty hours in the saddle and covering at least two hundred miles of Virginia countryside, it is hard to believe that Dahlgren had "white horses" on hand in sufficient number and condition to mark the way for his retreating column. Most likely, Lieutenant Mattison had the story right. There were no guides posted on "white horses"—or horses of any other color—to help Mitchell's men follow Dahlgren and Cooke's trail.[33]

Cooke was the one to realize that the column had been split, it was said later. He asked Dahlgren for permission to search for the missing men, but the colonel refused, predicting that the soldiers would close up eventually. They never did. Mitchell's contingent actually trod part of the path Dahlgren's men had taken in the darkness without realizing it, an easy oversight given that "[t]he storm had set in with a renewed fury," making it impossible to see tracks in the mud and rain. The column pressed on: "Tired and exhausted men fell asleep upon their horses. It became necessary to march by file, the jaded animals stumbling and falling down; and when we finally reached Hungary Station we discovered that half the command had become separated from us."[34]

Still Dahlgren pushed on, grabbing a local citizen and forcing him to guide his shrinking command to Hungary Station, where he hoped to link up with Lieutenant Bartley, who he had dispatched earlier in the day to find Kilpatrick. Dahlgren probably found his signal officer somewhere south of the depot. The lieutenant had stumbled upon a slave coming from Richmond with a letter for his master, John Stewart, a prominent tobacco merchant who lived near the Confederates' outer works. Bartley rode over to Stewart's house at Brook Hill, where he opened the letter in front of its intended recipient. The confiscated correspondence described "the Yankees to be as thick as hops and more coming"—stale news since Bartley could hear Hampton's attack at Atlee's Station. The crack of carbine fire and the boom of artillery shells from that direction told him the Federals were no longer at the gates of Richmond. Bartley camped for the night in an "old frame church" to await Dahlgren, who arrived during the night. Since Little Kil was nowhere to be found, the ninety-odd troopers with the colonel forged on in the direction of Atlee's Station, dodging Confederate patrols as they sought a juncture with the main body. To unburden the column, Dahlgren destroyed his two ambulances. Not waiting to hear from Mitchell, he started for the Pamunkey River at a speed born of desperation. "We rode the whole of the night as fast as the men and horses could stand it," Captain Dement, still Dahlgren's prisoner, confirmed. The colonel hoped to run around Richmond and reunite with Kilpatrick east of the city.[35]

The only Union soldiers Dahlgren encountered on that circuitous ride were in a Confederate wagon train of wounded, Yankee prisoners taken by Hampton near Atlee's Station. This occurred sometime after three o'clock in the morning on March 2, near Booker Hazelgrove's store. At first Dr. Thomas E. Williams, surgeon of the 2nd North Carolina Cavalry, mistook the mud-spattered Dahlgren for Captain William P. Roberts of his Tar Heel regiment. After a busy night, Dr. Williams must have been a little groggy, for he "had quite a conference" with the colonel before realizing his error. Moving to the wounded men in the wagons, Dahlgren questioned several captured officers, including the commander of the 7th Michigan, Allyn Litchfield. He signaled the Southern surgeon to proceed with his wagons, apparently unwilling to burden his wayward column with the Federal wounded. The doctor implored Dahlgren not to destroy the store since he meant to use it as a temporary hospital. The colonel agreed, even allowing the doctor to keep his horse, then started his men toward the Pamunkey. Dahlgren sat gracefully on his horse until nearly all his trooper had passed him, then trotted to the front of the column.[36]

Captain Mitchell had made better use of the night. After countermarching, the New Yorker hid his men in a swampy thicket until morning, giving his scouts a better chance at finding a safer route. To disguise their position, Mitchell wisely ordered his men not to speak above a whisper and forbade camp fires, an effective but painful tactic whose value would pay dividends in the hours to come.[37]

Between eight and nine o'clock in the morning of March 2, Dahlgren's ragged column reached the Pamunkey River. He had marched his men throughout the night on twisting, tree-clogged, wood-cutting roads and country lanes in his bid to find Kilpatrick. Finally, his troopers approached a crossing at Hanovertown Ferry. The river was running high; a flatboat was visible on the opposite shore. Two gutsy troopers stripped down and swam the near-freezing water to secure it. They rigged a tow rope, shuttling the men and horses onto the far bank in about two hours. Dahlgren's dauntless band of bluecoats was on its way across King William County, making for the Mattaponi River and hoping to shake their foes. But first they would have to get to the Mattaponi and cross it into King and Queen County.[38]

CHAPTER 12

KILPATRICK ON THE MOVE

A t dawn on March 2, Captain John Mitchell's column of about 250 Yankee troopers moved out from their sheltering position in the swampy thickets east of Glen Allen plantation in Hanover County. The 5th New York took the advance. Mitchell's column seems to have skirted the outer works of Richmond near the Brook Turnpike. According to a Michigan officer's recollection, the Federals took fire from a small redoubt on top of a hill near the pike. Most of the Rebel shots missed their marks, but one round severely wounded an officer. Galloping out of range as quickly as they could, the Federal cavalrymen continued their search for either Dahlgren or Kilpatrick until they finally halted for the night.

The night was a miserable one. The rain turned to sleet and snow until around midnight, when the sky cleared and the temperature plunged. As the snow was tapering off, Dahlgren was taking a circuitous route east with ninety-odd horse soldiers, while Mitchell was calling a halt and funneling his detachment into a densely wooded swamp. Mitchell's men "were not allowed to build a fire— although it was snowing—not even to speak louder than a whisper for the rebels were passing in force just a few rods from us," a Maine captain wrote later. Men "threw themselves upon the wet ground with a single blanket or an overcoat over them, and some slept in their saddles, overcome by fatigue and numbness." Others stood by their mounts, holding the horses' snouts to keep them from whinnying and alerting searching Confederates. In their stupor the raiders hardly knew what they were doing. A man from the 1st Maine remembered a bone-drenched cavalryman hanging his belt and saber on what he thought was a tree stump only to find at dawn that he had draped his gear on another soldier sleeping so deeply that he did not realize he was serving as a nightstand.[1]

Overnight, Captain Smith Hastings of the 5th Michigan approached scout Anson B. Carney. "Carney, you are an old scout," Hastings whispered. "Get us out of this scrape, if you can." Carney immediately picked up his gear and his carbine, pushing through a dense thicket at the edge of the camp. He nosed around until he found a slave cabin. There he convinced a slave, who probably lived on the grounds of Glen Allen plantation near the Mountain Road, to guide Mitchell's column. Back at the Federal camp, the soldiers gave the black man a horse. He led a ten-man advance party east and almost immediately ran into an ambush. The handful of Rebels might have been with the Henrico Light Dragoons; their surprise volley wounded all ten Yankees and their guide. The weary, injured troopers pulled back into the woods to wait for dawn. With a bullet in his hip, the twenty-three-year-old scout made medicinal use of some captured spirits.[2]

Shortly after daybreak, Mitchell enlisted another slave as a guide and resumed searching for either Dahlgren or Kilpatrick. After the early morning ambush, officers made sure that the troopers had their weapons at the ready, their saddles tight, and their ranks closed up lest they wind up at Libby Prison or Belle Isle. This search party quickly found the big house at Glen Allen, and the cavalrymen gathered there for their breakfast—or pillage, as Southern accounts have it. Memoirs describe the bluecoats breaking into the Allens' icehouse; stealing bacon, horses, and mules; killing chickens; taking forage for their mounts; and generally plundering the plantation.

Nourished and with the 2nd New York leading the way, the Northerners, led by Mitchell's latest contraband guide, steered along a remote bridle path through the woods until they came to an "obscure ford" at Riles's Mill that offered a route across the Chickahominy. Near the crossing a Union sympathizer offered to put them on the road to Atlee's Station, where Kilpatrick and Hampton had clashed the previous night. This farmer had a wealth of invaluable information for Mitchell about local roads and Confederate cavalry in the area. The captain could see from the fading embers of a burned train that Kilpatrick had been through the area. The farmer also passed along plausible intelligence that Pickett's Division had come up from Petersburg to confront the raiders. At Atlee's Station Mitchell's column surprised a thirty-five-man Rebel picket that scattered, later circling around to bushwhack the 1st Vermont, which was serving as a rear guard. As the column moved on in search of Kilpatrick's main body, the captain now knew that he would not find them inside or even near Richmond.[3]

As Mitchell's men spent their soggy night hiding from the enemy, Kilpatrick's troopers had a miserable march through White Oak

Swamp en route toward Old Church in eastern Hanover County. A New York officer vividly remembered how he and his men were "[s] leepy and tired almost beyond endurance, and so cold our feet would rattle in the stirrups; the half frozen mud so deep we could not walk. . . . Few of the men had anything left to eat."[4]

Throughout the night the Rebels pecked at Kilpatrick's column, sometimes from "within 'Spenser' [sic] and 'Sharps' speaking distance." The harrying let up briefly at Old Church until, around dawn, Bradley Johnson's dogged Maryland trackers, who had outrun Hampton and his broken-down mounts, attacked Yankee pickets about a mile from Old Church Tavern. Kilpatrick turned to his chief aide, Captain Llewellyn Estes, and said, "Send me one squadron of the 1st Maine." Companies A and C, led by the indomitable Estes, charged the Marylanders and "drove them back flying."[5] Also chasing the Rebels were some Vermont men, including a trooper named Hubbard Eastman, who took a bullet in the foot. Another Northerner was wounded by a saber slash, and three men went missing. The Confederates lost five killed and fifteen wounded, including Lieutenant Cyrus Ditty, a Baltimore lawyer shot through the thigh, and Captain George Emack, who lost a thumb; another five Marylanders were taken prisoner. After their repulse, the Rebels regrouped and shadowed Kilpatrick's column after his troopers resumed their march.

As the skirmish with Johnson's cavalrymen played out, the Federals' main body moved closer to Old Church Tavern for a brief respite. Once their comrades routed the Maryland force, the relaxation began in earnest, and the men jawed with each other about the previous night's incredible escape. For the first time in eighty-four hours, the troopers could boil coffee and cook rations. The horses feasted on corn blades while their riders roasted sweet potatoes and worked up more complicated fare like corn, ham, and chickens. "Turkeys were beheaded and laid upon the coals as burnt offerings," one diarist wrote. The Federals stayed the morning at Old Church, hoping to see Dahlgren and his men come in. Finally, Kilpatrick's two brigades moved on toward White House Landing, then Tunstall's Station, where they bivouacked again.[6]

Clearly regaining their confidence, Kill-Cavalry's troopers plundered their way through southeastern Hanover County. Reports circulated later that raiders snatched rings off a Mrs. Boyd's fingers and ordered a crippled man, Braxton Garlick, to hand over his watch. At

Marlbourne, home of ardent secessionist Edmund Ruffin, the troopers broke into the smokehouse and made off with as much bacon as they could carry along with butter and corn. "They ransacked the mansion from top to bottom, but found little to steal or destroy—as no furniture had been left," according to Ruffin, whose slaves the cavalrymen left behind, joking that Ben Butler would be by later for them. Along the way the troopers grabbed horses, meat, and corn whenever possible. They did not neglect their martial duties, however, pausing to burn a sawmill near Tunstall's Station and a depot on the Richmond and York River Railroad, but they had no energy left to wreck the tracks.[7]

Mitchell was not the only one looking for Kilpatrick. Robert E. Lee was on the case too. Hoping to intercept the Yankee general's retreat, Lee ordered Major General Edward Johnson to move his division to Wilderness Run on the Orange Turnpike, then move on to the Wilderness Church on the Plank Road. He assigned Johnson a company of couriers to keep information flowing and sent Jeb Stuart, with the brigades of Brigadier Generals Williams Wickham and Thomas Rosser, down the Plank Road to Parker's Store. Of course, Little Kil was far away.[8]

Meanwhile, Mitchell's blue-clad troopers followed a paper trail of Lincoln's amnesty proclamations like bread crumbs on a forest path in their search for the general's column. Smoking fence rails provided another sign for the Yankees to follow. Lieutenant Mattison of the 2nd New York thought Union troopers had torched the fences as a signal for Dahlgren to follow the main force of raiders.

Between two and three o'clock in the afternoon of March 2, this apparent trail also led Mitchell's troopers straight into Johnson's Marylanders about eight miles from Tunstall's Station. The mystery of the smoldering fences evaporated as the shooting started. The Confederates, two hundred to three hundred strong, were posted near Piping Creek Ferry in the woods on either side of the road, the same road Mitchell's men needed to use to reunite with Kilpatrick. On edge since their last skirmish, the Federals felt the genius of desperation, badly needing to link up with their commander. Their alternatives now were "Kilpatrick or Libby Prison," one officer noted. "Every man nerved himself for this new trial, and with suppressed hurrahs for Kilpatrick, demanded to be led on." Mitchell briefly spoke with his officers, then ordered his cavalrymen to close ranks to a twelve-man front, with horsemen in the middle baring sabers

and riders at the flanks unholstering revolvers. Riding down this column, the officers told the men that they would be making "a charge
for liberty." A lurking Rebel cavalryman was close enough to hear a
Yankee say, "We had better go to h—l than go back to Richmond."

Mitchell gave the command to move out. Two young lieutenants, John R. Andrews from Maine and Murt Cunningham from New
York, led the charge with "a genuine Indian war whoop." Slowly at
first, then gathering momentum, the Federal column broke out, gaining speed on the downhill slope as the troopers put their spurs to use
in meter to the gallop. Men and mounts became a single mass whose
aspect at the ground level was a thundering blur of legs, above which
strained tons of equine musculature topped by a muddied blue streak
of uniformed men, sidearms and sabers glinting as they used one
hand to hold a weapon and the other to hold the reins.

The Marylanders held their fire until the Yankees, yelling like
"a lot of Comanches," came within a hundred yards. In a blink a
carbine fusillade emptied a dozen saddles. The Yankee horsemen
thundered through the timber, emptying their revolvers into the
Southerners' ranks. Even the wounded army scout Carney rose up
in his stirrups and fired his pistol at the Rebels alongside the road.
The Yankees continued almost a mile down the road through the
woods. A Maine captain thought the charge "was one of the finest
[he had] ever witnessed." Johnson's startled Marylanders broke and
fled, leaving the raiders in control of the road. Some Yankee horses,
too weak to maintain the attack's speed, stumbled to the ground,
tossing their adrenalin-charged riders in all directions. The colonel
managed to rally his men, but it was too late. Mitchell's troopers
had successfully cut their way through the blocking Rebels, sus-
taining a loss of about twenty men, and continued on to Kilpatrick's
main body, arriving near Tunstall's Station between four and five
o'clock in the afternoon. The beaten Marylanders were able to gob-
ble up a few dismounted Federal prisoners, including the gallant
Lieutenant Harris, who had been painfully wounded in the charge
near Green's farm the previous day. Despite support from several
fellow Michiganders during the charge, the courageous lieutenant
was unable to stay in the saddle, tumbling into the roadbed during
the melee. Nevertheless, Mitchell now victoriously delivered some
236 Union cavalrymen back to the general.[9]

Though muscled aside yet again, the Marylanders felt no sting
of defeat. They had harried their foe long and well. A corporal in

the 1st Maryland Cavalry wrote home to say that "the most glorious sport was pushing Kilpatrick for three days at his rear, driving and scattering them. We had but a handful of men, but with
these annoyed their rear constantly and with so much vigor that the
[Federal] ranks thought a brigade was fighting them." He posited
that if Fitzhugh Lee's division had not been disbanded for winter rest
and refitting, Kill-Cavalry's command never would have escaped.[10]

One of the men Mitchell saved was "Pat," a prototypical Irishman
who had fallen out of Kilpatrick's column short of Tunstall's Station,
overcome by applejack or peach brandy. When the captain and his
troopers, exhilarated by their charge and so muddied that their uniforms looked butternut, rode up, Pat unsteadily offered a shout of
resistance and made to draw his saber, which became tangled with
his scabbard and cost him his balance. Enjoying a sort of afterglow,
two of Mitchell's men amiably hoisted their drunken compatriot
over an empty saddle and soon reunited him with his comrades in
the 7th Michigan.[11]

Mitchell had led his horse soldiers "with great judgment and cool-
ness as well as with determined courage in rejoining Gen. Kilpatrick
with but slight loss," in the words of his old regimental commander,
Henry Davies. Beyond gallantry, the captain had also shown wisdom, waiting out the rotten night after losing touch with Dahlgren
and proceeding at dawn, which put him closer to Kilpatrick's main
column, offered his troopers some rest, and allowed his men to fight
their way through to the safety of the larger Union force. As happy
as Kilpatrick must have been to see Mitchell and his men, their
arrival only underscored the gravity of Dahlgren's situation, which
was unknown but clearly bad. When he and the captain first came
face to face, the general asked what he knew of Dahlgren. Mitchell
had no answer.[12]

Kilpatrick's troopers spent the midday hours of March 2 fending off Confederate harassment before reaching Tunstall's Station.
At one point the Yankees charged the Rebels to prevent further
annoyance, after which "they staid [sic] away." A warm winter sun
quickly melted the snow from the previous evening. Even the troopers' spirits began to improve as the warmer weather dried out their
clothing and chilled bodies. But Kilpatrick, recalling the chagrin
of being routed by Wade Hampton, ordered a line of battle maintained as the raiders retreated, with units covering one another's
advance. "One brigade would take a defensive position, while the

other would march about five miles to a commanding point, where it in turn would form a line," a staff officer described. "The first brigade would then give way, pass through the second, and take position well to the rear."

Throughout the afternoon the Federals pushed on, stopping briefly to feed famished mounts "in a beautiful valley near the Pamunkey River" where they found an abundance of corn. Kilpatrick figured to cross the Pamunkey at White House, but the Rebels had burned the bridge and no boats were in sight. He then countermarched from the river but soon concluded that his column was lost; a council of war confirmed the obvious. A staff officer retrieved the situation by recruiting a local guide, an elderly black man, who reassured the general that he was within a half mile of Tunstall's Station. Kilpatrick had not recognized the area, having last seen it before war's ravages had obliterated every railway landmark and a year's vegetation growth had changed the visual contours of the locale beyond recognition except to the locals. About 9:00 P.M., after a shout of appreciation, the Federals finally camped for the night at Tunstall's Station on the Richmond and York River Railroad. Their commander spent the night "at a Mr. Temple's" house about a half mile from the depot. The last of the weary troopers finally staggered into camp closer to two o'clock the next morning.[13]

But for friendly bondsmen like the old slave at Tunstall's Station, the raiders might have fared far worse. Countless times during the raid, with Union scouts shrugging in confusion, black saviors stepped in to decode the mystifying terrain, read spoor, point out stocks of corn, and expose the victuals and horses local whites had tried to conceal. They offered intelligence on Rebel positions, explaining what and where they had seen Confederate activity. These "contrabands" freely and without hesitation put their shoulders to the task of wrecking Southern railroads; once a group waved as the raiders were pulling out, saying they would keep at the job a while longer. "We'll catch up," one called to the departing bluecoats.[14] The other side of the equation was that sticking with the Federals meant escape to a better life. No malice to match Dahlgren's cruelty to Martin Roberson occurred in Kilpatrick's ranks.

As the column straggled into Tunstall's Station, scouts reported seeing a large cavalry force's campfires nearby. Remembering Hampton's surprise attack, Little Kil ordered his artillery positioned and the men formed in line of battle before they dismounted.

His resolve rippled through the ranks. "I expected every moment the test would come, examined my pistols, tightened my saddle and made up my mind that if they took me to Richmond, it would be as a cold corpse," an officer of the 5th New York wrote. It went without saying that they would not have fires, and the sleep-deprived troopers stood to horse until daylight, never hearing any enemy approach.[15]

By March 3, still with no word from Dahlgren, Kilpatrick's now-ragged brigades staggered toward New Kent Court House. General Butler had ordered a relief column to march as far as New Kent but to go no farther. In a letter to Secretary of War Stanton, he wrote, "Upon being notified of the intended movement of Genl Kilpatrick I ordered Col. West . . . to march to New Kent C. H. & remain there to render such aid as might be necessary." Even if Butler had had mischief in mind for Richmond, his troops did not leave Williamsburg until nearly midnight on March 1, long after they could have thrown in on an attack of the Confederate capital.

Any plans Kill-Cavalry had entertained for a cooperative effort from the southeast apparently went astray through puzzling communications within the army's chain of command. Butler's orders to West show that the Massachusetts general had no intent to attack Richmond from the southeast—a strategy difficult to fathom, given Kilpatrick's original plan and his history with Butler. Kill-Cavalry fully expected a simultaneous attack on Richmond from the southeast to confuse and distract the city's defenders. Early in the war he had served under the older general on the Peninsula; they got on well enough for Kilpatrick to ask Butler for a letter of recommendation when seeking the rank of lieutenant colonel in the Harris Light Cavalry. The general obliged, writing an appreciative letter to Stanton and helping the young officer climb another rung. But Kilpatrick also tried and failed to persuade the War Department to assign his new regiment to Butler's command. So the timing miscue for Butler's troops to march toward Richmond and the fact that they would never attack the city remains a great mystery of the raid. Moreover, it is difficult to pin down who may have been the responsible party in this blunder—Meade, Halleck, Butler, or all three. At least in circumstantial terms, the upper ranks clearly displayed an indifferent, if not resistant, attitude toward the raid before and during its execution. Butler's failure to be at or even near the gates of Richmond on the morning of March 1 is a prime example.[16]

When Butler's column finally did move—but only as far as New Kent Court House—it consisted of about two thousand infantry and one thousand cavalry under Colonel Robert M. West. This force consisted of Colonel Samuel Duncan's infantry brigade of the 4th, 5th, 6th, and 22nd U.S. Colored Troops; the 1st New York Mounted Rifles and 11th Pennsylvania Cavalry under Colonel Samuel Spear; and Battery F, 1st Rhode Island Light Artillery. The artillery left Yorktown at 6:00 P.M. on the evening of March 1, arriving at Williamsburg about 9:30 P.M. The entire column started out of the old colonial capital about eleven o'clock that night. Interestingly, West would later report that while his orders did not authorize him to go beyond New Kent Court House, he took it upon himself to send cavalry beyond the county seat based on the circumstances he encountered. The colonel's instructions betray an indication that his force was never intended to attack Richmond from the southeast. That West's column was strictly a bailout force raises questions about who decided to leave Kilpatrick in front of Richmond's fortifications without the planned diversionary attack from Butler's sector. The record is silent on this, and only circumstantial evidence points to a possible conspiracy in the upper echelon of the Union high command. But it makes for interesting speculation about how the raid might have gone if Butler had come up as Kilpatrick expected.[17]

The middle section of the Peninsula was getting the same miserable weather as inland, "a cold rain that lasted all night," according to a Pennsylvania trooper. A Rhode Island cannoneer later remembered his "clothing being completely wet, [and] frozen, this adding to the discomforts of the march." The rain stopped, but the air got no warmer. Halting about 7:00 A.M. to make breakfast, this same man said that his overcoat "would have stood alone, frozen, had I taken it off." West's command continued on until two o'clock in the afternoon of March 2, when they finally reached New Kent Court House. They had spent twenty-four hours marching forty-two miles.[18] Spear arrived at New Kent Court House about 7:30 A.M. on March 2. After a short rest he dispersed small detachments to search for the raiders. Near evening, not far from Tunstall's Station, Spear's troopers made contact with advance units from Little Kil's cavalry.[19]

On the morning of March 3, Kilpatrick's main column stumbled into Duncan's soldiers on the road to New Kent. Thinking they were hearing enemy riders, the exhausted raiders braced for another fight, this time against an entire brigade. The horsemen closed ranks, threw down fences, and formed up a regiment for a charge—until Kilpatrick raised his binoculars and spied the Stars and Stripes fluttering above the infantrymen's ranks, allaying all fears. The general ordered the column forward, and around noon the troopers arrived at New Kent. The rest of West's command soon joined with the Army of the Potomac's horsemen at the county seat. "Many of the men were without hats or caps, wearing handkerchiefs tied over their heads. . . . Their route could have been traced by the horses, dead from hard riding and exhaustion, lying by the roadside," an artilleryman with the relief column said later. Kilpatrick got a rousing cheer from the 1st New York Mounted Rifles, whose colonel, along with another of the unit's officers, had served under Little Kil back in 1861. The troopers behind the general were a sight to behold. Observing the "rollicking devil-may-care appearance of the returning raiders covered with dust and mud," a soldier of the relief force noted "the relaxed discipline indulged by their officers. Some of the gayer troopers wore conspicuous regalia, made up of civilian apparel, spoils taken not for their value, but in a spirit of wanton mischief." One raider's horse wore "a net armour [*sic*] made out of a hoop skirt; another wore a lady's 'skoop-bonnet' with a huge bow. A large number wore stove pipe beaver hats of antique models, piling them up one upon another." A disorderly raider, who was balancing atop his head a telescoping array of headgear, "waggishly asserted that the top one was Jeff Davis's Sunday-go-to-meeting hat." After a halt of two to three hours at the courthouse, the combined blue column started for Williamsburg, with the general's horsemen "riding by fours and retaining their regalia until they passed through Yorktown." Kilpatrick drolly reported to Major General Pleasonton that he arrived inside Butler's lines "with my command in good order."[20]

The black soldiers among the relief column occasioned no ill feeling from the troopers. In fact, the presence of Duncan's brigade may have helped change a few minds among the white cavalrymen, who were sincerely glad to see the black troops as they marched into the village. "Arriving at New Kent CH, we met a brigade of colored troops. The first we have ever seen. . . . [N]o brigade . . . presented a better appearance," one Pennsylvanian wrote. "A mountain of prejudice was removed in an instant. . . . Heretofore the cavalry of the Army of the Potomac entertained a marked dislike for colored troops . . . [but now] the mutual cheers were deafening."

Others had the same feeling. A New York cavalryman penned in his diary that "some of the colored troops are the best drilled troops I ever saw—they make good soldiers—the very best." This entry improved on one written four days earlier, when he scribbled, "I never [saw] Niggers look so good to me before." Another New Yorker described them as "fine-looking colored men. . . . [W]e could see their faces and knew we had met friends." A Michigan trooper wrote home shortly after the raid, "Our boys did not have many prejudices against colored troops just then, and we gave them some hearty cheers as we ever gave anybody." Another Wolverine was a little more reserved, writing: "We were glad to see them ([even] if they were black). They make good looking soldiers, and are well drilled." One of Kilpatrick's aides observed: "It was the first time we had seen negro troops, but as the long line of glistening bayonets and light-blue uniforms came into view, prejudices, if there were any, vanished at once, and a cheer from the begrimed troopers rang down our line. . . . It was a pleasant thing to march past that array of faces, friendly though black, and know we were safe."[21]

Duncan's infantrymen were happy to share rations with Kilpatrick's famished troopers. "The brave black fellows emptied their haversacks to us in a generous providence, then formed in rear of the jaded cavalry, in this manner escorting us to Yorktown and safety," one Michigan cavalryman wrote home. By nightfall on March 3, the combined commands reached Burnt Ordinary (present-day Toano), about nine miles from Williamsburg. The Federals spent a cold night camped near an old tavern—the first time since they jumped off, a Vermont soldier told his diary, that the men unsaddled their mounts. Kilpatrick and his escort used the halt to search for Dahlgren, in the process drawing fire from Rebel bushwhackers in an adjoining woodlot. The Rebel shots drew a sharp response, and the guerrillas fled, leaving three of their number in Union hands. The next morning the column marched through Williamsburg before turning onto the road to Yorktown, which they reached at about five o'clock in the afternoon on March 4. A Michigan sergeant found the town to be an impregnable fort with thirty-six-pounders placed all around it, "their ugly looking mouths pointing in every direction."[22]

The raid was over for these troopers. The men drew their first rations and forage since leaving Stevensburg. But the adrenaline of the preceding days was still with them. "We find ourselves here in this dismal place called Yorktown and ready for something else," a

Vermonter wrote. A Mainer was more positive, claiming that he felt "a little shaky when going into battle, don't think anything about it while fighting, but to come out of it all right, makes me feel good all over." Another Vermonter used the respite to gather some oysters, a rare treat for Green Mountain men.[23]

The raid's end surely left Judson Kilpatrick feeling relieved. While still in Williamsburg, he telegraphed Pleasonton at 9:00 P.M. on March 3. The message had a tempered tone, short on his typical swagger. Kilpatrick admitted flat out that he had failed to accomplish the "great object" of his operation, but he had destroyed the enemy's communications at various points, including railroad lines, mills, canal locks, and "other valuable property." He proudly reported that he had lost "less than 150 men" but did not or could not say what Dahlgren's losses had been. Regaining form, he claimed that his "entire command [was] in good order, and [needed] but a few days' rest." A concerned Pleasonton immediately pleaded that General Meade have Kilpatrick's "picked troops" shipped back to Alexandria to bolster the Cavalry Corps. An hour before Kilpatrick had sent his telegram, Butler, in an 8:00 P.M. wire, was telling Secretary of War Stanton the raid's particulars. No one, however, knew where Ulric Dahlgren was.[24]

Two days later Kilpatrick reported new information to Pleasonton, giving his commander the impression that Colonel Dahlgren was alive near King and Queen Court House. The general optimistically claimed that he was in a position to send a relief force to help the young colonel. But two days later, on March 8, Little Kil came face to face with reality when a dozen raiders from Dahlgren's party reached Union lines with bad news. An ambush in King and Queen County had left Dahlgren dead, his command scattered. Then the colonel's servant came in, describing the officer's naked corpse lying by a roadside "horribly mutilated."[25]

Kilpatrick wanted revenge—and now—for what he termed Dahlgren's "murder." The general got his way several days later. Safely aboard a gunboat, McClellan-style, Kill-Cavalry sent his troopers against Confederate cavalry units in King and Queen County. Aided by horsemen from Colonel Spear's cavalry brigade and two artillery batteries, the Yankees attacked the 9th Virginia Cavalry and part of the 5th Virginia Cavalry. The assault routed the Confederates, under Colonel R. L. T. Beale, from their camps near Carlton's Store. A Vermonter haughtily penciled in his diary,

"Old Kill keeps the enemy doing all the running." Unchallenged, the Yankees rode on to King and Queen Court House, where they burned public buildings and several private structures. Many public documents were also consumed in the flames. As one Michigan trooper wrote home, when "the pillaging started the houses were demolished, to tell the truth it was a real celebration (treat) to the plunderer." Not even a child's musical instrument was safe. "Even a piano, which [William Martin's] daughter begged might be saved, was smashed in wantonness," a Richmond paper reported. "And the parlor carpet was taken from the floor, cut into strips, and divided among the robbers."[26]

The only building not burned was the Courthouse Tavern, its survival becoming a local legend. The story goes that with the courthouse next door aflame and Union cavalrymen about to burn the tavern, a citizen told an officer that a sick man was upstairs in the tavern. The officer ordered his men to save the bedridden fellow until his neighbor revealed that he had smallpox, a common ploy civilians used to save a building from burning, whether true or not. Leaving the man and tavern be, the Northerners moved on, never learning that there was no one upstairs at the tavern.[27]

Judson Kilpatrick was proud of what his men did in King and Queen County. A day after his troopers returned from this raid he reported to Butler that the people "have been well punished for the murder of Colonel Dahlgren." The revenge was little succor for Dahlgren's men, though, captured and marched to Stevensville, a few miles from the ambush site, on March 3.[28]

Two weeks after Kilpatrick returned to Yorktown, most of his raiders were back with the Army of the Potomac. A New York trooper wrote home that he had ridden to within cannon shot of Richmond. "It was a long and fatiguing march," the cavalryman wrote, "our troops only halted to feed the horses, either by day or night, all were nearly worn out when they reached Fortress Monroe." Dr. Charles Hackley, a Federal surgeon who rode with the raiders, provided more details on their condition: a "number of cases of painfully swelled feet came under my observation. These were partly attributable to the boots not having been removed and the spur straps being tight, and partly, doubtless, to the McClellan saddles interfering with the circulation of the legs." Hackley found numerous cases of enlisted men with hemorrhoids caused by saddle blankets lumping up in the space cut in the saddle trees, with no support for a constantly battered perineum. Officers fared better, though, their saddle seats being padded with leather. On March 11 the saddle-sore troopers boarded transports bound for Alexandria. Two days later they docked at the Virginia town, which had been in Union hands since early in the war. By March 16 the troopers were back at their camps around Stevensburg in Culpeper County.[29]

CHAPTER 13

DAHLGREN ATTEMPTS AN ESCAPE

A round 8:00 A.M. on March 2, as Kilpatrick's troopers were enjoying smoked ham, roasted turkey, and sweet potatoes at Old
Church, Ulric Dahlgren's jaded horse soldiers were crossing the
Pamunkey River. As Dahlgren and his ninety-odd men made their
way over the river at Hanovertown Ferry, the admiral's son was less
than ten miles from his commander, but they might as well have
been a continent apart. After spending several hours traversing
the river, Dahlgren's men and their prisoners—Captain Dement of
the 1st Maryland Battery and Lieutenant Blair of the Salem Light
Artillery—were on their way again, riding the flat farmlands of King
William County. Dement and Blair could have escaped long ago but
apparently chose to stick with their captors to gain more information. Their next crossing, of the Mattaponi, would put the raiders in
King and Queen County. Dahlgren seems to have been heading for
Gloucester Point on the York River, where Union gunboats offered
protection. Perhaps Kilpatrick had mentioned this route to the young
colonel while regaling his adventures during Stoneman's Raid the
previous May.[1]

Shortly after entering King William County, the raiders spied
two horsemen coming their way. One was Benny Fleet, a headstrong
seventeen-year-old who lived on the far shore of the Mattaponi
at Green Mount plantation. He had recently told a friend that he
intended to join Confederate John Mosby's famed partisan rangers
up in Loudoun County. Fleet and William Taliaferro, a neighbor and
a member of the Confederate Signal Corps, had heard that Yankees
were afoot and had gone out scouting for them. Fleet's dog, Stuart,
had come along for the romp. As the Union riders spotted them,
the two young Rebels also saw the column. Mistaking mud-caked
Federals for Confederates, they put on a gallop, realizing too late
that they were riding straight at the enemy. Raiders shot Taliaferro's
horse from under him and took the youth prisoner. Fleet got away,
though with a bad wound to his left arm that may have severed
an artery. He stayed in the saddle as his horse carried him into the

woods, but blood loss sent him tumbling to the ground. One story has his horse returning to Green Mount later that day, though it does not explain how the animal would have navigated the high river with no rider to spur it on. Searchers found Fleet's body the next morning, assisted by Stuart's barking. The dog apparently had remained by his master's side all night.[2]

After this dustup, despite being trailed by the 42nd Virginia Cavalry Battalion, the exhausted raiders made a fairly easy transit across King William County to the Mattaponi, where they encountered another challenge. It was afternoon, perhaps two or three o'clock, when they reached Aylett's Ferry and found there what one officer called "an old scow." In small groups the fatigued cavalrymen rowed the boat across, their mounts swimming alongside. The crossing took an hour or so, a quiet interlude for the raiders, who were nearly done when bushwhackers interrupted the calm by firing "shotguns, carbines and rifles," scattering the Federals as they took cover. Infuriated, Dahlgren ordered his men to return fire. None did. He shouted more forcefully, using harsher language, until they began to use their weapons. As ever, the colonel was in the thick of it, upright on crutches on the west bank of the river, firing his revolver until the boat returned for one last run to fetch him. Federal fire by now had pinned down the Rebels, who were not able to hit Dahlgren before he hobbled into the boat and was rowed across the Mattaponi. On the opposite bank, comrades hoisted him into his saddle, and Dahlgren resumed the march for Gloucester Point. The bushwhackers who had interrupted the crossing bedeviled the bluecoats the rest of the day and into the evening, forcing them into delays and detours that kept them marching into another inky night through unfriendly country.[3]

The narrow country roads of "thoroughly and universally rural" King and Queen County enforced a slower pace on the column. The plantation economy, originally heavy in tobacco but by the outbreak of war a mix of wheat, corn, and cotton, had discouraged the development of any "settlement that ever approached the dimensions of a town."[4] Only one hamlet, Stevensville, stood between the Union cavalrymen's path and Gloucester Point. The county was as unabashedly Rebel as it was uninterruptedly rural. Residents were "ardently devoted to the Confederate cause and ready to assert their devotion." Many young men had gone to wear the gray, but their elders who remained on the home front were just as ready to take up arms—and did, firing randomly at Dahlgren and his men. In retaliation the colonel ordered his troopers to burn every dwelling from which a shot had come. Remembering a comrade's confronta-tion with an elderly woman whose home seemed to have harbored a sniper, Lieutenant Reuben Bartley wrote, "The old lady would not condescend to reply to any of his questions at all but elevated her nose in a very unmistakable manner at him as though he was not worthy to be addressed by one of the F.F.V." When at the officer's order one of her slaves fetched some straw and a shovel of coals, it was "magical" how quickly the Southern dame relented. After that no one fired a round from any houses along Dahlgren's route.[5]

Soon after the troopers crossed the Mattaponi, according to a local tale, Dahlgren rode into the front yard of Glenwood plantation, where a slave boy named John Seger saw him. In a story Seger told at age eighty-two, the colonel "had on a red cap, and there were ten or fifteen other horse-soldiers with him. He was tired and he seemed in a hurry. He told us the war was about over and we'd soon be free. They rode off after a while in the direction of Walkerton," a village several miles away. What kind of soldier wears a bright red cap in enemy territory? Whether or not Dahlgren had on such headgear, what had become of his other troopers? Had he done as he did not so long before near Greencastle, Pennsylvania, when he had left his men? The former slave's story, which emphasizes the Union colo-nel's fatigue, also casts him as avid about the war and its cause. True or apocryphal, Seger's story, while beloved of those who still retell it, does not reveal much.[6]

En route to Stevensville, the raiders encountered a hastily orga-nized mounted force assembled by Lieutenant James Pollard, com-manding Company H, 9th Virginia Cavalry, who happened to be home on furlough to refit his company's horses. Pollard was "one of the bravest and truest of men," a Southerner said. "As a soldier, I think he was unexcelled. He was a man who could be relied upon to do the right thing at the right time—a Virginia gentleman of gravity and of character." A recurring bout with argue that caused malar-ial fever, chills, and sweats sometimes sidelined him, however. For the last several weeks, Pollard had been following orders to picket King William County against U.S. Navy marauders coming up the Rappahannock River in gunboats. As a headquarters, the lieuten-ant picked King William Court House to station his men for duty. Pollard had been in Richmond acquiring carbines for his unit when news spread through the city that mounted raiders were throughout the area. He hastened back to his troopers to make dispositions to meet the enemy if they came his way. Thinking the bluecoats would cross at Dunkirk, two miles north of Aylett's, he stationed his men there, but Dahlgren crossed the river downstream. An undaunted Pollard was soon joined by Captain William McGruder and about thirty men of the 42nd Virginia Cavalry Battalion, a unit from Richmond that had been tracking the Yankees.

Despite their exhaustion, the Federals easily brushed aside Pollard's makeshift force. They continued on the road to Stevensville until Pollard attacked again, this time hitting their rear guard about a mile west of Bruington Church. The Yankees took up a defensive position as desultory firing began on both sides. Soon Dahlgren decided to break off the engagement, which had left one blue-coated corporal dead. Pollard's harassing action caused the raiders to turn onto the River Road at Butler's Tavern, away from the route to Gloucester Point. Pollard then stole a march on the Northerners, pushing his men four miles directly east, then south another mile or so to a point where he planned to challenge the Yankee raiders again. As they marched Pollard's troopers collected a force of untried men and young boys mustering as the King and Queen County Home Guards. This unit, thirty-two-men strong, comprised "old or middle-aged men," including "six preachers, five doctors and two lawyers." They had been formed in July 1863 at Dr. Watson Walker's house. Walker, a thirty-seven-year-old physician, served as the company's first lieutenant, while a local Baptist preacher, the Reverend Richard H. Bagby, commanded the home guards with the rank of captain. Bagby's company was soon be joined by other King and Queen County home-guards units and some cavalrymen from the 5th Virginia.[7]

Knowing only that his harassers had moved away, Dahlgren would have been entitled to feel relief. At about 6:00 P.M. the bone-weary Northerners, "prostrated with fatigue and hunger," crossed Anseamancock (now Garnett's) Creek and halted near Hockley Neck to eat and feed their broken-down mounts. Three pickets were posted to guard against surprises. In a cold drizzle the other troopers rested in Gresham's clover field, cooking their first meal in thirty-six hours while Dahlgren slept on a pallet of fence rails. Major Cooke inventoried the men's stock of ammunition, which was nearly exhausted; many of the seventy remaining troopers had not a round left.[8]

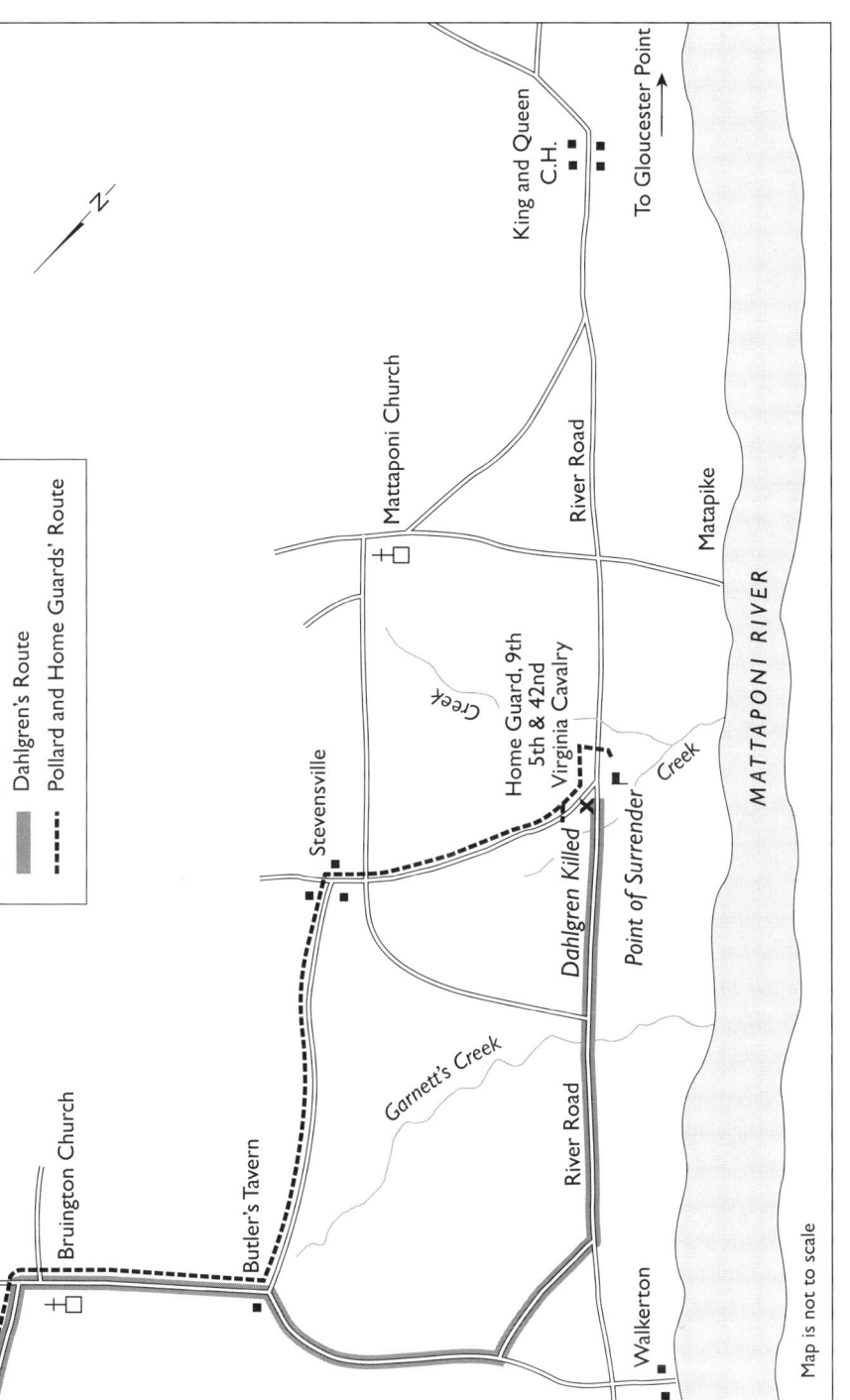

Legend

Dahlgren's Route

Pollard and Home Guards' Route

N

Bruington Church

Butler's Tavern

Stevensville

Mattaponi Church

King and Queen C.H.

To Gloucester Point

Garnett's Creek

River Road

Walkerton

Creek

Home Guard, 9th 5th & 42nd Virginia Cavalry

Dahlgren Killed

Point of Surrender

Creek

River Road

Matapike

MATTAPONI RIVER

Map is not to scale

Dahlgren Is Ambushed in King and Queen County. Map by Bill Nelson. *Copyright © 2016 by the University of Oklahoma Press.*

233

As Cooke was counting bullets around 9:00 P.M., a pair of Rebel irregulars was spying on the raiders from under cover about thirty feet away. With campfires silhouetting the tired troopers, the Southerners easily counted their ranks, watched for some time, fired a few shots, and then "hastened to Stevensville" to report to Pollard. The lieutenant quickly moved his 150-man patchwork command to a fork west of King and Queen Court House. Pollard's cavalry company was made up of "seasoned veterans," and "nearly every man in the company was a crack shot, . . . some were expert marksmen." But a home-guards officer remembered the motley force as "a strange medley of regulars, raw troops, old farmers, preachers, schoolboys, etc." Pollard set up his surprise—an improvised barricade of fallen tree limbs—near the intersection of the Stevensville and River Roads. A Bagby relative later claimed that the ambuscade was set "on the northeast angle of" where the Stevensville Road met that leading to King and Queen Court House. Feeling ill, Pollard turned command over to Captain Edward Fox of the 5th Virginia Cavalry, who arrived at the scene "a few minutes before the enemy advanced."[9]

Midnight was nearing as the raiders broke camp. They had only just gotten underway when they realized that their three pickets had disappeared. Even so, the Yankees proceeded up the River Road, sending a scout ahead. That man soon returned, reporting the road impassable. A clatter of hoofs, spurs, and sabers soon drew the Rebels closer to the road. As Dr. Bernard H. Walker remembered it, "We were soon behind trees on a rising ground overlooking the road."[10]

Dahlgren ordered an advance guard of six men, all who could be spared. To buck up his exhausted men's morale, the colonel "placed himself at their head" in the front rank, accompanying the scouts Martin Hogan and Jake Swisher; Dahlgren rode his "splendid bay." Major Cooke, 1st Lieutenant Merritt of the 5th New York, and Lieutenant Bartley joined the second set of four riders in the roadway. The one-legged colonel "had undaunted courage to a fault; his voice was like magic through the ranks" despite his "crippled condition," according to his signal officer. Dahlgren also brought along the two Confederate officers captured at the Frederick's Hall court-martial— Captain Dement and Lieutenant Blair—perhaps thinking that having the Rebels along might offer protection in a tight spot. The old country road, sunken between four-foot banks topped by a thick growth of mature cedar trees, was close quarters for men riding by fours at a trot. As their horses plunged down the muddy road, sabers rattling at their sides, the four Union officers suddenly encountered a man in their path, probably 1st Sergeant Fleming Meredith of the 9th Virginia Cavalry.[11]

The colonel reined in his mount. In the underbrush some-thing rustled. Private George Ward of the 1st Maine said later that Dahlgren asked the stranger his unit. "The Tenth New York," the Southerner drawled. "You are a liar!" Dahlgren snapped, drawing his pistol. "Surrender you damned rebel or I'll shoot you." From the woods a Southern voice shouted back that the Northerner should surrender. "Give them h—l boys," Dahlgren shouted, pulling the trigger of his own revolver. It misfired.

Suddenly pandemonium broke out. "[F]rom the surrounding thickets which lined the road a hundred rifles flashed a reply," one chronicler wrote. Carbines, pistols, "squirrel rifles," and dou-ble-barreled shotguns loaded with buckshot blazed away from the cover of the trees. "The bushes poured forth a sheet of fire" on the Yankees' left flank and rear, a Union officer recounted later. "The woods seemed to be alive with the enemy, who fired on us," another said. Signal officer Bartley thought the Southerners' vol-ley was "so close the flashes almost reached our horses." Dahlgren went down with as many as five bullets ripping into his body. "Oh, I am hurt so bad," he moaned. "Damn you, make haste, then, and die," a Rebel retorted. Cooke's horse went down, pinning him. Cap-tain Dement's horse was killed in the fusillade, but the Confed-erate officer remained unhurt. As Lieutenant Merritt shouted to the remaining Federals to pepper the bushes, he caught a round in the leg. Scrambling to reverse field in a tiny space, the surviving Yankees stampeded, wildly running a gauntlet of musketry as they streamed back down the road. In the melee both Dement and Blair finally made their escape to friendly lines.[12]

The minute or so it took Cooke to pull himself from beneath his dead horse must have seemed like hours. Now in command, he made his way back to his men on foot. The Northerners had broken through a fence line and were huddling in a field near the road. Cooke ordered them to tighten their girths and prepare to cut their way out. "The men stood perfectly firm though almost all of them were utterly destitute of ammunition, and fully aware of the hopelessness of our position," a New York officer wrote later. They were surrounded and on terrible terrain. "The country was broken up in rough hills and thickly wooded or dense jungles, rendering it utterly impracticable to make our way across the country mounted," another officer recalled. Bisecting the field was a man-made waterway large and deep enough to discourage any effort to cross it. It might have been worse for the bluecoats if Pollard, overcome by ague, had not retired from the field. His successor, Captain Fox was not as aggressive. Two locals, Christopher B. Fleet and A. C. Acree, found the Yankees in the murky darkness, but Fox decided to wait until morning to attack.[13]

With Dahlgren dead in the mucky roadbed a few hundred yards away, his officers plotted their next move. They had little to be optimistic about. The enlisted men realized that they were surrounded. Additionally, they had only thirty rounds of ammunition left among them. The only way out was to break up into groups of three, four, or five, trying "to baffle the pursuit." The men shoved their sabers into the wet ground to the hilt and picketed their horses to the handles, not wanting to use what little ammunition they had to kill the horses and perhaps draw the Confederates to their location. They stripped their carbines and buried the chambers, breaking the magazine tubes to make them useless. Some men were so exhausted that they decided to surrender. Of the surviving members of Dahlgren's column, forty or so would make a run for it, keeping only their belts, revolvers, and haversacks.[14]

Those attempting to reach Union lines departed in groups of three and four. One man collected two revolvers' worth of cartridges for Lieutenant Merritt, who never forgot the gesture. Major Cooke, the wounded Merritt, Bartley, and the three army scouts crept half a mile "like cats" on their hands and knees until they had cleared the enemy's pickets. They hid all day in a pine thicket on March 3, the first time Bartley had slept in more than ninety hours. The signal officer had kept his compass and a decent topographical map of Virginia but had made sure to destroy his secret codebooks and private papers as Dahlgren should have done after he was defeated outside Richmond by the Local Defense Troops.[15]

Toward daybreak, a bluecoat attached a handkerchief to a branch and waved this white flag at the head of the ragged column. Lieutenant William Nunn conveyed the survivors' wish to surrender to Captain Dement, their former prisoner. Dement conferred with Fox, who agreed to let the artillery officer accept the surrender. At daylight he brought the Federals in. Fox's men found

"large quantities of silverware, rings and watches" and other valuables in the raiders' saddlebags. Some troopers gave up their boots
to the Rebels along with their freedom. Now walking under guard
to Richmond, the bluecoats received only water from their captors until about two o'clock in the afternoon, when they got a little
bacon and cornmeal, which they mixed with water and baked over
a fire. Afterward the march continued, with men giving out from
exhaustion. Soon at Belle Isle, the enlisted men would be shuffled
into a putrid camp, where they would endure a rough time.[16]

After walking about three or four miles, the hungry little band
of escaping officers and scouts stopped at a small log cabin. They
concealed their pistols under their coats and knocked, asking for
food. The resident, an old overseer named McFarland, bade them
welcome and ushered them into his house. His wife set about preparing a meal while her husband stoked the fire to warm his unexpected guests. Mrs. McFarland soon excused herself, saying she had
to find one of the slaves they managed.

The Federals had happened onto Milton, the plantation owned
by Richard Bagby, the preacher and militia officer who had ambushed
their commander. While McFarland occupied the Yankees, his wife
sent a "small colored boy" to alert Bagby, whose house was two
hundred yards away, that Yankees were at her cabin for the taking.
Bagby; his sixteen-year-old son, John; and Jim Boler, a faithful slave,
came running with weapons and burst through the cabin door. The
Federals, their pistols impossible to reach, raised their hands. Major
Cooke surrendered his revolver and gave Bagby a silver watch rather
than lose it eventually to a prison guard. Local lore has it that the
preacher allowed his prisoners to wash their grimy faces and, blessing the meal with pistol in hand, fed them pancakes. Bagby kept
his prisoners overnight in his parlor after nailing the windows shut.
Later they were marched to Stevensville, then on to Libby under
a guard provided by Captain McGruder's 42nd Virginia Battalion.[17]

As Bagby was capturing Cooke and his cohorts, the preacher's
fellow home guardsmen were starting Dahlgren's body on a surreal
journey. Shortly after the submissive raiders surrendered to Dement
and Fox, some Confederates began stripping Dahlgren's corpse, emptying his pockets of eight hundred dollars in greenbacks. A Rebel
trooper named Cornelius Martin used a knife to slice off the dead
colonel's left pinky finger to remove his gold ring. A lock of hair
was snipped off his bloodstained head by Moore B. Wright, a home

guardsman. A local doctor named Taylor grabbed the artificial limb, leaving it with a Mrs. James for safekeeping. The good doctor's purpose was sincere; he wanted to take the leg to Richmond to show his colleagues. Taylor was amazed with the instrument's manufacture and thought Confederate surgeons could benefit from seeing the device before it was buried with the officer's remains. The prosthetic limb would never be buried with its original owner, however. Dr. Taylor also conducted an informal autopsy, finding "three bullets had entered [Dahlgren's] back, and one, if not two balls had penetrated his heart." Other accounts claim that Dahlgren received three buckshots in the spine. Still others delineate that there were two bullet holes in his head, two in his body, and one in his leg or hand. There were no exit wounds, probably because Dahlgren's heavy overcoat had slowed the rounds before they entered him. However many bullets hit the one-legged colonel, the result was immediate death.[18]

The morning after the ambush, Dahlgren lay where he had fallen. Frost had settled over the corpse and mud around it. The King and Queen County home guards had remained near the scene of the skirmish, among them thirteen-year-old William Littlepage. He served with his teacher, Edward Halbach, whose frailty had exempted him from regular service but did not keep him from forming a homeguards company with himself as captain. Halbach's "troops" were mostly boys like Littlepage who took naturally to having their schoolmaster as their commanding officer. The dead Yankee colonel, minus the pinky on his left hand, drew Littlepage's attention. He knelt by the mutilated corpse and, with a boy's industry, rifled through the pockets. He found trophies galore: a gold watch, a cigar case, a memorandum book with folded papers inserted among its pages, and other papers jammed into the Yankee's jacket pocket. Jauntily, perhaps even offering Captain Halbach a stogie, he handed over what he had found. A glance at the papers was enough to convince his teacher to move them rapidly up the chain of command.[19]

In no time Richmond was atwitter over the papers Littlepage had found on Dahlgren's body. Speeding news of the ambush across Federal lines, Union sympathizers got a copy of the March 5 *Richmond Sentinel*, with its account of the already notorious orders, to General Meade the day after it appeared. A *New York Herald* reporter at Army of the Potomac headquarters spied the Southern newspaper, and by March 9 the story was in the *Herald*, complete with the *Sentinel*'s inflammatory editorial. Things were soon heating up for Meade and Kilpatrick.[20]

While the boy soldier was turning over his extraordinary find to Halbach, other fleeing troopers made it to the York River near West Point, Virginia. Four troopers and Dahlgren's black body servant had encountered a local slave who guided them to Brick House Farm and the banks of the Mattaponi, where they secured a skiff. A Union gunboat, the *Morse*, was anchored in the river. The five put their backs into rowing and quickly reached the warship. Once on board, Dahlgren's servant gave Lieutenant Commander Charles A. Babcock, the ship's captain, a firsthand account of the Southerners' attack. As far as these Union soldiers knew, about half their comrades had surrendered.

Like Cooke and the rest at Bagby's plantation, other risk-taking Federals attempting to return to Union lines soon were caught and herded with the others to Libby Prison or Belle Isle under a scowling Confederate escort. About thirty-five slaves who had been following in Dahlgren's path also lost their short-lived freedom with the surrender of the Union cavalrymen.[21]

Once the Confederate home guards and cavalrymen had pillaged Dahlgren's corpse, Captain Dement asked them to bury the remains by the roadside. John South, a farmer who lived nearby, dug a shallow grave and threw the body into it, shoveling dirt over the dead colonel without so much as a bed sheet to cover him. Dr. Walker commented on that indignity. "Good enough for a Yankee," South replied. Others thought differently and acted on their notions. The next day someone dug up Dahlgren's muddy body. Thomas Dunstan, a local carriage maker serving with the home guards, made a proper pine coffin. Dr. Walker assured Lieutenant Merritt that it would be made by the "best joiner in the neighborhood," of "stained wood, [and] the best material available." Without pay Dunstan washed the body and cleaned Dahlgren's filthy uniform. In a later account Captain Bagby's son claimed that Dahlgren's "underclothes which were much soiled by blood stains from his wound were replaced by a Richmond youth named George P. Stacey from his scanty knapsack." Dunstan laid the dead man in the pine box with his clothing. Confederate troops transported Dahlgren's corpse to Richmond, where it was displayed for ridicule. A Union prisoner said that he had heard the body was exhibited "nude"—not likely, given Southerners' sense of formality. A Richmond newspaper reported that Dahlgren was clothed in Confederate shirt and pants and shrouded in a blanket, his features wearing "an expression of agony." The young colonel was buried secretly, at President Davis's personal order, in Richmond's Oakwood Cemetery. The rite was handled by a detail from the 10th and 19th Virginia Heavy Artillery Battalions under Lieutenant Colonel John W. Atkinson.

Twenty years later a Michigan sergeant who had surrendered to Dement vividly recalled how the colonel's body "was perfectly naked, with the exception of the bandages on his amputated leg." If this man's recollection is close to accurate, it suggests that the wound Dahlgren suffered at Hagerstown had not healed enough to keep his prosthesis attached to the stump. Perhaps for some or even all of the raid he could not wear his wooden leg, which means that Kilpatrick might have erred in giving him so prominent a role in the action. Even had the general or others pressed him about it, Dahlgren would not have been inclined to admit that he was unable to lead troops or even to ride.[22]

Dahlgren's body was not in the ground long before Union operatives tried to get it back. Ben Butler was a key figure in negotiating with Confederate officials for the return of the corpse after Admiral Dahlgren offered one hundred dollars in gold for his son's remains. But the body soon disappeared from Oakwood. Union sympathizers led by Elizabeth Van Lew disinterred the body and clandestinely smuggled it to a farm north of the Confederate capital near Hungary Station connected with Union supporter Robert Orrick. The coffin stayed there until months after Robert E. Lee's surrender at Appomattox. The admiral finally saw his son's remains reburied with full military honors in the family plot at Laurel Hill Cemetery in Philadelphia in November 1865.[23]

CHAPTER 14

Unintended Consequences

Following the raid that burned most of the structures at King and Queen Court House on March 10, Kilpatrick's cavalrymen prepared to depart for Alexandria on U.S. Navy transports; the horses were assigned to barges. The voyage to Alexandria was "quite pleasant" compared to the strenuousness of the recent raid, according to one observer. Another trooper had a different opinion. He claimed that the landlubbers faced some "rough waters which made some of the boys feed the fishes." Upon disembarking at Alexandria's wharf about 10:00 A.M. on March 13, the troopers were given some time to paint the town "red, white and blue." When several of the men ended up in jail, General Kilpatrick ordered them released immediately, then issued his own orders giving his men the run of the city. In words guaranteed to endear him to his troopers, the general wrote that his soldiers' recent arduous service "should entitle them to the freedom of any city in the United States."[1] One can only wonder what deprecations Alexandrians experienced that went unrecorded.

Back in King and Queen County, Edward Halbach did not spend much time studying the papers Will Littlepage gave him before passing them along to higher authorities. As the schoolmaster perused the documents, he did note that one document, undated, was addressed to "Officers and Men" and neatly written in ink on two sheets of official stationery printed with the title "Headquarters Third Division, Cavalry Corps," which Halbach might not have recognized as Kilpatrick's division headquarters. The message covered the front side of each sheet and continued onto the back of the first page. The signature read "U. Dahlgren." Another two-sheet document, in the same handwriting and also undated, though with no signature, listed instructions to "Guides—Pioneers (with oakum, turpentine, and torpedoes), signal officer, quartermaster, commissary. Scouts and pickets. Men in rebel uniform." Halbach read the first document with mounting shock. In flat military prose it described how the Yankee raiders were to put Richmond to the torch and capture Jefferson Davis along with his cabinet. On the other document, unsigned, the author said that once the capital was aflame, the bluecoats were to kill Davis and his cabinet officers.[2] The memo book Littlepage had found was marked up with writing in pencil. On the dated first page was the name "Ulric Dahlgren," noted as being a colonel in the Union army. Deeper in the pocket-sized volume was what seemed to be the same message as on the stationery sheets but in different language. At the end of the pencil draft, one sentence jumped out at Halbach: "Jeff Davis and Cabinet must be killed on the spot."[3]

Halbach brought the papers and memo book to Captain Richard H. Bagby, the county's home-guards commander. That afternoon Bagby found Lieutenant James Pollard, who had recovered from the previous night's indisposition, and gave him the dead Yankee's papers and artificial leg. Pollard immediately went to look for his regimental commander, Colonel Richard L. T. Beale of the 9th Virginia Cavalry, finding him at his camp near Old Church. Keeping the memo book, Beale sent Pollard on to Richmond with orders to deliver the loose papers to Major General Fitzhugh Lee in keeping with the cavalry's chain of command. The captain rode to the capital, found the general, and turned over the inflammatory documents. Scanning them, Lee went directly to Jefferson Davis's home, where he found the president in conference with Secretary of State Judah P. Benjamin. Davis read them aloud in front of Benjamin and Lee, saying nothing until he came to the sentence that ended, "Jeff. Davis and cabinet killed." "That means you, Mr. Benjamin," Davis said with a laugh, according to Lee.[4]

Dahlgren's papers and later the accompanying memo book, with its penciled draft, lit a firestorm. The papers were orders, and they called for extreme actions. First, Federal soldiers were to raze "the hateful city" of Richmond. With the Rebel capital ablaze, Dahlgren was to seize President Davis and his cabinet, apparently with orders to shoot anyone who tried to escape. This new brutal approach incensed Confederate officials. Secretary of War James Seddon wanted the captured Union raiders executed on the spot. So did presidential military advisor General Braxton Bragg, who found the contents so "extraordinary and diabolical" and the raid of such "fiendish and atrocious conduct of our enemies" as to argue for "an execution of the prisoners and [an official] publication [of the papers] as justification." The government made fifty photographic copies of the papers, sending sets to the Vatican and other European capitals.[5]

Confederate officialdom's reaction was disingenuous, papering over as it did their own responses to the raid, such as mining Libby Prison. Not only was "a sufficient quantity of gunpowder" placed in Libby's cellar, but with cruelty "pains were taken to inform the prisoners that any attempt at escape made by them would be effectually defeated"; that is, if Yankee cavalry got into the city, guards would blow up the prison. "The plan succeeded perfectly. The prisoners were awed and kept quiet," a later report concluded. Had the Rebels made good on that threat, Federal reaction would have been harsh. But the Confederate contingency for Libby was based on a mindset that had been building since 1863, when Davis excoriated the "general orders of the enemy" to burn houses and "plunder . . . everything moveable." This latest raid fit the mode to evoke such a Southern reaction due to the atrocities outlined in Dahlgren's orders.[6]

Robert E. Lee became involved in the situation within days of the ambush, dampening emotions. Seddon ordered him to get to the bottom of the Yankee plot, but the Army of Northern Virginia's commander counseled restraint. His son, Brigadier General William H. F. "Rooney" Lee, was a prisoner of war at Fort Monroe, awaiting exchange for a Union general. "God grant that he could be released," the elder Lee wrote his wife shortly before the raid. To satisfy Seddon, the commanding general decided to contact General Meade—once Rooney was safe. Whether or not the father may have been trying to keep his son from being made a pawn in the furor, Lee's instincts were right. Inflammatory accounts of the raid in the Southern press led Federal authorities to react as the general had feared, picking Rebel POWs and shuffling them from one Northern prison to another. "There were sixty of us held as hostages for Dahlgren's men," B. F. Foley of the 6th Virginia Cavalry wrote later. "We were taken from different Southern States. . . . We were held nine weeks, with a gallows ready to hang us if Dahlgren's men were executed."[7]

Lee waited nearly a month to contact Meade, sending him one of the copies made of the papers. Meade received five photographs, though none of Dahlgren's memo book. Beale, who had received the volume from Pollard soon after the Union colonel's death, kept it until March 31, when he sent it to Fitzhugh Lee. The general then forwarded it to General Samuel Cooper, Confederate adjutant and inspector general. Cooper offered access to the book to Richmond newspapermen. The press quickly printed the fateful sentence: "Jeff Davis and Cabinet must be killed on the spot," a highlight of the next spasm of reporting from Richmond. Cooper then dispatched the notebook to Robert E. Lee, who on April 1 again contacted Meade. The raid had brought a military and political firestorm down on the Union general's head. He put off dealing with Lee's communiqué for two weeks.[8]

Shortly after Kilpatrick returned to Culpeper, Meade probably quizzed him about the commotion raised by the Richmond newspapers. When he received Lee's official query, the Army of the Potomac's commander again handed the matter over to the raid's mastermind for an explanation. Perhaps Little Kil called Henry Davies, his loyal brigade commander and a lawyer, to his headquarters for advice. In both of his careful answers to Meade, Kilpatrick obfuscated the circumstances to the point that his now-dead one-legged subordinate came under unofficial suspicion for alleged heinous acts that were never carried out. Kilpatrick admitted that just before his command moved out from Stevensburg, Dahlgren had showed him a draft of a speech he wanted to read to his men. The general said that he had endorsed the address by writing "Approved" in red ink over his signature. He added that the copies Lee had sent Meade of the controversial papers were of material he had approved except for the phrase in the photographic copy "exhorting the prisoners to destroy and burn the hateful city and kill the traitor Davis and his cabinet." This last phrase he put in quotation marks for emphasis. Neither of the two copies of documents Lee had sent Meade contained the exact wording that Kilpatrick employed in his response. Might he have purposely misquoted one or both documents, or erred in haste? No one has ever answered the question as to whether either document contained Kilpatrick's signature endorsed in red ink, as he claimed. Since the originals no longer exist thanks to Edwin Stanton, who removed them from the War Department in November 1865, Kilpatrick's account cannot be refuted, though Meade later called him a liar. The photographic copies were black and white but still should have shown the word "Approved" with the general's signature if it was present, but no one seems to have raised that point, and Kilpatrick got off the hook.

Having extricated himself, Kilpatrick, after a full investigation of his division, claimed that he found no Union officer or enlisted man who rode with Dahlgren who could corroborate the Confederate claim that the colonel had delivered the incendiary speech. The blue ranks closed behind their diminutive commander. Thus began the demonization of Ulric Dahlgren. "Now that Dahlgren has failed to carry out his orders, the Yankees disown him," a Southern diarist wrote. "They disavow it all." With reputations tainted by the scandal, Lincoln, Stanton, Meade, and Kilpatrick remained essentially blameless.[9]

Fitzhugh Lee later told General Cooper that Dahlgren's papers came to him without any alterations. Lee felt that Dahlgren's "memoranda and address to his troops were probably based upon the general instructions to the *whole* command" (italics in original). His sentiments were seconded by Major Heros Von Borcke, who was on hand when Pollard delivered the papers. The Prussian soldier of fortune, an aide to Jeb Stuart, had no reason to embellish, and he believed the handwriting was Dahlgren's; how he knew the colonel's hand is unrecorded. Von Borcke remembered Fitzhugh Lee taking the papers to Davis within thirty minutes of receiving them.[10]

Weeks later, Major Josiah Gorgas, the Confederacy's chief of ordnance, wrote in his diary of seeing Dahlgren's memo book, which Colonel Beale had finally transmitted to Fitzhugh Lee. Gorgas said the penciled "rough draft" differed slightly in places from the recently published address appearing in Richmond newspapers; he identified the phrase "Jeff Davis and his Cabinet must be killed on the spot" as from the memo book.[11] Major General Wade Hampton was still in the area recently traversed by the Yankee raiders on their retreat. The night the home guards and cavalrymen had killed Dahlgren, Hampton found shelter as a guest of Dr. William Braxton near Old Church, where Colonel Beale was camped. A Confederate courier from Beale with Dahlgren's memo book was looking for the general but decided to rest for the night at the neighboring home of Lewis Washington rather press his search. The courier let Washington read the dead Yankee's notes. The next day, March 4, Washington ran into Hampton near Old Church. Washington told the South Carolinian that he had had a chance to read Dahlgren's memo book. Later Hampton said that Washington's description of the notebook's contents was "precisely similar" to the details published in the Richmond newspapers. It seemed to him afterward that unless the men who found the papers on Dahlgren's body or the weary courier had altered the memo book—"a supposition entirely incredible"—he believed that "Dahlgren was the originator of a plot to burn and sack Richmond, and to assassinate the President of the Southern Confederacy."[12]

Kilpatrick may have thought his arm-twisting among the men relieved him of responsibility. But his report to Meade smacks at the truth. One Southern newspaper alluded to an address given by the colonel when he offered "his men the privilege of withdrawing if they had no stomach for the business." Apparently Dahlgren warned them that "if they permitted themselves to be taken prisoners they would meet 'an ignominious death.'" Another paper reported, "A prisoner states that it was read out to the men engaged in the raid." Some captured raiders may have spoken to Confederate authorities and probably told the truth about Dahlgren addressing his men. Years later Charles Bunker Dahlgren asked an army scout who had been on the raid whether his brother gave such a speech. The scout, James Wood, who after the war had become a private detective in Boston, replied murkily. He could not "say to there being written orders. I know he had some memorandums or orders which he referred to several times."[13] At least two postwar accounts mention the colonel giving an address to his men, similar to the one reported in the Richmond journals, after Ely's Ford had been captured the night of February 28. Another account also mentions Dahlgren reiterating his objective when his command rested in the late afternoon of March 1, before the attack on the western side of the Confederate capital. In each instance the colonel stated the goal of capturing Davis and his cabinet, though he did not mention murdering them. Dahlgren may have given the speech but withheld the more sinister reference to killing Davis because someone other than his field commander had approved that step.[14]

Meade showed the photographic copies received from Lee to Lieutenant Colonel Lyman. The opinionated staff officer wrote in his private journal that the documents troubled the general, who "considered the weight of evidence in favor of the authenticity, and plainly said he did not consider Kilpatrick a trustworthy person." He offers no explanation for Meade's opinion of the cavalry general's involvement with the orders. Lyman himself lost no love for Kilpatrick. Meade's reticence suggests the delicacy of the situation created by the different copies of the orders.[15]

Another Kilpatrick critic, Brigadier General Marsena Patrick, the army's provost marshal general, heard an earful about Kill-Cavalry from Captain John McEntee, an army intelligence officer, veteran of the raid, and no fan of Kilpatrick. Entering Patrick's headquarters tent, McEntee raged at Kilpatrick's handling of the Dahlgren papers. Patrick wrote in his diary that the captain "has the same opinion of Killpatrick [sic] that I have and says he managed just as all cowards do—He further says, that he thinks the papers are correct that were found upon Dahlgren, as they correspond with what D. told him" before the raid. Patrick never explains specifically why McEntee thought the papers were genuine, however. Did Dahlgren tell McEntee who proposed to kill Davis? No chain of connection, however, links these tantalizing nuggets of evidence.[16]

"This is a pretty ugly piece of business; for in denying having authorized or approved 'burning of Richmond, or killing Mr. Davis and Cabinet,' I necessarily threw odium on Dahlgren," Meade wrote in a letter to his wife. "But I regret to say Kilpatrick's reputation, and collateral evidence in my possession rather go against this theory." This is Meade's only mention of such "collateral evidence." He went on to write that he "was determined my skirts should be clean," a clear indication of the perils of army politics. The general concluded that he "promptly disavowed having ever authorized, sanctioned or approved by any act not required by military necessity, and in accordance with the usages of war."[17]

On the Confederate side, Robert E. Lee, who had an eye on the imminent spring campaign, was content to accept Kilpatrick's explanation and let the matter drop. One of Lee's staff officers was less forgiving. Walter Taylor thought it was disingenuous for Meade, Kilpatrick, and Washington officials to deny they meant to torch Richmond. "That rascal Kilpatrick . . . says that the copies (photographic) of the address which we sent . . . lacked [his] approval," Taylor wrote, "intimating that we had forged these copies & interpolated the objectionable exhortations." Kilpatrick, "the low wretch—he approved the whole thing I am confident *now*," he added. No record exists of Lee's opinion.[18]

The raid galvanized some Southern officials. The "Confederate government, it seems had undergone a change of heart in the spring of 1864 after the Kilpatrick-Dahlgren raid on Richmond," one chronicler of Confederate espionage concluded. During 1864, Rebel operatives with Davis's sanction and knowledge tried in June, August, and September to grab the president of the United States. By then, triggered by Kilpatrick's raid and Dahlgren's papers, "direct action against Lincoln himself was not unthinkable"—operations termed "Black Flag Warfare." No matter who conceived the plan to kill the Confederate president, Southerners, besieged by their own press with endless lurid reports, came to feel that the Dahlgren papers "reflected the personal attitude of President Lincoln . . . , [and the] Confederate government felt considerable domestic pressure to seek retribution for the atrocities that sprang from Lincoln's policies." The anti-Lincoln *New York World* stoked this fire by claiming that the raid's dark goals were "planned by Mr. Lincoln, Mr. Kellogg of the Military Committee of the House and Gen. Kilpatrick." It is clear from the president's own dispatch to Major General Hooker and his approval of Butler's early February 1864 raid on Richmond that he had no problem taking Davis prisoner, but no evidence exists that Lincoln wanted him dead. None among a cadre of Lincoln historians gives credence to the idea of the Great Emancipator ordering the assassination of his Confederate counterpart.[19]

CHAPTER 15

AFTERMATH

"The grand Yankee fandango is over at last. Dalgreen [*sic*] is shot as highwaymen deserve," Confederate lieutenant John Esten Cooke wrote in his journal on March 7, 1864. "This raid will be historic," Jeb Stuart's aide added. "Dalgreen sought immortality and has found it." "The Kilpatrick-Dahlgren campaign is ended," another Confederate horse soldier wrote. "The Yankee nation is indelibly disgraced by the objects of the expedition, and Stuart's laurels wilted by his failure to annihilate the whole party."[1] But according to Cooke, talk at Confederate headquarters was of capturing Kilpatrick. What he wrote just days after the raid ended is hard to dispute even more than seven score years later. However ignominious his end, Dahlgren would be immortalized and the raid remembered, albeit layered in myths, legend, truth, and confection.

After their brief fling in Alexandria, Kilpatrick's men collected their mounts and proceeded to Fairfax Court House for a night's rest, followed by a ride to Warrenton Junction and into Culpeper County. By March 18 most of the returning raiders had settled back into their camps near Stevensburg. They were welcomed by comrades who had not ridden with them by singing "When Johnny Comes Marching Home Again," but instead replacing the chorus "hurrah, hurrah" with "forlorn, forlorn," a wry touch after a hard ride.

Losses were pegged at 340, about 10 percent of the force. Seventy men were missing in action. Six hundred horses were gone, either shot or strayed. Even so, a Vermonter wrote home, "The boys enjoyed the raid highly, even the recruits." A Maine cavalryman of a more sanguine outlook said his regiment had "lost some of their best men and it . . . seemed more than a miracle [that] any of us ever returned." But the 1st Maine's chaplain painted a more dire picture for the state's governor two weeks after the raid, reporting, "I suppose I have heard a hundred persons, mostly officers, speak of Killpatrick [*sic*] with the utmost contempt, but never one who seemed to have any respect for him either as an officer or man!" "Genl Kilpatrick is with us and we rejoice," another man declared.

"The Genl looks well but somewhat chagrined at his recent failure and the loss of 'poor little Dahlgren.'"[2] Someone asked a sergeant if the raiders had freed any Union prisoners. "No," he said. "But we reinforced them."

Kilpatrick had to admit in a preliminary report to Major General Alfred Pleasonton that he had "[f]ailed to accomplish the great object of the expedition." That the raid had floundered was "through no fault of the officers and men accompanying it," the general affirmed. This statement seemed like false praise to one Federal officer, who confided in a letter home that it appeared to him that Henry Davies's "Brigade of this division gets from Kilpatrick and his staff all the good opportunities to do themselves credit." It was Brigadier General George A. Custer, according to this Michigander, who "gives us all the credit we are entitled to." In seeming defense of the failed foray, Kilpatrick carefully listed a great many amounts of enemy property destroyed, meanwhile taking credit for strewing copies of President Lincoln's amnesty proclamation all along his path. He blamed Dahlgren's unfortunate guide for failing to get that column across the James River. He complained that if only Ben Butler had done his anticipated part in putting pressure on the enemy at Bottom's Bridge southeast of Richmond, the main force easily could have entered the Rebel capital and freed the Union prisoners. That sentiment was echoed by many of Kilpatrick's troopers, including a Vermonter who recorded in his diary that the general failed to take Richmond "owing to a delay of Gen. Butler in cooperation with his force."[3]

Instead of returning immediately to his headquarters in Stevensburg, General Kilpatrick made a bee line for the nation's capital, across the Potomac River from Alexandria. No record indicates whether he visited Lincoln or Secretary of War Stanton, but the press found him registered at the National Hotel, at the corner of Pennsylvania Avenue and Sixth Street NW, for several days while his troopers were traveling to Culpeper County. Before leaving for the capital, Kilpatrick told Colonel Edward Sawyer, who had commanded a brigade on the raid, that officers should remain with their units and "in no case will you permit them to visit Washington," a strong hint that the general meant his version of the story to be the only one told in high places. Whoever Kilpatrick talked to among Federal officialdom, he let slip to a reporter that his force had penetrated Richmond's outer defenses, a gambit foiled by Dahlgren's failure to cross the James. As a measure of his confidence in all those best-laid plans, Little Kil told the journalist that he had with him "an order for the surrender [of Richmond] already penned."[4]

While Kilpatrick was explaining away his failure and his weary troopers were meandering back to the Army of the Potomac, it was a very different story for the men left behind as captives. Dahlgren's signal officer, Reuben Bartley, lost all his belongings except an old comb. When the feisty lieutenant objected, asking his captors if they wanted his clothes too, they told him that he would be hanged in the few days and they would "get the clothes anyhow." According to Richmond papers, the captured raiders were thrown in irons, the officers singled out for further humiliation—in the Confederates' imagination anyway—by being confined with soldiers from Butler's U.S. Colored Troops recently captured in James City County.

Lieutenant Colonel Litchfield of the 7th Michigan, captured near Atlee's Station, recalled the horrors he and five other officers faced in the dungeons of Libby Prison. The six officers and "four negro soldiers captured from Butler's command" were squeezed into a "dungeon measuring about 7 feet by 11 feet," perhaps the first time Rebels had treated black Union troops as POWs. The only "sanitary arrangement was an open tub in one corner, emptied once a day." The white officers remained with these black troops more than a week before a first-floor room was partitioned off to serve as their quarters for four and a half months. No plates, knives, forks, or spoons were allowed. Feeling he was being treated like a "felon," Litchfield wrote to the prison warden, Major Thomas Turner, who ignored him. When finally questioned directly by the Union offi-cer, Turner begged bureaucratic shuffling at the War Department had failed to provide an answer to his entreaties. In July Litchfield's complaints were finally resolved when all of Libby Prison's res-idents were moved to Macon, Georgia. Ending up in Columbia, South Carolina, the officer remained a prisoner until nearly the end of the war. Although he long outlived the raid's other captured offi-cers, Litchfield was a broken man. Shuttling from job to job, war-time deprivations had bankrupted him physically and mentally. Litchfield claimed on his 1906 pension application that he still suf-fered from torpor, a condition he called a "stupid, dull feeling," as well as insomnia, a nervous disease, irritability, and depression.[5]

Though contrary to his jailors' assumptions, Edwin Cooke relished his time penned up with the black soldiers, declaring he "infinitely preferred the company of loyal negroes to that of white traitors." The slightly built Cooke seemed to suffer physically the most. He and other wounded and sick men had to subsist on one-third rations and were denied hospital care. He too spent most of the remaining months of the war as a POW, brevetted brigadier general of volunteers in March 1865 for "faithful and meritorious service" to his country. He returned to New Jersey shortly before his young wife died. Cooke did not endure mental illness, but his body was a wreck. After the war he accompanied his good friend Judson Kilpatrick to a new assignment as secretary of the U.S. Legation in Chile, where he died in 1867, a month shy of his thirty-second birthday.[6]

Hearing of white officers confined in leg irons along with black soldiers with a death sentence hanging over their heads, Ben Butler huffed and puffed for verification by the Confederate commissioner of exchange, giving to imply that if this were true, he would exact the "promptest and severest retaliation for the treatment of those officers" from Rebel prisoners. Such threats would have been taken seriously by General Robert E. Lee because arrangements had been underway for several weeks to exchange his son, Rooney, for a comparably ranked Federal officer. Lee had a further concern because both Braxton Bragg and James Seddon were calling for the raiders to be hanged as a warning to future Yankee designs on assassination and mayhem.[7]

Adding to the officers' humiliation, gawking Richmonders were allowed access to the prisoners and heaped scorn upon the raiders "as a kind of [carnival] show." Richmond mayor Joseph Mayo and Sallie Seddon, chatelaine of Sabot Hill, which Dahlgren's raiders had hit, took the opportunity to visit Libby. The wife of the secretary of war was "extremely violent with her tongue, applying in rapid succession such epithets as 'inhuman monsters, hellhounds' etc., and expressing in language more forcible than elegant, the hope that the Confederate government was strong enough to hang them all, and if this could not be done they ought to be thrown into prison and left there to rot," a newspaperman reported. Lieutenant Bartley took note of Mrs. Seddon's diatribe about "Thieves, Murderers, Fiends, Hell Monsters, Assassins, etc." He blamed the harsh treatment accorded him and his fellow officers on "pure revenge to satisfy Mrs. J. A. Seddon and a few others of the FFVs."[8]

Other Richmond residents had their own ideas about what to do with the captured raiders. Firebrand secessionist Edmund

Ruffin wrote in his diary that they should hang, acknowledging that Jefferson Davis, "our tender-conscience & imbecile President," lacked the will to put them on the gibbet. Rather than hang the lot of them, the Federals should have to draw lots, with every tenth man shot, said Confederate postmaster general John Henninger Reagan.[9] It speaks well of Lee and Davis that they did not succumb to their compatriots' bloodlust.

Between the debate over the captured raiders' fate and Kilpatrick's machinations to save his career, another thread of the raid's aftermath unspooled. Ulric Dahlgren's body and personal effects made a journey that until now has not been told in full.

The record is clear that within days of his death, Dahlgren's corpse was on display in Richmond, then secretly buried in Oakwood Cemetery. Under cover of darkness, Elizabeth Van Lew and her associates in the Richmond underground exhumed and spirited away the body, a story that needs to be recapitulated here briefly.[10] By the evening of March 6, Lieutenant Thomas Jefferson Christian, a native of King and Queen County, with an escort from his 9th Virginia Cavalry delivered Dahlgren's corpse in a rude pine coffin to Richmond. At the York River and West Point Railroad station in the city, the coffin, bearing the stenciled name "Ulric Dahlgren," remained opened, the body "dressed in an unbleached cotton shirt, and in green pants, apparently uniform pants," according to Colonel John W. Atkinson. With six soldiers, Atkinson took charge of the corpse, which they buried clandestinely in Oakwood Cemetery. A month later, as agreed in talks with Butler, orders went out from Davis to exhume the body. But Captain Samuel MacCubbin, who received the order, found the grave empty. On April 6, Union sympathizers orchestrated by Van Lew—among them F. W. E. Lohman, William S. Rowley, Martin M. Lipscomb, and a black servant—had dug up the body, loaded it on a spring-board wagon, and hauled it to Rowley's house in Richmond. The plotters moved Dahlgren's body into a metal coffin. In moving the remains, the men noticed bullet holes at the back of the skull. Before they closed the lid, Van Lew clipped a lock of the young officer's hair, which she sent to his father as confirmation that his son's remains were safe. They loaded the metal coffin onto the wagon, camouflaging it with a load of peach saplings, then drove it past Confederate sentries to Hanover County. Dahlgren's third resting place was at the "root of a sassafras tree in a very unfrequented spot near Hungary Station."

Ironically, not far away was the place where Dahlgren had crossed the Richmond, Fredericksburg, and Potomac Railroad after his repulse on the Westham Plank Road. The body remained buried there until June 1865, when troops brought Dahlgren's remains to Washington for identification by his grieving father, who had his son laid to final rest in Laurel Hill Cemetery in Philadelphia the following November.[11]

Two days after Lee surrendered at Appomattox in April 1865, Stanton ordered Dahlgren's remains retrieved—an odd gesture given that Jefferson Davis was still on the run and General Joe Johnston's army still active in the field in North Carolina. Lincoln was still alive, so perhaps Admiral Dahlgren had spoken to his friend. Whoever initiated the order, Stanton wanted the body brought to Washington as soon as possible.[12]

Before getting his son's body back, John Dahlgren himself took some incredible steps that illustrate his political influence, war or no war. Trying to collect his son's effects, the admiral, with Stanton's help, brought the U.S. Military Detective Police Agency to bear on former Confederates. The effort also enlisted units of the Adjutant General's Office and the Provost Marshal General's Office, which were able to locate and return or report on the status of the young colonel's prosthetic leg, overcoat, sack coat, vest, pants, boots, crutch, watch, gold ring, and even his horse. Shortly after Dahlgren was killed, Lieutenant Robert Hart of the 5th Virginia Cavalry started divvying up the colonel's possessions. Joining him was Private Cornelius Martin of Company H, 9th Virginia Cavalry, who saw a gold ring on Dahlgren's pinky finger, a gift from his deceased sister. When it would not slip off, Martin sliced off the dead man's finger and pocketed the bloody piece of jewelry.

Admiral Dahlgren particularly wanted to know what had become of this ring. In October 1865, well after he had taken delivery of his boy's corpse from an honor guard and uniformed escort ordered by Stanton, the admiral telegraphed inquiries about the ring to Major General Alfred Terry, commanding the Department of Virginia, and Brigadier General Edward D. Townsend, assistant adjutant general. He had read a newspaper report that month suggesting authorities had recovered the ring, to which he referred in his telegram as a "relic."[13] Federal officials knew by July 4, 1865, that Martin had mutilated Dahlgren's body and stolen the ring, but they also heard that Martin had died in May 1864 in the fighting at Yellow Tavern.

Then word came that he was alive and living in Caroline County, Virginia. Military Detective F. W. Lohman was assigned to locate Martin and retrieve the ring. Lohman and H. M. Jones found the former cavalryman, who at first gave a false name and denied knowledge of the ring, but soon he came clean. He pointed the investigators to a Dr. Saunders of Essex County who had the ring, now valued at fifty dollars. The detectives took Martin into custody, bringing him along as they searched for and found Saunders, who "after some difficulty" produced the ring. Martin vouched for its authenticity. On October 25, the same day the admiral was telegraphing Terry and Townsend, his son's ring was being shipped to Washington via the Adams Express Company.[14]

The lock of Dahlgren's hair that a home guardsman had snipped as he lay freshly dead wound up in the care Mrs. Juliet Pollard, who intended to send it to Ulric's father. After Appomattox Mrs. Pollard gave the memento to the provost in Stevensville for delivery to Admiral Dahlgren. And there the trail goes cold. Whether or not John Dahlgren ever received his son's lock of hair remains one of the many unresolved mysteries of the raid.[15]

Ulric Dahlgren's below-the-knee prosthesis, taken soon after his death by a local doctor who wanted his colleagues to examine it with an eye toward making better artificial limbs for Confederate amputees, wound up in another Pollard's possession. Lieutenant James Pollard took the artificial limb to Richmond when he delivered the Dahlgren orders to Major General Fitzhugh Lee. On June 24, 1864, Pollard was wounded in action at Nance's Shop, Virginia. He lost his right leg. Ironically, the officer who had set up the ambush that killed Dahlgren somehow got hold of the colonel's prosthesis again. However Pollard secured the limb, he took it to John Wills's Leg Factory in Charlottesville, Virginia, hoping to have Dahlgren's prosthesis retooled to fit his stump, but it was too small. Another one-legged Confederate, Captain John N. Ballard, was living near Charlottesville at the time. Ballard, who had ridden with Mosby, apparently had a stump that was a better fit. He and Pollard negotiated an arrangement in which Ballard got Dahlgren's prosthetic and covered the price of a new artificial limb for the lieutenant.

Ballard made no secret that he was using Dahlgren's famous leg. The ex-partisan's indiscretion eventually caught up with him. In addition to the efforts of Federal detectives like Lohman and William Vernon, an informal network of friends and acquaintances had formed to help Admiral Dahlgren in his time of need. One was a Virginia doctor named Archer, beholden to the admiral for a "past obligation." Archer enlisted the good offices of Colonel William B. Woolridge, former commander of the 4th Virginia Cavalry, in his search. The doctor heard from Woolridge that Ballard had traveled to Richmond, hoping to obtain a replacement leg but was unable to make a trade. He also learned that there might be a warrant out for his arrest over possession of the artificial leg. When detectives Lohman and Vernon showed up at Ballard's house in Albermarle County, the former guerrilla "gave up the leg with [willingness] and felt relieved . . . [to be] rid of it." By November 1865 the prosthesis too was on its way back to Washington.[16]

Other items owned by the young officer were more elusive. By July 1865 it was known that Rebel soldiers had confiscated Dahlgren's vest, pants, and boots and had worn them out in the service of the lost cause. As far as anyone knew, Dahlgren's horse, a handsome specimen, had survived him, but it was unclear as to what end. By June 1865 Captain C. W. Coffin of the Assistant Provost Marshal's Office in Yorktown reported that the horse had been seized by Lieutenant Christian Nunn of the 5th Virginia Cavalry at the time of the ambush. Yet Nunn's possession of the mount was short lived. Confederate authorities soon honored a claim by Dr. William Walker of Goochland County, returning the horse to him. Since a definitive description of the animal was unavailable, detectives dropped the search for the colonel's steed. Dahlgren's crutch and overcoat also were not recovered, although a good story supports the crutch's provenance. George W. Bagby, the son of the King and Queen County's home-guards commander, gave a fairly detailed account of what happened to that item. George said that his father, Richard, gave the crutch to Thomas H. Wynne, treasurer of the Southern Telegraph Company and an avid wartime souvenir hunter, for safekeeping. When downtown Richmond burned on April 3, 1865, Wynne's office was among many that went up in flames. Federal investigators were satisfied with Bagby's story, which Wynne corroborated.[17] As for the colonel's overcoat, it left the ambush site in the hands of Lieutenant Robert Hart of the 5th Virginia Cavalry, who gave it to his commander, Captain Fox. But Fox would only possess it a few months before he was killed at Yellow Tavern, Virginia—the battle in which Jeb Stuart was mortally wounded. The overcoat then went with his other effects to his

widow, who sold it to a man named Ryland, who left it on the battlefield at Hatcher's Run in December 1864.[18]

Authorities would recover two other items among Dahlgren's
personal effects. Lieutenant Hart, who took the colonel's gold
watch, two months later gave it to Edwin T. Powell, a clerk in
the Quartermaster Department. Powell in turn gave the watch to
Archy Gwathney, a pharmacist living in Norfolk, Virginia; there
is no record of whether money changed hands when the watch
did. General Townsend retrieved the watch from Gwathney and
returned it to Admiral Dahlgren, as he did the young colonel's sack
coat, another war prize grabbed by Lieutenant Hart. Hart had given
the coat to Captain Marius Pendleton Todd of the King and Queen
County Home Guards, who had previously been a captain in the
5th Virginia Cavalry, Hart's unit, suggesting that the two were
friends. Todd retained the sack coat until March 1865, when he
traded it to another familiar officer in the 5th Virginia, Christian
Nunn. The lieutenant later traded the coat to Charles Davis of the
42nd Battalion Virginia Cavalry, who also may have had ties to the
5th Virginia. By August 1865 the sack coat was tracked to Davis in
Norfolk, Virginia. When Townsend got the coat back, he noted that
it contained four bullet holes.[19]

Colonel Dahlgren's saber was the genesis of two fabulist tales.
The weapon, which disappeared in 1864, was not referred to in
any official reports supplied by government detectives at the time
they were locating his other personal affects. However, one scenario puts the weapon in the hands of a black man in King and
Queen County. At some point the slave gave the sword to Alex
Thomlinson, a Richmond detective, who gave it to Kirk Matthews
in 1888. Matthews then contacted a Dahlgren relative in an effort
to establish the weapon's provenance but was unable to nail down
the connection. He gave the blade to W. D. Cardwell, after which
the weapon became lost in the mists of history and hearsay. A
more bizarre explanation of the saber's disappearance appears in
a newspaper clipping kept by Madeleine Vinton Dahlgren, the colonel's stepmother. The article states that Mrs. Dahlgren kept a
sword on display beneath a portrait of her stepson, claiming that
she obtained it in 1876 through the good offices of a Catholic
priest who had received it from a penitent in the confessional
box. According to her, the priest, who would not betray his sacred
vow, said only: "This is returned to you through the confessional.

No questions can be answered." The fate of Ulric Dahlgren's sword remains a mystery.[20]

Judson Kilpatrick seems not to have participated in efforts to secure his subordinate's body or personal affects, nor did he comment on the postraid tribulations of the men who ended up in Libby Prison or on Belle Isle. But the general did busy himself with explanations, rationales, suppositions, arguments, and perhaps even prevarications as to why his grand scheme flopped. Some have credence, such as Butler's half-hearted effort, though here it is difficult to pinpoint who was responsible, Meade, Halleck, Butler, or all three. At least circumstantially, the upper ranks clearly displayed indifference if not resistance to the raid before and during the operation. Kilpatrick fully expected Butler to provide a coordinated attack, which failed to materialize. It seems that any plans Kilpatrick had entertained for a cooperative effort with Butler apparently went astray through the army's chain of command. A Northern newspaper used stronger words, though, calling the War Department incompetent and declaring that "the President, his military board of directors and the commander of the Army of the Potomac" were responsible for ensuring that a strong infantry force was sent up the Peninsula from Fort Monroe. The absurdity of blaming Dahlgren's black guide is matched only by the transparency of scapegoating the fellow, whose competence or incompetence could have done little to affect the James River in flood and Virginia's mercurial weather in full winter exuberance. Besides, Dahlgren was way off schedule long before he arrived at the James; it hardly mattered what side of the river he was on by the afternoon of March 1.

But another Northern newspaper raised an interesting twist on the guide issue. An article in the *New York Herald* claimed that Kilpatrick's raid failed "chiefly from the neglect of the War Department to provide suitable guides," a line of reasoning absent from previous analyses. Since both Kilpatrick's and Dahlgren's guides, including the notorious and dead black man, were provided by Army of the Potomac headquarters, perhaps Meade deserves a share of blame. A Federal officer associated with the Bureau of Military Information assessed one of the army scouts sent with the raiders: "[Joseph] Humphries [*sic*] is not worth a——. He does not know a road in Virginia not anything about the works about Richmond nor could he answer a question which the Gen. asked him. He has been a perfect nuisance and a consummate bore to

me. I have continually wished that he was in——." The guides provided by the army, particularly to Dahlgren's column, once they got
beyond certain points simply did not know the territory, an arguable
but not a game-changing factor in such a complex operation.[21]

In fact, no single factor can explain the raid's failure. A host of
reasons, logistics prominent among them, doomed from the start
what one report called a "daring and well-planned raid." Kilpatrick's
plan appeared splendid on paper but failed due to bad weather, command-and-control issues, ignorance of terrain, logistical mishaps,
and nearly a total lack of secrecy. An astute observation concerning
the raid's failure comes from the general's loyal subordinate Henry
Davies. While most historians blame Kilpatrick's poor leadership as
the salient flaw, a previously unremarked-upon postwar report by
Davies lays out why things went awry. After the war, when Davies
was free to criticize his commander, the New York lawyer offered
a logical argument based on the military principle of command and
control. Recalling the number of units brigaded together (eighteen
to twenty by his count) from the three different cavalry divisions,
the former brigadier reasoned that "the force consisting of this large
number of details from separate regiments was not at all fitted for
an enterprise requiring disciplined confidence strictly and implicit
obedience to orders." Moreover, he said, "Officers and men were
to a great extent strangers to each other and such organizations as
could be improved in such a body of troops could not give confidence to the men or the authority and power to the officers." In
addition, the raid "seriously impaired the efficiency of the cavalry
in the approaching [spring] campaign."[22] Kilpatrick did not say in
official reports whether he realized how the problem of command
and control would affect his force during the operation, but there is
little doubt it did.

Two poor selections for principal subordinates compounded
Kilpatrick's command-and-control problems. The unpopular
Colonel Edward Sawyer, who was no George Custer, commanded
one of the mixed brigades. The general then further complicated
the situation by assigning (or perhaps acquiescing to the appointment of) the inexperienced Ulric Dahlgren to the major subordinate
role of commanding the detached western column. As the Yankee
troopers trotted out of Stevensburg, problems were bound to mul-
tiply, not diminish—and did. "General Kilpatrick's idea was all
right and would have succeeded if the other side hadn't objected," a

Michigan officer wrote. A fellow Wolverine scoffed in a letter home that Kilpatrick's "ruling wish is to be made a Major General, and he urged this last raid expressly to manufacture capital for himself." Kill-Cavalry left Custer behind because he "did not want to share any glory he might achieve," the Michigander added, and "cares nothing about the lives of men, sacrificing them with cool indifference, his only object being his own promotion and keeping his name before the public."[23] Of course, it was not unusual for Michigan men to censure Kilpatrick in favor of Custer.

For the raid to succeed, it required secrecy, and from the outset that rarest of military commodities was compromised. Well before the jump off, Meade's staff officer Theodore Lyman was mentioning the planned action in his private letters. A Washington diarist noted it in her daily record. Brigadier General Davies also identified this as an problem in his later account of the expedition. Newspapers cited breaches of secrecy too. Immediately after the raid the *New York World* invoked the weather and "the fact that its nature was noised too much in the army" as two reasons for failure. The *Baltimore Sun* said that the operation "was a matter of conversation here for some time before the movement actually took place." The *New York Herald* even claimed that by the Friday before its launch, "every Secesh woman in Culpeper knew of the raid." In all these instances the blame rests squarely with Kilpatrick. He spoke openly, if by innuendo, about the operation, a case of hubris at play to the advantage of his foe. A Union artillery officer put it best when he wrote in his diary, "These raids make a big noise in the papers, and so glorify their commander; who is generally a man of that kind who court[s] newspaper renown."[24]

It is also difficult to reconcile the strength of the opposing sides. A timeworn characterization has Richmond defended by a ragtag bunch of old men, schoolboys, invalids, and government clerks who should have fallen prostrate at the thought of Kilpatrick and his 3,500 veteran cavalrymen charging on the city. But in the opinion of Union major William Wells, to capture Richmond the raiders needed "double the force" they brought. Three weeks earlier Isaac Wistar, with nearly twice Kilpatrick's strength, had failed to take Richmond once his operation had been compromised. Lieutenant Colonel Ebenezer Gould, before the war a Michigan lawyer, wrote shortly after the raid, "I've done a little speech making and a very little fighting and from that little I have come to the conclusion

that I'd rather take Richmond in speech than in a fight." Three
months later Major General Philip H. Sheridan, with virtually the
entire Cavalry Corps, a force three times larger than Kilpatrick had,
managed to kill Jeb Stuart but failed to punch through Richmond's
defenses and capture the city. For many of Little Phil's troopers, this
was the second time they were chastened by home guards and government clerks, albeit with some help from Lee's cavalry.[25]

Not only the character but also the quantity of resistance was
a key factor, and one not easily analyzed. Confederate trimonthly
returns for the Department of Richmond indicate troop levels on
February 10 as an "effective total" of 5,160 men. On March 31 this
figure had risen to an "effective total" of 7,500. These counts do
not include the Department of Henrico, comprising the county surrounding Richmond, which reported 1,593 effectives on March 10.
The Richmond Defenses, part of the former department, consisted
of the 10th, 18th, 19th, and 20th Virginia Heavy Artillery Battalions,
units not filled with government workers, ancients, and striplings
but soldiers in their midtwenties, prime military age. While surely
not the equals in quality, combat experience, or reputation of Army
of Northern Virginia veterans, the capital's defenders had advantages over their attackers. These heavy artillerymen served as infantrymen fighting from behind formidable defensive works. They had
sufficient artillery support, putting them at least on an equal foot-
ing with the Federal cavalrymen. Their value cannot be disregarded
in the March 1 confrontations. A new revelation shows that battle-
tested Confederate troops from Lee's army also were present that
day. Even the government clerks and factory workers who defeated
Dahlgren on the west end of the capital proved themselves in crisis
more capable than "d—d melish." They were, in fact, mostly former
regular-army men who, for disability or expertise, now served in the
local defense of Richmond.

Apparently, Federal intelligence was wrong about Richmond's
vulnerability, but more probably that information was stale, as noted
by Kilpatrick's first biographer. In 1865 Dr. James Moore wrote that
the raid failed chiefly due to the "possession of *data*" (italics in original) or really a lack thereof. Before the raid Bet Van Lew had cautioned Butler that to take Richmond he would need 40,000 soldiers.
Her warning had its counterpart in an opinion from a Confederate
War Department clerk who wrote in his diary, "In a few hours we
can muster men enough to defend the city against 25,000." This

man estimated that the Federals would need "a column of 15,000 bold men in the assault, [if] they might have penetrated [the city]." Union colonel Abel Streight, who recently had escaped from Libby Prison, freely told whoever would listen that "Kilpatrick couldn't take Richmond." The city had not only adequate manpower but also sufficient advance notice and a surplus of heart among its defenders, who answered the call to fight with pluck and determination on a day that required precisely those elements.[26]

Kilpatrick had advocates such as the *Army Navy Journal*, the Union military's official news purveyor, which insisted that the raid "was brilliant, it was gallant, and though a failure . . . it was not altogether barren in results." The editor hesitated "to criticize so bold and dashing an attempt to accomplish so praiseworthy an object as the liberation of our soldiers pining in Richmond prisons" and concluded that had Butler come up the Peninsula with the anticipated support, Kilpatrick would have succeeded. An army scout who was with the raiders also sided with the general. Comparing Kilpatrick's performance with Dahlgren's decisions, this man concluded that the general "did not get lost, hung no negro, but did arrive in front of Richmond on time as planned."[27]

Undoubtedly, Union leaders chose poorly in selecting Ulric Dahlgren for so important a part in the raid. The record is murky as to which generals or general in particular is to blame for that decision. Should a politician share the blame? The colonel's father claimed shortly after the raid that "the reluctant consent of the authorities was at last yielded to [Ulric's] earnest entreaties." But Admiral Dahlgren never identified these "authorities." Long after the raid an army scout offered the opinion that Kilpatrick never would have gone outside his own division for subordinate commanders for the operation if the decision had been his alone.[28]

Clearly, Lincoln's friendship with Admiral Dahlgren opened the door for his son to join the expedition; Stanton may have had a hand in the choice as well. Kilpatrick, a consummate politician, fell prey to his ambition by agreeing to accept in such a critical role a young officer clearly not up to the task. No doubt Dahlgren was courageous and bold, but he lacked the seasoning and maturity demanded in such an undertaking. He was "brave almost to rashness," one editor declared. A former Confederate termed the colonel "a gallant and dashing officer, a man of polish and education, but of unbounded ambition which induced him to undertake the desperate adventure he was on." And physically, he was not equal to the task. Throughout the raid, his men noted his fatigue and discomfort, often having to help him mount his horse. "Everyone was aware that he was in no condition to take the field just then," his father wrote in a letter. "The wound was not perfectly healed; he was still weak and could only move on crutches." His stepmother admitted eight months after his amputation that Ulric was "so feeble as to require to be helped into his saddle."[29] Physical debilitation clouded his judgment, leading to decisions at odds with success. Kilpatrick needed, as any field commander requires in any combat situation, a key subordinate able to complement his skills and compensate for his shortcomings, not an inexperienced young officer with more liabilities than assets.

Given the looming exigencies, Judson Kilpatrick's plan was too ambitious. In many ways it showed up his character and demeanor, reflecting as it did a tangential grasp of reality. "Our cavalry had marched too far and too rapidly to be in trim for a fight," a New York trooper wrote home in a letter shortly after the raid. Any plan hinging on speed, secrecy, expediency, and a substantial absence of problems was destined to fail. For example, Major General Wade Hampton, who believed a Federal force with the proper plan could take Richmond, credited Colonel Bradley Johnson's interception of the couriers Dahlgren sent to Kilpatrick as a key factor in the expedition's failure. Apparently, in planning the raid no one questioned whether there might be problems crossing the James River, a shock to Dahlgren when he discovered it unfordable. Add the punishing weather, Federal leaks (including from Kilpatrick himself to the press), Washington gossips, and faulty and out-of-date intelligence on Richmond's defensibility, and you have a recipe for disaster regardless of the commander. And even if the raid had succeeded in its most overt aspect—freeing Union prisoners—it seemingly included no operational preparations for handling their escape. Federal authorities knew from exchanged soldiers that conditions were deplorable in Libby and on Belle Isle. If anything, the raid's failure probably saved Union POWs from a bloodbath.[30] "The rationale of the raid was a hurried ride, timely arrival, great daring, a surprise, a sudden charge without a moment's hesitation—success," a Michigan officer wrote after the war. It was a debacle foretold in its own limited vision.[31]

But few men criticized their commander, while some mourned the fallen Dahlgren. Briefly chastened, Kilpatrick endured several weeks of uncertainty before being transferred to William T. Sherman's command in the West. There the plucky little general went on to command the Union cavalry during the famed March to the Sea and north through the Carolinas, ending the war with a second star as brevet major general of volunteers. Immediately afterward, Kilpatrick became U.S. ambassador to Chile, where he met and married the lovely Louisa Valdevieso, niece of Santiago's archbishop. He returned from his stint in diplomacy to enter politics, toggling between parties and running for governor of New Jersey. He made a small fortune on the lecture circuit, and on his farm in Sussex, New Jersey, the former general organized the first reenactment of a Civil War battle between veterans and the New Jersey National Guard. Kilpatrick returned to Chile in 1880, again as minister. Within a year, though, he was dead of Bright's disease, a condition of kidney failure now called nephritis. On hand for his burial in the cemetery at West Point three years later were his wife, his two daughters, General Sherman, and a host of friends and comrades, including veterans of what has come to be called the Kilpatrick-Dahlgren Raid on Richmond.[32]

"The boys enjoyed the raid highly, even the recruits, although they were much fatigued with the constant riding of the first two or three days," a resolute veteran of the 1st Vermont wrote in a letter home shortly after the events of late February and early March 1864. This cavalryman knew such experiences were all part of service in Kilpatrick's Third Cavalry Division. He summed up the raid persuasively when he asserted, "Were another such raid in prospect[,] but few would 'play off' to get excused I'm sure."[33]

CHAPTER 16

THE DAHLGREN PAPERS
RECONSIDERED

James O. Hall established the authenticity of the Dahlgren papers, the orders found on the colonel's body in King and Queen County on March 3, 1864, by William Littlepage, with some certainty. This longtime student of the topic conducted an exhaustive study, results of which have been endorsed by historian Stephen W. Sears. A popular author who wrote on the raid, Virgil Jones, came to the same conclusion through his own research years earlier, including the observation that Admiral John Dahlgren never denied that the papers or the name on the memo book "legibly set down on its cover were" those of his fallen son. Likewise, a recent biographer of Colonel Dahlgren has concluded, "it appears that the Dahlgren Papers were, in fact, authentic documents written by Ulric Dahlgren."[1]

Two other writers contend, far less convincingly, that Confederate officials forged the papers associated with Dahlgren to advance a scheme to release Rebel prisoners of war, burn Northern cities, and undertake other secret operations against the United States. Even an awarding-winning Lincoln scholar has said, "the genuineness of the Dahlgren papers is contestable." In the raid's aftermath some Northern newspapers, citing aberrations such as the official orders' lack of a date, use of a shortened signature for the young colonel's name when he habitually used his full name on army documents, the misspelling of his surname, and the ease with which the closing line could have been altered to add the phrase about killing Davis, seconded the forgery theory. E. A. Paul, a newspaper reporter and intimate of General Kilpatrick, claimed to have seen the notorious orders prior to the expedition. Paul insisted that Rebels inserted the inflammatory words out of rancor at the extent of the destruction the raiders visited on them. Spinning his favorite general's predicament like a current-day crisis consultant, Paul described how the Federals pulled off the raid under secessionist leadership's noses, "and what is worse than all, by troops led by Kilpatrick and

Dahlgren—two men who, next to Butler, are the most cordially hated and feared by all opposed to the Union cause." But most contemporaneous evidence holds overwhelmingly that Southern military leaders and Confederate government officials lacked the time to fabricate the documents before making them public. To conclude that the Dahlgren papers were other than authentic strains the limits of credibility and logic.[2]

Other evidence not cited by Hall argues for the papers being genuine. In a letter written only seven years after the action, the Confederate partisan famously known as the "Gray Ghost," John S. Mosby, himself renowned as a cavalry raider, told a friend about a conversation he had had with Brigadier General Isaac Wistar. Mosby wrote that Wistar confided to him that "the infernal purposes of Kilpatrick and Dahlgren were correctly disclosed in the papers found on Dahlgren's body." According to the general, Kilpatrick, as yet unaware of Dahlgren's death, revealed identical facts about the expedition's intent while at Wistar's Yorktown headquarters soon after the raid. In addition, a note found in the personal papers of Captain John Babcock, the intelligence officer who provided Dahlgren with his guide for the raid, said in effect that the documents found on the colonel's corpse as reproduced in the Richmond newspapers were an "authentic report of the contents."[3]

The most provocative scrap of evidence consists of secondhand testimony by Brigadier General George Armstrong Custer, who contributed the raid's diversionary element. A literal fragment of writing in the hand of the unknown author of an untitled diary or memoir purports to recapitulate a conversation between Custer and a West Point classmate's wife, Mrs. Thomas Rosser. Rosser, despite being a Confederate cavalry general, remained a close friend of Custer's. According to this fragment, "the night before [Custer] and Dahlgren parted, Dahlgren told him [Custer] that he would not take the President and his cabinet, but would put them to death and that he would himself set fire to the first house in Richmond and burn the city. He, Custer, did not think this purpose right."[4]

Considering the contemporary descriptions of the headstrong Ulric Dahlgren as a "holy warrior," it is entirely likely that the reckless one-legged colonel decided on his own to assassinate Davis. Regrettably, the Custer fragment, the best evidence pinning down culpability, bears no corroborating identification. Yet cross-referenced with other documents, it is useful as a tool for scrutinizing the validity of Dahlgren's express and implied intentions while also a touchstone for the Richmond raid's violent, enigmatic, and enduring mystique. Given the young officer's acknowledged personality, it is feasible that he would take it upon himself to expand his orders to include murder and mayhem.[5]

An aspect of the Dahlgren papers that has heretofore been overlooked by historians and analysts is the language used—specifically, the employment of a personal pronoun in one set of the orders but not in the other. In Dahlgren's address to his "Officers and Men" written on Third Division Cavalry headquarters stationary, he encourages his troopers to "burn the hateful city" and "not allow the rebel leader Davis and his traitorous crew to escape." This order was signed "U. Dahlgren, Colonel, Commanding." But in another special order, directed to his command's various components (that is, "Guides—Pioneers . . . scouts and pickets," and the like), Dahlgren mentions that General Custer and his men may follow his column.[6] The orders read: "As General Custer may follow *me,* be careful not to give a false alarm" (italics added). It seems obvious that Dahlgren himself wrote this particular order, employing as he did the first-person singular pronoun. An officer on Kilpatrick's staff would have been unlikely to cast the order in such personal terms. More likely, Dahlgren penned this document himself. Since Custer was sent to wreck havoc near Charlottesville, which is some thirty-five miles west of Goochland County, he would have been nearer Dahlgren than Kilpatrick were he to follow either of the Federal contingents. No written orders extant tell Custer to cut toward Dahlgren's trail after doing mischief near Charlottesville, but the colonel may have believed this to be the plan. More significantly for this analysis is that the order employing the personal pronoun "me" also contains the directive to the raiders that "once in the city it must be destroyed and Jeff. Davis and cabinet killed." The second order, invoking assassination, seems to have been written by Dahlgren. This interpretation of both orders also explains why Kilpatrick answered Robert E. Lee's inquiry as he did. Kilpatrick probably expected an attempt would be made to capture Davis and his cabinet, but there was no official order to kill the Confederate president.[7]

More evidence exists to verify the nature of Dahlgren's papers. Hall argues convincingly that the original documents disappeared from a Federal repository after Secretary of War Edwin Stanton pulled them in late November 1865, ironically, the same month that

Ulric's body was returned for burial in Philadelphia. Neither the War Department nor the Archive Office ever got the papers back, but a clear lithographic set of Dahlgren's orders exist as part of Admiral Dahlgren's personal papers, along with other correspondence from his son. The handwriting in a February 26, 1864, letter from Ulric to his father closely resembles the penmanship on both sets of orders. It would be difficult to prove authenticity, even through professional handwriting analysis, without the original documents, but it is reasonable to conclude that the young colonel may have written the controversial orders himself. This determination is partly embraced by another analyst of the Dahlgren papers. The body of material and analysis therefore suggests that we should not view Colonel Dahlgren as a sacrificial scapegoat but rather as a more engaged and sinister participant, as Confederate officials originally claimed.[8]

Hall's research points, at least circumstantially, to Edwin Stanton as a figure in the plot to kill Davis. Why remove official documents from a government office and not return them unless he had nefarious motives? A link to Hall's findings may exist in a statement made by Stuyvesant Fish, the son of a prominent New York politician of the day. Fish said that he remembered seeing among his father's papers a reference pointing to a cabinet member sending orders to Kilpatrick. One could surmise, albeit skeptically, that Secretary of War Stanton may have been that cabinet officer. If his name was indeed the one the younger Fish saw, we can speculate that Stanton issued orders to murder Jefferson Davis. Sears, likewise, points an accusing finger at the secretary of war.[9]

Another explanation for Stanton behaving this way hinges on the chance that Dahlgren's papers contained a rather flippant but harshly incriminating statement about the colonel's intent. In an article written more than forty years after the raid, William Preston Cabell claimed that in a memorandum Dahlgren wrote, he "had made a wager that he would hang Jeff Davis and his cabinet on the raid." No reference to a wager on Davis's life appeared in the Richmond papers in the raid's aftermath. This could mean that Cabell's information was based on later hearsay but ran in his article because it made a good story better, or it could mean that incriminating evidence appeared in Dahlgren's memo book, which Colonel Richard Beale held off on transporting to Richmond until April, when tempers had cooled. If Cabell had it right, and there is no credible reason to believe he did, Stanton had good reason to destroy

Dahlgren's papers, particularly if the secretary held the other half of the wager. Such tantalizing speculation continues to make the Kilpatrick-Dahlgren Raid a billiard table of caroming conjecture.[10]

Judson Kilpatrick was no man to devise so morbid a scheme on his own. The young general was all about show. Some fellow officers in the Army of the Potomac deemed him a boaster who hunted headlines the way some men hunted quail. One staff officer said Kilpatrick was "a frothy braggart, without brains and not over-stocked with the desire to fall on the field; and that he gets all his reputation by newspapers and political influence."[11] Others said that he lusted after loftier military rank as well as political office at the highest levels. Echoing these sentiments, a former Confederate general wrote years later that for any officer who could have captured or killed Jefferson Davis and burned Richmond to the ground, the presidency of the United States would have been but "meager compensation for him, in the hearts of the masses of the people."[12]

But a manipulator is not necessarily a murderer, and Kilpatrick's actions prior to the raid indicate no evidence of zealotry or bloody intent toward Confederate officials. Undoubtedly, Little Kil would have relished frog-marching Jeff Davis back to Washington in leg irons, but his personality and previous actions do not point at any desire to haul him back in a pine box. As one Northern editor wrote, a raid that could "have gone into Richmond, and snaked Jeff. Davis from his bed—such a dash upon that city has been the dream of our enterprising cavalry officers." Though it fingered the wrong man, a New York newspaper editorial came up with this same scenario, "the rebel President would have been too rich a prize to bring North for Colonel Dahlgren to wish to put an end to him in any such summary manner." In addition, a New York officer who rode with Kilpatrick's main column later remembered sending word to the general that "I could carry the works in front of me and asked permission to try, but was ordered to hold until dark when the advance would be made. We were told that we would be ordered to work our way to Jeff Davis's house *and make him prisoner*, while the others were to go to the different prisons and release the prisoners" (italics added). Moreover, an observant Southerner, captured by the raiders near Richmond, later said, "So far as I was able to discover on the march to Williamsburg, and my eyes were open all the time, nothing happened to indicate that General Kilpatrick or any of his officers knew of any such order [to kill Davis]." Even Kill-Cavalry's harshest critic, Theodore Lyman, confided in his private journal that the raid was intended to "liberate the prisoners" and "grab all the M.C.'s possible." Lyman seems convinced that the plan was to capture, not kill, Confederate officials. Plausibly, Kilpatrick rather than Dahlgren would have been more keenly interested in delivering Davis into Lincoln's hands alive, not dead. Unlike Dahlgren, Kilpatrick was no "holy warrior" but instead a self-interested pragmatist and heady politician. As a topic of conversation and a goad to press coverage, Davis in irons trumped Davis shot dead. In addition, Dahlgren did not arrive at army headquarters in Culpeper until February 18, affording him plenty of time to pay an unrecorded visit to Stanton at the War Department. If there is a presidential connection to the orders found on the colonel's body, it is more likely that Stanton devised them and, perhaps, sent them through a willing acolyte like young Ulric Dahlgren.[13]

It is not difficult to see the secretary using the young officer because Dahlgren did not always use the best judgment. Beset by deteriorating conditions after midday on March 1, why keep such devastating documents on his person? His signal officer, Lieutenant Reuben Bartley, had the good sense to destroy his secret codes and documents, yet Dahlgren clung to materials that could (and tacitly did) indict by implication the highest officials in the Federal government and the army in an assassination plot. There is no denying Dahlgren's bravery, swagger, and verve. But along with those attributes sometimes come, as they did in him, arrogance and foolishness. By the evening of March 2, only a fool or a knave would have been holding on to such incriminating papers. One might even use a harsher word—it was stupid. As a Northern newspaper pointed out, no matter what the source of the orders, keeping the papers reflected "youthful indiscretion. . . . It was certainly careless to carry any orders upon his person." The colonel's other missteps on the road to and from Richmond aside, this assessment supports the conclusion that army brass should not have included Dahlgren in the operation, let alone assign him a major command role. The Southern press agreed. A Richmond newspaper opined, "The serious part of the work was committed by Kilpatrick to an *inexperienced boy*, who had not the sense to conceal the infamous orders under which they came, and who seems to have had no intelligent idea of what he had to perform" (italics added). The journalist understood as well that Dahlgren had no business being in the saddle: "But his amazing ignorance of the geography of the country is the most striking fact on the face of his programme [*sic*]. . . . Dahlgren was, perhaps not a reasonable man" for this mission.[14]

Kilpatrick may have been correct when, in a shout to his trusted comrade, Major Edwin Cooke, at the expedition's start, he intimated that he would have preferred one of his own subordinates heading the detached contingent. Perhaps the general had no choice. Perhaps the man running the War Department capitalized on an opportune situation, much as he might have exploited a young firebrand like Ulric Dahlgren. Without doubt, the Dahlgren papers are authentic, and most evidence points to the colonel as the perpetrator of the idea of killing Jeff Davis "on the spot."

Whatever truth lurks in the raid's dense forest of subterfuge and surmise, its elusiveness will continue to entice minds inclined to wonder what flickers in shadows and among darkling pathways. The sound of hooves, the roar of cannon, the scream of frightened civilians bent on defending their city, and the shouts of cavalrymen on a desperate sprint to capture it come together. Fact and conflation, intimation and assumption, guilt and innocence all come into play. No wonder we keep poking at the Kilpatrick-Dahlgren Raid for answers that are elusive. It reflects life itself.

APPENDIX

THE DAHLGREN PAPERS

Shortly after the incriminating orders to capture or kill Confederate president Jefferson Davis were found on Colonel Ulric Dahlgren's body in King and Queen County, Virginia, the documents were printed in Richmond newspapers.

The version of Dahlgren's papers presented here was printed in the *Official Records* from copies that appeared in the Richmond press:[1]

The following papers and memoranda were found on [Colonel] Dahlgren's person, and contain the indisputable evidence of the diabolical designs of the enemy.

The following address to the officers and men of the command was written on a sheet of paper having in printed letters on the upper corner, "Headquarters Third Division, Cavalry Corps,—[1864]:"

OFFICERS AND MEN:
You have been selected from brigades and regiments as a picked command to attempt a desperate undertaking—an undertaking which, if successful, will write your names on the hearts of your countrymen in letters that can never be erased, and which will cause the prayers of our fellow-soldiers now confined in loathsome prisons to follow you and yours wherever you may go. We hope to release the prisoners from Belle Island first, and having seen them fairly started, we will cross the James River into Richmond, destroying the bridges after us and exhorting the released prisoners to destroy and burn the hateful city; and do not allow the rebel leader Davis and his traitorous crew to escape. The prisoners must render great assistance, as you cannot leave your ranks too far or become too much scattered, or you will be lost. Do not

allow any personal gain to lead you off, which would only bring you to an ignominious death at the hands of citizens. Keep well together and obey orders strictly and all will be well; but on no account scatter too far, for in union there is strength. With strict obedience to orders and fearlessness in the execution you will be sure to succeed. We will join the main force on the other side of the city, or perhaps meet them inside. Many of you may fall; but if there is any man here not willing to sacrifice his life in such a great and glorious undertaking, or who does not feel capable of meeting the enemy in such a desperate fight as will follow, let him step out, and he may go hence to the arms of his sweetheart and read of the braves who swept through the city of Richmond. We want no man who cannot feel sure of success in such a holy cause. We will have a desperate fight, but stand up to it when it does come, and all will be well. Ask the blessing of the Almighty, and do not fear the enemy.

U DAHLGREN,
Colonel, Commanding.

The following special orders were written on a similar sheet of paper and on detached slips, the whole disclosing the diabolical plans of the leaders of the expedition:[2]

Guides.—Pioneers (with oakum, turpentine, and torpedoes), signal officer, quartermaster, commissary. Scouts and pickets. Men in rebel uniform. These will remain on the north bank and move down with the force on the south bank, not getting ahead of them, and if the communication can be kept up without giving an alarm it must be done; but everything depends upon a surprise, and no one must be allowed to pass ahead of the column. Information must be gathered in regard to the crossings of the river, so that should we be repulsed on the south side we will know where to recross at the nearest point. All mills must be burned and the canal destroyed, and also everything which can be used by the rebels must be destroyed, including the boats on the river. Should a ferry-boat be seized and can be worked, have it moved down. Keep the force on the south side posted of any important movement of the enemy, and in case of danger some of the scouts must swim the river and bring us information. As we approach the city the party must take great care that they do not get ahead of the other party on the south side, and must conceal themselves and watch our movements. We will try and secure the bridge to the city, 1 mile below Belle Isle, and release the prisoners at the same time. If we do not succeed they must then dash down, and we will try and carry the bridge from each side. When necessary, the men must be filed through the woods and along the river bank. The bridges once secured, and the prisoners loose and over the river, the bridges will be secured and the city destroyed. The men must keep together and well in hand, and once in the city it must be destroyed and Jeff. Davis and cabinet killed. Pioneers will go along with combustible material. The officer must use his discretion about the time of assisting us. Horses and cattle which we do not need immediately must be shot rather than left. Everything on the canal and elsewhere of service to the rebels must be destroyed. As General Custer may follow me, be careful not to give a false alarm.

The signal officer must be prepared to communicate at night by rockets, and in other things pertaining to his department.

The quartermasters and commissaries must be on the lookout for their departments, and see that there are no delays on their account.

The engineer officer will follow to survey the road as we pass over it, &c.

The pioneers must be prepared to construct a bridge or destroy one. They must have plenty of oakum and turpentine for burning, which will be rolled in soaked balls and given to the men to burn when we get in the city. Torpedoes will only be used by the pioneers for destroying the main bridges, &c. They must be prepared to destroy railroads. Men will branch off to the right with a few pioneers and destroy the bridges and railroads south of Richmond, and then join us at the city. They must be well prepared with torpedoes, &c. The line of Falling Creek is probably the best to work along, or as they approach the city Goodes Creek, so that no re-enforcements can come up on any cars. No one must be allowed to pass ahead for fear of communicating news. Rejoin the command with all haste, and if cut off cross the river above Richmond and rejoin us. Men will stop at Bellona Arsenal and totally destroy it, and anything else but hospitals; then follow on and rejoin the command at Richmond with all haste, and if cut off cross the river and rejoin us. As General Custer may follow me, be careful not to give a false alarm.

The following is an exact copy of a paper written in lead-pencil, which appears to have been a private memorandum of the programme which Dahlgren had made to enable him to keep his work clearly in mind:

Saturday—Leave camp at dark (6 P.M.). Cross Ely's Ford at 10 P.M.
Twenty miles—Cross North Anna at 4 A.M. Sunday. Feed and water one hour.
Three miles—Frederick Hall Station 6 A.M. Destroy arts 8 A.M.
Twenty miles—Near James River 2 P.M. Sunday. Feed and water one hour and a half.
Thirty miles to Richmond—March toward Kilpatrick for one hour, and then as soon as dark cross the river, reaching Richmond early in the morning (Monday).
One squadron remains on north side and one squadron to cut the railroad bridge at Falling Creek, and join at Richmond; 83 miles.
General Kilpatrick—Cross at 1 A.M. Sunday; 10 miles.
Pass river 5 A.M. Resistance.
Chilesburg—Fourteen miles; 8 A.M.
Resistance at North Anna; 3 miles.
Railroad bridges at South Anna; 26 miles; 2 P.M. Destroy bridges, pass the South Anna, and feed until after dark; then signal each other. After dark move down to Richmond and be in front of the city at daybreak.
Return—In Richmond during the day. Feed and water men outside.
Be over the Pamunkey at daybreak. Feed and water and then cross the Rappahannock at night (Tuesday night), when they must be on the lookout.
Spies should be sent on Friday morning early, and be ready to cut.

The following paper was inclosed in an envelope directed to Col. U. Dahlgren, etc., at General Kilpatrick's headquarters, and marked "Confidential." The letter is not dated:

Colonel DAHLGREN, etc.:
DEAR COLONEL: At the last moment I have found the man you
want; well acquainted with the James River from Richmond
up. I send him to you mounted on my own private horse. You
will have to furnish him a horse. Question him five minutes,
and you will find him the very man you want.
Respectfully and truly, yours,
JOHN C. BABCOCK.

On the margin of this letter is written:
He crossed at Rapidan last night, and has late information.

The *Richmond Daily Examiner* printed the following text, written in pencil, from Dahlgren's memorandum book in its April 1,
1864, issue:[3]

Pleasonton will govern details.
Will have details from other commands, (four thousand).
Michigan men have started.
Colonel J. H. Devereux has torpedoes.
Hanover Junction (B. T. Johnson). Maryland Line.
Chapin's Farm—Seven miles below Richmond.
One brigade (Hunton's relieved, Wise sent to Charleston).
River can be forded half a mile above the city. No works on south
side. Hospitals near them. River fordable. Canal can be crossed.

Fifty men to remain on north bank, and keep in communication if possible. To destroy mills, canal, and burn everything of
value to the Rebels. Seize any large ferry boats, and note all crossings, in case we have to return that way. Keep us posted of any
important movement of the Rebels, and as we approach the city,
communicate with us, and do not give the alarm before they see us
in possession of Belle Isle and the bridge. If engaged there or unsuccessful, they must assist in securing the bridges until we cross. If
the ferry boat can be taken and worked, bring it down. Everything
that cannot be secured or made use of must be destroyed. Great
care must be taken not to be seen or any alarm given. The men
must be filed along off the road or along the main bank. When we
enter the city the officer must use his discretion as to when to
assist in crossing the bridges.

The prisoners once loosed and the bridges crossed, the city
must be destroyed, burning the public buildings, etc.

Prisoners to go with party.

Spike the heavy guns outside.

Pioneers must be ready to repair, destroy, etc. Turpentine will be provided. The pioneers must be ready to destroy the Richmond bridges, after we have all crossed, and to destroy the railroad near Frederick's Hall (station, artillery, etc.).

Fifteen men to halt at Bellona Arsenal, while the column goes on, and destroy it. Have some prisoners. Then rejoin us at Richmond, leaving a portion to watch if anything follows, under a good officer.

Will be notified that Custer may come.

Main column, four hundred.

One hundred men will take the bridge after the scouts, and dash through the streets and open the way to the front, or if it is open destroy everything in the way.

While they are on the big bridges, one hundred men will take Belle Isle, after the scouts, instructing the prisoners to gut the city. The reserve (two hundred) will see this fairly done and everything over, and then follow, destroying the bridges after them, but not scattering too much and always having a part well in hand.

Jeff. Davis and Cabinet must be killed on the spot.

Notes

Abbreviations

ALPL	Abraham Lincoln Presidential Library
BHL-UM	Bentley Historical Library, University of Michigan
BHL-UV	Bailey/Howe Library, University of Vermont
CHL	Clarke Historical Library, Central Michigan University
CMR	Confederate Military Records
Cronin, "Vest Mansion"	Daniel Edward Cronin, "The Vest Mansion: Its Historical and Romantic Associations as Confederate and Union Headquarters (1862–1865) in the American Civil War," 1908–10, John D. Rockefeller, Jr., Library, Colonial Williamsburg Foundation
Davies Report	Henry E. Davies, Jr., "Report," 1874, U.S. Army Generals' Reports of Civil War Service, 1864–87, RG 94, NA
HSP	Historical Society of Pennsylvania
ISL	Indiana State Library
LC	Library of Congress
LV	Library of Virginia
NA	National Archives
Official Records	U.S. War Department, *Official Records of the Union and Confederate Armies in the War of the Rebellion*, 128 vols. (Washington, D.C.: Government Printing Office, 1880–1901). All citations are to series 1 unless otherwise noted.
RG 94	Record Group 94, Records of the Adjutant General's Office, 1780s–1917
RG 107	Record Group 107, Records of the Office of the Secretary of War
RG 393	Record Group 393, Records of U.S. Army Continental Commands, 1821–1920
Supplement	Janet B. Hewett et al., *Supplement to the Official Records of Union and Confederate Armies*, 100 vols. in 3 pts. plus index (Wilmington, N.C.: Broadfoot, 1994–2001)
USAHEC	U.S. Army Heritage and Education Center, Military History Institute
VHS	Virginia Historical Society
WL	Waldo Library, Western Michigan University

Chapter 1

1. *Philadelphia Daily Evening Bulletin,* Apr. 18, 1864; *Burlington Free Press,* Apr. 23, 1864; Nathan Webb Diary, Nathan Webb Papers, ALPL, transcript, 414.
2. Charles Blinn Diary, Apr. 17, 1864, BHL-UV.
3. Kidd, *Riding with Custer,* 164–65.
4. Pickerill, *Third Indiana Cavalry,* 137; *Baltimore American* quoted in *Alexandria Gazette,* Mar. 4, 1864.
5. Owens, *Sword and Pen,* 125.
6. *New York Herald,* Jan. 7, 1864; Lyman, *Meade's Headquarters,* 79.
7. Howard, *Civil-War Echoes,* 214.
8. Styple, *Generals in Bronze,* 48, 50.
9. Kidd, *Riding with Custer,* 164–65.
10. Glazier, *Three Years in the Federal Cavalry,* 135–36.
11. Meyer, *Civil War Experiences,* 97–98; Glazier, *Three Years in the Federal Cavalry,* 135–36.
12. G. A. Custer, *Custer Story,* 76–77; Hamilton, *Recollections of a Cavalryman,* 152.
13. Lyman, *Meade's Army,* 35, 55, 103; Lyman, *Meade's Headquarters,* 76.
14. Philip Neher to Dear Old Friend, Apr. 17, 1864, Phillip Neher Papers, Albany Institute of History and Art.
15. Joseph Douglas to George Douglas, Apr. 24, 1864, Douglas-Nellis Papers, BHL-UM.
16. Davenport, *Camp and Field Life of the Fifth New York Volunteer Infantry,* 429–30, 438, 452, 458.
17. Southwick, *Duryee Zouave,* 29.
18. Quarstein, *Big Bethel,* 136.
19. Frank Gross Diary, Apr. 16, 1864, BHL-UM; Culpeper Historical Society, *Historic Culpeper,* 114; Jeffries, *Survey Report, Rose Hill.*
20. Styple, *Generals in Bronze,* 50; Kidd, *Riding with Custer,* 165; Philip Neher to Dear Old Friend, Apr. 17, 1864, Neher Papers; William B. Hutton to Mary Mills, Apr. 17, 1864, Mary Mills Papers, Duke Univ.
21. Victor Comte to Elise Comte, Apr. 20, 1864, Victor Comte Papers, BHL-UM; Wickman, *Letters to Vermont,* 2:165.
22. Isham, *Seventh Regiment of Michigan Volunteer Cavalry,* 40.
23. Letter, Apr. 22, 1864, in *Rutland Daily Herald,* Apr. 28, 1864. Another Union veteran put a positive spin on the general's reputation: "Kilpatrick always proved the dashing and ready but level headed fighter that soldiers pin their faith to and the crowd goes mad over. His troops idolized him, and to this day, from Maine to Michigan, the Grand Army comrades take for the hero of their campfire tales this young Jerseyman of the Sussex hills." Kilmer, *Miscellaneous War Sketches,* 82.
24. Letter, Apr. 17, 1864, in *Burlington Free Press,* Apr. 23, 1864.
25. Philip Neher to Dear Old Friend, Apr. 17, 1864, Neher Papers.
26. Isham, *Seventh Regiment of Michigan Volunteer Cavalry,* 40; Gross Diary, Apr. 16, 1864; Ide, *First Vermont Cavalry Volunteers,* 158.

27. Blinn Diary, Apr. 17, 1864; F. J. Bellamy to Fletcher Bellamy, Apr. 20, 1864, F. J. Bellamy Papers, ISL.
28. Edward Corselius to George Corselius, Apr. 21, 1864, G. Corselius Papers, BHL-UM; Foster, *New Jersey in the Rebellion*, 745.
29. Wilson, *Under the Old Flag*, 1:368–71.
30. *Philadelphia Daily Evening Bulletin*, Apr. 18, 1864; *Burlington Free Press*, Apr. 23, 1864; Foster, *New Jersey in the Rebellion*, 745. For difficulties between Kilpatrick and Custer, see various items in Miscellaneous Letters, Reports, pt. 2, vol. 35, RG 393, NA; and Wert, *Custer*, 121–22.
31. Wainwright, *Diary of Battle*, 324.

Chapter 2

1. William Martin to his wife, n.d., William H. Martin Papers, Harrisburg Civil War Round Table Collection, USAHEC.
2. Averell, *Ten Years in the Saddle*, 328–29.
3. Starr, *Union Cavalry in the Civil War*, 1:243–52, 257–58; Thiele, "Evolution of Cavalry in the American Civil War," 524–30.
4. Mewborn, "Wonderful Exploit," 6–21, 46–54; *Official Records*, ser. 1, 2(1):1042; Hubbard, *Civil War Memoirs*, 47; Cox, *Military Reminiscences*, 2:290.
5. *Official Records*, 12(2):729–33; McClellan, *Life and Campaigns of Major-General J. E. B. Stuart*, 89–96.
6. Longacre, *Mounted Raids*, 21–45.
7. Longacre, *Lee's Cavalrymen*, 163–66; McClellan, *Life and Campaigns of Major-General J. E. B. Stuart*, 201; Wert, *Cavalryman of the Lost Cause*, 195–98. For a thorough, well-documented discussion of Stuart's winter raids, see O'Neill, *Chasing Jeb Stuart and John Mosby*.
8. For a discussion and analysis of Stuart's raid into Pennsylvania, see Nesbitt, *Saber and Scapegoat*. Also see Wittenberg and Petruzzi, *Plenty of Blame to Go Around*.
9. Freeman, *Lee's Lieutenants*, 2:xxiv, 397–408; Thiele, "Evolution of Cavalry in the American Civil War," 530–31.
10. *Officials Records*, 12(3):476, 481–82, 484–86, 488–91.
11. Thiele, "Evolution of Cavalry in the American Civil War," 309–11, 531; Warner, *Generals in Blue*, 53, 216–17.
12. *Official Records*, 21:895–96.
13. Ibid.
14. Ibid., 902.
15. Thiele, "Evolution of Cavalry in the American Civil War," 392.
16. Warner, *Generals in Blue*, 481–82; Longacre, *Mounted Raids*, 149–51; O'Neill, "Cavalry on the Peninsula," 6–22, 38–51; *Official Records*, 25(2):51.
17. Longacre, *Mounted Raids*, 151–57.
18. Ibid., 156–63.
19. *Official Records*, 25(1):1060.
20. Ibid.; Longacre, *Mounted Raids*, 163–65.

21. Longacre, *Mounted Raids*, 166–71; J. Moore, *Kilpatrick and Our Cavalry*, 49–50.
22. *Official Records*, 25(2):449, 528; *Burlington Free Press*, Mar. 9, 1864. Lincoln had interviewed Brig. Gen. August Willich about the condition of Richmond. For a previous, rather dubious, plot to capture Jefferson Davis, see Vifquain, *1862 Plot to Kidnap Jefferson Davis*.
23. *Official Records*, 25(1):1064.
24. Johnston, *Virginia Railroads in the Civil War*, 149.
25. For a description of how to permanently destroy bridges and locomotive engines, see memorandum, Brig. Gen. Herman Haupt, Nov. 1, 1862, *Official Records*, ser. 3, 2:709–10. Haupt was in charge of the U.S. Military Railroads.
26. Starr, *Union Cavalry in the Civil War*, 1:368–461, 2:1–34; Longacre, *Lincoln's Cavalrymen*, 147–236; Longacre, *Lee's Cavalrymen*, 188–268.
27. *Official Records*, 29(1):919–73. For a detailed study of this raid, see Collins, *Averell's Salem Raid*.

Chapter 3

1. Furgurson, *Ashes of Glory*, 58–59, 155–56, 214–15; Wheelan, *Libby Prison Breakout*, 31–33.
2. *Official Records*, ser. 2, 6:241–42.
3. Ibid., 475, 977–78, 1087–89.
4. Wheelan, *Libby Prison Breakout*, 65–74; *Official Records*, ser. 2, 6:439, 510–11. Exchanges of POWs had been standard early in the war, but to discomfit the Rebels by forcing them to care for captured Union troops and to deprive the Southern armies of reinforcements, the Federals had reduce their frequency.
5. *Richmond Daily Examiner*, Nov. 24, 1863; *Official Records*, 29(2):231–32, 236–37, 779.
6. *Richmond Daily Examiner*, Nov. 23, 24, 1863.
7. *Official Records*, ser. 2, 6:438–39.
8. *Daily National Republican*, Nov. 25, 1863; *Philadelphia Inquirer*, Jan. 28, 1864.
9. *Official Records*, 29(2):446–47.
10. Nevins, *War for the Union*, 1:81–83.
11. Lyman, *Meade's Army*, 227.
12. *Official Records*, 29(2):446–47; Warner, *Generals in Blue*, 60–61.
13. *Official Records*, 51(1, supplement):1286.
14. Warner, *Generals in Blue*, 568–69; Welsh, *Medical Histories of Union Generals*, 373–76; Wistar, *Autobiography*, 408–409.
15. Warner, *Generals in Blue*, 568–69; Welsh, *Medical Histories of Union Generals*, 373–76; Cronin, "Vest Mansion," 130; Butler, *Private and Official Correspondence*, 3:158–59.
16. John Wilson to Butler, Feb. 16, 1864, Letter Book 210, Box 25, Benjamin F. Butler Papers, LC; Newspaper Clips File 259, ibid.; Butler, *Private and Official Correspondence*, 3:158–59.
17. Hunt and Brown, *Brevet Brigadier Generals in Blue*, 662; Sifakis, *Who Was Who in the Civil War*, 705–706; *Official Records*, 51(1,

supplement):1282. After the war West served under Custer on the frontier, "where he took up drinking and came into conflict with Custer over the shooting of deserters. He pressed charges against Custer and in return was charged by him with drunkenness. He was suspended from rank for two months. Obtaining a sutlership, he resigned in 1869 but died six months later." Sifakis, *Who Was Who in the Civil War,* 706.

18. *Official Records,* 51(1, supplement):1283–84.
19. Ibid., 1282–83.
20. Ibid.
21. Ibid. West's viewpoint appears to be uncannily similar to the impression Kilpatrick would have of Confederate defenses three months later when he pitched his own plan for a raid to Lincoln and Stanton. Unfortunately for the Federals, things did not remain static in Richmond.
22. Ibid. In his autobiography Wistar also claims credit for the plan without attaching West's name to it. See Wistar, *Autobiography,* 426.
23. J. B. Jones, *Rebel War Clerk's Diary,* 2:91.
24. *Official Records,* 29(1):974–77; *Richmond Daily Examiner,* Dec. 15, 16, 1863.
25. *Official Records,* 29(2):537, 554, 571, 581, 595–98; Butler, *Private and Official Correspondence,* 3:154, 159, 171, 180–82, 193, 216, 351.
26. Varon, *Southern Lady, Yankee Spy,* 57, 109; Van Lew, *Yankee Spy in Richmond,* 8–11.
27. Varon, *Southern Lady, Yankee Spy,* 109–12; Butler, *Private and Official Correspondence,* 3:228–29.
28. See Vifquain, *1862 Plot to Kidnap Jefferson Davis.*
29. Stuart, "Of Spies and Borrowed Names," 310–11. In late January 1864 Butler was receiving intelligence from "a table servant" named James Pemberton, who formerly worked for Jefferson Davis before he absconded. Pemberton's information that Vice Pres. Alexander Stevens had fled to Europe was patently false. *Official Records,* 33:406.
30. *Official Records,* 33:519–21; Stuart, "Colonel Ulric Dahlgren and Richmond's Union Underground, April 1864," *Virginia Magazine of History and Biography* 72 (Apr. 1964): 187; Stuart, "Of Spies and Borrowed Names," 310–11.
31. Cronin, "Vest Mansion," 129.
32. Telegram, Benjamin Butler to Isaac Wistar, Feb. 2, 1864, Box 25, Butler Papers. This seemingly innocuous question would have relevance to another Yankee raid on Richmond three weeks later. Prior to that foray, its commander did not check the water level in the James River, an oversight that would be a major factor in its failure.
33. *Official Records,* 33:519–21.
34. *Army Navy Journal,* Feb. 13, 1864.
35. *Official Records,* 33:502, 506, 511, 518–19; telegram, Benjamin Butler to Edwin Stanton, Feb. 3, 1864, Box 25, Butler Papers. In his autobiography Butler reveals in a spurious conversation with Lincoln, allegedly in the spring of 1863, that he spurned an assignment with the Army of the Potomac because of the West Point attitude toward political generals:

"McClellan has put almost all brigades in charge of lieutenants, captains and majors of the regular army, and they all think they are very much my superior in the knowledge of everything pertaining to the art of war." He told Lincoln that he even saw this demeanor in his own staff. The Massachusetts general felt that army was full of "jealousies, feuds and embroilments" and wanted no part of it at the time. Butler, *Autobiography and Personal Reminiscences*, 577–78.

36. Lyman, *Meade's Army*, 95; *Official Records*, 33:523–24; Humphreys, *From Gettysburg to the Rapidan*, 72–73; Hall, Besley, and Woods, *Sixth New York Cavalry*, 172; *Richmond Sentinel*, Feb. 15, 1864.

37. *Official Records*, 33:483–84, 521; telegrams, Benjamin Butler to Edwin Stanton, Feb. 2, 3, 4, 1864, Box 25, Butler Papers; Cronin, "Vest Mansion," 135–36; *Supplement*, pt. 2, 58:855; Hunt and Brown, *Brevet Brigadier Generals in Blue*, 177, 575.

38. Lyman, *Meade's Army*, 95; Humphreys, *From Gettysburg to the Rapidan*, 73; Welsh, *Medical Histories of Union Generals*, 359; *Richmond Sentinel*, Feb. 15, 1864; *Official Records*, 33:114–21, 126–27, 141–43; Beaudry, *Wartime Journal*, 89; Apperson, *Repairing the "March of Mars,"* 504–505; Fleming, *Life and Letters of Alexander Hays*, 540–43; letter, Feb. 19, 1864, in *Wyoming County Mirror*, Feb. 24, 1864. Army rumors later circulated that the indignant Hays was "severely censured for his conduct," but they were just that—rumors.

39. Favill, *Diary of a Young Officer*, 278.

40. William Martin to his wife, Feb. 12, 1864, postmark, William H. Martin Papers, Harrisburg Civil War Round Table Collection, USAHEC; *Army Navy Journal*, Feb. 13, 1864.

41. Gracey, *Annals of the Sixth Pennsylvania Cavalry*, 222. The present-day Robinson River appears in the *Official Records* and the *Atlas of the Official Records* as the Robertson River.

42. Beaudry, *Wartime Journal*, 89; *Official Records*, 33:114–18, 525.

43. Taylor, *Lee's Adjutant*, 116; *Army Navy Journal*, Feb. 13, 1864.

44. Isaac Wistar to Benjamin Butler, Feb. 4, 1864, Letter Book 210, Box 25, Butler Papers.

45. *Official Records*, 33:521. It appears that Wistar was in error about the battery number. Battery No. 3 was directly on the Williamsburg Road; Battery No. 2 was about a mile south of the road. See G. B. Davis et al., *Official Military Atlas*, Plate XCII.

46. *Official Records*, 33:521–22.

47. Ibid.

48. Ibid., 522.

49. Butler, *Autobiography and Personal Reminiscences*, 620–21.

50. Ibid., 146, 532; Chase, "Service with Battery F, 1st Rhode Island," 113; Day, *My Diary*, 118–19.

51. *Official Records*, 33:146–47.

52. Ibid., 146–48, 1158; *Richmond Sentinel*, Feb. 9, 1864.

53. *Richmond Daily Examiner*, n.d., reprinted in *Rockland Gazette*, Feb. 13, 1864; Paradis, *Strike the Blow for Freedom*, 44; William Joyner to

his mother, Feb. 11, 1864, William Joyner Papers, Richmond National Battlefield Park Library; J. B. Jones, *Rebel War Clerk's Diary*, 2:145.

54. *Official Records*, 33:147, 149, 1160; Taylor, *Lee's Adjutant*, 116; Stearns, *Civil War Diary*, 35; Chase, "Service with Battery F, 1st Rhode Island," 114–15; Paradis, *Strike the Blow for Freedom*, 44–45; *Army Navy Journal*, Feb. 13, 1864.

55. *Official Records*, 33:145–46; Stearns, *Civil War Diary*, 34.

56. *Official Records*, 33:539.

57. Ibid., 147–48.

58. Ibid., 1074, 1081, 1125, 1131; Taylor, *Lee's Adjutant*, 116.

59. *Official Records*, 33:144; Boyle quoted in Lowery, *Don't Shoot That Boy!*, 152; Butler, *Autobiography and Personal Reminiscences*, 619–20; telegram, Benjamin Butler to Isaac Wistar, Feb. 8, 1864, Box 25, Butler Papers; Chase, "Service with Battery F, 1st Rhode Island," 116; *Old Dominion Daily*, Mar. 4, 1864. David Cronin claims that Abraham helped Boyle by "filing his manacles." He also contends that Boyle was spotted by a comrade from his regiment some years after the war in New York City, though after the fugitive had been reported killed in a mining accident out west. Cronin, "Vest Mansion," 140.

60. Cronin, "Vest Mansion," 141; *New York World*, Feb. 10, 1864.

61. Butler, *Autobiography and Personal Reminiscences*, 621. Butler and Davis had been political friends before the war. See W. C. Davis, *Jefferson Davis*, 281.

62. *Official Records*, 33:149, 541, 552; Newspaper Clips File 259, Butler Papers; *Springfield Republican*, Mar. 12, 1864; *Army Navy Journal*, Feb. 13, 1864; *New York World*, Feb. 10, 1864.

63. *Official Records*, 33:149.

64. Letter, Feb. 20, 1864, in *The Caledonian*, Mar. 4, 1864.

Chapter 4

1. *Boston Globe*, May 13, 1910, copy in Maud Wood Park Papers, LC.

2. Ibid.

3. *Grand Rapids Daily Democrat*, Feb. 6, 1887.

4. W. L. Curry, *Four Years in the Saddle*, 243.

5. Wainwright, *Diary of Battle*, 324.

6. Letter, Feb. 20, 1864, in *The Caledonian*, Mar. 4, 1864.

7. Letter, Feb. 14, 1864, in *Michigan Argus*, Feb. 26, 1864.

8. *Official Records*, 33:140–41.

9. Edward Whitaker to Adeline Whitaker, Feb. 10, 1864, Edward W. Whitaker Civil War Letters, Babcock Library, typescript.

10. *Supplement*, pt. 3, 3:328–31; Reuben Bartley Memoir, Reuben Bartley Papers, VHS, 1. Bartley's memoir is a ninety-eight-page handwritten document of his experiences on the Richmond raid and in a Confederate prison.

11. Gorgas, *Civil War Diary*, 84.

12. *Army Navy Journal*, Feb. 13, 1864; Davies Report; E. B. Custer, *Civil War Memories*, 49.

13. Nathan Webb Diary, Nathan Webb Papers, ALPL, transcript, 378, 388.
14. *Official Records*, 33:144, 170, 551–52; Welsh, *Medical Histories of Union Generals*, 225; Humphreys, *From Gettysburg to the Rapidan*, 74; Perret, *Lincoln's War*, 338.
15. Eugene Beaumont Letter Book, Special Collections, U.S. Military Academy Library, 199. Beaumont observed that as early as September 1862, Kilpatrick was unpopular for using his "political influence" in the army.
16. Letter, Feb. 14, 1864, in *Michigan Argus*, Feb. 26, 1864.
17. Ibid.
18. *Official Records*, 25(1):1062.
19. Beaumont, "Monument to General H. J. Kilpatrick."
20. Shenk, *Lincoln's Melancholy*, 28; Goodwin, *Team of Rivals*, 6; Beaumont, "Monument to General H. J. Kilpatrick."
21. *Official Records*, 33:170; Abraham Lincoln to Edwin Stanton, Feb. 10, 1864, Russell A. Alger Papers, Clements Library, Univ. of Michigan. Alger was colonel of the 5th Michigan Cavalry in Custer's Second Brigade of the Third Cavalry Division.
22. *New York Times*, Feb. 6, 1864. This same article also references a tightening of discipline and weeding out of incompetent officers within the division, thus readers (and politicians) would know that Kilpatrick's command was ready for a difficult operation, if one was to be undertaken.
23. *Official Records*, 33:172; Welles, *Diary*, 1:531–32.
24. Goodwin, *Team of Rivals*, 115.
25. Styple, *Generals in Bronze*, 279.
26. Ibid.; J. Moore, *Kilpatrick and Our Cavalry*, 27–28, 32, 201–206.
27. *Official Records*, 33:172–73.
28. Ibid., 25(1):1069.
29. Dowdey, *Wartime Letters of R. E. Lee*, 672–73.
30. *Official Records*, 25(2):725. One historian has postulated that the major reason for Lee's second invasion of the North in June 1863 was to gather much-needed supplies, including food for his army, because the Confederacy's supply system could not keep pace with the demands of war. "The idea for the Pennsylvania campaign . . . was born in a desperation caused by the looming collapse of the Army of Northern Virginia if it remained in war-ravaged central Virginia without adequate food and supplies for its horses and mules. . . . Virginia had virtually run out of surplus food for Lee's army." K. M. Brown, *Retreat from Gettysburg*, 12–13.
31. *Official Records*, 33:172–73.
32. Ibid.
33. F. J. Bellamy to Fletcher Bellamy, Mar. 1, 1864, F. J. Bellamy Papers, ISL.
34. O'Dell, *Chesterfield County*, 383, 388–90; *Official Records*, 25(2):517–18.
35. *Official Records*, 33:172–73, 598–99.
36. Warner, *Generals in Blue*, 108–10, 146–49, 321–22.
37. Lyman, *Meade's Army*, 35.
38. Hanson, "Civil War Custer," 24–28.

39. *Official Records*, 27(1):997–1001; *Culpeper Star Exponent*, Mar. 13, 2008; Wert, *Custer*, 122; Whittaker, *Complete Life of General George A. Custer*, 1:214.

40. G. A. Custer, *Custer Story*, 81–85.

41. Wert, *Custer*, 230; Urwin, *Custer Victorious*, 278; *Culpeper Star Exponent*, Mar. 13, 2008. For an extensive analysis of Custer's Civil War leadership, see Urwin, *Custer Victorious*, 265–86.

42. Kidd, *Riding with Custer*, 132–33; Whittaker, *Complete Life of General George A. Custer*, 2:611; Pleasonton quoted in Urwin, *Custer Victorious*, 278.

43. For these reprimands, see vol. 35, pt. 2, Miscellaneous Letters, Reports, RG 393, NA.

44. Ibid.

45. For a balanced discussion of the Annie Jones incident, see Wert, *Custer*, 142–44. See also Anna Jones Statement, Mar. 14, 1864, Provost Marshal's File, RG 107, NA.

46. *Official Records*, 25(1):1084, 33:172–73.

47. *New York Herald*, Jan. 7, 1864.

48. Ebenzer Gould to William Gould, Feb. 27, 1864, Ebenezer Gould Papers, CHL.

49. Telegram, Judson Kilpatrick to Francis W. Kellogg, Feb. 17, 1864, Telegrams Sent to the War Department, RG 393, NA; *Wyoming County Mirror*, Mar. 2, 1864.

50. Howard, *Civil-War Echoes*, 214.

51. *Detroit Free Press*, Mar. 16, 1864.

52. Letter, Feb. 14, 1864, in *Michigan Argus*, Feb. 26, 1864; *Wyoming County Mirror*, Mar. 2, 1864; *Essex County Republican*, Apr. 27, 1899; Kidd, *Riding with Custer*, 236.

53. *Wyoming County Mirror*, Mar. 2, 1864; Charles Blinn Diary, Feb. 21, 1864, BHL-UV; Kidd, *Riding with Custer*, 234; Howard, *Civil-War Echoes*, 214.

54. Howard, *Civil-War Echoes*, 214. The cannonball hole described by Howard is still evident at Rose Hill. See also Culpeper Historical Society, *Historic Culpeper*, 114.

55. Edward Whitaker to Adeline Whitaker, Feb. 26, 1864, Whitaker Civil War Letters, typescript; *Essex County Republican*, Apr. 27, 1899; letter, Feb. 14, 1864, in *Michigan Argus*, Feb. 26, 1864.

56. Favill, *Diary of a Young Officer*, 278–81; Ward, *One Hundred and Sixth Regiment Pennsylvania Volunteers*, 233; Robertson, "From the Wilderness to Spottsylvania," 252–55; *Detroit Free Press*, Mar. 16, 1864.

57. Robertson, "From the Wilderness to Spottsylvania," 254; Favill, *Diary of a Young Officer*, 280; Kidd, *Riding with Custer*, 234; *Bangor Whig and Courant*, Mar. 8, 1864.

58. Favill, *Diary of a Young Officer*, 280; *Richmond Daily Examiner*, Mar. 7, 1864.

59. Howard, *Civil-War Echoes*, 221.

60. Ward, *One Hundred and Sixth Regiment Pennsylvania Volunteers*, 233; Favill, *Diary of a Young Officer*, 280–81; Theodore Lyman Private

Notebook, Feb. 23, 1864, Lyman Family Papers, Massachusetts Historical Society, microfilm; Howard, *Civil-War Echoes*, 216–21.
61. Lyman Private Notebook, Feb. 23, 1864; Favill, *Diary of a Young Officer*, 281.

Chapter 5

1. Lyman, *Meade's Army*, 107; *Richmond Daily Examiner*, Mar. 7, 1864.
2. *National Tribune*, Mar. 12, 1896; J. A. Dahlgren, *Memoir of Ulric Dahlgren*, 168–70; Trowbridge to J. Allen Bigelow, n.d., Luther Trowbridge Letters, Gettysburg National Military Park Library; Rodenbough, *Eighteenth Regiment of Cavalry Pennsylvania Volunteers*, 17–18, 38; Sunderland, *Sermon in Memory of Colonel Ulric Dahlgren*, 23; *New York Times*, Mar. 9, 1864. Paul frequently rode with Kilpatrick's division.
3. W. L. Curry, *Four Years in the Saddle*, 244. The quote is attributed to Capt. Noah Jones, commander of Company A, 1st Ohio Cavalry, Kilpatrick's Headquarters Guard.
4. J. A. Dahlgren, *Memoir of Ulric Dahlgren*, 11–19; Sunderland, *Sermon in Memory of Colonel Ulric Dahlgren*, 6–13; V. Davis, *Jefferson Davis, Ex-President*, 2:472. Admiral Dahlgren died before his biography of his son was completed. His widow, who was Ulric's stepmother, saw that it was published and perhaps wrote most of the text from the admiral's notes and documents.
5. J. A. Dahlgren, *Memoir of Ulric Dahlgren*, 11–19; Sunderland, *Sermon in Memory of Colonel Ulric Dahlgren*, 6–13; *New York Herald*, Aug. 8, 1864. Gower, *Charles Dahlgren of Natchez*, 240; Schneller, *Quest for Glory*, 134.
6. J. A. Dahlgren, *Memoir of Ulric Dahlgren*, 20–21.
7. Gower, *Charles Dahlgren of Natchez*, 36–37.
8. Ibid., xvi, 12–14, 38.
9. Welles, *Diary*, 1:475.
10. *New York Times*, Mar. 9, 1864.
11. Quoted in Gower, *Charles Dahlgren of Natchez*, 37–38.
12. Sunderland, *Sermon in Memory of Colonel Ulric Dahlgren*, 14–16; J. A. Dahlgren, *Memoir of Ulric Dahlgren*, 25–52.
13. Perret, *Lincoln's War*, 147.
14. Schneller, *Quest for Glory*, 186.
15. Hay, *At Lincoln's Side*, 133.
16. Quoted in Schneller, *Quest for Glory*, 186–89.
17. Quoted in Burlingame, *Inner World of Abraham Lincoln*, 106; Scrapbook, Box 1, Madeleine Vinton Dahlgren Papers, Special Collections, Georgetown University, 7.
18. Schneller, *Quest for Glory*, 215.
19. "Case of Ulric Dahlgren," Entry 496, Box 207, Staff Officers Papers, RG 94, NA.
20. J. A. Dahlgren, *Memoir of Ulric Dahlgren*, 92–113; *Official Records*, 19(2):162–63; O'Reilly, *Fredericksburg Campaign*, 14–15.
21. O'Reilly, *Fredericksburg Campaign*, 16, 48.

22. Wainwright, *Diary of Battle*, 395; Perret, *Lincoln's War*, 266; Hennessy, *Return to Bull Run*, 6.
23. J. A. Dahlgren, *Memoir of Ulric Dahlgren*, 92–113; *Official Records*, 19(2):579, 21:971.
24. J. A. Dahlgren, *Memoir of Ulric Dahlgren*, 117–21; *Official Records*, 21:971.
25. John A. Dahlgren to Joseph Hooker, Mar. 12, 1863, Box 16, Staff Officers Papers, RG 94, NA.
26. J. A. Dahlgren, *Memoir of Ulric Dahlgren*, 124–42; *Official Records*, 25(2):167.
27. *Official Records*, 25(2):517–18.
28. *Supplement*, pt. 1, 4:474–75; Robert F. O'Neill, interview by the author, Jan. 22, 2014. O'Neill spent considerable time trying to find out if Lincoln knew of the potential raid and its goals during research for his most recent book on the Federal cavalry in 1862–63, but he was unsuccessful. See O'Neill, *Chasing Jeb Stuart and John Mosby*.
29. Memorandum Book, May 23, 1863, Container 19, John A. Dahlgren Papers, LC; J. A. Dahlgren, *Memoir of Ulric Dahlgren*, 142. Since the naval officer's biography of his son seldom failed to praise Ulric's accomplishments, Hooker's opinion never saw print.
30. Smith, *"We Have It Damn Hard Out Here,"* 95–96.
31. *Official Records*, 29(2):1046.
32. *New York Times*, June 11, 1863.
33. John A. Dahlgren to Joseph Hooker, June 15, 1863, Box 16, Staff Officers Papers, RG 94, NA; Joseph Hooker to John A. Dahlgren, [?] 1863, ibid.
34. *Official Records*, 27(3):86–87.
35. J. A. Dahlgren, *Memoir of Ulric Dahlgren*, 158–60.
36. Ibid., 161–63.
37. Coddington, *Gettysburg Campaign*, 451–53, 773–74; Fishel, *Secret War for the Union*, 532; Sears, *Gettysburg*, 354, 576. In Dahlgren's defense another writer feels that his "feat was nevertheless a *coup de main.* His intelligence provided uncontestable proof that Lee could expect no reinforcements and that at present Confederates were on their own in Pennsylvania." Wittenberg, "Ulric Dahlgren in the Gettysburg Campaign," 105.
38. Newhall, *Dedication of the Monument of the Sixth Pennsylvania Cavalry*, 18–19; Gracey, *Annals of the Sixth Pennsylvania Cavalry*, 189.
39. Ibid., 189–92.
40. Kidd, *Riding with Custer*, 239; *Official Records*, 27(1):995.
41. *New York Times*, Mar. 9, 1864.
42. Ibid.; Sunderland, *Sermon in Memory of Colonel Ulric Dahlgren*, 23–27; J. A. Dahlgren, *Memoir of Ulric Dahlgren*, 173–76; "Case of Ulric Dahlgren," File D-167 (VS) 1863, Entry 496, Box 207, RG 94, NA; Welles, *Diary*, 1:380, 470; Abraham Lincoln to Edwin Stanton, Box 22, Staff Officers Papers, RG 94, NA.
43. G. V. Fox to the President, July 15, 1863, Box 22, Staff Officers Papers, RG 94, NA; *New York Herald*, Aug. 8, 1864. Dahlgren's stepmother,

Madeleine Vinton Dahlgren, took issue with the War Department in 1895 over the missing order, claiming that she possessed a copy of it signed by Stanton. In turn, the War Department responded, not to Mrs. Dahlgren, but to her other stepson, Charles Bunker Dahlgren, who claimed that he was the proper representative of his brother's legacy. The official answer was anything but conclusive. The army colonel who researched the files stated with an equal degree of embarrassment and conviction that Ulric Dahlgren's rank may have been "a questionable one; but it is not the desire of this Department to make that question a debatable one unless its discussion should become unavoidable." In 1895 the department was obtusely saying that the young Dahlgren may not have been a colonel, at least officially, after all. Some evidence suggests that the appointment letter rested on his coffin during a memorial service after his body had been recovered by U.S. authorities. What happened to the document after that is puzzling. It is unclear whether the copy on the coffin is the one referred to by Mrs. Dahlgren or an official copy that should have been returned to his War Department file. Why such a simple order of promotion disappeared from army records, or was never acted upon by the U.S. Senate as required by military law, is a mystery. It is only one of many uncertainties surrounding the career of Ulric Dahlgren after his wounding during the Gettysburg Campaign. Other original documents connected with Dahlgren also disappeared after his death, making him perhaps one of the more enigmatic figures of the Civil War period. F. C. Ainsworth to C. B. Dahlgren, Aug. 12, 1895, Box 22, Staff Officers Papers, RG 94, NA; Scrapbook, Madeleine Vinton Dahlgren Papers.

44. Sunderland, *Sermon in Memory of Colonel Ulric Dahlgren*, 23–27; J. A. Dahlgren, *Memoir of Ulric Dahlgren*, 173–76.
45. "Case of Ulric Dahlgren"; Ulric Dahlgren to Brig. Gen. L. Thomas, Jan. 4, 1863 [*sic*], Box 22, Staff Officers Papers, ibid.; Memorandum Book, Nov. 30, 1863, Container 19, John A. Dahlgren Papers; M. V. Dahlgren, *Memoir of John A. Dahlgren*, 437; J. A. Dahlgren, *Memoir of Ulric Dahlgren*, 183–204.
46. *New York Times*, Mar. 9, 1864.
47. Letter Book, Jan. 29, 1864, Container 19, John A. Dahlgren Papers.
48. Stoddard, *Inside the White House in War Times*, 128; Sunderland, *Sermon in Memory of Colonel Ulric Dahlgren*, 33; J. A. Dahlgren, *Memoir of Ulric Dahlgren*, 204–205; E. B. Lee, *Wartime Washington*, 355; Lyman, *Meade's Headquarters*, 77.
49. Sunderland, *Sermon in Memory of Colonel Ulric Dahlgren*, 33. Thirty years after the war, a former Confederate cavalryman claimed in a mythical reminiscence that Colonel Dahlgren was part of an elaborate masquerade to gather intelligence as a spy observing the Rebel capital's defenses in early 1864. Thad Walker's article included the word "romantic" in the title, which is the best caveat for an unsuspecting reader. Based on Dahlgren's physical condition and the well-documented itinerary of his movements after the amputation of his leg,

it was virtually impossible for him to have accompanied Walker as a paroled soldier around the Richmond area, let alone sneak in and out of the city as a clandestine operative. In fact, more than forty years after the war, a Richmond newspaper disputed Walker's story by quoting a Gen. George W. Davis, who seemed to know something about Dahlgren's activities. Davis contended that the one-legged colonel "was in Washington all the time between the date of his arrival there from Charleston [on January 24] and the time he left [on February 18] to join the army on the Rapidan." Walker's story is a hoax, the product of a vivid postwar imagination, and without any credible connection to the Richmond raid of 1864. T. J. Walker, "A Romantic Incident of the War," 330–32; *Richmond Times Dispatch*, June 9, 1909.

50. Ulric Dahlgren to John A. Dahlgren, Feb. 1, 1864, Container 19, John A. Dahlgren Papers.

51. J. A. Dahlgren, *Memoir of Ulric Dahlgren*, 210; *Detroit Advertiser and Tribune*, Mar. 21, 1864; *New York Herald*, Aug. 8, 1864.

52. *National Tribune*, May 31, 1894.

53. *Richmond Times Dispatch*, Aug. 1, 1897; *New York Herald*, Aug. 8, 1864.

54. Howard, *Civil-War Echoes*, 222.

55. *Philadelphia Inquirer*, Nov. 1, 1865.

56. V. Jones, *Eight Hours before Richmond*, 29. Unfortunately, Jones does not provide a source for this statement, but it would be entirely logical for such a mission to occur at the time.

57. *Official Records*, 33:171–72.

58. Ibid.; George G. Meade, Jr., to Mr. Johnson, Sept. 14, 1888, George G. Meade, Jr., Papers, Duke Univ.

59. Davies Report.

60. *Official Records*, 33:170; Humphreys, *From Gettysburg to the Rapidan*, 75; Lyman, *Meade's Army*, 105.

61. James Biddle to his wife, Feb. 29, 1864, James Biddle Papers, HSP.

62. *Official Records*, 33:172–73; Lyman, *Meade's Army*, 104–105. Clearly, the Yankee raiders intended more harm to the Confederacy than just liberating POWs and distributing political flyers.

63. Ulric Dahlgren to John A. Dahlgren (with cover note to Martha Dahlgren), Feb. 26, 1864, Container 19, John A. Dahlgren Papers.

64. Telegram, Henry Davies, Jr., to Enos Parsons, Feb. 28, 1864, Telegrams Collected by the Secretary of War, RG 393, NA, M504, roll 244; Wells to his parents, Feb. 25, 1864, William Wells Papers, BHL-UV.

65. Ebenezer Gould to William Gould, Feb. 27, 1864, Ebenezer Gould Papers, CHL.

66. Kidd, *Riding with Custer*, 238.

67. Davies Report.

68. Moyer, *Seventeenth Regiment of Pennsylvania Cavalry*, 233; *Rutland Daily Herald*, Mar. 9, 1864; William O'Brien to his brother, Mar. 16, 1864, William H. O'Brien Papers, BHL-UM; Robertson, "From the Wilderness to Spottsylvania," 253.

69. James Wood Memoir, 3, Maud Wood Park Papers, LC. This was true for the most part, though not completely. Confederates were able to contact the capital via a circuitous route through Gordonsville once it appeared a Yankee cavalry operation was underway.

70. *Supplement*, pt. 1, 10:566–67; *Philadelphia Weekly Times*, Apr. 30, 1880.

71. *Richmond Daily Examiner*, Feb. 27, 1864. An obvious question arises, though: was there any particular reason why these officials would be inspecting Richmond's defenses at the same time Kilpatrick was assembling his requisite number of troopers for a raid on the city two days later? There is no evidence to support a specific intelligence leak that would tip off Confederate officials, but it was widely known that a raid was afoot.

72. Wainwright, *Diary of Battle*, 323–24; *Official Records*, 33:174; Meade, *Life and Letters*, 2:170.

73. Nehemiah Mann Diary, in *Fifth Report of the New York State Bureau of Military Statistics*, 618; *Official Records*, 33:607.

74. Longacre, *Custer and His Wolverines*, 195–99; *Official Records*, 29(2):556–57.

75. "My Experiences in the First Maine Cavalry," Charles E. Gardiner Papers, Maine Historical Society, transcript; Davies Report. Davies counted eighteen to twenty regiments in Kilpatrick's total command for the raid.

76. This detachment included men from Companies C, E, F, G, H, I, L, and M. *Supplement*, pt. 2, 30:10–11.

77. Whitman and True, *Maine in the War for the Union*, 368; Merrill, *Campaigns of the First Maine*, 170–71; Hyndman, *History of a Cavalry Company*, 185; *Maine Farmer*, Apr. 7, 1864; Tobie, *First Maine Cavalry*, 235–36; George L. Kilmer, "Heroes in the Saddle," *First Maine Bugle* 2, no. 9 (July 1892): 71–72; "My Experiences in the First Maine Cavalry," Gardiner Papers.

78. Mohr, *Cormany Diaries*, 401.

79. Moyer, *Seventeenth Regiment of Pennsylvania Cavalry*, 231–33, 334; *Supplement*, pt. 2, 57:462; Cheney, *Ninth Regiment, New York Volunteer Cavalry*, 146; William Hill Diary, Feb. 27, 1864, LC; Mann Diary, 681.

80. William Martin to his wife, Mar. 3, 1864, William H. Martin Papers, Harrisburg Civil War Round Table Collection, USAHEC.

81. Harris, *Personal Reminiscences*, 70–71; Dufur, *Over the Dead Line*, 12; W. O. Lee, *Personal and Historical Sketches*, 28; John Connor to his brother, Mar. 11, 1864, in Bush, *Articles from Wyoming County Newspapers*; *Maine Farmer*, Apr. 7, 1864; Frobel, *Civil War Diary*, 161.

82. Martin Quiatt Diary, Feb. 28, 1864, Folder 4, Box 1, LC; James Biddle to his wife, Feb. 29, 1864, Biddle Papers.

83. *Philadelphia Weekly Times*, Apr. 3, 1880; Beaudry, *Wartime Journal*, 97; *National Tribune*, Mar. 29, 1894; *Supplement*, pt. 1, 6:287; *Official Records*, 29(2):487–88, 33:183, 761.

84. Wood Memoir, 3. Biographical information about Martin Hogan is found in V. Jones, *Eight Hours before Richmond*, 157n5.
85. *Official Records*, 33:194, 221; *Maine Farmer*, Apr. 7, 1864.
86. During the month of February, Cooke's promotion to lieutenant colonel in the 2nd New York Cavalry was announced, but most accounts refer to him as a major. See *Sussex Register*, Feb. 19, 1864. Cooke is listed as a major in Hunt and Brown, *Brevet Brigadier Generals in Blue*, 127.
87. *Philadelphia Weekly Times*, Apr. 3, 1880; *Grand Rapids Daily Democrat*, Feb. 6, 1887; *National Tribune*, May 31, 1894; Glazier, *Three Years in the Federal Cavalry*, 311; *Official Records*, 33:194.
88. *Philadelphia Weekly Times*, Sept. 29, 1877; Scrapbook, Madeleine Vinton Dahlgren Papers; *Michigan Argus*, Mar. 18, 1864. Was Kilpatrick here revealing a concern about the young colonel's ability to lead such an important part of the operation? Would Dahlgren's performance impugn the general's personal reputation, depending on its outcome? Thirty years later an army scout named J. W. Landegon, who commanded Kilpatrick's scouts during the raid, voiced a corroborating question in hindsight: "Does any soldier who knew or served under General Kilpatrick believe, had the selection been left to him, would have gone outside his old Third Cavalry Division for a leader?" The scout's opinion was echoed by another chronicler's observation shortly after the war that Kilpatrick "knew how to put 'the right man in the right place,' and always kept the right sort of men about him, even to his orderly, his servant and his cook." With this acknowledged acumen for selecting talent, it is difficult to understand how an inexperienced, crippled officer was entrusted with such an important assignment on an operation that surely promised to be perilous. These accounts suggest that someone in Washington may have had a hand in determining Kilpatrick's command structure. Did Lincoln assign Dahlgren to the raid without the general's wholehearted assent? There is no documented evidence to prove the president or any other high-ranking government official sponsored the young colonel's assignment, but it leaves open serious speculation as to how a decidedly disabled officer managed to gain the most important role on such a hazardous expedition. If speculation is allowed, Stanton fits the bill more than Lincoln. Dahlgren was well known to him and was also a susceptible pawn that the secretary of war could use, if Stanton had any nefarious plans for the operation. Since Kilpatrick spent more time in his meeting with Stanton than with Lincoln, it is not beyond possibility that a tacit agreement was reached to use the naive and arrogant twenty-one-year-old colonel to accomplish sinister results. *National Tribune*, May 31, 1894; Foster, *New Jersey in the Rebellion*, 840.
89. Dufur, *Over the Dead Line*, 12; Moyer, *Seventeenth Regiment of Pennsylvania Cavalry*, 234; Kidd, *Riding with Custer*, 245; John Morey Diary, Feb. 28, 1864, John Morey Papers, BHL-UM, transcript; William O'Brien to his brother, Mar. 16, 1864, O'Brien Papers; Letter Book,

2nd New York Cavalry, RG 94, NA; Athearn, "Civil War Diary of John Wilson Philips," 96; *National Tribune*, July 22, 1886, Sept. 8, Oct. 10, 1887, Dec. 6, 1888; Urwin, *Custer Victorious*, 94–95; John Connor to his brother, Mar. 11, 1864, in Bush, *Articles from Wyoming County Newspapers.*

Chapter 6

1. *Official Records*, 33:470, 599; Gracey, *Annals of the Sixth Pennsylvania Cavalry*, 223; Hunt and Brown, *Brevet Brigadier Generals in Blue*, 583. Custer did not command any of his own Michigan Brigade on this expedition. Why? The major thrust toward Richmond was Kilpatrick's. It was his plan, his political clout, and it was going to be his glory. Since the Michigan regiments were under his command and control, it is logical to see why he wanted them. Libbie Custer claimed that Kilpatrick "demanded and fought for Autie's Michigan Brigade, as it had electrified the country by its successes the previous summer," in his discussions with his superiors. Custer had been absent during most of the early planning for the raid, so it could be justified that he was not up to speed on the preparations. But more importantly, Kilpatrick probably wanted to sideline his brigadier from the main operation. Giving him an independent command far from the more important action was the commanding general's solution. Apparently, Little Kil preferred to work with a less than exemplar brigade commander like Edward Sawyer, trying to make the best of it, rather than risk dealing with a subordinate who might cause him difficulty during the operation but who surely would want to snatch any laurels that might be won along the way. Ulric Dahlgren, with close ties to Lincoln and Stanton, provided a convenient foil to Custer. While it is impossible to get inside Kilpatrick's mind and no written records exist to support how Custer ended up heading in the opposite direction from his Wolverines, it is not unreasonable to speculate, based on past frictions between the two boy generals, that the Third Cavalry Division was not big enough for their egos. E. B. Custer, *Civil War Memories*, 49.
2. *Official Records*, 33:470, 597–98, 51(1):1149.
3. Ibid., 33:605, 609, 626–27; letter, Mar. 1, 1864, in *The Caledonian*, Mar. 11, 1864; F. Moore, *Rebellion Record*, 8:570.
4. *Official Records*, 33:162; F. Moore, *Rebellion Record*, 8:570; Culpeper Historical Society, *Historic Culpeper*, 112; J. O. Moore, "Custer's Raid into Albemarle County," 342; Gracey, *Annals of the Sixth Pennsylvania Cavalry*, 223.
5. *Official Records*, 33:162, 169, 599; Munford, "Cavalry Raid," 157; Smith, *"We Have It Damn Hard Out Here,"* 112–13; McMahon, "From Gettysburg to the Coming of Grant," 93–94. Whether Custer actually made this statement is speculative because it is based on a postwar recollection. But if he did indeed say something similar, then his query to Sedgwick and his bravado statement are interesting to consider for two reasons. First, it is another example of how Kilpatrick excluded his

subordinate from important innercircle discussions about the impending raid on Richmond. Second, it gives some credibility to a phrase later
repeated twice in Colonel Dahlgren's orders, "General Custer may follow me," which provides an intriguing hint as to who may have written them.

6. *Supplement*, pt. 1, 6:284–85; *Official Records*, 33:616; Gracey, *Annals
   of the Sixth Pennsylvania Cavalry*, 223–24; Smith, *"We Have It Damn
   Hard Out Here,"* 114.

7. Jordan, *Charlottesville and the University of Virginia in the Civil War*,
   1, 12–15; Neese, *Three Years in the Confederate Horse Artillery*, 81–82.

8. McClellan, *Life and Campaigns of Major-General J. E. B. Stuart*, 399;
   J. C. Wise, *Long Arm of Lee*, 2:578; *Official Records*, 33:167, 201; Neese,
   Three Years in the Confederate Horse Artillery, 245.

9. Lt. Charles R. Phelps to his aunt, Mar. 2, 1864, in Trout, *Galloping
   Thunder*, 445–47; Trout, *Memoirs of the Stuart Horse Artillery*, 80.

10. Trout, *Galloping Thunder*, 442. Trout provides a detailed footnote doc-
    umenting this event. Jennings Wise claims that the captured men were
    fishing at the time, but Trout's documentation makes a better case that
    the order from Moorman was to wash their mounts. J. C. Wise, *Long
    Arm of Lee*, 2:726–27.

11. Trout, *Galloping Thunder*, 442, 446; *Philadelphia Inquirer* article, n.d.,
    quoted in *Richmond Whig*, Mar. 7, 1864. See also *Richmond Daily
    Examiner*, Mar. 7, 1864; J. C. Wise, *Long Arm of Lee*, 2:728; and Neese,
    Three Years in the Confederate Horse Artillery, 249. Rio Mills Bridge
    is also called Berner's Mill Bridge or Burnley's Mill Bridge in some
    accounts.

12. *Lynchburg Daily Republican*, Mar. 5, 1864; letter, Mar. 2, 1864, in
    Richmond Sentinel, Mar. 8, 1864.

13. *Official Records*, 33:162, 167; letter, Mar. 2, 1864, in *Pottstown Min-
    ers Journal*, Mar. 12, 1864; *Richmond Whig*, Mar. 7, 1864. Fuqua's
    statement is quoted in Trout, *Galloping Thunder*, 444. The regimen-
    tal historian of the 6th Pennsylvania Cavalry also thought that "[t]rain
    after train of cars . . . had arrived from Gordonville, all loaded with
    troops," but there is no Confederate documentation to substantiate his
    conclusion. Gracey, *Annals of the Sixth Pennsylvania Cavalry*, 226.

14. *Official Records*, 33:162, 167–68, 51(2):823; Neese, *Three Years in the
    Confederate Horse Artillery*, 249–51; Trout, *Galloping Thunder*, 443–
    44; Trout, *Memoirs of the Stuart Horse Artillery*, 80; letter, Mar. 2,
    1864, in *Pottstown Miners Journal*, Mar. 12, 1864; *Richmond Dispatch*,
    Mar. 7, 1864; J. C. Wise, *Long Arm of Lee*, 2:727–28; Munford, "Cavalry
    Raid," 158. Dulany's 7th Virginia Cavalry was at Mount Crawford in
    the Shenandoah Valley at the time. Neese, *Three Years in the Confed-
    erate Horse Artillery*, 251. A Confederate horse artilleryman who was
    a witness to the fight claimed that Chew and Breathed mounted only
    fifteen men sporting four pistols and three sabers among them, a truly
    remarkable display of bravery. *Richmond Sentinel*, Mar. 8, 1864. Major
    Mason's participation was also noted in *Richmond Daily Examiner*,

Mar. 2, 1864. He was quartermaster for Wickham's Brigade. R. E. L. Krick, *Staff Officers in Gray*, 217. At least one furloughed lieutenant from the 19th Virginia Infantry recorded his fight with the Federals, although he was not part of Mason's contingent. See Wood, "Personal Encounter in the Rio Hill Battle," 35–36.

15. *Official Records*, 33:161, 163–64, 168, 616; *Richmond Dispatch*, Mar. 7, 1864; letter, Mar. 3, 1864, in *Lynchburg Daily Republican*, Mar. 5, 1864; letter, Mar. 2, 1864, in *Richmond Sentinel*, Mar. 8, 1864; letter, Mar. 2, 1864, in *Pottstown Miners Journal*, Mar. 12, 1864; Trout, *Memoirs of the Stuart Horse Artillery*, 80, 157n3; Neese, *Three Years in the Confederate Horse Artillery*, 250. For an opinion that Chew intentionally blew up his own caisson, based on a descriptive card associated with the flag awarded the battalion (discussed below), see J. R. Brown, "Battle of Rio Hill," 33.

16. *Official Records*, 33:162–65; letter, Mar. 2, 1864, in *Lynchburg Daily Republican*, Mar. 5, 1864; Smith, "We Have It Damn Hard Out Here," 115; Gracey, *Annals of the Sixth Pennsylvania Cavalry*, 226–27; *Alexandria Gazette*, Mar. 3, 1864.

17. J. O. Moore, "Custer's Raid into Albemarle County," 346; Jordan, *Charlottesville and the University of Virginia in the Civil War*, 72. For a more detailed description regarding the flag, see J. R. Brown, "Battle of Rio Hill," 33.

18. *Official Records*, 51(2):823; Munford, "Cavalry Raid," 158.

19. *Official Records*, 33:162–63, 165; letter, Mar. 2, 1864, in *Pottstown Miners Journal*, Mar. 12, 1864; Garnett, *Riding with Stuart*, 41–42.

20. *Official Records*, 33:162–63, 165; Smith, "We Have It Damn Hard Out Here," 115; Garnett, *Riding with Stuart*, 41–42; *Alexandria Gazette*, Mar. 3, 1864. Custer's report claims that he was attacked by the 1st and 5th Virginia Cavalry, but the 5th Virginia was not part of Wickham's Brigade, being in Brig. Gen. Lunsford Lomax's brigade instead. The 1st Virginia and 2nd Virginia were the regiments Custer's troopers fought in this action. For an analysis of the rosters of the various regiments that prove the general's error, see J. O. Moore, "Custer's Raid into Albemarle County," 347. Yates's report claims that Captain Ash of the 5th Cavalry led the initial attack.

21. *Official Records*, 33:165; Gracey, *Annals of the Sixth Pennsylvania Cavalry*, 227.

22. *Official Records*, 33:165–66, 628; Gracey, *Annals of the Sixth Pennsylvania Cavalry*, 225, 227.

23. *Official Records*, 33:161. A Confederate horse artilleryman later claimed, "We had no support whatever in the way of sharpshooters or cavalry." Neese, *Three Years in the Confederate Horse Artillery*, 250. Custer would have more to say about his run-in with the Confederates at Rio Hill, but his story about being severely outnumbered would remain unchanged.

24. *Official Records*, 33:165–66, 628; F. Moore, *Rebellion Record*, 8:570; letter, Mar. 2, 1864, in *Lynchburg Daily Republican*, Mar. 5, 1864;

Smith, *"We Have It Damn Hard Out Here,"* 116; letter, Mar. 2, 1864, in *Pottstown Miners Journal*, Mar. 12, 1864; Gracey, *Annals of the Sixth Pennsylvania Cavalry*, 228.

25. *Official Records*, 33:162–63.

26. Munford, "Cavalry Raid," 159.

27. Kidd, *One of Custer's Wolverines*, 76.

28. *Official Records*, 33:1191; Longacre, *Lee's Cavalrymen*, 264–66; Driver, *5th Virginia Cavalry*, 71; R. E. L. Krick, e-mail message to author, Mar. 31, 2010. For F. Lee's documented presence in Richmond, see chapter 8 below. Sgt. Thomas Smith of the 6th Pennsylvania Cavalry also mentions "Rebel infantry marching in three columns on our Left to get possession of the Bridge in our Rear," but Lieutenant Yates's official report does not state that he saw the enemy; he only surmises infantry detraining at the railroad station. Smith, *"We Have It Damn Hard Out Here,"* 114; *Official Records*, 33:164.

29. For a soldier's opinion of Custer as being unfit to be an independent commander based on his "inconsistent and tyrannical orders," see *National Tribune*, Apr. 28, 1892.

Chapter 7

1. *Daily Morning Chronicle*, Feb. 6, 1865; *Richmond Daily Examiner*, Mar. 5, 1864; J. A. Dahlgren, *Memoir of Ulric Dahlgren*, 212; *Philadelphia Weekly Times*, Sept. 29, 1877, Apr. 3, 1880; *Grand Rapids Daily Democrat*, Feb. 6, 1887; *National Tribune*, Dec. 3, 1885; *Boston Sunday Globe*, June 5, 1904; *Boston Globe*, May 10, 1910. The number of volunteers who crossed the river varies from six to fifteen, twenty, or twenty-three, depending on the source. Fifteen is used here because it comes from an article written by Merritt, who likely knew how many men he led across.

2. *Daily Morning Chronicle*, Feb. 6, 1865; *National Tribune*, May 29, 1894.

3. *Daily Morning Chronicle*, Feb. 6, 1865; *Boston Globe*, May 14, 1910; *Official Records*, 33:181, 202–204; *Grand Rapids Daily Democrat*, Feb. 6, 1887; James Wood Memoir, Maud Wood Park Papers, LC, 4–5. Three days later Confederate brigadier general Pierce M. B. Young, whose brigade was responsible for the picket line in that area, defended the unruly captain as "the best picket officer" in his brigade and a man he would have selected for any "reliable" assignment. Obviously, General Young did not know firsthand the true condition of Captain Young's unguarded reserve post on the night of February 28. Some sources describe the reserve headquarters as a log hut.

4. *Grand Rapids Daily Democrat*, Feb. 6, 1887; *National Tribune*, Nov. 15, 1888; *Official Records*, 33:178–79; *Richmond Whig*, Mar. 7, 1864.

5. *Grand Rapids Daily Democrat*, Feb. 6, 1887; *National Tribune*, Dec. 3, 1885; *Rutland Daily Herald*, Mar. 18, 1864; William O'Brien to his brother, Mar. 16, 1864, William H. O'Brien Papers, BHL-UM.

6. McEntee to Sharpe, Mar. 4, 1864, Box 11, Miscellaneous Letters, Reports, RG 393, NA; Albert Fisher to Fisher Humphrey, Mar. 30, 1864, Albert H. Fisher Papers, WL.

7. *National Tribune,* Sept. 20, 1888. Lt. S. A. Clark remembered that "Gen. Butler, with the Army of the James, was to advance from that side of Richmond and the three columns were to attack at the same time."

8. *Official Records,* 33:181–82; Kidd, *Riding with Custer,* 240; Meade, *Life and Letters,* 2:168.

9. Wood Memoir, 96–98.

10. Merrill, *Campaigns of the First Maine,* 171; *Official Records,* 33:188–89; William O'Brien to his brother, Mar. 16, 1864, O'Brien Papers; Kidd, *Riding with Custer,* 240; G. Crosby Diary, Feb. 29, 1864, Vermont Historical Society; *National Tribune,* Sept. 20, 1888.

11. *Boston Globe,* May 14, 1910, copy in Maud Wood Park Papers, LC; *National Tribune,* Mar. 29, 1894.

12. Roe, *E. P. Roe,* 65–66; *American Tribune,* Nov. 23, 1888.

13. *Official Records,* 33:189; *National Tribune,* Sept. 20, 1888.

14. Brooks, *Butler and His Cavalry,* 102, 136; *Official Records,* 33:203.

15. It is possible that the telegraph lines Hampton was using may have been cut by Union scouts sent out on February 20 in addition to Stuart being distracted by Custer. Confederates were also able to contact Richmond by a circuitous route through Gordonsville once it appeared a Yankee cavalry operation was underway.

16. *Official Records,* 29(2):727, 33: 199–202; Goldsborough, *Maryland Line,* 188–91; Miller, "Civil War Memoirs of Henry C. Mettam," 150. The Maryland Line consisted of the 2nd Maryland Infantry, 1st Maryland Cavalry, 2nd Maryland Battery, and Cooper's (Virginia) Battery prior to the Kilpatrick-Dahlgren Raid. See *Official Records,* 33:1058.

17. *Philadelphia Weekly Times,* Apr. 3, 1880.

18. *Official Records,* 33:616. See also Col. George Sharpe to Benjamin Butler, Telegrams Collected by the Secretary of War, 1864, RG 393, NA, M504, roll 303.

19. *Philadelphia Weekly Times,* Apr. 3, 1880; Moyer, *Seventeenth Regiment of Pennsylvania Cavalry,* 235; Crosby Diary, Feb. 29, 1864; *Detroit Advertiser and Tribune,* Mar. 17, 1864.

20. *Rutland Daily Herald,* Mar. 7, 1864; *Oneida Weekly Herald,* Mar. 8, 1864.

21. *Philadelphia Weekly Times,* Apr. 3, 1880; Moyer, *Seventeenth Regiment of Pennsylvania Cavalry,* 234–35; W. O. Lee, *Personal and Historical Sketches,* 175–76.

22. *Philadelphia Weekly Times,* Apr. 3, 1880; Moyer, *Seventeenth Regiment of Pennsylvania Cavalry,* 234–35; J. A. Dahlgren, *Memoir of Ulric Dahlgren,* 212.

23. G. B. Davis et al., *Official Military Atlas,* plate XLV; *Official Records,* 25(1):1060. The area where Dahlgren's column crossed is partly flooded by a twentieth-century nuclear power plant's cooling pond.

24. *Richmond Times Dispatch,* July 15, 1906; *National Tribune,* Dec. 3, 1885; *Detroit Free Press,* Jan. 21, 1882; *Maine Farmer,* Apr. 7, 1864; *Official Records,* 33:21, 194; Reuben Bartley Memoir, Reuben Bartley Papers, VHS, 4; L. A. Wallace, *Richmond Howitzer Battalion,* 238; J. W. Jones, "Kilpatrick-Dahlgren Raid," 521. Jones concludes: "Colonel Dahlgren might have made his raid a brilliant success, if (instead of putting so much confidence in the statement of the 'intelligent contraband') he had dashed into camp, . . . [capturing] the guns and equipments of Ewell's artillery." The first black man Dahlgren encountered was most likely a slave owned by a Colonel Claybrook, an area landowner. *Field and Post Room* 1, no. 4 (1886): 50–51. Another account puts the Confederate artillery reserve at ninety-six guns. *Official Records,* 33:194.

25. *Richmond Daily Examiner,* Mar. 1, 1864; "Dahlgren's Famous Raid," George Clarke Papers, VHS, typescript, 1–11; Dowdey, *Wartime Letters of R. E. Lee,* 675; J. B. Jones, *Rebel War Clerk's Diary,* 2:161; Taylor, *Lee's Adjutant,* 129.

26. *Richmond Dispatch,* Mar. 7, 1864; telegram from Garnett's Mountain, 6:00 P.M., Feb. 29, 1864, Box 6, Miscellaneous Letters, Reports, RG 393, NA. The Richmond press' comment about Ewell raises an interesting observation about his ability.

27. Taylor, *Lee's Adjutant,* 131; Dowdey, *Wartime Letters of R. E. Lee,* 675; *Official Records,* 33:1205.

28. Harris, *Personal Reminiscences,* 71–72; *Richmond Times Dispatch,* July 15, 1906; L. A. Wallace, *Richmond Howitzer Battalion,* 238; *Official Records,* 33:210; John W. Daniel, "Kilpatrick's Celebrated Raid," n.d., Box 23, John W. Daniel and the Daniel Family Papers, Adelman Library, Univ. of Virginia.

29. *Official Records,* 33:210–11; Harris, *Personal Reminiscences,* 71–72; *Rutland Daily Herald,* Mar. 18, 1864.

30. Lt. Col. Hilary P. Jones served under Ewell. The thirty-year-old, a native of Hanover County, was a University of Virginia graduate and a teacher before the war. His battlefield experience included most of the Army of Northern Virginia's major campaigns, including the Seven Days, Antietam, Chancellorsville, and Gettysburg. His wife was the granddaughter of Chief Justice John Marshall. A fellow artillery officer characterized Jones as "a moderately good officer; no very strong points, nor yet any objectionable ones." R. K. Krick, *Lee's Colonels,* 183.

31. Dahlgren's signal officer claimed that no shots were fired when the Federals attacked the house. Bartley Memoir, 4.

32. *Richmond Daily Examiner,* Mar. 1, 7, 1864; *Richmond Times Dispatch,* June 10, 1906; Harris, *Personal Reminiscences,* 73; *Philadelphia Weekly Times,* Apr. 3, 1880; *Detroit Free Press,* Jan. 21, 1882; *National Tribune,* Dec. 3, 1885; Bartley Memoir, 5; Wood Memoir, 6; A. L. Long, *Memoirs of Robert E. Lee,* 319. There is some evidence that one R. J. "Bob" Dryden of the 1st Maryland Artillery tried to warn a Lieutenant Hill in Jones's court-martial proceeding that the Federals were near

but was told "there is not a Yankee on that side of the Rapidan." *Field and Post Room*, 1, no. 4 (1886): 50–51. In addition to Jones, Captains Dement, Garner, Channing, Page, and Watson and Lieutenants Lambie and Walthall were bagged by the raiders. *Richmond Daily Examiner*, Mar. 2, 1864; *Official Records*, 33:210–11.

33. *Richmond Dispatch*, Mar. 3, 1864.

34. Bartley Memoir, 5; *Richmond Enquirer*, Mar. 1, 1864; Merrill, *Campaigns of the First Maine*, 180; *Official Records*, 33:194; Wood Memoir, 7. It appears that Dahlgren's raiders did a less-than-perfect job when wrecking the tracks because a newspaper later reported that "the road was not damaged at Frederick's Hall." *Richmond Whig*, Mar. 4, 1864.

35. Wood Memoir, 6–7.

36. *Richmond Times Dispatch*, June 10, 1906. Jones's infant son, born November 14, 1863, would grow up to be a decorated rear admiral in the U.S. Navy.

37. *Maine Farmer*, Apr. 7, 1864; Tobie, *First Maine Cavalry*, 236; Harris, *Personal Reminiscences*, 71; *Grand Rapids Daily Democrat*, Feb. 6, 1887; *Philadelphia Weekly Times*, Sept. 29, 1877.

38. Bartley Memoir, 6.

39. John Sheahan to his father, Mar. 5, 1864, John Sheahan Papers, Maine Historical Society; Bartley Memoir, 6; Wood Memoir, 8.

40. *Official Records*, 33:211; *National Tribune*, Dec. 3, 1885; Wood Memoir, 7; *Richmond Daily Examiner*, Mar. 8, 1864. The traditional story identifies the guide hanged by Dahlgren as Martin Robinson. Chapter 9 will discuss the discovery of a new, more accurate identification for the unfortunate man.

41. *Richmond Times Dispatch*, June 10, 1906; *Official Records*, 33:194; *Philadelphia Weekly Times*, Sept. 29, 1877; Bartley Memoir, 6; Wood Memoir, 7–8.

42. Merrill, *Campaigns of the First Maine*, 180; J. A. Dahlgren, *Memoir of Ulric Dahlgren*, 213.

43. Glatthaar, *General Lee's Army*, 212.

44. Letter from William Kemp, Mar. 5, 1864, in *Detroit Advertiser and Tribune*, Mar. 16, 1864.

45. *Michigan Argus*, Mar. 18, 1864; Tobie, *First Maine Cavalry*, 242; Crosby Diary, Feb. 29, 1864; *Richmond Daily Enquirer*, Mar. 3, 1864; *Richmond Daily Examiner*, Mar. 3, 1864. An itinerary published in the *Official Records* states that Kilpatrick arrived at Beaver Dam Station at 1:00 P.M., which appears too early based on soldier accounts and the fact that the same entry claims that he arrived at Spotsylvania Court House at 10:00 A.M. Another entry for Davies's command states that he arrived at the station at 4:00 P.M., which is more reasonable. *Official Records*, 33:622.

46. *Official Records*, 33:190–91, 189; *Michigan Argus*, Mar. 18, 1864; William O'Brien to his brother, Mar. 16, 1864, O'Brien Papers; Munford, "Cavalry Raid," 160; Moyer, *Seventeenth Regiment of Pennsylvania Cavalry*, 235–36; *Richmond Daily Examiner*, Mar. 3, 1864; Baily, "Civil

War," unpublished article based on Isaac W. Scherich's memoirs, in possession of the author. Brig. Gen. Rufus King had burned Beaver Dam Station on July 29, 1862; Sheridan and Custer burned it again on May 9, 1864. *Hanover Herald,* n.d., in Hanover County Historical Society, *Hanover County, Virginia,* 16. A short time later the three black men were recaptured and sent to Castle Thunder, a Richmond prison.

47. *Official Records,* 33:191; Kidd, *Riding with Custer,* 243; Tobie, *First Maine Cavalry,* 242.

48. Kidd, *Riding with Custer,* 244; *Supplement,* pt. 2, 27:9.

49. Reminiscences, Mar. 15, 1878, Edward H. Harvey Papers, WL, typescript; *Detroit Advertiser and Tribune,* Mar. 17, 1864; Cheney, *Ninth Regiment, New York Volunteer Cavalry,* 147.

50. *Official Records,* 33:184, 189, 191; Moyer, *Seventeenth Regiment of Pennsylvania Cavalry,* 236, 240–41; *Michigan Argus,* Mar. 18, 1864.

51. *National Tribune,* Mar. 29, 1894. Another army scout, J. W. Landegon, who claimed to be in charge of the scouts under Kilpatrick, disputed Carney's peach-brandy story. Ibid., May 31, 1894.

52. Hall, Besley, and Woods, *Sixth New York Cavalry,* 174–75; Cheney, *Ninth Regiment, New York Volunteer Cavalry,* 146–47; Moyer, *Seventeenth Regiment of Pennsylvania Cavalry,* 237–40, 335–36; Pickerill, *Third Indiana Cavalry,* 136–37; Nehemiah Mann Diary, in *Fifth Report of the New York State Bureau of Military Statistics,* 619; *Official Records,* 33:191; Davies Report. A postwar chronicle claims that Johnson fought off Hall's dismounted troopers with only sixty men from the 1st Maryland Cavalry and two guns from the Baltimore Light Artillery because the rest of his force was out searching for the raiders. Goldsborough, *Maryland Line,* 189.

53. *Official Records,* 33:212–13, 201; Goldsbourough, 191; Moyer, *Seventeenth Regiment of Pennsylvania Cavalry,* 241.

54. McDonald, *Laurel Brigade,* 222–23; *Official Records,* 33:1003.

55. Gillespie, *Company A, First Ohio Cavalry,* 194; *Official Records,* 33:191.

Chapter 8

1. Cabell, "Woman Saved Richmond City," 354; Agee, *Facets of Goochland,* 65–78; Gibson, *Cabell's Canal,* 272; J. S. Wise, *End of an Era,* 138.

2. After Lee's surrender General Meade asked Maj. Gen. Godfrey Weitzel, commanding at Richmond, on April 13, 1865, to take special care of the "daughters of Brig. Gen. Henry A. Wise, one of them my niece." Annie Jennings Wise Hobson was the wife of Plumer Hobson, the owner of Eastwood. Meade's wife, Margaret Sergeant Meade, was the sister of Mary Elizabeth Wise, the Confederate general's wife. The Pennsylvanian sent an ambulance loaded with supplies, two mules, and fifty dollars in cash to the Wise family shortly afterward. *Official Records,* 46(3):740; Cleaves, *Meade of Gettysburg,* 52, 335.

3. Warner, *Generals in Gray,* 341–42.

302 NOTES TO PAGES 150–54

4. Cabell, "Woman Saved Richmond City," 354–55; J. S. Wise, *End of an Era*, 139–40; Auditor of Public Accounts, Personal Property Tax Books—Goochland County, 1860–63, LV, reel 533.
5. Letter, Mar. 11, 1864, in *New Jersey Herald*, Mar. 24, 1864; Tobie, *First Maine Cavalry*, 236; *Richmond Whig*, Mar. 2, 1864; Ide, *First Vermont Cavalry Volunteers*, 584; *National Tribune*, Dec. 3, 1885; *Philadelphia Weekly Times*, Sept. 29, 1877.
6. Letter, Mar. 24, 1864, in *Maine Farmer*, Apr. 7, 1864. This letter mentions the arrival time, though later accounts put it at between 9:00 and 10:00 A.M.
7. James Wood Memoir, Maud Wood Park Papers, LC, 8; *Richmond Times Dispatch*, Aug. 1, 1897; *Philadelphia Weekly Times*, Sept. 29, 1877; *Rutland Daily Herald*, Mar. 18, 1864; *Official Records*, 33:195; *Richmond Whig*, Mar. 2, 1864. The *Richmond Whig* reported the next day that a large number of blacks were "mounted and armed." This early provocative report, however, is not substantiated by any Federal accounts scribbled at the time or written after the war. Undoubtedly, liberated blacks were following the Yankee column, but most likely they were unarmed, basically just refugees from slavery.
8. Cabell, "Woman Saved Richmond City," 353–54; Bullard, *Goochland*, 27, 60–63; J. S. Wise, *End of an Era*, 141; A. Brown, *Cabells and Their Kin*, 362–65.
9. "What Is the Truth of Dahlgren's Raid?," 68; Cabell, "Woman Saved Richmond City," 357; Munford, "Cavalry Raid," 166; J. W. Jones, "Kilpatrick-Dahlgren Raid," 538; Wight, *Story of Goochland*, 23.
10. *National Tribune*, Dec. 3, 1885; Harris, *Personal Reminiscences*, 73–74; *Philadelphia Weekly Times*, Sept. 29, 1877. Obviously, some looting of silverware occurred, based on later newspaper accounts of raiders captured with saddlebags or sack-coat pockets stuffed with valuables. A number of outbuildings and mills were undoubtedly burned in an effort to retard the war effort. Likewise, horse stealing was a necessity due to the celerity of the pace the cavalrymen were keeping. It is, however, unlikely that there was wholesale looting of plantation homes by Dahlgren's men.
11. The Morson mansion did burn, though not until 1933. Bullard, *Goochland*, 60–62.
12. Anne Hobson Diary, Apr. 3, 1864, Anne Jennings Wise Hobson Papers, VHS, transcript; Cabell, "Woman Saved Richmond City," 355–56; Mayo, "War-Time Aurora Borealis," *Tyler's Quarterly*, 73.
13. This was the same Schofield who had helped the army scouts capture Ely's Ford two days earlier. David H. Schofield would win the Medal of Honor for capturing the battle flag of the 12th Virginia Infantry at the Battle of Cedar Creek on October 19, 1864. Boudrye, *Fifth New York Cavalry*, 306.
14. *National Tribune*, Dec. 3, 1885; Boudrye, *Fifth New York Cavalry*, 102; Cabell, "Woman Saved Richmond City," 356; Hobson Diary, Apr. 3, 1864.

15. Hobson Diary, Apr. 3, 1864. Unlike the Southern tales attached to the Yankee freebooting at Dover, at least one Federal officer later verified the circumstances of Wise's escape. Undoubtedly true, it raises a very pertinent question about Dahlgren's leadership and common sense during the raid: why would he be worrying about Henry Wise when he was on a very tight schedule to join Kilpatrick at Richmond with the specific purpose of freeing 13,000 Union prisoners and perhaps capturing a bigger prize? Surely the raid's main objective outweighed any reason for capturing a lower-echelon general officer in Confederate service, notwithstanding Wise's prewar notoriety.

16. Bullard, *Goochland*, 60–64; Cabell, "Woman Saved Richmond City," 358; Auditor of Public Accounts, Personal Property Tax Books—Goochland County, 1860–63, reel 553. Seddon also owned twenty-seven horses, three carriages, thirty-two cattle, seventy-six sheep, and forty hogs in 1863. Sabot Hill was named for a nearby island in the James River that was shaped like a shoe (in French, "sabot").

17. R. W. Curry, "James A. Seddon," 123–50; Thomas, *Confederate Nation*, 192, 286–87; Malone, *Dictionary of American Biography*, 16:545.

18. William Preston Cabell, "How a Woman Helped to Save Richmond," *Confederate Veteran* 31, no. 1 (Jan. 1923): 177–78; Cabell, "Woman Saved Richmond City," 353, 357–58.

19. Cabell, "Woman Saved Richmond City," 354.

20. "What Is the Truth of Dahlgren's Raid?," 67–69.

21. Hobson Diary, Apr. 3, 1864; Mayo, "War-Time Aurora Borealis," *Tyler's Quarterly*, 70–76; *Richmond Daily Enquirer*, Mar. 3, 1864.

22. *Philadelphia Weekly Times*, Sept. 29, 1877.

23. On November 7, 2004, Robert E. Lee Camp 1589, Sons of Confederate Veterans, Midlothian, Virginia, through the S.C.V. national organization, posthumously awarded Pvt. James Pleasants the Confederate States of America Medal of Honor. Pleasants's recognition was partially attributed to the author's article in *Blue & Gray* (Winter 2003) on the Kilpatrick-Dahlgren Raid, which highlights his exploits.

24. Stiles, *4th Virginia Cavalry*, 1, 131.

25. Ibid., 42–42.

26. Bowles, "Private James Henry Pleasants," 9–14; "A Goochland Hero," *Confederate Veteran*, 33 (1925): 366–68. James Pleasants survived a subsequent wound and surrendered at Appomattox. Unfortunately, cavalry service was hard on his body, and the local hero succumbed to tuberculosis at age twenty-eight. The United Daughters of the Confederacy honored Goochland's hero with a stone pyramid erected in 1929 near his uncle's home in Cardwell.

27. M. H. Walker, "Oak Grove," 13–19; Pilcher, "Some Incidents of the Kilpatrick-Dahlgren Raid," 77.

28. *Official Records*, 33:194; letter, Mar. 11, 1864, in *New Jersey Herald*, Mar. 24, 1864.

29. Couture, *Powhatan*, 79, 306–10. Jude's Ferry operated until at least 1923. It was also notable during Gabriel's Insurrection in 1800, when

slaves revolted in the Richmond area. One slave named Frank Goode organized a local plot "to begin at Jude's Ferry and put to death every man on both sides of the river to Richmond." Ibid., 145.

30. *National Tribune*, Dec. 3, 1885; "Dahlgren's Famous Raid," 1–11, George Clarke Papers, VHS; *Philadelphia Weekly Times*, Sept. 29, 1877.

31. *National Tribune*, May 31, 1894; *Philadelphia Weekly Times*, Apr. 3, 1880.

Chapter 9

1. Catton, *Stillness at Appomattox*, 1, 14, 17–18; V. Jones, *Eight Hours before Richmond*, 46, 74, 157; Longacre, *Mounted Raids*, 247–48; Schultz, *Dahlgren Affair*, 118–20; Crouch, "Dahlgren Raid," 184.

2. Crouch, "Dahlgren Raid," 184; James Wood Memoir, Maud Wood Park Papers, LC, 7–8; *Daily Morning Chronicle*, Feb. 6, 1865; *National Tribune*, Dec. 3, 1885; Cabell, "Woman Saved Richmond City," 353–58; Ide, *First Vermont Cavalry Volunteers*, 153. This last remarkable identification was from a man who was on the raid and helped hang the guide.

3. *Official Records*, ser. 2, 6:1053.

4. Ide, *First Vermont Cavalry Volunteers*, 153; *Army Navy Journal*, Mar. 12, 1864.

5. *Official Records*, ser. 4, 3:325.

6. Godwin Scudamore, Pension Record, NA. Interestingly, Scudamore lived to be eighty-three years old, had two wives who predeceased him, six children, twenty-six grandchildren, and "several great grandchildren." Scudamore's pension narrative of these events is substantiated by a letter written by Capt. James Biddle in 1864, long before Scudamore made his application. James Biddle to his wife, Mar. 8, 1864, James Biddle Papers, HSP; Meade, *Life and Letters*, 2:168.

7. Anne Hobson Diary, Apr. 3, 1864, Anne Jennings Wise Hobson Papers, VHS, transcript.

8. James Biddle to his wife, Feb. 28, 29, 1864, Biddle Papers; Lyman, *Meade's Army*, 107; *Philadelphia Weekly Times*, Sept. 29, 1877. A New York officer added that the man was "very shrewd and intelligent" but "considered faithful and reliable." *National Tribune*, Dec. 3, 1885.

9. *Official Records*, 33:221. For background on Babcock, see Fishel, *Secret War for the Union*, 153–54, 257–59, 558. The organizational status of the Bureau of Military Information was subsumed into the Provost Marshal General Department when Meade took command of the Army of the Potomac.

10. Identification of the man sent by Babcock is slightly muddied by a Richmond newspaper naming "John A. Hogan" as the "very man [Dahlgren] wanted" as a guide. The man referred to by the journalist was probably Martin Hogan, but the Irishman was so full of himself he probably relished the notoriety he could garner by being associated with Babcock's captured note. *Richmond Daily Examiner*, Mar. 8, 1864. *National*

Tribune, Dec. 3, 1885. A postwar narrative of the 2nd New York Cavalry, most likely written by Maj. William Mattison, an officer of the regiment, states that "Dahlgren's guide—a negro sent to him from Gen. Meade's headquarters on Sunday night—had volunteered to lead him to the James River." Mattison was on the raid and is listed as a contributor to Snell, *History of Sussex and Warren Counties,* iii, 99.

11. No free black man named Martin Robinson is listed for Goochland County in the 1858, 1860, or 1863 slave records. See Boxes 1, 2, Goochland County Free and Slave Records, 1726–1867, LV. No one named Martin Robinson appears in 1860 or 1862 as having personal property. Auditor of Public Accounts, Personal Property Tax Books—Goochland County, 1860–63, LV, reel 553.

12. *Richmond Sentinel,* Mar. 3, 1864; *Richmond Daily Examiner,* Mar. 5, 1864.

13. The 1860 special census for Goochland County shows David Mimms as the owner of nine male slaves ages twelve to seventy-five. 1860 Special Census—Slave Schedules, LV, roll VA 192, frame 223.

14. Crouch, "Dahlgren Raid," 184; Pilcher, "Some Incidents of the Kilpatrick-Dahlgren Raid," 77–79. A history of Goochland County published in 1943 refers to the guide as "Robson," which is a closer match to Roberson, but this story has the man pulled from working on a stone wall at Sabot Hill, which is unlikely based on other evidence. Wight, *Story of Goochland,* 9–10.

15. *National Tribune,* Dec. 3, 1885; Harris, *Personal Reminiscences,* 75; *Richmond Whig,* Mar. 2, 1864; *Philadelphia Weekly Times,* Apr. 3, 1880; Thomas J. Young, 56th Va. Inf., to James Walters, Apr. 16, 1864, Walters Papers, VHS.

16. *Richmond Daily Enquirer,* Mar. 3, 1864; *Richmond Whig,* Mar. 2, 1864; Snell, *History of Sussex and Warren Counties,* 99.

17. J. A. Dahlgren, *Memoir of Ulric Dahlgren,* 214; *Grand Rapids Daily Democrat,* Feb. 6, 1887.

18. Thompson, "Brief History of Tuckahoe," 15. This article is part of a guidebook for the house and property, with no sources cited for the information written about Dahlgren and Allen. No Federal contemporary or postwar accounts mention the event.

19. *National Tribune,* Dec. 3, 1885; *Boston Globe,* May 16, 1910, in Maud Wood Park Papers, LC; *Richmond Times Dispatch,* Aug. 1, 1897; *Philadelphia Weekly Times,* Sept. 29, 1877; *New Jersey Herald,* Mar. 24, 1864; *Richmond Whig,* Mar. 2, 1864; Reuben Bartley Memoir, Reuben Bartley Papers, VHS, 7–8; Harris, *Personal Reminiscences,* 72–73; Nathan Webb Diary, Nathan Webb Papers, ALPL, transcript, 395; Snell, *History of Sussex and Warren Counties,* 99. Even General Lee's former staff officer and artillerist, Armistead Long, agreed with these Federals when he later wrote, "Dahlgren put in the responsible position of guide, a contraband who showed his fidelity to the Southern cause by misleading him from his proposed line of march, and thus created a delay which prevented his forming a junction with Kilpatrick." A. L. Long, *Memoirs*

of Robert E. Lee, 319. This scenario raises the question of whether or not Martin was sent specifically to mislead the expedition. Although somewhat farfetched, could his assistance to Lieutenant Scudamore been discovered and a deal struck with James Seddon, the cousin of his wife's master? See *National Tribune,* Apr. 6, 1894. An early report of the raid endorsed by a captain in the Provost Marshal General's Department claimed that Dahlgren "was deceived by the negro guide (whom the report says he hung)." John McEntee to Col. George H. Sharp, Mar. 4, 1864, Box 11, Miscellaneous Letters, Reports, RG 393, NA.

20. *National Tribune,* Apr. 6, 1894; *Boston Globe,* May 16, 1910; Wood Memoir, 8–9; Ide, *First Vermont Cavalry Volunteers,* 153.

21. Harris, *Personal Reminiscences,* 73; *Grand Rapids Daily Democrat,* Feb. 6, 1887.

22. *New Jersey Herald,* Mar. 24, 1864; Snell, *History of Sussex and Warren Counties,* 99; *Philadelphia Weekly Times,* Sept. 29, 1877; *National Tribune,* Dec. 3, 1885; J. W. Jones, "Kilpatrick-Dahlgren Raid," 538; Cabell, "Woman Saved Richmond City," 356; *Richmond Times Dispatch,* Apr. 29, 1906. "The tree where the Negro Martin was hung was in existence until the last few years between 'Tuckahoe' and St. Mary's Church." The date when this statement was written is unknown. "What Is the Truth of Dahlgren's Raid?," 67. "Mr. and Mrs. Powell Wesley have presented to the Society the stump of the famous oak tree on which Col Ulric Dahlgren, of the Union Army, hung a negro slave for having directed him to a ford of the James River that was not passable because of a spring freshet." "President's Report," 4. The stump has since disappeared.

Chapter 10

1. Meade, *Life and Letters,* 2:169.

2. Kidd, *Riding with Custer,* 245; W. O. Lee, *Personal and Historical Sketches,* 176; G. Crosby Diary, Mar. 1, 1864, Vermont Historical Society; Athearn, "Civil War Diary of John Wilson Philips," 97.

3. *Official Records,* 33:184, 189, 213, 216; Moyer, *Seventeenth Regiment of Pennsylvania Cavalry,* 236, 240–41; *American Tribune,* Nov. 23, 1888; Gillespie, *Company A, First Ohio Cavalry,* 194–95; Davies Report; letter, Mar. 7, 1864, in *Michigan Argus,* Mar. 18, 1864.

4. Ford, "Wade Hampton's Strategy," 280; *Supplement,* pt. 2, 27:9; *Detroit Advertiser and Tribune,* Mar. 17, 1864. Kilby Station was named for John Kilby, a Hanover County resident who had served during the Revolutionary War as commander of the quarterdeck on John Paul Jones's ship *Bonhomme Richard. Hanover Herald,* n.d., in Hanover County Historical Society, *Hanover County, Virginia,* 16.

5. Cheney, *Ninth Regiment, New York Volunteer Cavalry,* 147–48; Nehemiah Mann Diary, in *Fifth Report of the New York State Bureau of Military Statistics,* 619; Moyer, *Seventeenth Regiment of Pennsylvania Cavalry,* 239.

6. *Official Records*, 33:191–92, 212; W. L. Curry, *Four Years in the Saddle*, 244; Kidd, *Riding with Custer*, 246; Nelson, "Brook Hill Fortifications Remembered," 46; W. O. Lee, *Personal and Historical Sketches*, 28. This intelligence officer was probably Capt. John McEntee.

7. John McEntee to Col. George H. Sharp, Mar. 4, 1864, Box 11, Miscellaneous Letters, Reports, RG 393, NA.

8. J. B. Jones, *Rebel War Clerk's Diary*, 2:162; F. Lee, "Death of Colonel Dahlgren," 256; Davies Report; Hyndman, *History of a Cavalry Company*, 186.

9. Warner, *Generals in Gray*, 292; *Official Records*, 33:212–13. Stevens would be an unreconstructed Rebel, going to Mexico after the war and dying there in 1867. He is buried in Hollywood Cemetery in Richmond. Stevens may have been assisted in his work on the defenses by Custis Lee, who in addition to his staff duties and being commander of the Local Defense Brigade, used his "trained engineering skill, and so improved the discipline and general efficiency of the heavy artillery." See McCabe, "Major-General George Washington Custis Lee," 6–7.

10. J. B. Jones, *Rebel War Clerk's Diary*, 2:164; *Bangor Weekly Whig and Courier*, Mar. 14, 1864; Potter, *Memoirs of the Civil War*, Special Collections, Univ. of California Santa Barbara, 15; Starr, "In and Out of Confederate Prisons," 85; *Lewiston Evening Journal*, Mar. 25, 1864. Neal Dow, a recently exchanged POW, made a speech shortly after the raid in which he confirmed that Libby was mined. He was empathic about this: "Turner said, 'I know d—d well that a thousand pounds of powder was put under here last night, though I didn't do it. . . . It was a nice thing for you [Kilpatrick] did not come in—you would all have been blown to h—l.'" *The Liberator*, May 6, 1864. Another prisoner vividly remembered years later that "our anxiety was not a little heightened by the well-authenticated information that the cellars of the prison had been mined," adding, "some of the prison officials, after the retreat of the raiders, made no secret of it." Whether Confederate authorities would have followed through with their horrific threat remains unknown, but the consequences of such a diabolical action would certainly have had far-reaching implications for the war. *Maine Farmer*, Mar. 31, 1864; Cavada, *Libby Life*, 195–96.

11. Davies Report; *Essex County Republican*, Apr. 27, 1899; *National Tribune*, May 31, 1894.

12. *Official Records*, 33:191; Davies Report.

13. Weaver, *10th and 19th Battalions of Heavy Artillery*, 2, 60–61; Chernault and Weaver, *18th and 20th Battalions of Virginia Heavy Artillery*, 3, 50.

14. *National Tribune*, Sept. 20, Nov. 15, 1888; *Richmond Whig*, Mar. 2, 1864; *Richmond Enquirer*, Mar. 8, 1864; Athearn, "Civil War Diary of John Wilson Philips," 97; letter, Mar. 21, 1864, in *Detroit Free Press*, Mar. 26, 1864; letter, Mar. 9, 1864, in *Detroit Advertiser and Tribune*, Mar. 17, 1864; *Richmond Daily Examiner*, Mar. 3, 4, 1864.

15. *Official Records*, 33:184, 192, 212; Merrill, *Campaigns of the First Maine*, 175; Tobie, *First Maine Cavalry*, 526–27. Heald would not survive the war, being killed in action at Sayler's Creek on April 6, 1865. William Baker to his father, Mar. 20, 1864, William Baker Papers, Southern Historical Collection, Univ. of North Carolina; Athearn, "Civil War Diary of John Wilson Philips," 97.

16. *Official Records*, 33:212; *Richmond Daily Enquirer*, Mar. 8, 1864.

17. *Richmond Daily Enquirer*, Mar. 8, 11, 1864; Chernault and Weaver, *18th and 20th Battalions of Virginia Heavy Artillery*, 93. Chaplain would later be wounded at Drewry's Bluff on May 16, 1864, and retire from the service. Porter, *Record of Events in Norfolk County*, 132–33.

18. *Official Records*, 33:213; William Baker to his father, Mar. 20, 1864, Baker Papers; Compiled Service Records, 20th Battalion Virginia Heavy Artillery, NA, roll 249; Kidd, *Riding with Custer*, 249; Athearn, "Civil War Diary of John Wilson Philips," 97; Gilbert Chapman to dear friend, n.d., Gilbert W. Chapman Papers, Burton Historical Collection, Detroit Public Library; F. J. Bellamy to his parents, brothers, and sisters, Mar. 20, 1864, F. J. Bellamy Papers, ISL.

19. Rodenbough, *Eighteenth Regiment of Cavalry Pennsylvania Volunteers*, 47; Nelson, "Brook Hill Fortifications Remembered," 46; R. C. Wallace, *A Few Memories*, 33; Baily, "Civil War," 29.

20. J. B. Jones, *Rebel War Clerk's Diary*, 2:164; John W. Stott Diary, Mar. 2, 1864, Civil War Times Illustrated Collection, USAERC; *Richmond Daily Enquirer*, Mar. 2, 1864; F. Lee, "Death of Colonel Dahlgren," 256; *American Tribune*, Nov. 23, 1888; letter, Mar. 21, 1864, in *Detroit Free Press*, Mar. 26, 1864. As a Pennsylvania officer who was with Hall put it, "We afterwards learned that Kilpatrick was correspondingly anxious about our command." Moyer, *Seventeenth Regiment of Pennsylvania Cavalry*, 240.

21. *National Tribune*, Sept. 20, 1888; *American Tribune*, Nov. 23, 1888; R. C. Wallace, *A Few Memories*, 33;Tobie, *First Maine Cavalry*, 242–43.

22. Longacre, *Lincoln's Cavalrymen*, 242. David Long also made this point strongly during "Dahlgren's Raid," a Civil War Education Association field tour, June 7–9, 2002.

23. Kidd, *Riding with Custer*, 249; W. L. Curry, *Four Years in the Saddle*, 244; McEntee to Sharpe, Mar. 4, 1864, Box 11, Provost Marshal's File, RG 107, NA.

24. *Official Records*, 33:185, 192; *Washington Daily Morning Chronicle*, Mar. 7, 1864; Hunton, *Autobiography*, 107; roll of Company K, 19th Virginia Infantry, Folder 33, Box 22, CMR, LV; *Richmond Whig*, Mar. 2, 1864; *Supplement*, pt. 2, 71:194, 356, 362, 367, 383, 391, 400; Burgwyn, *Captain's War*, 125.

25. *Official Records*, 33:1157–59, 1216, 1247–49; Crute, *Units of the Confederate States Army*, 361–70.

26. Victor Comte to Elise (wife), Mar. 19, 1864, Victor E. Comte Papers, BHL-UM; William O'Brien Diary, Mar. 1, 1864, William H. O'Brien Papers, BHL-UM; *Detroit Advertiser and Tribune*, Mar. 17, 1864;

Detroit Free Press, Mar. 26, 1864, Jan. 21, 1882; "History of the First Michigan Cavalry," Regimental File, Box 18, Michigan State Library and Archives; "Reminiscences of My Army Life," newspaper article printed in the *Mt. Clemens Monitor,* Mar. 15, 1878, copy in Edward H. Harvey Papers, WL; W. O. Lee, *Personal and Historical Sketches,* 29; John McEntee to Col. George Sharp, Mar. 4, 1864, Box 11, Miscellaneous Letters, Reports, RG 393, NA; Compiled Service Records, 20th Virginia Heavy Artillery, NA, roll 249; *Supplement,* pt. 2, 70:355; *Richmond Daily Examiner,* Mar. 2, 1864; Moyer, *Seventeenth Regiment of Pennsylvania Cavalry,* 241; R. C. Wallace, *A Few Memories,* 33.

27. Evans, *Confederate Military History,* 2:117; Goldsborough, *Maryland Line,* 189–90; Hyndman, *History of a Cavalry Company,* 186.

28. *National Tribune,* May 31, 1894.

29. Hampton, "Twelve Months in Rebel Prisons," 233.

30. Dufur, *Over the Dead Line,* 14; Kidd, *One of Custer's Wolverines,* 72; narrative of the raid from various Richmond newspapers, n.d., London Family Papers, VHS; *Official Records,* 33:185, 192; Davies Report; letter, Mar. 9, 1864, in *Detroit Advertiser and Tribune,* Mar. 17, 1864; Isham, *Seventh Regiment of Michigan Volunteer Cavalry,* 38; R. C. Wallace, *A Few Memories,* 33–34. The destruction of the Meadow Bridges was less than perfect. A Richmond newspaper later reported that the spans would be repaired by March 5. *Richmond Whig,* Mar. 4, 1864. For details of the property stolen by the Federals, see *Richmond Daily Enquirer,* Mar. 2, 1864; *Richmond Whig,* Mar. 2, 1864; *Richmond Dispatch,* Mar. 3, 1864; and *Richmond Daily Examiner,* Mar. 2, 1864. For a detailed description of the Federals' savage treatment of one William Chesterman, a carpenter with five children, see Munford, "Cavalry Raid," 172.

31. William Hill Diary, Mar. 1, 1864, LC; *Richmond Dispatch,* Mar. 3, 1864; *Washington Daily Chronicle,* Mar. 7, 1864.

32. Davies Report; *Essex County Republican,* Apr. 27, 1899; Crosby Diary, Mar. 1, 1864; Moyer, *Seventeenth Regiment of Pennsylvania Cavalry,* 242; Hill Diary, Mar. 1, 1864; Dufur, *Over the Dead Line,* 14; Kidd, *Riding with Custer,* 250.

33. W. O. Lee, *Personal and Historical Sketches,* 29; *Official Records,* 33:85; *National Tribune,* May 31, 1894; Moyer, *Seventeenth Regiment of Pennsylvania Cavalry,* 242–43; Merrill, *Campaigns of the First Maine,* 177; Tobie, *First Maine Cavalry,* 243–44; Kidd, *Riding with Custer,* 252; *Rutland Daily Herald,* Jan. 11, 1864; letter, Apr. 17, 1864, in *Burlington Free Press,* Apr. 23, 1864; Constantine Taylor, Pension File, NA. Merrill's account is most interesting because it was written in 1866, only two years after the raid. It states that one of Kilpatrick's objectives was to send Preston and Taylor back into the city to capture Jefferson Davis.

34. W. O. Lee, *Personal and Historical Sketches,* 29–30, 200; Brooks, *Butler and His Cavalry,* 102–103; *Official Records,* 33:201; Athearn, "Civil War Diary of John Wilson Philips," 97; *National Tribune,* Sept. 20, 1888;

Clark, *Histories of the Several Regiments and Battalions from North Carolina,* 1:460–61; Hill Diary, Mar. 1, 1864; letter, Mar. 9, 1864, in *Detroit Advertiser and Tribune,* Mar. 17, 1864; Dufur, *Over the Dead Line,* 15; Ford, "Wade Hampton's Strategy," 281–82; Isham, *Seventh Regiment of Michigan Volunteer Cavalry,* 38; letter from William Kemp, Mar. 5, 1864, in *Detroit Advertiser and Tribune,* Mar. 16, 1864.

35. W. O. Lee, *Personal and Historical Sketches,* 29–32; Allyn Litchfield, Pension File, NA; Ide, *First Vermont Cavalry Volunteers,* 36, 60–61, 67, 76. After the raid Kilpatrick would replace Sawyer with Addison Preston during the first week of March 1864. Custer and Sheridan forced Sawyer's resignation from the service on April 24, 1864. Ibid., 77.

36. W. O. Lee, *Personal and Historical Sketches,* 29–32, 199, 212–13; letter, Mar. 9, 1864, in *Detroit Advertiser and Tribune,* Mar. 17, 1864; Ford, "Wade Hampton's Strategy," 280–82.

37. W. O. Lee, *Personal and Historical Sketches,* 170–72.

38. Isham, *Seventh Regiment of Michigan Volunteer Cavalry,* 39; letter, Mar. 9, 1864, in *Detroit Advertiser and Tribune,* Mar. 17, 1864; Samuel B. Carll, Pension File, NA; W. O. Lee, *Personal and Historical Sketches,* 200. Because the 7th Michigan no longer had any field-grade officers, Maj. William Wells of the 1st Vermont was temporarily assigned to command it. Ibid.

39. R. C. Wallace, *A Few Memories,* 34; Dufur, *Over the Dead Line,* 15–16; *Supplement,* pt. 2, 69:159; Kidd, *One of Custer's Wolverines,* 72, 74; Kidd, *Riding with Custer,* 250; Munford, "Cavalry Raid," 163.

40. Hill Diary, Mar. 1, 1864; Crosby Diary, Mar. 1, 1864; Kidd, *Riding with Custer,* 254; *Official Records,* 33:189, 193, 201; Victor Comte to Elise (wife), Mar. 19, 1864, Comte Papers; *National Tribune,* Sept. 20, Nov. 15, Dec. 6, 1888; Moyer, *Seventeenth Regiment of Pennsylvania Cavalry,* 242–43; *Washington Daily Chronicle,* Mar. 7, 1864; R. C. Wallace, *A Few Memories,* 35.

41. W. O. Lee, *Personal and Historical Sketches,* 32; Davies Report; *Official Records,* 33:185, 193; Kidd, *Riding with Custer,* 255; Athearn, "Civil War Diary of John Wilson Philips," 97; *Supplement,* pt. 2, 6:289.

42. W. O. Lee, *Personal and Historical Sketches,* 32–33; Allyn Litchfield, Pension File.

43. *Richmond Dispatch,* Mar. 4, 1864; John McAnerney Memoir, ca. 1900, John McAnerney Papers, VHS, transcript; Clark, *Histories of the Several Regiments and Battalions from North Carolina,* 1:462–63.

Chapter 11

1. *Grand Rapids Daily Democrat,* Feb. 6, 1887; *Philadelphia Weekly Times,* Sept. 29, 1877, Apr. 3, 1880; *National Tribune,* Dec. 3, 1885; Nelson, "Coal Mines of Henrico's West End," 16–28. To confirm the information about Dahlgren passing the Franklin farm, the author conducted interviews with Richard Forrester of Richmond, Virginia, on April 26, 2004 and C. Southall Wallace of Manakin-Sabot, Virginia, in March 2004, both of whom were familiar with Douglas Pitts's research on Dahlgren's route.

2. Pitts, "Dahlgren's Raid Route," 1–6; *Official Records*, 33:195; Tobie, *First Maine Cavalry*, 236–37; *Rutland Daily Herald*, Mar. 18, 1864; Reuben Bartley Memoir, Reuben Bartley Papers, VHS, 10; *Maine Farmer*, Apr. 7, 1864; Nelson, "Laurel," 6–7, 10–11; *Philadelphia Weekly Times*, Sept. 29, 1877. The Three Chopt, or Three Notch'd, Road followed the path of an ancient Indian trail and ran from Richmond to the Shenandoah Valley. It was a main east–west route from the early eighteenth century until the 1930s. "Numbered mile markers were incised or painted on trees along the road, probably by Peter Jefferson, a surveyor and father of Thomas [Jefferson]." It was first called "three notched road" in 1742. Pawlett, "Three Notch'd Road Revisited," 6–7.

3. *National Tribune*, Dec. 3, 1885; *Official Records*, 33:195; *Philadelphia Weekly Times*, Apr. 3, 1880; *Richmond Daily Examiner*, Mar. 2, 1864.

4. *Grand Rapids Daily Democrat*, Feb. 6, 1887. This revelation is indeed a provocative one. After the raid the issue of who knew what and when they knew it would become critically important. How much more Dahlgren revealed to his officers from what was originally shared at Ely's Ford is unclear. In the immediate aftermath of the expedition, the information that this Michigander recalled was kept quiet. But his willingness to share his observations years later adds one more clue to the mystery of the raid's actual intent. Lieutenant Bartley said later that he saw that Dahlgren had orders on his person, but the colonel did not share the specific contents with his signal officer.

5. *Philadelphia Weekly Times*, Sept. 29, 1877; Snell, *History of Sussex and Warren Counties*, 99; Foster, *New Jersey in the Rebellion*, 742; J. A. Dahlgren, *Memoir of Ulric Dahlgren*, 215–16.

6. *Rutland Daily Herald*, Mar. 18, 1864; *Grand Rapids Daily Democrat*, Feb. 6, 1887; Harris, *Personal Reminiscences*, 75; Cronin, "Vest Mansion," 112.

7. Joseph R. Haw, "The Armory Battalion at Green's Farm," *Confederate Veteran* 16, no. 4 (Apr. 1908): 153–54; "What Is the Truth of Dahlgren's Raid?," 75; Crute, *Units of the Confederate States Army*, 349; "That Fight at Green's Farm, near Richmond," *Confederate Veteran*, 17 (1909): 452; *Detroit Free Press*, Jan. 21, 1882; J. B. Jones, *Rebel War Clerk's Diary*, 2:166; Watts, "Last Battles," 70.

8. John McAnerney Memoir, Feb. 23, 1914 (transcript), 1–6, Richmond National Battlefield Park Library; McAnerney Memoir (ca. 1900); J. B. Jones, *Rebel War Clerk's Diary*, 2:144–45, 164; Miles Cary, "How Richmond Was Defended," *Confederate Veteran* 15, no. 2 (Dec. 1907): 557–58; *Richmond Sentinel*, Mar. 10, 1864; *Richmond Dispatch*, Sept. 16, 1894; *Mobile Advertiser & Register*, Mar. 10, 1864; *Richmond Daily Enquirer*, Mar. 4, 8, 1864. The Officers' Battalion would not see action against Dahlgren or Kilpatrick but provided moral support to the troops leaving for the intermediate works.

9. Adamson, "Old Brick House," 13–17. Green died in 1872.

10. Haw, "Armory Battalion at Green's Farm," 153–54; P. J. Davies, *C.S. Armory Richmond*, 123; "What Is the Truth of Dahlgren's Raid?," 75;

Crute, *Units of the Confederate States Army*, 349; *Richmond Whig*, Mar. 4, 1864; *Detroit Free Press*, Jan. 21, 1882; Custis Lee to James Seddon, Apr. 1, 1864, quoted in P. J. Davies, *C.S. Armory Richmond*, 199–200.

11. James Wood Memoir, Maud Wood Park Papers, LC, 10; letter, Mar. 11, 1864, in *New Jersey Herald*, Mar. 24, 1864; *Grand Rapids Daily Democrat*, Feb. 6, 1887; letter, Mar. 5, 1864, in *Rutland Daily Herald*, Mar. 18, 1864.

12. Wood Memoir, 10; *Richmond Whig*, Mar. 7, 1864; letter, Mar. 24, 1864, in *Maine Farmer*, Apr. 7, 1864; Harris, *Personal Reminiscences*, 76; Merrill, *Campaigns of the First Maine*, 181–82.

13. Letter, July 24, 1864, in *New York Herald*, Aug. 8, 1864. A Confederate reminiscence also claimed to have seen Dahlgren mounted and directing the attack. See Cary, "How Richmond Was Defended," 558.

14. *Grand Rapids Daily Democrat*, Feb. 6, 1887; Tobie, *First Maine Cavalry*, 237; Gilbert Chapman to dear friend, n.d., Gilbert W. Chapman Papers, Burton Historical Collection, Detroit Public Library; Haw, "Armory Battalion at Green's Farm," 153–54; *Rutland Daily Herald*, Mar. 18, 1864; Wood Memoir, 10; *National Tribune*, Dec. 3, 1885; letter, Mar. 24, 1864, in *Maine Farmer*, Apr. 7, 1864; Munford, "Cavalry Raid," 166: Cary, "How Richmond Was Defended," 559. By his own account, Harris found thirteen bullet holes in his overcoat and two in his slouch hat. Harris, *Personal Reminiscences*, 76–79.

15. Charles B. Kenny letter, Oct. 20, 1890, in *First Maine Bugle* 2, no. 2 (Oct. 1890): 54–58; John P. Sheahan to his father and mother, Mar. 30, 1864, John Sheahan Papers, Maine Historical Society; Tobie, *First Maine Cavalry*, 237–38.

16. Letter, Mar. 24, 1864, in *Maine Farmer*, Apr. 7, 1864; Harris, *Personal Reminiscences*, 76, 79; Tobie, *First Maine Cavalry*, 238.

17. Salmon Adams to Maj. F. F. Jones, Mar. 8, 1864, reproduced in P. J. Davies, *C.S. Armory Richmond*, 199.

18. Letter, Mar. 24, 1864, in *Maine Farmer*, Apr. 7, 1864; John B. Purcell Memoirs, [1910], Venter Personal Collection, transcript.

19. For a complete list of each company's departmental affiliation, see *Supplement*, pt. 2, 70:733–40.

20. *National Tribune*, Dec. 3, 1885; *Richmond Whig*, Mar. 3, 4, 1864; Purcell Memoirs; Chesnut, *Mary Chesnut's Civil War*, 580; William Joyner to his mother, Mar. 12, 1864, William H. Joyner Papers, Richmond National Battlefield Park Library; *Southern Punch*, Mar. 12, 1864; James, "Dahlgren's Raid," 67; Reagan, *Memoirs*, 180; article from *Richmond Times Dispatch*, Mar. 1, 1914, Folder 17, Box 31, CMR, LV. The members of Company G later became Richmond's leading bankers, merchants, and professional men after the war. McAnerney Memoir (1914), 1–6; *Richmond Dispatch*, Sept. 16, 1894. McAnerney commanded the battalion because Henley was sick. *Richmond Dispatch*, Mar. 4, 1864.

21. Cary, "How Richmond Was Defended," 558. Cary made some factual errors in his narrative, so it is questionable whether or not he actually encountered Dahlgren on March 1 at Hicks's farm.

22. McAnerney Memoir (ca. 1900); *Richmond Dispatch*, Sept. 16, 1894. After the battle with Dahlgren, McAnerney would be hosted at a banquet at Richmond's American Hotel and promoted to colonel by order of President Davis, who saluted him as the "Savior of Richmond." McAnerney would marry a Richmond woman in 1866 but later moved to New York City, where he became successful in banking and railroads, was treasurer of St. Patrick's Cathedral, and remained a prominent member of the "Friendly Sons of St. Patrick." He lived to be eighty-nine years old. R. K. Krick, *Lee's Colonels*, 211–12; *New York Times*, Mar. 23, 1928.

23. *Detroit Free Press*, Jan. 21, 1882; *Richmond Examiner*, Mar. 3, 1864; James, "Dahlgren's Raid," 66–67; William Joyner to his mother, Mar. 12, 1864, Joyner Papers; A. B. Carney to James Wood, July 29, 1908, Maud Wood Park Papers, LC; J. B. Jones, *Rebel War Clerk's Diary*, 2:163; McAnerney Memoir (1914), 1–6; Munford, "Cavalry Raid," 167; John W. Carter to Clement Sulivane, Mar. 5, 1864, Carter Family Papers, VHS; *Maine Farmer*, Apr. 7, 1864; Purcell Memoirs; *Richmond Dispatch*, Sept. 16, 1894.

24. *Detroit Free Press*, Jan. 21, 1882; *Richmond Examiner*, Mar. 3, 1864; *Richmond Times Dispatch*, Feb. 18, 1906; Haw, "Armory Battalion at Green's Farm," 452; Thomas C. Gray, "Thomas Gray's Experience on the Dahlgren Raid," *First Maine Bugle* 2, no. 2 (Oct. 1890): 58.

25. Purcell and Ward escorted their prisoner to Libby Prison, an episode that lived in Purcell's memory for over a half century. Purcell Memoirs; *Richmond Sentinel*, Mar. 3, 9, 1864; William Walter Cleary Diary, Mar. 2, 1864, VHS, microfilm; *Richmond Dispatch*, Mar. 3, 1864; *Richmond Daily Enquirer*, Mar. 3, 1864.

26. *Detroit Free Press*, Jan. 21, 1882; letter, Mar. 11, 1864, in *New Jersey Herald*, Mar. 24, 1864; Bartley Memoir, 10; *Richmond Daily Examiner*, Mar. 3, 7, 1864; J. Davis, *Rise and Fall of the Confederate Government*, 2:506; Harris, *Personal Reminiscences*, 76; *Richmond Sentinel*, Mar. 3, 1864, quoted in "War Time Story of Dahlgren's Raid," 201; Clement Sulivane, "Miles Cary Report Criticised," *Confederate Veteran* 16, no. 8 (Aug. 1908): 398.

27. James, "Dahlgren's Raid," 65–67; report, Mar. 5, 1864, Carter Family Papers, VHS; *Richmond Whig*, Mar. 3, 1864; *New Jersey Herald*, Mar. 24, 1864; Wood Memoir, 10; *National Tribune*, Dec. 3, 1885; Peter B. Law to his uncle, Mar. 8, 1864, Box 1, Correspondence: 1860–69, Holland Family Papers, Adelman Library, Univ. of Virginia; Nathan Webb Diary, Nathan Webb Papers, ALPL, transcript, 394; *Philadelphia Weekly Times*, Sept. 29, 1877, Apr. 3, 1880; McAnerny Memoir (1914); McAnerney Memoir (ca. 1900); John Anderson to Maj. Robert W. Hunter, June 9, 1905, Folder 21, Box 31, CMR; *Richmond Dispatch*, Sept. 16, 1894.

28. Sulivane, "Miles Cary Report Criticised," 398.
29. *Detroit Free Press*, Jan. 21, 1882; letter, Mar. 11, 1864, in *New Jersey Herald*, Mar. 24, 1864; Bartley Memoir, 10–11; *Richmond Daily Examiner*, Mar. 3, 7, 1864; J. Davis, *Rise and Fall of the Confederate Government*, 2:506; Harris, *Personal Reminiscences*, 76; *Richmond Sentinel*, Mar. 3, 1864, quoted in "War Time Story of Dahlgren's Raid," 201; Sulivane, "Miles Cary Report Criticised," 398. Kilpatrick would lump all his losses for the raid together, so we have no clear record of Dahlgren's battlefield losses. Dahlgren's signal officer thought the colonel had lost about forty men in killed and wounded. *Philadelphia Weekly Times*, Apr. 3, 1880. Jefferson Davis also recalled that "one three-inch Napoleon gun was captured," but no Federal reports, letters, or memoirs mention that Dahlgren had any artillery with him. If he had, it would seem likely that the colonel would have used a gun against the barricaded Confederates. See J. Davis, *Rise and Fall of the Confederate Government*, 2:506.
30. *Boston Globe*, June 5, 1904; *Grand Rapids Daily Democrat*, Feb. 6, 1887; *Boston Globe*, May 17, 1904, copy in Park Papers.
31. Redwood, "Following Stuart's Feather," 118; *Boston Globe*, May 17, [1910], in Park Papers. Wood would eventually make an escape from Libby Prison. See also Goldsborough, *Maryland Line*, 189.
32. *Grand Rapids Daily Democrat*, Feb. 6, 1887; *Philadelphia Weekly Times*, Sept. 29, 1877; *Richmond Sentinel*, Mar. 3, 1864, quoted in "War Time Story of Dahlgren's Raid," 202; letter, Mar. 5, 1864, in *Rutland Daily Herald*, Mar. 18, 1864; *Detroit Advertiser and Tribune*, Mar. 16, 1864; Merrill, *Campaigns of the First Maine*, 183; G. W. Beale, *Lieutenant of Cavalry in Lee's Army*, 138; letter, Mar. 11, 1864, in *New Jersey Herald*, Mar. 24, 1864.
33. J. A. Dahlgren, *Memoir of Ulric Dahlgren*, 217. Postwar sources vary as to whether the colonel turned left or right and vice versa for Mitchell. The fact remains that whatever way Dahlgren turned, the major took the opposite way. The two never reunited. *National Tribune*, Oct. 25, 1894; Foster, *New Jersey in the Rebellion*, 742. Samuel Harris claims that Mitchell's men took the left-hand road because it "was more in line of the rocket sent up by General Kilpatrick; also it would take us outside the breastworks." Harris, *Personal Reminiscences*, 80.
34. Snell, *History of Sussex and Warren Counties*, 99; *National Tribune*, Dec. 3, 1885; *Philadelphia Weekly Times*, Sept. 29, 1877.
35. *Philadelphia Weekly Times*, Sept. 29, 1877, Apr. 3, 1880; Bartley Memoir, 11; Snell, *History of Sussex and Warren Counties*, 99; Foster, *New Jersey in the Rebellion*, 742; J. W. Jones, "Kilpatrick-Dahlgren Raid," 539.
36. *Philadelphia Weekly Times*, Sept. 29, 1877, Apr. 3, 1880; *National Tribune*, Dec. 3, 1885; Clark, *Histories of the Several Regiments and Battalions from North Carolina*, 2:100; Ford, "Wade Hampton's Strategy," 282–83; Anderson, "Trains Running for the Confederacy," 210–11. Reuben Bartley put the arrival at Hanovertown Ferry at 7:00 A.M.

37. Merrill, *Campaigns of the First Maine*, 184; *Grand Rapids Daily Democrat*, Feb. 6, 1887; John Morey Diary, Mar. 2, 1864, John Morey Papers, BHL-UM; *Rutland Daily Herald*, Mar. 18, 1864; *Official Records*, 33:195.
38. Boudrye, *Fifth New York Cavalry*, 106–107; *National Tribune*, Dec. 3, 1885.

Chapter 12

1. Harris, *Personal Reminiscences*, 80–81; *Essex County Republican*, Apr. 27, 1899; John Morey Diary, Mar. 2, 1864, John Morey Papers, BHL-UM; letter, Mar. 24, 1864, in *Maine Farmer*, Apr. 7, 1864; Tobie, *First Maine Cavalry*, 240.
2. *National Tribune*, Apr. 6, 1894; Anson B. Carney, Pension File, NA; *Richmond Whig*, Mar. 2, 1864. Carney would survive the war and live to be ninety years old, dying in 1932.
3. *Rutland Daily Herald*, Mar. 18, 1864; *Official Records*, 33:196; newspaper narratives, n.d., London Family Papers, VHS; letter, Mar. 24, 1864, in *Maine Farmer*, Apr. 7, 1864; Tobie, *First Maine Cavalry*, 240; Snell, *History of Sussex and Warren Counties*, 100; *Grand Rapids Daily Democrat*, Feb. 6, 1887.
4. *Essex County Republican*, Apr. 27, 1899.
5. Capt. John Myrick thought that Captain Cole deserved credit for driving the Marylanders, writing, "Capt. Estes is a very gallant officer, and has laurels enough, but he had nothing to do with the affair, the honor of which belongs to Capt. Cole." Letter, Mar. 24, 1864, in *Maine Farmer*, Apr. 7, 1864.
6. *National Tribune*, Dec. 6, 1888; Cheney, *Ninth Regiment, New York Volunteer Cavalry*, 148; Moyer, *Seventeenth Regiment of Pennsylvania Cavalry*, 243–44; *Official Records*, 33:185–86, 193, 202; *Supplement*, pt. 1, 6:286–87, 289, pt. 2, 27:11; *Richmond Whig*, Mar. 5, 1864; *Richmond Daily Examiner*, Mar. 7, 1864; Ruffner, *Maryland's Blue & Gray*, 305–306; Tobie, *First Maine Cavalry*, 244; G. Crosby Diary, Mar. 2, 1864, Vermont Historical Society; William Hill Diary, Mar. 2, 1864, LC; *Rockland Gazette*, Mar. 26, 1864.
7. Ruffin, *Diary*, 3:364–65; *Richmond Whig*, Mar. 5, 1864; *Richmond Daily Examiner*, Mar. 5, 1864.
8. Dowdey, *Wartime Letters of R. E. Lee*, 677.
9. *Official Records*, 33:196–97; *Rutland Daily Herald*, Mar. 18, 1864; *Grand Rapids Daily Democrat*, Feb. 6, 1887; *Richmond Dispatch*, Mar. 7, 1864; R. C. Wallace, *A Few Memories*, 35; *National Tribune*, Apr. 6, 1894; letter, Mar. 24, 1864, in *Maine Farmer*, Apr. 7, 1864; Snell, *History of Sussex and Warren Counties*, 100; Morey Diary, Mar. 3, 1864; Peck, *Revised Roster of Vermont Volunteers*, 219. Peck's work identifies the 1st Vermont Cavalry's action on March 2, 1864, as occurring at "Piping Tree, Virginia," thus connecting the location of Mitchell's fight with a geographic location. Samuel Harris would end up in Libby

Prison. Harris, *Personal Reminiscences,* 82–83. Mitchell claims that he brought in 260 men. *Official Records,* 33:196.

10. Charles S. Kettlewell to unknown, n.d., in Driver, *First and Second Maryland Cavalry,* 73, 250.

11. *Grand Rapids Daily Democrat,* Feb. 6, 1887.

12. Davies Report; *Grand Rapids Daily Democrat,* Feb. 6, 1887. Even twenty years after the raid, Capt. H. A. Haire claimed that he had "never seen, nor could [he] gather while in the service, a detailed service account of Dahlgren's march from the point of our separation until he was ambuscaded." Ibid.

13. Athearn, "Civil War Diary of John Wilson Philips," 97–98; *American Tribune,* Nov. 23, 1888; letter, Mar. 7, 1864, in *Michigan Argus,* Mar. 18, 1864; letter, Mar. 9, 1864, in *Detroit Advertiser and Tribune,* Mar. 17, 1864; Crosby Diary, Mar. 3, 1864; *Richmond Whig,* Mar. 5, 1864; *Official Records,* 33:186; "History of the First Michigan Cavalry," Regimental File, Box 118, Michigan State Library and Archives.

14. *Corning Journal,* Mar. 24, 1864.

15. Hall, Besley, and Woods, *Sixth New York Cavalry,* 176; *Essex County Republican,* Apr. 27, 1899.

16. *Official Records,* 1:182, 33:198, 615, 618; Chase, "Service with Battery F, 1st Rhode Island," 118; Butler, *Private and Official Correspondence,* 3:487.

17. *Official Records,* 33:198–99.

18. Daniel C. Sheckler Diary, Mar. 2, 1864, HSP; Chase, "Service with Battery F, 1st Rhode Island," 118–19; Stearns, *Civil War Diary,* 37; Gillespie, *Company A, First Ohio Cavalry,* 199. Another account claims that West arrived at New Kent Court House at 7:30 A.M. If this is correct, he must have accompanied Spear's cavalry. See Regimental Historical Committee, *Eleventh Pennsylvania Volunteer Cavalry,* 103.

19. *Official Records,* 33:198–99.

20. Ibid., 182, 198–99; Gillespie, *Company A, First Ohio Cavalry,* 199; Chase, "Service with Battery F, 1st Rhode Island," 120–21; letter, Mar. 7, 1864, in *Michigan Argus,* Mar. 18, 1864; Cronin, "Vest Mansion," 143.

21. Moyer, *Seventeenth Regiment of Pennsylvania Cavalry,* 247; Connor, "Colored Troops," 78; Hill Diary, Mar. 2, 1864; *Essex County Republican,* Apr. 27, 1899; letter, Mar. 9, 1864, in *Detroit Advertiser and Tribune,* Mar. 17, 1864; letter, Mar. 7, 1864, in *Michigan Argus,* Mar. 18, 1864; *American Tribune,* Nov. 23, 1888.

22. Letter, Mar. 7, 1864, in *Michigan Argus,* Mar. 18, 1864. This Michigan sergeant was also intrigued with Slabtown, a settlement Butler had established near Yorktown for emancipated slaves. The neatly swept streets were laid out in a regular grid, with each one-story cabin measuring about twelve-by-eighteen feet. The cabins' floors and roofs were built with pine slabs, many were whitewashed and boasted neat fences around the perimeters. Slabtown had its own stores, post office, schools, and a church. There were some 2,000 to 3,000 blacks living

there, the Wolverine cavalryman describing these inhabitants as rang-
ing from "the darkest ethiops to the fairest octoroons." The former
slaves now worked for the U.S. government in several trade-type jobs
or dragging oysters. It seems that Butler had worked hard to provide a
stable and productive environment for his contrabands.

23. "Reminiscences of My Army Life," Mar. 15, 1878, Edward H. Harvey Papers, WL; Crosby Diary, Mar. 4, 1864; *Washington Daily Morning Chronicle*, Mar. 7, 1864; Tobie, *First Maine Cavalry*, 244; Moyer,
Seventeenth Regiment of Pennsylvania Cavalry, 249; Hall, Besley,
and Woods, *Sixth New York Cavalry*, 176–77; letter, Mar. 5, 1864, in
Rutland Daily Herald, Mar. 18, 1864; Merrill, *Campaigns of the First
Maine*, 185.

24. *Official Records*, 33:182.

25. Ibid., 182–83.

26. Ibid., 182, 240–47; Crosby Diary, Mar. 10, 1864; Victor Comte ot Elise
(wife), Mar. 19, 1864, Comte Papers; *Richmond Daily Examiner*, Mar.
16, 1864; R. L. T. Beale, *Ninth Virginia Cavalry*, 112–15.

27. Chowning, *Soldiers at the Doorstep*, 43–47. In 2015 the Courthouse
Tavern still stands.

28. *New York Times*, May 1, 1864.

29. *Corning Journal*, Mar. 24, 1864; *Supplement*, pt. 1, 6:288; Moyer, *Seventeenth Regiment of Pennsylvania Cavalry*, 249; Benedict, *Vermont
in the Civil War*, 2:631.

Chapter 13

1. *Philadelphia Weekly Times*, Sept. 29, 1877; *National Tribune*, Dec. 3,
1885. Lieutenant Bartley puts the time at 7:00 A.M. when they arrived at
the Pamunkey River. Reuben Bartley Memoir, Reuben Bartley Papers,
VHS, 11–12.

2. Fleet, *Green Mount*, 310–12; *Philadelphia Weekly Times*, Apr. 3, 1880,
Sept. 17, 1887; *Richmond Sentinel*, Mar. 5, 1864; Bartley Memoir, 12.

3. Munford, "Cavalry Raid," 168; *Philadelphia Weekly Times*, Sept. 17,
1887; J. W. Jones, "Kilpatrick-Dahlgren Raid," 539; letter, July 24, 1864,
in *New York Times*, Aug. 8, 1864; Barley Memoir, 12–13.

4. "Dahlgren's Famous Raid," George Clarke Papers, VHS, typescript,
4–5; Kaplan, *Land and Heritage*, 85.

5. Bagby, *King and Queen County*, 134; Bartley Memoir, 13–14.

6. *Bulletin of the King and Queen County Historical Society* 66 (Jan.
1989).

7. *Philadelphia Weekly Times*, Sept. 17, 1887, Apr. 3, 1880; *Official
Records*, 33:205, 208; Crouch, "Dahlgren Raid," 182–86; "Dahlgren's
Famous Raid," Clarke Papers, 5–7; *Southside Sentinel*, Feb. 12, 1909,
Box 33, RG 46, CMR, LV; Weaver, *Virginia Home Guards*, 66; *King
and Queen County Historical Society Bulletin* 27 (July 1969). Pollard's
attack was near Norwood, the home of Samuel P. Ryland, a prominent
citizen of King and Queen County. The corporal had a two-dollar bill in
his pocket with "50" pasted over it, perhaps to deceive an unsuspecting

Southerner if he had had a chance to use it. By 1864 Bagby had served the Bruington congregation for twenty-two years.

8. *Philadelphia Weekly Times*, Sept. 29, 1877, Apr. 3, 1880; Munford, "Cavalry Raid," 169; *National Tribune*, Dec. 3, 1885.

9. *New York Times*, May 1, 1864; *Philadelphia Weekly Times*, Sept. 17, 1887; *Southside Sentinel*, Feb. 12, 1909. One account puts the Confederate force at 153 men. See "Dahlgren's Famous Raid," Clarke Papers, 6–7. Another claims that it was 167 strong, including fourteen "school boys." See Bagby, *King and Queen County*, 136. Dr. Bernard H. Walker and William F. Harrison were the Southerners spying on the raiders at Garnett's Creek.

10. *Philadelphia Weekly Times*, Sept. 29, 1877; *National Tribune*, Aug. 14, 1884; Bagby, *King and Queen County*, 135; *New York Times*, May 1, 1864; *Philadelphia Weekly Times*, Sept. 17, 1887; *Southside Sentinel*, Feb. 12, 1909.

11. *Official Records*, 33:209; *Philadelphia Weekly Times*, Sept. 29, 1877, Apr. 3, 1880; *National Tribune*, Aug. 14, 1884, Dec. 3, 1885; Bagby, *King and Queen County*, 135; Crouch, "Dahlgren Raid," 182; J. W. Jones, "Kilpatrick-Dahlgren Raid," 549; "Dahlgren's Famous Raid," Clarke Papers, 7; *Southside Sentinel*, Feb. 12, 1909; Tobie, *First Maine Cavalry*, 239; Munford, "Cavalry Raid," 169.

12. Tobie, *First Maine Cavalry*, 239; *Richmond Daily Examiner*, Mar. 7, 1864; *Richmond Whig*, Mar. 8, 1864; *National Tribune*, Dec. 3, 1885; *Official Records*, 33:206; *Philadelphia Weekly Times*, Apr. 3, 1880; *New York Times*, May 1, 1864; Bartley Memoir, 14–15; *Grand Army Review* (Dec. 1885); *Richmond Daily Dispatch*, Mar. 21, 1864; J. W. Jones, "Kilpatrick-Dahlgren Raid," 539. Another account claimed that Dahlgren was hit three times, all in the back—two rounds entered his heart and one his right lung. Dr. Watson Walker to the editor, *Richmond Times Dispatch*, Apr. 11, 1909. Still another chronicler claimed that the colonel could have been killed "by his own men." This is a possibility considering the darkness and fatigue of the remaining raiders but somewhat unlikely based on the number of Southerners prepared to fire on the Union column. See Pollard, *Lost Cause*, 502. An incredulous postwar story written by an officer who was not present claimed that Dahlgren was only wounded in the attack, and when a Rebel attempted to pull off his boots, the colonel "with insult, took off the wooden leg and struck the rebel over the head with it, who then completed the murder." W. L. Curry, *Four Years in the Saddle*, 244. The site of the ambush has been known as "Dahlgren's Corner" since at least 1918. See G. W. Beale, *Lieutenant of Cavalry in Lee's Army*, 139.

13. *Philadelphia Weekly Times*, Apr. 3, 1880; *National Tribune*, Dec. 3, 1885, Oct. 25, Dec. 3, 1894; *Official Records*, 33:208–209; *New York Times*, May 1, 1864; Bagby, *King and Queen County*, 135.

14. *Philadelphia Weekly Times*, Apr. 3, 1889; *National Tribune*, Dec. 3, 1885; Tobie, *First Maine Cavalry*, 239; Bagby, *King and Queen County*, 136; Munford, "Cavalry Raid," 169.

NOTES TO PAGES 236–41

15. *National Tribune*, Dec. 3, 1885; Munford, "Cavalry Raid," 169; *Philadelphia Weekly Times*, Apr. 3, 1880; J. W. Brown, *Signal Corps*, 381; Bartley Memoir, 15; *Supplement*, pt. 1, 10:566. Judson McKnight to James Wood, June 9, 1895, Maud Wood Park Papers, LC.
16. *Philadelphia Weekly Times*, Apr. 3, 1889; *National Tribune*, Dec. 3, 1885; Tobie, *First Maine Cavalry*, 239; Bagby, *King and Queen County*, 136; Munford, "Cavalry Raid," 169; *New York Times*, May 1, 1864.
17. Bartley Memoir, 15–16; Kaplan, *Land and Heritage*, 139–40; *New York Times*, Mar. 9, 1864; "Dahlgren's Famous Raid," Clarke Papers, 7–9; Bagby, *King and Queen County*, 136; Cox and Weathers, *Old Houses of King and Queen County*, 159; *Philadelphia Weekly Times*, Apr. 3, 1880. The overseer's cabin is no longer standing.
18. Union lieutenant Henry A. D. Merritt later claimed that Lt. Robert Benjamin Hart of the "7th Va Cav" was the culprit who cut off Dahlgren's finger to get the ring, but this identification is doubtful. *National Tribune*, Dec. 3, 1885. Hart actually served in the 5th Virginia Cavalry and was a native of King and Queen County. See Driver, *5th Virginia Cavalry*, 215. Later evidence proved that it was Cornelius Martin of Company H, 9th Virginia Cavalry, who cut the ring off. See Stuart, "Colonel Ulric Dahlgren," 169; *Richmond Daily Dispatch*, Mar. 21, 1864; *Southside Sentinel*, Feb. 12, 1909; *National Tribune*, Aug. 14, 1884; Bagby, *King and Queen County*, 135; "What Is the Truth of Dahlgren's Raid?," 79; and *Philadelphia Weekly Times*, Oct. 27, 1877.
19. Crouch, "Dahlgren Raid," 187–90; J. W. Jones, "Kilpatrick-Dahlgren Raid," 547–48; Weaver, *Virginia Home Guards*, 71; *New York Herald*, Aug. 8, 1864.
20. Hall, "Dahlgren Papers," 35.
21. U.S. Navy Department, *Official Records of the Union and Confederate Navies*, ser. 1, 9:540–42; Kaplan, *Land and Heritage*, 139–40; *Richmond Whig*, Mar. 7, 1864.
22. Munford, "Cavalry Raid," 169; *Richmond Dispatch*, Mar. 7, 1864; *Richmond Daily Examiner*, Mar. 7, 1864; *Southside Sentinel*, Feb. 12, 1909; Bruce Dunstan to Editor, *Richmond Times Dispatch*, July 25, 1955, VHS; A. F. Bagby to John W. Daniel, n.d., Box 24, John W. Daniel and the Daniel Family Papers, Adelman Library, Univ. of Virginia; *National Tribune*, Dec. 3, 1885; *Richmond Daily Dispatch*, Mar. 21, 1864; *National Tribune*, Aug. 14, 1884.
23. Stuart, "Colonel Ulric Dahlgren," 152–204; *Richmond Whig*, Mar. 8, 1864; Munford, "Cavalry Raid," 169; *Richmond Dispatch*, Mar. 7, 1864; *Richmond Daily Examiner*, Mar. 7, 1864; *Southside Sentinel*, Feb. 12, 1909; *Richmond Times Dispatch*, Nov. 17, 1901; John A. Dahlgren to Benjamin Butler, Mar. 10 and 15, 1864, Box 25, Butler Papers, LC; *Official Records*, 33:180–81; *Philadelphia Inquirer*, Nov. 2, 1865.

Chapter 14

1. Tobie, *First Maine Cavalry*, 244; Gillespie, *Company A, First Ohio Cavalry*, 202; Moyer, *Seventeenth Regiment of Pennsylvania Cavalry*, 249, 251–58.

2. *Official Records*, 33:219–21.
3. Hall, "Dahlgren Papers," 33.
4. *Official Records*, 33:207, 218–21; F. Lee, "Death of Colonel Dahlgren," 256–57.
5. *Official Records*, 33:218–21; ibid., ser. 2, 6:1017; "Case of Ulric Dahlgren," File D-167 (VS) 1863, Entry 496, Box 207, RG 94, NA; *National Unionist*, June 10, 1864. The Dahlgren papers were printed in both English and French.
6. *Official Records*, ser. 2, 8:344; Grimsley, *Hard Hand of War*, 219. For a conceptual discussion of Confederate reaction to the North's proclivities, see ibid., 205–25.
7. Dowdey, *Wartime Letters of R. E. Lee*, 670; B. F. Foley, "Prisoners Taken in Dahlgren's Raid," *Confederate Veteran* 16, no. 6 (June 1908): 280.
8. *Official Records*, 33:222–24. Maj. Albert H. Campbell, C.S.A. Engineers, was in charge of the Department of Virginia's Topographical Department and verified in a letter dated March 7, 1874, that he had made fifty copies of Dahlgren's papers. J. W. Jones, "Kilpatrick-Dahlgren Raid," 558; Hall, "Dahlgren Papers," 36. Varina Davis later claimed that Lee would have sent Meade the originals if there was any question regarding the authenticity of the photographic copies, but the general's letter to Meade never mentions this overture. *Official Records*, 33:178; V. Davis, *Jefferson Davis, Ex-President*, 471–72.
9. *Official Records*, 33:176–80, 197; Chesnut, *Mary Chesnut's Civil War*, 586. It is not unusual that Kilpatrick's officers, those who were with Mitchell and made it back, denied seeing the orders. Dahlgren's signal officer, Lt. Reuben Bartley, who was captured and went to Libby Prison, later confirmed that he "never saw the papers nor even a copy of them as they were carefully kept from us." Reuben Bartley Memoir, Reuben Bartley Papers, VHS, 32. But as one modern commentator has concluded, "Few friends of the South doubted it [the intent to kill Davis and burn Richmond] and many were certain that the already much-hated president of the United States was himself responsible." Hanchett, *Lincoln Murder Conspiracies*, 34.
10. Heros Von Borcke, "The Death of Colonel Dahlgreen [*sic*]," *The Historical Magazine . . .* 6, no. 6 (Dec. 1869), 361; F. Lee, "Death of Colonel Dahlgren," 257.
11. Gorgas, *Civil War Diary*, 89 (Apr. 1, 1864).
12. Wells, *Hampton and His Cavalry in '64*, 121–22. Hampton did not tag Kilpatrick with the dirty deed. He was no fan of Little Kil, based on the personal interaction they had near Bennett's Place shortly before Gen. Joseph Johnston surrendered to Sherman in April 1865. But instead of indicting the leader of the raid, Hampton placed blame on Dahlgren for the scheme to kill Davis. For a description of the nasty encounter between the two cavalry generals, see Cisco, *Wade Hampton*, 160.
13. Wood's answers to Charles Bunker Dahlgren's questionnaire were written in an arcane shorthand style called Pittman, which in some ways makes it all the more mysterious. C. B. Dahlgren to James Wood, Apr. 12, 1894, Maud Wood Papers, LC.

14. *Richmond Whig*, Mar. 7, 1864; *Richmond Enquirer*, Mar. 8, 1864; *Grand Rapids Daily Democrat*, Feb. 6, 1887; *National Tribune*, Nov. 15, 1888.

15. Lyman, *Meade's Army*, 123–24.

16. Patrick, *Inside Lincoln's Army*, 347.

17. Meade, *Life and Letters*, 2:190–91.

18. Taylor, *Lee's Adjutant*, 152–53.

19. Tidwell et al., *Come Retribution*, 236–38, 246; *New York World*, Mar. 8, 1864. The author has personally queried Lincoln scholars Michael Burlingame, Gerald Perrot, and James McPherson, all three of whom believe that Lincoln had no part in an assassination order. See also Sears, "Dahlgren Papers Revisited," 63–85. A Richmond editorial condemned the papers by stating, "these orders were for war under the Black Flag." *Richmond Whig*, Mar. 7, 1864.

Chapter 15

1. Trout, *With Pen and Saber*, 231; Myers, *The Comanches*, 253.

2. *Official Records*, 33:182; Tobie, *First Maine Cavalry*, 244; Gillespie, *Company A, First Ohio Cavalry*, 202; Moyer, *Seventeenth Regiment of Pennsylvania Cavalry*, 249, 251–58; Baily, "Civil War," 33; R. C. Wallace, *A Few Memories*, 36; G. Crosby Diary, Mar. 18, 1864, Vermont Historical Society; letter, Mar. 19, 1864, in *Vermont Journal*, Mar. 26, 1864; Charles F. Dam Papers, Maine Historical Society; George W. Bartlett to Governor Samuel Cony, Mar. 14, 1864, Folder 17, Maine Adjutant General Correspondence, Maine State Library; J. C. Smith Papers, LC. Another tabulation puts the losses at 335 men. *Official Records*, 33:174.

3. *Official Records*, 33:182, 186–87; *Alexandria Gazette*, Mar. 11, 1864; Ebenezer Gould to his wife, Mar. 16, 1864, Ebenezer Gould Papers, CHL; Charles Blinn Diary, Mar. 4, 1864, BHL-UV.

4. John Beazell to "My own little Pet"(wife), Mar. 30, 1864, John S. Beazell Papers, Venter Private Collection, transcripts provided by Tony Klingensmith; telegram, Mar. 5, 1864, Telegrams Sent to the War Department, RG 393, NA; *Alexandria Gazette*, Mar. 14, 1864; *Sussex Register*, Mar. 18, 1864.

5. Allyn Litchfield, Pension File, NA; Isham, *Seventh Regiment of Michigan Volunteer Cavalry*, 38–39. The other officers in the confined space were Maj. Edwin Cooke, Lt. Henry Merritt, Lt. Reuben Bartley, Capt. John A. Clarke, and Asst. Surgeon Samuel Kingston. *Old Dominion Daily*, Mar. 12, 1864. The four black soldiers were Pvt. James W. Corn, Co. C, 5th USCT; Pvt. P. F. Lewis, Co. I, 5th USCT; and Pvts. R. P. Armistead and John Thomas, Co. H, 6th USCT. Litchfield probably suffered from post-traumatic stress disorder. See chapter 10.

6. Hunt and Brown, *Brevet Brigadier Generals in Blue*, 127; Foster, *New Jersey in the Rebellion*, 744–45.

7. *Official Records*, ser. 2, 6:1025, 1034, 975; *Richmond Whig*, Mar. 8, 1864; Reuben Bartley Memoir, Reuben Bartley Papers, VHS, 30–33. See

also *Official Records*, ser. 2, 7:566. Brig. Gen. Neal Dow eventually would be exchanged for Rooney Lee, who had been wounded during the Battle of Brandy Station. Lee was recuperating at his home, White House, when he was captured by Union cavalry under Col. Samuel Spear in late June 1863. *Official Records*, 27(2):794.

8. *Detroit Free Press*, Mar. 25, 1865; Bartley Memoir, 30–33.

9. Ruffin, *Diary*, 3:363, 366; Reagan, *Memoirs*, 182.

10. Stuart, "Colonel Ulric Dahlgren," 152–204; Wittenberg, *Like a Meteor Blazing Brightly*, 215–16.

11. *Richmond Dispatch*, Mar. 7, 1864; Atkinson, "Col. Ulric Dahlgren," 351; Harry Moore to A. W. Smith, July 4, 1864, Box 16, Staff Officers Papers, RG 94, NA; *Richmond Times Dispatch*, Mar. 21, 1909; J. A. Dahlgren, *Memoir of Ulric Dahlgren*, 274–75.

12. *Official Records*, 46(3):712.

13. Harry Moore to A. W. Smith, July 4, 1864, Box 16, Staff Officers Papers, RG 94, NA.

14. Ibid.

15. Bagby, *King and Queen County*, 135; "What Is the Truth of Dahlgren's Raid?," 79; *Philadelphia Weekly Times*, Oct. 27, 1877.

16. Harry Moore to A. W. Smith, July 4, 1864, Box 16, Staff Officers Papers, RG 94, NA.

17. Ibid.

18. Ibid.

19. Ibid.; Weaver, *Virginia Home Guards*, 66. Not mentioned in official government documents is the whereabouts of Dahlgren's sash and gauntlets. Historical artist Don Troiani has the sash and one gauntlet in his collection. He believes that the other glove is still held by a Dahlgren family member. Don Troiani, e-mail message to the author, Jan. 2, 2013.

20. "What Is the Truth of Dahlgren's Raid?," 79; Scrapbook, Box 1, Madeleine Vinton Dahlgren Papers, Special Collections, Georgetown University, 9.

21. *New York World*, n.d., quoted in *Richmond Enquirer*, Mar. 15, 1864; *Richmond Daily Examiner*, Mar. 14, 1864; *New York Herald*, n.d., quoted in *Richmond Daily Examiner*, Mar. 14, 1864; *Frank Leslie's Illustrated Weekly*, Mar. 26, 1864; McEntee to Sharp, Mar. 4, 1864, Box 11, Miscellaneous Letters, Reports, RG 393, NA.

22. *Grand Rapids Daily Democrat*, Feb. 6, 1887; Davies Report.

23. R. C. Wallace, *A Few Memories*, 36; *Detroit Free Press*, Mar. 26, 1864.

24. *New York World*, Mar. 3, 1864; *Baltimore Sun*, n.d., as reported in *Alexandria Gazette*, Mar. 5, 1864; *New York Herald*, n.d., quoted in *Richmond Sentinel*, Mar. 12, 1864; Wainwright, *Diary of Battle*, 325. Ironically, the raid's secrecy may have been maintained better at the cabinet level than anywhere else. Secretary of the Navy Gideon Welles recorded in his diary that he only heard of the operation "spoken of indefinitely and vaguely, but with no certainty till the expedition had started." Apparently, the War Department in Washington was keener

to such matters than the commander in the field. Welles, *Diary*, 3:536, 538.

25. William Wells to "Friend Anna," Mar. 25, 1864, Wells Papers; Ebenezer Gould to his wife, Mar. 20, 1864, Gould Papers; Rhea, *To the North Anna River*, 37, 40–31.

26. *Official Records*, 33:1157–59, 1216, 1247–49; Crute, *Units of the Confederate States Army*, 361–70; J. O. Moore, "Custer's Raid into Albemarle County," 149; J. B. Jones, *Rebel War Clerk's Diary*, 2:162–63; *Alexandria Gazette*, Mar. 5, 1864.

27. *Army Navy Journal*, Mar. 12, 1864; *National Tribune*, May 31, 1894.

28. Letter, July 24, 1864, in *New York Herald*, Aug. 8, 1864; *National Tribune*, May 31, 1894.

29. Letter, July 24, 1864, in *New York Herald*, Aug. 8, 1864; *New York Times*, Mar. 9, 1864; Munford, "Cavalry Raid," 169–70; newspaper clipping, Scrapbook, Madeleine Vinton Dahlgren Papers, 79.

30. W.C.M. to "Mr. Editor," Mar. 7, 1864, 5th New York Cavalry File, New York State Military Museum; *Official Records*, 33:199–200.

31. Kidd, *Riding with Custer*, 246.

32. See Venter, "General Judson Kilpatrick."

33. Letter, Mar. 19, 1864, in *Vermont Journal*, Mar. 26, 1864.

Chapter 16

1. Hall, "Dahlgren Papers," 30–39; Sears, "Dahlgren Papers Revisited," 63–85; V. Jones, *Eight Hours before Richmond*, 174; Wittenberg, *Like a Meteor Blazing Brightly*, 247.

2. Swigget, *Rebel Raider*, 213–16; Schultz, *Dahlgren Affair*, 239–57; McPherson, "Failed Richmond Raid," 130, 133; *Sussex Register*, Mar. 18, 1864; *National Unionist*, June 10, 1864.

3. John S. Mosby to Major Stiles, Jan. 13, 1871, John S. Mosby Papers, VHS; note by Babcock, n.d., John C. Babcock Papers, LC.

4. Untitled Diary, n.d., MSS: 1 UN 3: 12, VHS.

5. A recent biographer of Wade Hampton comes to the conclusion that "Dahlgren had apparently ordered his men not only to open the prisons, but also to assassinate President Davis and his cabinet and 'burn the hateful city.'" Andrew, *Wade Hampton*, 185.

6. See the appendix for a transcription of the Dahlgren papers.

7. *Official Records*, 33:219–21.

8. Hall, "Dahlgren Papers," 38–39; Ulric Dahlgren to his father, Feb. 26, 1864, John A. Dahlgren Papers, LC; Riggs, "Dahlgren Papers Reconsidered," 658–66.

9. Stuart, "Colonel Ulric Dahlgren," 35. The younger Fish noted, "I have a vague memory of finding among my father's papers the story that the orders were sent to Kilpatrick by a member of Lincoln's cabinet without Meade's knowledge." Stewart, "Colonel Ulric Dahlgren," 35. It would seem a logical conclusion that the cabinet member was Edwin Stanton, but Fish is silent on the name.

10. Cabell, "Woman Saved Richmond City," 356. Cabell's article must have been so good that it warranted republication in its entirety. See

Cabell, "How a Woman Helped to Save Richmond," *Confederate Veteran* 31, no. 1 (Jan. 1923): 177–78.

11. Lyman, *Meade's Headquarters*, 79.

12. F. Lee, "Death of Colonel Dahlgren," 257.

13. *Burlington Free Press*, Mar. 9, 1864; *New York World*, Mar. 11, 1864; *Essex County Republican*, Apr. 27, 1899; *Richmond Times Dispatch*, June 17, 1906; Lyman, *Meade's Army*, 104–105. Lyman probably meant "members of the cabinet" when he wrote "M.C.'s" It was Jeb Stuart's immediate opinion that Lincoln was to blame, but he provided no concrete evidence. In a letter dated March 7, 1864, Stuart wrote, "There is every reason to believe that the expedition was planned under the immediate direction of President Lincoln, himself." J. E. B. Stuart Papers, VHS.

14. *Springfield Weekly Republican*, Mar. 19, 1864; *Richmond Whig*, Mar. 10, 1864.

Appendix

1. *Official Records*, 33:219–21.

2. These instructions were given to Capt. John F. B. Mitchell, 2nd New York Cavalry, who was to lead a separate detachment along the north bank of the James in Goochland County after Dahlgren crossed the river.

3. The memorandum book was held by Colonel Beale, 9th Virginia Cavalry, until the end of March, when it was brought to Richmond and printed in the newspaper.

Bibliography

Manuscript Sources

Adelman Library, University of Virginia, Charlottesville
    John W. Daniel and the Daniel Family Papers
    Holland Family Papers
Abraham Lincoln Presidential Library, Springfield, Ill.
    Nathan Webb Diary (transcript), Nathan Webb Papers
Albany Institute of History and Art Library, Albany, N.Y.
    Philip Neher Papers
Babcock Library, Ashford, Conn.
    Edward W. Whitaker Civil War Letters (typescript)
Bentley Historical Library, University of Michigan, Ann Arbor
    Victor Comte Papers
    G. Corselius Papers
    Douglas-Nellis Papers
    Frank Gross Diary
    John Morey Papers
    William H. O'Brien Family Papers
Bailey/Howe Library, University of Vermont, Burlington
    Charles Blinn Diary
    William Wells Papers
Burton Historical Collection, Detroit Public Library, Mich.
    Gilbert W. Chapman Papers
Clarke Historical Library, Central Michigan University, Mount Pleasant
    Ebenezer Gould Papers
Clements Library, University of Michigan, Ann Arbor
    Russell A. Alger Papers
Duke University, Durham, N.C.
    George G. Meade, Jr., Papers
    Mary Mills Papers
Fredericksburg-Spotsylvania National Military Park Library, Va.
    Daniel Isaac Underhill Letters (transcript)
Gettysburg National Military Park Library, Pa.
    Luther Trowbridge Letters
Historical Society of Pennsylvania, Harrisburg
    James Biddle Papers
    Daniel C. Sheckler Diary, James S. Schoff Collection
Indiana State Library, Indianapolis
    F. J. Bellamy Papers
Library of Congress, Washington, D.C.
    John C. Babcock Papers

Benjamin F. Butler Papers
John A. Dahlgren Papers
William Hill Diary
Frank A. Moran Collection (notes written by Reuben Bartley)
Maud Wood Park Papers
Martin Quiatt Diary
J. C. Smith Papers
Library of Virginia, Richmond
Auditor of Public Accounts Personal Property Tax Books, Goochland
County, 1860–63
Confederate Military Records
Goochland County Free and Slave Records, 1726–1867
1860 Special Census, Slave Schedules
Maine Historical Society, Portland
Charles F. Dam Papers
Charles F. Gardiner Papers
John Sheahan Papers
Maine State Library, Augusta
Maine Adjutant General Correspondence
Massachusetts Historical Society, Boston
Lyman Family Papers, Theodore Lyman Private Note Book (microfilm)
Michigan State Library and Archives, East Lansing
Regimental Files, First Michigan Cavalry
National Archives, Washington, D.C.
Record Group 15, Records of the Veterans Administration
Pension Records
Record Group 94, Records of the Adjutant General's Office,
1780s–1917
Compiled Service Records
Office of the Adjutant General, Letter Book, 2nd New York
Cavalry
Office of the Adjutant General, Staff Officers Papers
U.S. Army Generals' Reports of Civil War Service, 1864–87,
Microcopy M1098
Record Group 107, Records of the Office of the Secretary of War
Provost Marshal's File
Telegrams Collected by the Secretary of War
Telegrams Sent to the War Department
Record Group 393, Records of U.S. Army Continental Commands,
1821–1920
Miscellaneous Letters, Reports
New York State Military Museum, Saratoga Springs
5th New York Cavalry File
Richmond National Battlefield Park Library, Va.
William H. Joyner Papers (copy, original in Southern Historical
Collection, University of North Carolina, Chapel Hill)
John McAnerney Memoir, February 23, 1914 (transcript/copy, original

in Museum of the Confederacy Library, Richmond)
 Col. John McAnerney Memoir, ca. 1900, (transcript/copy)
John D. Rockefeller, Jr., Library, Colonial Williamsburg Foundation, Va.
 Daniel Edward Cronin, "The Vest Mansion: Its Historical and
 Romantic Associations as Confederate and Union Headquarters (1862–
 1865) in the American Civil War," 1908–1910 (typescript). Original in
 Collection of the New-York Historical Society, New York City.
Southern Historical Collection, University of North Carolina, Chapel Hill
 William Baker Papers
Special Collections, Georgetown University, Washington, D.C.
 Madeleine Vinton Dahlgren Papers
Special Collections, U.S. Military Academy Library, West Point, N.Y.
 Eugene Beaumont Letter Book
Special Collections, University of California, Santa Barbara
 Harry Clay Potter, *Memoirs of the Civil War* (n. p., 196[?])
U.S. Army Heritage and Education Center, Military History Institute,
 Carlisle Barracks, Pa.
 William H. Martin Papers, Harrisburg Civil War Round Table
 Collection
 John W. Stott Diary, Civil War Times Illustrated Collection
Bruce M. Venter Private Collection, Goochland, Va.
 John W. Beazell Papers (transcript)
 John B. Purcell Memoirs (transcript)
Vermont Historical Society, Burlington
 G. Crosby Diary
Virginia Historical Society, Richmond
 Reuben Bartley Papers
 Carter Family Papers
 George Clarke Papers
 William Walter Cleary Diary (microfilm)
 Bruce Dunsten Letter
 Anne Jennings Wise Hobson Papers (diary transcript)
 London Family Papers
 John McAnerney Papers
 John Mosby Letter
 J. E. B. Stuart Papers
 Untitled Diary
 Walters Papers
Waldo Library, Western Michigan University, Kalamazoo
 Albert H. Fisher Papers
 Joseph H. Gillet Papers
 Edward H. Harvey Papers

Primary Sources

Anderson, C. S. "Trains Running for the Confederacy." *Hanover County
 Historical Society Bulletin* 33 (November 1985).

Apperson, John Samuel. *Repairing the "March of Mars": The Civil War Diaries of John Samuel Apperson, Hospital Steward in the Stonewall Brigade, 1861–1865.* Edited by John Herbert Roper. Macon, Ga.: Mercer University Press, 2001.

Athearn, Robert G., ed. "The Civil War Diary of John Wilson Philips." *Virginia Magazine of History and Biography* 62, no. 1 (January 1954).

Atkinson, John Wilder. "Col. Ulric Dahlgren, the Defeated Raider." *Southern Historical Society Papers* 37 (1909).

Averell, William Woods. *Ten Years in the Saddle: The Memoir of William Woods Averell, 1851–1862.* Edited by Edward K. Eckert and Nicolas J. Amato. San Rafael, Calif.: Presidio, 1978.

Baily, Chuck, Jr. "Civil War: The 18th Pennsylvania Cavalry Rides Again!" Unpublished paper, n.d. Greene County Historical Society, Waynesburg, Pa.

Beale, G. W. *A Lieutenant of Cavalry in Lee's Army.* Reprint. Baltimore: Butternut and Blue, 1994.

Beale, R. L. T. *History of the Ninth Virginia Cavalry in the War between the States.* Richmond: B. F. Johnson, 1899.

Beaudry, Louis N. *Wartime Journal of Louis N. Beaudry, Fifth New York Cavalry: The Diary of a Union Chaplain, Commencing February 16, 1863.* Edited by Richard E. Beaudry. Jefferson, N.C.: McFarland, 1996.

Beaumont, Eugene. "A Monument to General H. J. Kilpatrick." Wilkes-Barre, Pa.: n.p., 1897.

Boudrye, Louis. *Historic Records of the Fifth New York Cavalry.* Albany, N.Y.: J. Munsell, 1868.

Brooks, U. R. *Butler and His Cavalry in the War of Secession 1861–1865.* Reprint. Germantown, Tenn.: Guild Bindery, 1994.

Burgwyn, William H. S. *A Captain's War: The Letters and Diaries of William H. S. Burgwyn.* Edited by Herbert M. Schiller. Shippensburg, Pa.: White Mane, 1994.

Bush, B. Conrad, comp. *Articles from Wyoming County Newspapers and Letters from Soldiers of 5th New York Cavalry.* N.p., n.d.

Butler, Benjamin F. *Autobiography and Personal Reminiscences: Butler's Book.* Boston: A. M. Thayer, 1892.

———. *Private and Official Correspondence of Gen. Benjamin F. Butler during the Period of the Civil War.* Norwood, Mass.: Plimpton, 1917.

Cavada, F. F. *Libby Life: Experiences of a Prisoner in Richmond, Va., 1863–64.* Philadelphia: J. B. Lippincott, 1865.

Chase, Philip. "Service with Battery F, 1st Rhode Island Light Artillery." *Military Order of the Loyal Legion Rhode Island Commandery,* vol. 6. Reprint. Wendell, N.C.: Broadfoot, 1992.

Cheney, Newel. *History of the Ninth Regiment, New York Volunteer Cavalry, War of 1861 to 1865.* Jamestown, N.Y.: Martin Merz & Son, 1901.

Chesnut, Mary Boykin. *Mary Chesnut's Civil War.* Edited by C. Vann Woodward. New Haven, Conn.: Yale University Press, 1981.

Clark, Walter, ed. *Histories of the Several Regiments and Battalions from North Carolina.* 5 vols. Reprint. Wendell, N.C.: Broadfoot, 1982.

Connor, Selden. "The Colored Troops." *MOLLUS, Maine Commandery,* vol. 3. Wilmington, N.C.: Broadfoot, 1992.

Cox, Jacob D. *Military Reminiscences of the Civil War.* 2 vols. New York: Charles Scribner's Sons, 1900.

Crouch, Richard G. "The Dahlgren Raid." *Southern Historical Society Papers* 34 (1906).

Curry, W. L., comp. *Four Years in the Saddle: History of the First Regiment Ohio Volunteer Cavalry.* Reprint. Jonesboro, Ga.: Freedom Hill, 1984.

Custer, Elizabeth Bacon. *The Civil War Memories of Elizabeth Bacon Custer: Reconstructed from Her Diaries and Notes.* Edited by Arlene Reynolds. Austin: University of Texas Press, 1994.

Custer, George A. *The Custer Story: The Life and Letters of General George A. Custer and His Wife Elizabeth.* Edited by Marguerite Merington. Reprint. New York: Barnes & Noble Books, 1994.

Dahlgren, R.Adm. [John A.]. *Memoir of Ulric Dahlgren.* Philadelphia: J. B. Lippincott, 1872.

Dahlgren, Madeleine Vinton, ed. *Memoir of John A. Dahlgren, Rear-Admiral, United States Navy.* Boston: J. R. Osgood, 1892.

Davenport, Alfred. *Camp and Field Life of the Fifth New York Volunteer Infantry (Duryee Zouaves).* New York: Dick and Fitzpatrick, 1879.

Davis, Maj. George B., et al. *The Official Military Atlas of the Civil War.* Reprint. New York: Gramercy Books, 1983.

Davis, Jefferson. *Rise and Fall of the Confederate Government.* 2 vols. Reprint. Richmond, Va.: Garrett and Massie, 1938.

Davis, Varina. *Jefferson Davis, Ex-President of the Confederate States of America: A Memoir by His Wife.* 2 vols. Reprint. Freeport, N.Y.: Books for Libraries, 1971.

Day, David L. *My Diary of Rambles with the 25th Massachusetts Volunteer Infantry.* Milford, Mass.: King & Billings, Printers, 1884.

Dowdey, Clifford, ed. *Wartime Letters of R. E. Lee.* Boston: Little, Brown, 1961.

Dufur, S. M. *Over the Dead Line or Tracked by Blood-Hounds.* Burlington, Vt.: Free Press Assoc., 1902.

Evans, Clement, ed. *Confederate Military History: A Library of Confederate States History.* 12 vols. Reprint. Dayton, Ohio: Morningside Bookshop, 1975.

Favill, Josiah Marshall. *The Diary of a Young Officer Serving with the Armies of the United States during the War of the Rebellion.* Chicago: R. R. Donnelley & Sons, 1909.

Fifth Report of the New York State Bureau of Military Statistics 11, no. 148 (1868).

Fleet, Benjamin Robert. *Green Mount: A Virginia Plantation Family during the Civil War: Being the Benjamin Robert Fleet Diary and Letters of His Family.* Edited by Betsy Fleet and John D. P. Fuller. Lexington: University of Kentucky Press, 1962.

Fleming, George Thornton, ed. *Life and Letters of Alexander Hays: Brevet Colonel United States Army, Brigadier General and Brevet Major General, United States Volunteers.* Pittsburg, Pa.: n.p., 1919.

Ford, Worthington Chauncey, ed. *A Cycle of Adams Letters, 1861–1865*. 2 vols. Boston: Houghton Mifflin, 1920.

Frobel, Anne S. *The Civil War Diary of Anne S. Frobel.* Edited by Mary H. Lancaster and Dallas M. Lancaster. McLean, Va.: EPM, 1992.

Garnett, Theodore S. *Riding with Stuart: Reminiscences of an Aide-de-Camp.* Edited by Robert J. Trout. Shippensburg, Pa.: White Mane, 1994.

Gillespie, Samuel L. *History of Company A, First Ohio Cavalry, 1861–1865.* Washington, Ohio: Ohio State Register, 1898.

Glazier, Willard. *Three Years in the Federal Cavalry.* New York: R. H. Ferguson, 1873.

Goldsborough, W. W. *The Maryland Line in the Confederate Army, 1861–1865.* Reprint. Gaithersburg, Md.: Olde Soldier Books, 1987.

Gorgas, Josiah. *Civil War Diary of General Josiah Gorgas.* Edited by Frank E. Vandiver. Tuscaloosa: University of Alabama Press, 1947.

Gracey, Samuel L. *Annals of the Sixth Pennsylvania Cavalry.* Philadelphia: E. H. Butler, 1878.

Hall, Hillman A., W. B. Besley, and Gilbert G. Woods, comps. *History of the Sixth New York Cavalry (Second Ira Harris Guard).* Worcester, Mass.: Blanchard, 1908.

Hamilton, William D. *Recollections of a Cavalryman of the Civil War after Fifty Years, 1861–1865.* Columbus, Ohio: F. J. Heer Printing, 1915.

Hampton, Charles G. "Twelve Months in Rebel Prisons." *MOLLUS, Michigan Commandery,* vol. 2. Wilmington, N.C.: Broadfoot, 1992.

Harris, Samuel. *Personal Reminiscences of Samuel Harris.* Chicago: Rogerson, 1897.

Hay, John. *At Lincoln's Side: John Hay's Civil War Correspondence and Selected Writings.* Edited by Michael Burlingame. Carbondale: Southern Illinois University Press, 2000.

Hewett, Janet B., et al., eds. *Supplement to the Official Records of Union and Confederate Armies.* 100 vols. in 3 pts. plus index. Wilmington, N.C.: Broadfoot, 1994–2001.

Howard, Hamilton Gay. *Civil-War Echoes: Character Sketches and State Secrets by a United States Senator's Son.* Reprint. Tuscaloosa, Ala.: Confederate Publishing, 1960.

Hubbard, Robert T., Jr. *The Civil War Memoirs of a Virginia Cavalryman.* Edited by Thomas P. Nanzig. Tuscaloosa: University of Alabama Press, 2007.

Humphreys, Andrew A. *From Gettysburg to the Rapidan: The Army of the Potomac, July, 1863 to April, 1864.* New York: Charles Scribner's Sons, 1883.

Hunton, Eppa. *Autobiography of Eppa Hunton.* Richmond, Va.: William Byrd, 1933.

Hyndman, William. *History of a Cavalry Company: A Complete Record of Company A, 4th Pennsylvania Cavalry.* Philadelphia: J. B. Rodgers, Printer, 1870.

Ide, Horace K. *History of the First Vermont Cavalry Volunteers in the War of the Rebellion.* Edited by Elliott W. Hoffman. Baltimore: Butternut and Blue, 2000.

Isham, Asa B. *An Historical Sketch of the Seventh Regiment of Michigan Volunteer Cavalry.* Reprint. Huntington, W.Va.: Blue Acorn, 2000.

Jones, J. B. *A Rebel War Clerk's Diary at the Confederate States Capital.* 2 vols. Philadelphia: J. B. Lippincott, 1866.

Kidd, James Harvey. *One of Custer's Wolverines: The Civil War Letters of Brevet Brigadier General James H. Kidd, 6th Michigan Cavalry.* Edited by Eric J. Wittenberg. Kent, Ohio: Kent State University Press, 2000.

———. *Riding with Custer: Recollections of a Cavalryman in the Civil War.* Edited by Paul F. Hutton. Reprint. Lincoln: University of Nebraska Press, 1997.

Kilmer, George Langdon. *Miscellaneous War Sketches.* New York: American Press Assoc., 1897.

Lee, Elizabeth Blair. *Wartime Washington: The Civil War Letters of Elizabeth Blair Lee.* Edited by Virginia Jeans Laas. Urbana: University of Illinois Press, 1991.

Lee, Fitzhugh. "The Death of Colonel Dahlgren." *The Historical Magazine,* 2nd ser., 7, no. 4 (April 1870).

Lee, William O., comp. *Personal and Historical Sketches and Facial History of and by Members of the Seventh Regiment Michigan Volunteer Cavalry, 1862–1865.* Detroit: 7th Michigan Cavalry Association, 1904.

Long, A. L. *Memoirs of Robert E. Lee: His Military and Personal History.* New York: J. M. Stoddart, 1887.

Lyman, Theodore. *Meade's Army: The Private Notebooks of Lt. Col. Theodore Lyman.* Edited by David H. Lowe. Kent, Ohio: Kent State University Press, 2007.

———. *Meade's Headquarters, 1863–1865: Letters of Colonel Theodore Lyman.* Edited by George R. Agassiz. Reprint. Salem, N.H.: Ayer, 1987.

Mayo, Ellen Wise. "A War-Time Aurora Borealis." *Cosmopolitan* 21, no. 2 (June 1896).

———. "A War-Time Aurora Borealis." *Tyler Quarterly Historical and Genealogical Magazine* 28, no. 2 (October 1946).

McClellan, H. B. *The Life and Campaigns of Major-General J. E. B. Stuart, Commander of the Cavalry of the Army of Northern Virginia.* Reprint. Secaucus, N.J.: Blue & Grey, 1993.

McDonald, William N. *A History of the Laurel Brigade.* Edited by Bushrod C. Washington. Reprint. Baltimore: The Johns Hopkins University Press, 2002.

McMahon, Martin T. "From Gettysburg to the Coming of Grant." *Battles and Leaders of the Civil War,* vol. 4. Reprint. New York: Thomas Yoseloff, 1956.

Meade, George Gordon. *The Life and Letters of George Gordon Meade, Major-General United States Army.* 2 vols. New York: Charles Scribner's Sons, 1913.

Merrill, Samuel H. *The Campaigns of the First Maine and First District of Columbia Cavalry.* Portland, Maine: Bailey & Noyes, 1866.

Meyer, Henry Coddington. *Civil War Experiences: Under Bayard, Gregg, Kilpatrick, Custer, Raulston, and Newberry.* New York: Knickerbocker, 1911.

Miller, Samuel H., ed. "Civil War Memoirs of Henry C. Mettam, 1st Maryland Cavalry, C.S.A." *Maryland Historical Magazine* 58, no. 2 (June 1963).

Mohr, James C., ed. *The Cormany Diaries: A Northern Family in the Civil War.* Pittsburgh: University of Pittsburgh Press, 1982.

Moore, Frank, ed. *The Rebellion Record: A Diary of American Events with Documents, Narratives, Illustrative Incidents, Poetry, etc.* 11 vols. New York: D. Van Nostrand, 1865.

Moore, James. *Kilpatrick and Our Cavalry.* New York: W. J. Middleton, 1865.

Moyer, H. P. *History of the Seventeenth Regiment of Pennsylvania Cavalry.* Lebanon, Pa.: n.p., 1911.

Myers, Frank M. *The Comanches: A History of White's Battalion, Virginia Cavalry, Laurel Brigadier, Hampton's Division, A.N.V., C.S.A.* Baltimore: Kelly, Piet, 1871.

Neese, George M. *Three Years in the Confederate Horse Artillery.* Reprint. Dayton, Ohio: Morningside Bookshop, 1983.

Newhall, Frederick C. *Dedication of the Monument of the Sixth Pennsylvania Cavalry on the Battlefield of Gettysburg, October 14, 1888.* Philadelphia: James Beale, Printer, 1889.

Owens, John Algernon. *Sword and Pen: Ventures and Adventures of William Glazier.* Philadelphia: P. W. Ziegler, 1882.

Patrick, Marsena Rudolph. *Inside Lincoln's Army: The Diary of Marsena Rudolph Patrick, Provost Marshal General, Army of the Potomac.* Edited by David S. Sparks. New York: Thomas Yoseloff, 1964.

Peck, Theodore S. *Revised Roster of Vermont Volunteers in the War of the Rebellion, 1861–1866.* Montpelier, Vt.: Watchman, 1892.

Pickerill, W. N. *History of the Third Indiana Cavalry.* Indianapolis: Aetna Printing, 1906.

Pollard, Edward A. *The Lost Cause: A New Southern History of the War of the Confederates.* New York: E. B. Treat, 1866.

Reagan, John H. *Memoirs, with Special Reference to Secession and the Civil War, by John H. Reagan.* Edited by Walter F. McCaleb. New York: Neale, 1906.

Regimental Historical Committee. *History of the Eleventh Pennsylvania Volunteer Cavalry Together with a Complete Roster of the Regiment and Regimental Officers.* Philadelphia: Franklin Printing, 1902.

Robertson, Robert Stoddart. "From the Wilderness to Spottsylvania." *MOLLUS, Ohio Commandery,* vol. 1. Reprint. Wendell, N.C.: Broadfoot, 1993.

Rodenbough, Theodore F., et al., comps. and eds. *History of the Eighteenth Regiment of Cavalry Pennsylvania Volunteers, 1862–1865*. New York: Committee 18th Pa. Cav. Ass'n, 1909.

Roe, Mary Abigail. *E. P. Roe: Reminiscences of His Life by His Sister.* New York: Dodd, Mead, 1899.

Roper, John L., Henry C. Archibald, and G. W. Coles. *History of the Eleventh Pennsylvania Volunteer Cavalry together with a Complete Roster of the Regiment and Regimental Officers.* Philadelphia: Franklin Printing, 1902.

Ruffin, Edmund. *The Diary of Edmund Ruffin.* Edited by William K. Scarborough. 2 vols. Baton Rouge: Louisiana State University Press, 1971.

Smith, Thomas W. *"We Have It Damn Hard Out Here": The Civil War Letters of Sergeant Thomas W. Smith, 6th Pennsylvania Cavalry.* Edited by Eric J. Wittenberg. Kent, Ohio: Kent State University Press, 1999.

Southwick, Thomas. *A Duryee Zouave.* Washington, D.C.: Acme Printing, 1930.

Starr, George H. "In and Out of Confederate Prisons." *MOLLUS, New York Commandery,* vol. 2. Wilmington, N.C.: Broadfoot, 1992.

Stearns, Amos E. *The Civil War Diary of Amos E. Stearns: A Prisoner at Andersonville.* Edited by Leon Basile. Rutherford, N.J.: Fairleigh Dickinson University Press, 1981.

Stoddard, William O. *Inside the White House in War Times: Memoirs and Reports of Lincoln's Secretary by William O. Stoddard.* Edited by Michael Burlingame. Lincoln: University of Nebraska Press, 2000.

Styple, William B., ed. *Generals in Bronze: Interviewing the Commanders of the Civil War.* Kearny, N.J.: Belle Grove, 2005.

Sunderland, Rev. B. *A Sermon in Memory of Ulric Dahlgren.* Washington, D.C.: n.p., 1864.

Taylor, Walter Herron. *Lee's Adjutant: The Wartime Letters of Colonel Walter Herron Taylor, 1862–1865.* Edited by R. Lockwood Tower. Columbia: University of South Carolina Press, 1995.

Tobie, Edward P. *History of the First Maine Cavalry, 1861–1865.* Boston: Press of Emery and Hughes, 1887.

Trout, Robert J., ed. *Memoirs of the Stuart Horse Artillery Battalion.* Vol. 1, *Moorman's and Hart's Batteries.* Knoxville: University of Tennessee Press, 2008.

———. *With Pen and Saber: The Letters and Diaries of J. E. B. Stuart's Staff Officers.* Mechanicsburg, Pa.: Stackpole, 1995.

U.S. Navy Department. *Official Records of the Union and Confederate Navies in the War of the Rebellion.* 30 vols. Washington, D.C.: Government Printing Office, 1896–1922.

U.S. War Department. *Official Records of the Union and Confederate Armies in the War of the Rebellion.* 128 vols. Washington, D.C.: Government Printing Office, 1880–1901.

Van Lew, Elizabeth L. *A Yankee Spy in Richmond: The Civil War Diary of "Crazy Bet" Van Lew.* Edited by David D. Ryan. Mechanicsburg, Pa.: Stackpole, 1996.

Vifquain, Victor. *The 1862 Plot to Kidnap Jefferson Davis.* Edited by Jeffery H. Smith and Philip Thomas Tucker. Mechanicsburg, Pa.: Stackpole, 1998.

Wainwright, Charles S. *A Diary of Battle: The Personal Journals of Colonel Charles S. Wainwright, 1861–1865.* Edited by Allan Nevins. New York: Harcourt, Brace, & World, 1962.

Walker, Thad J. "A Romantic Incident of the War, Ending in the Death of Colonel Ulric Dahlgren." *Blue and Gray* 3, no. 6 (June 1894).

Wallace, Lee A., comp. *History of the Richmond Howitzer Battalion.* Reprint. Baltimore: Butternut and Blue, 2000.

Wallace, Robert C. *A Few Memories of a Long Life.* Edited by John C. Carroll. Fairfield, Wash.: Ye Galleon, 1988.

Ward, Joseph R. C. *History of the One Hundred and Sixth Regiment Pennsylvania Volunteers.* Philadelphia: F. McManus, Jr., 1906.

"War Time Story of Dahlgren's Raid." *Southern Historical Society Papers* 37 (1909).

Welles, Gideon. *The Diary of Gideon Welles.* Edited by Edgar T. Welles. 3 vols. Boston: Houghton Mifflin, 1911.

Wells, Edward L. *Hampton and His Cavalry in '64.* Reprint. Richmond, Va.: Owens, 1991.

Wickman, Donald H., comp. and ed. *Letters to Vermont: From Her Civil War Soldier Correspondents to the Home Press.* 2 vols. Bennington, Vt.: Images from the Past, 1998.

Wilson, James H. *Under the Old Flag: Recollections of Military Operations in the War for the Union, the Spanish War, the Boxer Rebellion, etc.* 2 vols. Reprint. Westport, Conn.: Greenwood, 1971.

Wise, Jennings Cropper. *The Long Arm of Lee, or the History of the Artillery of the Army of Northern Virginia.* 2 vols. Reprint. Lincoln: University of Nebraska Press, 1991.

Wise, John S. *The End of an Era.* Boston: Houghton, Mifflin, 1899.

Wistar, Isaac J. *Autobiography of Isaac Jones Wistar, 1827–1905: Half a Century in War and Peace.* New York: Harper and Brothers, 1914.

Wood, William Nathaniel. "A Personal Encounter in the Rio Hill Battle." *Magazine of Albemarle County History* 22 (1963–64).

Newspapers and Magazines

Alexandria (Va.) Gazette
American Tribune
Army Navy Journal
Bangor (Maine) Weekly Whig and Courant
Boston Globe
Boston Sunday Globe
Burlington (Vt.) Free Press
Confederate Veteran
Corning (N.Y.) Journal

Culpeper Star Exponent
Daily Alta (Calif.)
Daily Morning Chronicle (Washington, D.C.)
Daily National Republican
Dawson's Historical Magazine
Detroit Advertiser & Tribune
Detroit Free Press
Essex County (N.Y.) Republican
Field and Post Room
First Maine Bugle
Frank Leslie's Illustrated Weekly
Grand Army Review
Grand Rapids (Mich.) Daily Democrat
Lewiston Evening Journal
Lynchburg (Va.) Daily Republican
Maine Farmer
Michigan Argus (Ann Arbor)
Mobile (Ala.) Advertiser & Register
National Tribune
New Jersey Herald
New York Herald
New York Times
New York World
Old Dominion Daily
Oneida (N.Y.) Weekly Herald
Philadelphia Daily Evening Bulletin
Philadelphia Inquirer
Philadelphia Weekly Times
Pottstown (Pa.) Miners Journal
Richmond Daily Examiner
Richmond Dispatch
Richmond Daily Enquirer
Richmond Sentinel
Richmond Times Dispatch
Richmond Whig
Rockland (Maine) Gazette
Rutland Daily Herald
Southern Punch
Southside Sentinel
Springfield (Mass.) Weekly Republican
Sussex (N.J.) Register
The Caledonian (St. Johnsbury, Vt.)
The Liberator
Vermont Journal
Wyoming County (N.Y.) Mirror

Secondary Sources

Adamson, Louise. "The Old Brick House at 6510 Three Chopt Road." *Richmond Quarterly* 10, no. 4 (1988).

Agee, Helene Barret. *Facets of Goochland (Virginia) County's History.* Richmond, Va.: Dietz, 1962.

Andrew, Rod, Jr. *Wade Hampton: Confederate Warrior to Southern Redeemer.* Chapel Hill: University of North Carolina Press, 2008.

Bagby, A. *King and Queen County, Virginia.* New York: Neale, 1908.

Benedict, G. G. *Vermont in the Civil War.* 2 vols. Burlington, Vt.: Free Press Association, 1886.

Bowles, J. C. "Private James Henry Pleasants of Goochland, His Life and Bravery." *Goochland County Historical Society* 34 (2002).

Brown, Alexander. *The Cabells and Their Kin: A Memorial Volume of History, Biography, and Genealogy.* Reprint. Harrisburg, Pa.: C. J. Carrier, 1978.

Brown, J. Willard. *The Signal Corps, U.S.A.* Boston: U.S. Veteran Corps Association, 1896.

Brown, John R. "The Battle of Rio Hill: February 29, 1864." *Magazine of Albemarle History* 22 (1963–64).

Brown, Kent Masterson. *Retreat from Gettysburg: Lee, Logistics, & the Pennsylvania Campaign.* Chapel Hill: University of North Carolina Press, 2005.

Bullard, Cece. *Goochland: Yesterday and Today: A Pictorial History.* Virginia Beach, Va.: Donning, 1994.

Burlingame, Michael. *The Inner World of Abraham Lincoln.* Urbana: University of Illinois Press, 1994.

Cabell, William Preston. "Woman Saved Richmond City." *Southern Historical Society Papers* 34 (1906).

Catton, Bruce. *A Stillness at Appomattox.* Garden City: Doubleday, 1953.

Chernault, Tracy, and Jeffery C. Weaver. *18th and 20th Battalions of Virginia Heavy Artillery.* Lynchburg, Va.: H. E. Howard, 1995.

Chowning, Larry S. *Soldiers at the Doorstep, Civil War Lore.* Centreville, Md.: Tidewater, 1999.

Cisco, Walter Brian. *Wade Hampton: Confederate Warrior, Conservative Statesman.* Washington: Brassey's, 2004.

Cleaves, Freeman. *Meade of Gettysburg.* Dayton, Ohio: Morningside Bookshop, 1980.

Coddington, Edwin B. *The Gettysburg Campaign: A Study in Command.* New York: Charles Scribner's Sons, 1968.

Collins, Darrell L. *General William Averell's Salem Raid.* Shippensburg, Pa.: Bird Street, 1998.

Couture, Richard T. *Powhatan: A Bicentennial History.* Richmond, Va.: Dietz, 1980.

Cox, Virginia D., and Willie T. Weathers. *Old Houses of King and Queen County Virginia.* Reprint. Richmond, Va.: Blue Water Printing, 1998.

Crute, Joseph, Jr. *Units of the Confederate States Army.* Reprint. Gaithersburg, Md.: Olde Soldiers Books, 1987.

Culpeper Historical Society. *Historic Culpeper.* Culpeper, Va.: Culpeper Historical Society, 1974.

Curry, Roy Watson. "James A. Seddon: A Southern Prototype." *Virginia Magazine of History and Biography* 63, no. 2 (April 1955).

Davies, Paul J. *C.S. Armory Richmond: A History of the Confederate States Armory.* Carlisle, Pa.: P. J. Davies, 2000.

Davis, William C. *Jefferson Davis: The Man and His Hour.* New York: Harper Collins, 1991.

Driver, Robert J., Jr. *5th Virginia Cavalry.* Lynchburg, Va.: H. E. Howard, 1997.

———. *First and Second Maryland Cavalry, C.S.A.* Charlottesville, Va.: Rockbridge, 1999.

———. *Richmond Local Defense Troops, C.S.A.* Wilmington, N.C.: Broadfoot, 2011.

Fishel, Edwin C. *The Secret War for the Union: The Untold Story of Military Intelligence in the Civil War.* Boston: Houghton Mifflin, 1996.

Ford, N. P. "Wade Hampton's Strategy." *Southern Historical Society Papers* 24 (1896).

Foster, John Y. *New Jersey in the Rebellion.* Newark: Martin R. Dennis, 1868.

Freeman, Douglas Southall. *Lee's Lieutenants: A Study in Command.* 3 vols. New York: Charles Scribner's Sons, 1943.

Furgurson, Ernest B. *Ashes of Glory: Richmond at War.* New York: Alfred A. Knopf, 1996.

Gibson, Langhorne, Jr. *Cabell's Canal: The Story of the James River and Kanawha.* Richmond, Va.: Commodore, 2000.

Glatthaar, Joseph T. *General Lee's Army: From Victory to Collapse.* New York: Free Press, 2008.

Goodwin, Doris Kearns. *Team of Rivals: The Political Genius of Abraham Lincoln.* New York: Simon & Schuster, 2005.

Gower, Herschel. "Charles Bunker Dahlgren (1839–1912)." Unpublished manuscript, n.d. Copy in author's possession.

———. *Charles Dahlgren of Natchez: The Civil War and Dynastic Decline.* Washington, D.C.: Brassey's, 2002.

Grimsley, Mark. *The Hard Hand of War: Union Military Policy toward Southern Civilians, 1861–1865.* New York: Cambridge University Press, 1995.

Hall, James O. "The Dahlgren Papers: A Yankee Plot to Kill President Davis." *Civil War Times Illustrated* (November 1983).

Hanchett, William. *The Lincoln Murder Conspiracies.* Urbana: University of Illinois Press, 1983.

Hanover County Historical Society. *Hanover County, Virginia: A Retrospective.* Hanover, Va.: Wadsworth, 1993.

Hanson, Joseph Mills. "The Civil War Custer." *Cavalry Journal* 43, no. 181 (May/June 1934).

Hennessy, John J. *Return to Bull Run: The Campaign and Battle of Second Manassas.* New York: Simon & Schuster, 1993.

Hunt, Roger D., and Jack R. Brown. *Brevet Brigadier Generals in Blue.* Rev. ed. Gaithersburg, Md.: Olde Soldiers Books, 1997.

James, G. Watson. "Dahlgren's Raid." *Southern Historical Society Papers* 39 (1914).

Jeffries, Margaret. *Survey Report, Rose Hill, Virginia, Historical Inventory.* Virginia Works Progress Administration, 1937. Digitized record, Richmond, VA, 1999.

Johnston, Angus James, II. *Virginia Railroads in the Civil War.* Chapel Hill: University of North Carolina Press, 1961.

Jones, J. William, comp. "The Kilpatrick-Dahlgren Raid against Richmond." *Southern Historical Society Papers* 13 (1885).

Jones, Virgil Carrington. *Eight Hours before Richmond.* New York: Henry Holt, 1957.

Jordan, Ervin L., Jr. *Charlottesville and the University of Virginia in the Civil War.* Lynchburg, Va.: H. E. Howard, 1988.

Kaplan, Barbara Beigun. *Land and Heritage in the Virginia Tidewater: A History of King and Queen County.* Richmond, Va.: Cadmus Fine Books, 1993.

Krick, Robert E. L. *Staff Officers in Gray: A Biographical Register of the Staff Officers in the Army of Northern Virginia.* Chapel Hill: University of North Carolina Press, 2003.

Krick, Robert K. *Civil War Weather in Virginia.* Tuscaloosa: University of Alabama Press, 2007.

———. *Lee's Colonels: A Biographical Register of the Field Officers of the Army of Northern Virginia.* 2nd rev. ed. Dayton, Ohio Morningside Bookshop, 1984.

———. *9th Virginia Cavalry.* Lynchburg, Va.: H. E. Howard, 1982.

Long, David E. "Lincoln, Davis, and the Dahlgren Raid." *North and South* 9, no. 5 (October 2006).

Longacre, Edward G. *Custer and His Wolverines: The Michigan Cavalry Brigade, 1861–1865.* Conshohocken, Pa.: Combined, 1997.

———. *Lee's Cavalrymen: A History of the Mounted Forces of the Army of Northern Virginia, 1861–1865.* Mechanicsburg, Pa.: Stackpole, 2002.

———. *Lincoln's Cavalrymen: A History of the Mounted Forces of the Army of the Potomac.* Mechanicsburg, Pa.: Stackpole, 2000.

———. *Mounted Raids of the Civil War.* Lincoln: University of Nebraska Press, 1994.

Lowery, Thomas. *Don't Shoot That Boy!: Abraham Lincoln and Military Justice.* Macon City, Iowa: Savas, 1999.

Malone, Dumas, ed. *Dictionary of American Biography.* New York: Charles Scribner's Sons, 1935.

McCabe, W. Gordon. "Major-General George Washington Custis Lee." *Annual Report of the Virginia Historical Society.* 1914.

McPherson, James M. "A Failed Richmond Raid and Its Consequences." *Columbiad* 2, no. 4 (Winter 1999).

Mewborn, Horace. "A Wonderful Exploit: Jeb Stuart's Ride around the
    Army of the Potomac, June 12–15, 1862." *Blue & Gray* 15, no. 6 (1998).
Moore, James O. "Custer's Raid into Albemarle County: The Skirmish
    at Rio Hill, February 29, 1864." *Virginia Magazine of History and
    Biography* 79, no. 3 (July 1971).
Munford, George W. "Cavalry Raid by Custer, Kilpatrick, and Dahlgren."
    Transactions of the Southern Historical Society. Baltimore: Turnbull
    Brothers, 1874.
Nelson, Henry Lee, Jr., ed. "Brook Hill Fortifications Remembered."
    Henrico County Historical Society Magazine 12 (1986).
———."The Coal Mines of Henrico's West End." *Henrico County
    Historical Society Magazine* 14 (1990).
———. "Laurel: Not Just Another Whistle Stop," *Henrico County
    Historical Society Magazine* 15 (1991).
Nesbitt, Mark. *Saber and Scapegoat: J. E. B. Stuart and the Gettysburg
    Controversy.* Mechanicsburg, Pa.: Stackpole, 1994.
Nevins, Allan. *War for the Union.* 4 vols. Reprint. New York: Konecky &
    Konecky, 1971.
O'Dell, Jeffery M. *Chesterfield County: Early Architecture and Historic
    Sites.* Chesterfield, Va.: Chesterfield County, 1983.
O'Neill, Robert F. "Cavalry on the Peninsula: Fort Monroe to the Gates of
    Richmond." *Blue & Gray* 19, no. 5 (2002).
———. *Chasing Jeb Stuart and John Mosby: The Union Cavalry in
    Northern Virginia from Second Manassas to Gettysburg.* Jefferson,
    N.C.: McFarland, 2012.
O'Reilly, Francis Augustin. *The Fredericksburg Campaign: Winter War on
    the Rappahannock.* Baton Rouge: Louisiana State University, 2003.
Paradis, James M. *Strike the Blow for Freedom: The 6th United States
    Colored Infantry in the Civil War.* Shippensburg, Pa.: White Mane,
    1998.
Pawlett, Nathaniel Mason. "The Three Notch'd Road Revisited." *Virginia
    Department of Transportation Bulletin* 49, no. 4 (April 1976).
Perret, Geoffrey. *Lincoln's War: The Untold Story of America's Greatest
    President as Commander in Chief.* New York: Random House, 2004.
Pilcher, William. "Some Incidents of the Kilpatrick-Dahlgren Raid on
    Richmond." *Tyler's Quarterly Historical and Genealogical Magazine.*
    28, no. 2 (October 1946).
Pitts, H. Douglas. "Dahlgren's Raid Route." *Richmond Journal of History
    and Architecture* 3, no. 1 (Spring 1996).
Porter, John W. H. *A Record of Events in Norfolk County, Virginia.*
    Portsmouth, Va.: W. A. Fiske, Printers, 1892.
"President's Report." *Goochland County Historical Society Magazine* 1,
    no. 1 (1969).
Quarstein, John V. *Big Bethel: The First Battle.* Charleston, S.C.: History
    Press, 2011.
Ramsdell, Charles W. "Lee's Horse Supply." *American Historical Review*
    35, no. 4 (July 1930).

Redwood, Allen C. "Following Stuart's Feather." *Journal of Military Service Institute of the United States* 49 (1911).

Rhea, Gordon. *To the North Anna: Grant and Lee, May 13–25, 1864.* Baton Rouge: Louisiana State University Press, 2000.

Riggs, David F. "The Dahlgren Papers Revisited." *Lincoln Herald* 83, no. 2 (1981).

Ruffner, Kevin Conley. *Maryland's Blue & Gray: A Border State's Union and Confederate Junior Officer Corps.* Baton Rouge: Louisiana State University, 1997.

Schneller, Robert J., Jr. *A Quest for Glory: A Biography of Rear Admiral John A. Dahlgren.* Annapolis, Md.: Naval Institute Press, 1996.

Schultz, Duane. *The Dahlgren Affair: Terror and Conspiracy in the Civil War.* New York: W. W. Norton, 1998.

Sears, Stephen W. *Gettysburg.* New York: Houghton Mifflin, 2003.

———. "The Dahlgren Papers Revisited." *Columbiad* 3, no. 2 (Summer 1999).

Shenk, Joshua Wolf. *Lincoln's Melancholy: How Depression Challenged a President and Fueled His Greatness.* New York: Houghton Mifflin, 2005.

Sifakis, Stewart. *Who Was Who in the Civil War.* New York: Facts on File Publications, 1988.

Snell, James P., comp. *History of Sussex and Warren Counties, New Jersey.* Philadelphia: Everts & Peck, 1881.

Starr, Stephen Z. *The Union Cavalry in the Civil War.* 3 vols. Baton Rouge: Louisiana State University Press, 1979–85.

Stewart, Lucy. "Colonel Ulric Dahlgren." *New-York Historical Society Quarterly* 30, no. 1 (1946).

Stiles, Kenneth L. *4th Virginia Cavalry.* Lynchburg, Va.: H. E. Howard, 1985.

Stuart, Merriwether. "Colonel Ulric Dahlgren and Richmond's Union Underground." *Virginia Magazine of History and Biography* 72, no. 2 (April 1964).

———. "Of Spies and Borrowed Names: The Identity of Union Operatives in Richmond Known as 'The Phillipses' Discovered." *Virginia Magazine of History and Biography* 89, no. 3 (July 1981).

Swigget, Howard. *The Rebel Raider: The Life of John Hunt Morgan.* Indianapolis: Bobbs-Merrill, 1934.

Thiele, Thomas F. "The Evolution of Cavalry in the American Civil War." Ph.D. diss., University of Michigan, 1951.

Thomas, Emory. *The Confederate Nation, 1861–1865.* New York: Harper & Row, 1979.

Thompson, Addison Baker. "A Brief History of Tuckahoe." In *Tuckahoe Plantation.* Tuckahoe Plantation Enterprises, 1997.

Tidwell, William A., with James O. Hall and Winfred Gaddy. *Come Retribution: The Confederate Secret Service and the Assassination of Lincoln.* Jackson: University Press of Mississippi, 1998.

Trout, Robert J. *Galloping Thunder: The Stuart Horse Artillery Battalion.* Mechanicsburg, Pa.: Stackpole, 2002.

Urwin, Gregory J. W. *Custer Victorious: The Civil War Battles of General George Armstrong Custer.* Lincoln: University of Nebraska Press, 1983.

Varon, Elizabeth. *Southern Lady, Yankee Spy.* New York: Oxford University Press, 2003.

Venter, Bruce M. "General Judson Kilpatrick: The First Civil War Reenactor." *Civil War* 72 (February 1999).

———. "The Kilpatrick-Dahlgren Raid." *Blue & Gray* 20, no. 3 (2003).

Walker, Margaret Henley. "Oak Grove: Manakin, Virginia." *Goochland County Historical Magazine* 25 (1993).

Warner, Ezra J. *Generals in Blue: Lives of the Union Commanders.* Baton Rouge: Louisiana State University Press, 1964.

———. *Generals in Gray: Lives of Confederate Commanders.* Baton Rouge: Louisiana State University, 1959.

Watts, Jeri Hanel "Last Battles: The Wartime and Postwar Careers of Custis Lee." *Virginia Cavalcade* 42, no. 2 (1992).

Weaver, Jeffery C. *10th and 19th Battalions of Heavy Artillery.* Lynchburg, Va.: H. E. Howard, 1996.

———. *The Virginia Home Guards.* Lynchburg, Va.: H. E. Howard, 1999.

Welsh, Jack D. *Medical Histories of Union Generals.* Kent, Ohio: Kent State University Press, 1996.

Wert, Jeffery D. *Cavalryman of the Lost Cause: A Biography of J. E. B. Stuart.* New York: Simon & Schuster, 2008.

———. *Custer: The Controversial Life of George Armstrong Custer.* New York: Simon & Schuster, 1996.

"What Is the Truth of Dahlgren's Raid?" *Tyler's Quarterly Historical and Genealogical Magazine* 28, no. 2 (October 1946).

Wheelan, Joseph. *Libby Prison Breakout: The Daring Escape from the Notorious Civil War Prison.* New York: Public Affairs, 2010.

Whitman, William E. S., and Charles H. True. *Maine in the War for the Union.* Lewiston, Maine: N. Dingly, Jr., 1865.

Whittaker, Frederick. *A Complete Life of General George A. Custer.* 2 vols. Reprint. Lincoln: University of Nebraska Press, 1993.

Wight, Richard C. *The Story of Goochland.* Richmond, Va.: Richmond Press, 1943.

Wittenberg, Eric J. *Like a Meteor Blazing Brightly: The Short but Controversial Life of Colonel Ulric Dahlgren.* Roseville, Minn.: Edinborough, 2009.

———. "Ulric Dahlgren in the Gettysburg Campaign." *Gettysburg Magazine* 22 (January 2000).

Wittenberg, Eric J., and J. David Petruzzi. *Plenty of Blame to Go Around: Jeb Stuart's Controversial Ride to Gettysburg.* New York: Savas Beatie, 2006.

Index

Illustrations are indicated with italicized page numbers.

59, 60, 90, 218, 250; and Butler,
28, 29, 35, 50–51, 283n35; and
Davis assassination orders,
247–48, 320n9, 321n19,
324n13; death sentences
commuted by, 49, 50; and idea
of Richmond raid, 21–22; and
John Dahlgren, 77–78, 262; and
Kilpatrick, 4, 12, 56, 57–60;
leadership style of, 57, 60; and
Ulric Dahlgren, 85–86, 87, 88,
89, 90, 294n1
Lipscomb, Martin M., 253
Litchfield, Allyn C.: during attack
on Richmond, 184, 188–
89, 190, 193; as Confederate
prisoner, 194, 214, 251, 321n5
Littlepage, William, 238, 241–42,
265
Local Defense Troops (LDT): in
battle, 201–10; mobilization of,
198–99, 200–201
Lohman, F. W. E., 253, 255, 256
Lomax, Lunsford, 296n20
Long, Armistead, 138, 305n19
Longstreet, James, 37
looting, 153, 217–18, 227, 302n10
Lyman, Theodore, 91, 165, 246,
260, 270, 324n13
Lyons, James, 178

MacCubbin, Samuel, 253
Madison Court House, 113, 114,
115, 122, 123–24
Magee, Ebenezer, 211–12
Manakin's Bend, 151
Manakin's Ferry, 159–60, 168, 170
Manassas (Second), Battle of, 15, 17
Mann, Nehemiah, 94–95
Martin, Cornelius, 237, 254–55,
319n18
Martin, William, 227
Martin Robinson/Roberson/Robson
(black guide), 98, 151, 167–69,
172, 250; hanging of, 169–71,
306n22; identification of, 162–
67, 300n40, 304n8, 305n11,
305n14

Mason, Robert Franklin, 120, 126,
295n14
Mattaponi River, 68, 214, 229, 230,
231, 239
Matthews, Kirk, 257
Mattison, William, 160, 212, 218,
304n10
Mayo, Ellen Wise, 147, 150, 157
Mayo, Joseph, 252
Mayo's Bridge, 44
McAnerney, John H., Jr., 312n20,
313n22; and defense of
Richmond, 194–95, 206–208,
209
McCamack (Union sympathizer),
53–54
McCamack, James (son), 131
McClellan, George B., 14, 17, 64,
80, 284n35
McEntee, John, 182, 185, 246–47
McFarland (overseer), 237
McGregor, William H., 117
McGruder, William, 232, 237
McKethan, Hector, 183
McKnight, Judson, 131
Meade, George G., 54, 57, 67, 72,
165; and Butler, 34, 38; and
Dahlgren, 83; and Dahlgren
papers, 243–44, 245, 246, 247,
320n8; and Gettysburg, 23, 84;
and Kilpatrick raid, 58, 90–91,
94, 130, 172, 222, 258; and
Wise, 149, 301n2
Meade, Margaret Sergeant, 301n2
Meadow Bridges, 21, 42, 68, 186,
187, 309n30
Meems (Mimms), David, 166,
305n13
Meigs, Montgomery C., 16
Meredith, Fleming, 235
Meredith, S. A., 25
Merrill, Samuel H., 309n33
Merritt, Henry A. D., 98, 127, 137,
235, 236, 321n5; and Dahlgren
body, 239, 319n18
Merritt, Wesley, 84, 189; and Butler's
raid, 39, 42; and Custer's
diversionary movement, 91,

185–86; escape efforts by, 164; exchanges of, 25, 27, 243, 282n4; from Kilpatrick-Dahlgren Raid, 194, 211–12, 214, 251–53, 258, 314n31, 321n5; Richmond raids' plan to free, 32, 33, 44, 45, 62, 130, 160. *See also* Belle Isle prison; Libby Prison
Purcell, John, 209, 313n25

Raccoon Ford, 39, 42
Ramsey, Alexander, 69
Randolph, Alfred, 151
Randolph, Thomas, 168
Ransom, Duncan, 97
Rapidan River, 54, 98; Butler's raid along, 41, 42, 45, 49, 51; crossings of, 16, 51, 53, 55, 116, 128, 131, 133; Lee's defenses along, 37, 38–39
Rappahannock River, 18, 23, 78, 113, 231; crossings of, 16, 20, 79, 80, 82
Reagan, John Henninger, 253
Reinhold, Martin, 145
Richmond, Fredericksburg, and Potomac Railroad, 19, 22, 44, 61–62, 144, 173, 196
Richmond, Va.: Butler's raid and, 31–33, 42–45, 46–47; casualties during battle of, 186, 205, 209, 210, 314n29; concerns about efforts to free POWs in, 26–28, 36, 56; Confederate artillery in, 145, 177–78, 184; Confederate troop strength in, 32–33, 36, 37, 145–46, 182–84, 260–62, 283n21; counterattack on Kilpatrick in, 188–93; Dahlgren attack on, 198, 201–10; Dahlgren orders to burn, 242, 267, 275, 323n5; Dahlgren retreat from, 211–13; Dahlgren's youthful visit to, 76; inspection of Confederate defenses in, 94, 292n71;

Kilpatrick attack on, 176–77, 178–79, 187–88, 196, 197, 309n33; Kilpatrick withdrawal from, 181–82, 185, 186; Local Defense Troops' mobilization in, 198–99, 200–201; "Officers' Battalion" in, 200, 311n8; popular response to attacks on, 46–47, 175, 198, 199–200; POWs' presence in, 25–28, 36, 56, 130, 160, 185–86, 190–91; proposed cavalry raid on, 18; reaction to Dahlgren papers in, 238; reasons for failure to capture, 192–94; Stoneman raid and, 21–22; Union intelligence network in, 33–35, 54, 283n29; vulnerability of, 21, 261
Richmond Daily Examiner, 27, 34, 277–78
Richmond Sentinel, 238
Rio Hill, Battle of, 119–21, 125–26, 296n23
Rivanna River, 114, 116, 117, 121, 124
Rives, J. Henry, 175
Roberson, Martin. *See* Martin Robinson/Roberson/Robson
Roberts, William P., 214
Robertson, Jerome, 200
Robinson, Martin. *See* Martin Robinson/Roberson/Robson
Rocketts Landing, 27, 43
Rockville, Md., 16
Roe, E. P., 132
Rose Hill, 8, 9. 11, 58, 70-74, 92, 99
Rosser, Thomas L., 115, 146, 218, 266
Rowley, Merritt, 35–36
Rowley, William S., 35, 36, 253
Ruffin, Edmund, 218, 252–53
Rush's Lancers, 82, 83–84
Russell, David A., 113
Ryland, Samuel P., 317n7

Sabot Hill Plantation, 106, 154–55, 156, 157–58, 159, 303n16